PERSPECTIVES ON
SOCIALLY
SHARED
COGNITION

PERSPECTIVES ON
SOCIALLY
SHARED
COGNITION

E D I T E D
BY
LAUREN B. RESNICK,
JOHN M. LEVINE,
AND
STEPHANIE D. TEASLEY

LEARNING RESEARCH
AND DEVELOPMENT CENTER

UNIVERSITY OF PITTSBURGH

American Psychological Association
Washington, DC

Second printing March 1993

Published by the
American Psychological Association
750 First Street, NE
Washington, DC 20002

Copies may be ordered from
APA Order Department
P.O. Box 2710
Hyattsville, MD 20784

Typeset in Times Roman by Harper Graphics, Waldorf, MD

Printer: BookCrafters, Chelsea, MI
Cover designer: Beth Schlenoff
Technical editing and production coordinator: Valerie Montenegro
Copyeditor: Naomi Thiers

Library of Congress Cataloging-in-Publication Data

Perspectives on socially shared cognition / edited by Lauren B. Resnick, John M.
   Levine, and Stephanie D. Teasley.
      p.   cm.
   Rev. papers presented at a conference, entitled Socially shared cognition, held at
the University of Pittsburgh, 1989.
      Includes bibliographical references and index.
      ISBN 1-55798-121-3 (hard : acid-free paper)
      1. Social perception—Congresses. I. Resnick, Lauren B.
   II. Levine, John M. III. Teasley, Stephanie D.
   BF323.S63S62   1991
   302′.12—dc20   91-17922
                                                                                CIP

Printed in the United States of America

CONTENTS

FOREWORD

Federal research agencies stopped most support of investigator-initiated state-of-the-art research conferences in scientific psychology over a decade ago. During this period, however, scientific psychology has continued to grow as well as to diversify into many new areas. Yet there have been relatively few opportunities for investigators in new and promising research areas to convene in special settings to discuss their findings.

As part of its continuing effort to enhance the dissemination of scientific knowledge in psychology, the American Psychological Association (APA) has undertaken a number of initiatives designed to foster scientific research and communication. In particular, the APA Science Directorate established in 1988 the Scientific Conferences program, from which this publication resulted.

The APA Scientific Conferences Program provides university-based psychological researchers with seed monies essential to organizing specialty conferences on critical issues in basic research, applied research, and on methodological issues in psychology. Deciding which conferences to support involves a competitive process. An annual call for proposals is issued by the APA Science Directorate to solicit conference ideas. Proposals from all areas of psychological research are welcome. These are then reviewed by qualified psychologists, who forward substantive suggestions and funding recommendations to the Science Directorate. At each stage, the criteria used to determine which conferences to support include relevance, timeliness, comprehensiveness of the topics, and qualifications of the presenters. From its inception in 1988 to mid-1991, 19 conferences have been funded, with a total outlay of more than $250,000. In the future, we expect to support several conferences annually.

This program has two major goals. The first is to provide, by means of the conferences, a broad view of specific topics and, when appropriate, to encourage interdisciplinary participation. The second goal is to assure timely dissemination of the findings presented, by publishing carefully crafted scholarly volumes based, in part, on the conferences. The information thus reaches the broader psychological and scientific communities as well as the audiences at the conferences. Psychology and related fields thereby benefit from the most current research on a given topic.

This volume presents findings reported at a February 1989 conference entitled "Socially Shared Cognition," held at the University of Pittsburgh. The emerging interdisciplinary research being conducted in this area demonstrated that the topic was ripe for a conference of its most active scholars. A focal point for the conference was to develop an overview volume to examine the diverse research program now under way on thinking as a sociocognitive activity, and to provide an agenda for future research endeavors.

The American Psychological Association is pleased to have sponsored this conference and now to make the research presented there available in book form. We hope you will enjoy and be stimulated by this volume and others to come.

A list of the conferences funded through this program follows:

Researching Community Psychology: Integrating Theories and Methodologies, September 1988

The Psychological Well-Being of Captive Primates, September 1988

Psychological Research on Organ Donation, October 1988

Arizona Conference on Sleep and Cognition, January 1989

Socially Shared Cognition, February 1989

Taste, Experience, and Feeding, April 1989

Perception of Structure, May 1989

Suggestibility of Children's Recollections, June 1989

Best Methods for Analysis of Change, October 1989

Conceptualization and Measurement of Organism–Environment Interactions, November 1989

Cognitive Bases of Musical Communication, April 1990

Conference on Hostility, Coping/Support, and Health, November 1990

Psychological Testing of Hispanics, February 1991

Study of Cognition: Conceptual and Methodological Issues, February 1991

Cardiovascular Reactivity to Psychological and Cardiovascular Disease: A Conference on the Evidence, April 1991

Maintaining and Promoting Integrity in Behavioral Science Research, October 1991

Developmental Psychoacoustics, August 1991

The Contributions of Psychology to Mathematics and Science Education, November 1991

Lives Through Time: Assessment and Theory in Personality Psychology from a Longitudinal Perspective, November 1991

LEWIS P. LIPSITT, PHD
Executive Director for Science

VIRGINIA E. HOLT
Manager, Scientific Conferences Program

PREFACE

Over the last several years, researchers from a number of disciplines have become intrigued by the reciprocal relations between cognition and social interaction. Within psychology, investigators interested in cognitive, social, and developmental processes have begun to identify important theoretical and empirical questions that bridge traditional research specialties. Such questions concern relationships between intrapersonal processes, such as memory and reasoning, and interpersonal processes, such as parent–child and peer interaction. In addition, investigators from other disciplines, such as anthropology, sociology, and linguistics, have begun systematic exploration of certain relationships between cognition and social interaction.

The conceptual foundation for much current work was laid down long ago by such theorists as Mead, Vygotsky, and Piaget. Only recently, however, have researchers begun to take seriously the ideas of these important thinkers regarding socially shared cognition. Rather than seeking to understand cognitive and social processes in isolation or treating one process as context for the other, a growing number of investigators are seeking to develop conceptual schemes and methodological techniques that allow the study of thinking as sociocognitive activity.

In 1988, we conducted an interdisciplinary faculty–student seminar on socially shared cognition. In the course of that seminar, we located many interesting bodies of relevant work. However, we found no comprehensive review or collection of papers that brought together the divergent points of view that characterize this emerging field and that provided a clear agenda for future research. We decided, therefore, to organize a conference on socially shared cognition and to provide a volume of conference papers suitable for publication.

With the support of the Science Directorate of the American Psychological Association, we invited a group of scholars from psychology and related disciplines to participate in this endeavor. The conference was held in February 1989 at the Learning Research and Development Center, University of Pittsburgh. The chapters of this volume are based on presentations at that conference. As the reader will discover, they present a range of thoughtful and interesting perspectives on socially shared cognition from investigators with diverse disciplinary backgrounds. The thematic content of the various chapters and of the book as a whole is described in some detail in the introductory chapter.

We gratefully acknowledge those individuals who contributed to planning and conducting the conference and to preparing this volume. Deborah Connell provided invaluable assistance in all phases of the project. Pat Stanton was of great help in running the conference. And Barbara Burge, the technical editor of this volume, made a major contribution in preparing the manuscripts for publication.

LAUREN B. RESNICK
JOHN M. LEVINE
STEPHANIE D. TEASLEY

CHAPTER 1

SHARED COGNITION: THINKING AS SOCIAL PRACTICE

LAUREN B. RESNICK

This volume is about a phenomenon that seems almost a contradiction in terms: cognition that is not bounded by the individual brain or mind. In most psychological theory, the social and the cognitive have engaged only peripherally, standing in a kind of figure–ground relationship to one another rather than truly interacting. This book aims to undo this figure–ground relationship between cognitive and social processes. In so doing, it looks beyond psychology to a number of allied disciplines that have traditionally taken a view of human phenomena that is less focused on the individual.

Of all the branches of scientific psychology, cognition is perhaps the last place we might have expected to see an explosion of interest in the social. For cognition is, by past consensus and implicit definition, an individual act bounded by the physical facts of brain and body. Why this press, even within the bastion of cognitive psychology, toward viewing cognition as a social phenomenon? The answer lies partly in a pervasive assumption of today's cognitive psychology: constructivism. The empiricist assumption that dominated many branches of psychology for decades, the assumption that what we know is a direct reflection of what we can perceive in the physical world, has largely disappeared. In its place is a view that most knowledge is an interpretation of experience, an interpretation based on schemas, often idiosyncratic at least in detail, that both enable and constrain individuals' processes of sense-making.

The constructivist assumption solves many traditional problems for psychology, but it raises some important new ones: How can people know the same

1

thing if they are each constructing their knowledge independently? How can social groups coordinate their actions if each individual is thinking something different? Some theorists place the answer to the first question in biological structures: Humans are speciated for certain forms of common knowledge. Most elaborated as a theory of language acquisition, the argument for biological or "hard-wired" structures that guide and constrain infants as they interpret their earliest experience is now being put forth for basic mathematical and physical concepts as well. Theorists making this argument propose that biologically grounded processes of interpretation and constraining structures will produce common ideas if individuals grow up in similar environments.

It is not clear yet how much of humans' apparently common knowledge and reasoning processes can be accounted for by such biologically grounded structures and processes. But however great the scope of these structures, it is clear that much of human cognition is so varied and so sensitive to cultural context that we must also seek mechanisms by which people actively shape each other's knowledge and reasoning processes. According to the strong constructivist assumption, everything an individual knows is personally constructed. But directly experienced events are only part of the basis for that construction. People also build their knowledge structures on the basis of what they are told by others, orally, in writing, in pictures, and in gestures. Our daily lives are filled with instances in which we influence each other's constructive processes by providing information, pointing things out to one another, asking questions, and arguing with and elaborating on each other's ideas. Furthermore, as Vygotsky (1978) and Mead (1934) have independently suggested, social experience can shape the kinds of interpretive processes available to individuals. Constructivism also makes cognition integral to social processes. Cognitions *about* social phenomena have long been of concern to social psychologists. But constructivism forces students of many social phenomena to treat social processes *as* cognition, leading them to analyze the ways in which people jointly construct knowledge under particular conditions of social purpose and interaction.

Psychologists' growing interest in the intersection of the social and cognitive is mirrored by changes in allied fields. Sociolinguistics, for example, a field of growing visibility outside its own small community, joins traditional concerns of linguistics with those of anthropology to address questions of how language works simultaneously to convey information and to situate people in a social system. A growing field of discourse linguistics includes a visible minority of linguists who study *dialogic discourse*—the ways in which linguistic communication between two or more individuals is structured. Other students of the structure of conversation and communication come from the discipline of sociology. Influenced to some extent by sociological and anthropological studies of scientific communities, philosophers of science today are struggling with the question of how the social distribution of knowledge and the importance of social rewards for scientific eminence interact with traditional standards of scientific rationality (see, e.g., Kitcher, 1990). Further afield, literary theorists are speaking of the role of interpretive communities in influencing the readings that individuals will give to texts (e.g., Fish, 1980).

In cognitive science, challenges to the dominant role of formal logic as an account of human rationality are producing growing concern for the role of argument, contradiction, and negotiation processes in reasoning. Challenges to the dominant cognitive science view that thought and mind can be fully accounted for in terms of symbol processing are leading some cognitive scientists to press for theories of cognition more connected to both the physical and the social world (e.g., Winograd & Flores, 1986). The metaphor of cognitive systems as social systems in connectionist and blackboard models of thinking (cf. Minsky, 1986) makes the entire cognitive science community more open than it was a decade ago to the idea of knowledge as distributed across several individuals whose interactions determine decisions, judgments, and problem solutions.

These intellectual murmurings are producing a sea change in the fields of investigation concerned with human thinking and social functioning. We seem to be in the midst of multiple efforts to merge the social and cognitive, treating them as essential aspects of one another rather than as dimly sketched background or context for a dominantly cognitive or dominantly social science. As this occurs, investigators seem to be reaching across disciplinary and subdisciplinary boundaries. This book is a sampler of what is happening. Reflecting the mix of disciplines involved in investigations that merge the social and the cognitive, this volume contains chapters not only by psychologists—social, developmental, and cognitive—but also by members of allied disciplines, including anthropology and sociology. It also reaches out to relations with linguistics, philosophy, and literature. Our book is organized in six parts, with this introductory chapter as the first. The chapters in Part One, by developmental, social, and educational psychologists and an anthropologist, explore the role of the immediate social situation in cognition, offering challenges from the mild to the deeply unsettling to psychologists' traditional assumptions about cognition, competence, and performance. In Part Two, chapters by a psychologist and an anthropologist explore from a linguistic perspective the various and often hidden ways in which the social permeates thinking, especially by shaping the forms of reasoning and language use available to members of a community. Part Three contains three chapters by psycholinguists, a sociologist, and social psychologists that examine the way language functions in face-to-face communication. Part Four, in chapters by an anthropologist, developmental psychologists, and social psychologists, examines the sources, individual and social, of shared cultural knowledge. Part Five contains chapters by an anthropologist and by social and cognitive psychologists examining the structure and processes of cognitive collaboration in work situations. In Part Six, several chapters by developmental psychologists consider the individual in sociocognitive activity, examining both how individuals learn from collaborative activity and what they must bring to that activity. Finally, a concluding essay reflects on the preceding chapters from a multidisciplinary perspective that takes human communication as its core.

SOCIALLY SITUATED COGNITION: THE SOCIAL CHARACTER OF MOTIVES AND TASK REPRESENTATIONS

Recent theories of *situated cognition* are challenging the view that the social and the cognitive can be studied independently, arguing that the social context in which cognitive activity takes place is an integral part of that activity, not just the surrounding context for it. Sharing with Soviet-origin *activity theory* (Leont'ev, 1981) an antifunctionalist point of view in which intentionality and affect are components of cognitive activity, North American theories of situated cognition (e.g., Brown, Collins, & Duguid, 1989; Greeno, 1973, 1988; Lave, 1988; Resnick, 1990; Suchman, 1987) challenge the dominant view in cognitive science that assumes a cognitive core can be found that is independent of context and intention. Instead, they argue, every cognitive act must be viewed as a specific response to a specific set of circumstances. Only by understanding the circumstances and the participants' construal of the situation can a valid interpretation of the cognitive activity be made.

Although at first glance they appear to be only simple efforts to take more of the complexity of human performance into account, theories of situated cognition turn out to challenge certain fundamental assumptions of psychology. For example, psychologists typically assume that performance in the special conditions of the laboratory is a valid way of discovering what people's true or basic cognitive competencies are. The laboratory is portrayed as a neutral environment rather than a specific place. It is this belief in the laboratory's nonspecificity that permits psychologists to claim that performances evoked there, often on tasks and apparatus never encountered elsewhere, provide valid information about what people can do "normally"—that is, outside the laboratory.

A contrary view is that performances in a laboratory or on a mental test require a particular social construal by subjects if they are to yield believable data. Yet, as Goodnow (1976) pointed out, that construal is often unavailable or unacceptable to people outside mainstream, middle-class, industrialized cultures. Many people, unused to the kind of total decontextualization taken for granted in much psychological testing and experimentation (Cole, Gay, Glick, & Sharp, 1971; Heath, 1983), will either refuse certain questions altogether or reinterpret them in more familiar terms. Such persons' failure to share our expected social construals of the testing situation, rather than any lack of knowledge or reasoning ability, may account for their failure to perform well on our tests and interviews.

In this volume, Siegal (chapter 2) pursues this possibility systematically, showing how forms of questioning meant by the experimenter to clarify or confirm children's belief commitments are often processed through "social lenses" that affect the child's performance. These studies show that young children's failure to construe the social intent of questioning in the terms meant by the experimenter may lead them to answer in ways that systematically underestimate what they know. Siegal notes that many features of the clinical cognitive interview violate the conventions of ordinary conversation (cf. Grice, 1975). For example, the interviewer often poses the same question several times to check the child's consistency or commitment to a response, but children may interpret the repeated questioning as asking for a different response, because in ordinary conversation one does not ask for information one already has. As a result, Siegal argues, children's conversational inexperience, rather than their conceptual incompetence, may be what produces the patterns of response typical in interview studies with preschoolers. The implications of this conclusion go well beyond the particular concepts that Siegal's experiments investigated. By showing that conversational knowledge plays a role even in the supposedly neutral laboratory interview, Siegal's data imply that researchers should reconsider the generality of many of psychology's laboratory findings.

Siegal's findings are likely to be unsettling to psychologists used to depending on the validity of properly conducted and replicated laboratory studies. Yet his interpretation of those findings is conservative, for he maintains a classic distinction, fundamental to cognitive developmental theory, between *competence* and *performance*. That is, he assumes that the special conversational conventions of the interview have interfered with the investigator's effort to assess children's knowledge, but he assumes the knowledge is there, intact and ready to be revealed by more suitable methods. A commitment to a situated cognition point of view, however, leads to some uncertainty about the very distinction between competence and performance. Strictly speaking, if one believes that all cognition is tailored to a specific situation, competence can only mean the capacity to act appropriately in a given situation. How then can it make sense to speak of a competence that *would* have been manifested *if* the situation—for example, the form of questioning—had been different?

Perret-Clermont, Perret, and Bell (chapter 3), in a chapter that describes experimental findings quite similar to Siegal's, go further than he does in questioning the standard interpretive constructs of developmental psychology. The authors begin with a review of their group's "first generation" of studies, which had as a central goal showing how social engagement might induce individual cognitive growth. As their work proceeded, however, they began to doubt that their construals of the situations studied matched those of their subjects. They suspected that subjects were not always struggling with the logical and symbolic features of the task, but rather with the social meaning of the situation, including

they are heavily influenced by the kinds of beliefs and reasoning schemas available in the individuals' surrounding culture (cf. Nersessian, 1989).

Not only theories but even ways of reasoning themselves are socially determined. Cognitive tools also include the forms of reasoning and argumentation that are accepted as normative in given cultures (see, for example, Grize and Pieraut-LeBonniec, 1983, for an analysis of the role of contradiction in francophone reasoning, and Ashley, 1990, for an analysis of the particular forms of case-based reasoning used by the American law community). Both Mead (1934) and Vygotsky (1978) proposed that mechanisms of thought are best conceived as internalizations of ways of behaving first engaged in externally, in interaction with others. Mead called thought a "conversation with the generalized other," implying that as we think individually we attempt to respond—internally and vicariously—to the imagined responses of others to our ideas and arguments. Vygotsky's central claim was that to understand individual psychological development it is necessary to understand the system of social relations in which the individual lives and grows. This system is itself a product of generations of development over time, so that the individual is, in effect, historically situated, an heir to a long cultural development. Primary among the tools that, for Vygotsky, are each individual's cultural patrimony is language, which mediates all thought.

Within our own culture, coming to us initially from literary disciplines but now beginning to command the attention of linguists and some psychologists, is the notion of discourse communities—communities that share preferred ways of speaking or writing and that judge the quality of ideas in part as a function of the extent to which they are felicitously expressed, according to community standards. Scholarly disciplines constitute discourse communities, as do ordinary people who share ways of talking and reasoning with people like themselves. The phenomenon of *code-switching* shows that people can belong to multiple discourse communities, each enabling and constraining thought in different ways. Which code individuals use, which discourse community they situate themselves within, depends on their social construal of particular cognitive situations, as well as on codes they have available as a result of their past social experience.

Wertsch (chapter 5) outlines Vygotsky's sociocultural perspective on the social situatedness of mind and cognition. Following Vygotsky, Wertsch suggests that the very representations available to the lone individual facing a cognitive task will have been socially shaped. Carrying his analysis beyond the now-familiar themes of Vygotsky, Wertsch looks to another Soviet figure, the literary theorist Bakhtin, to suggest how language itself contains a social history, so that even an utterance by a single individual can be construed as *dialogic*, an expression constructed to respond to particular audiences and expectations. From this flows the notion of *social languages*, particular forms of discourse that mark communities and that shape thought and cognition in fundamental ways.

Socialization through and into language has long been a theme of anthropologists interested in patterns of cognition. The notion—often expressed as the Sapir-Whorf (Mandelbaum, 1949) hypothesis—that certain thoughts cannot be expressed or perhaps even entertained in certain languages is now being extended in ways that suggest that language socialization profoundly shapes world views and social relationships. Children learn not only the grammar and vocabulary of their language but also a structure of social meanings and relationships. Ochs (1988), for example, shows how children's initial language learning in Western Samoa carries with it initiation into assumptions about social authority (e.g., who may speak when, who may express certain ideas), and psychology (e.g., whether there is a hidden meaning or intention that must be sought behind a person's expressed words). Heath (1983) documented similar processes of socialization into and through language in the United States in studies of two small Carolina Piedmont communities.

In this volume, Heath (chapter 6) shows how particular linguistic forms mark and shape a community that is only a part-time one for its participants. She provides an ethnographic account of the language usage of a Little League team studied over the course of a season of play. The study reported is part of a larger project examining learning—often through the medium of language—in nonschool community settings. These settings are always social ones, thus requiring that learning and, hence, cognition be examined as social processes. In addition to rejecting a distinction between the social and the cognitive—thus effectively treating cognition *as* a social process—Heath, like Lave, rejects the traditional association of learning with deliberate instruction. Her project aims to demonstrate the varied forms of learning opportunity available in the context of activities designed for pleasure or community maintenance rather than for instruction. Heath's analysis shows how a coach structures Little League participation in ways that make it into a series of occasions for practicing problem solving, conditional reasoning, and other forms of thinking valued in society at large.

COORDINATING COGNITION: LINGUISTIC TOOLS AND SOCIAL KNOWLEDGE

Language not only functions to shape and constrain world views, but it also embodies tools for coordinating multiple cognitions during direct social interaction. These social management features of language are the central concern of the field of *pragmatics* (see Levinson, 1983), developed initially by philosophers and linguists. A central question for pragmatics concerns how dialogic discourse (i.e., discourse involving two or more individuals, usually carried out in direct interaction) is structured so that participants know what the other is talking about, so that social roles and privileges are respected, and so that the conversation advances to a mutually shared end. Conventions of communication that govern conversation and other forms of linguistic interaction are tools that enable, but also inevitably constrain, socially shared cognition.

Two chapters in this volume explicitly examine this tool aspect of language. Clark and Brennan (chapter 7) examine the ways in which conversants establish and maintain common ground in communication, that is, how they coordinate the content or referential meaning of their talk. Analyzing conversation as pairs of utterances constituting *presentations* and *acceptances*, they show how participants in a conversation seek and use evidence that their partners have understood the intended meanings of successive contributions. They also show how speakers work collaboratively to honor principles of communication of the kind that Grice (1975) laid out. Extending Grice's analysis, Clark and Brennan argue that conversation functions under a principle, not of least effort for individual speakers, but of least *collaborative* effort. This principle produces conversational forms that take account of the difficulties that may be encountered en route to establishing common ground.

Schegloff (chapter 8) shows how a particular feature of conversation—*repair* of perceived miscommunications—serves as a means of maintaining both shared reference and appropriate social relationships during conversation. The availability of procedures for detecting and repairing miscommunications is part of what gives conversational language its enormous flexibility: It need not be precise and unambiguous, because the entire interactive and situational context, not just a speaker's words, is available for establishing shared understanding among participants.

The linguistic forms studied by Clark and Brennan and by Schegloff transcend the individual participants in the conversation and can be understood only as joint constructions in analyses that treat the group rather than individual members of the group as the primary unit of cognitive analysis. These forms are sensitive to shifts in the perceived purposes of the conversation and the medium of communication. As Clark and Brennan show, conversational conventions differ according to the medium of communication (e.g., face-to-face, telephone, electronic mail) and the goal of the communicators (e.g., sharing the gist of information; obtaining such exact information as telephone or credit card numbers). Elsewhere, a growing body of research on distributed cognition (e.g., Brown & Duguid, 1989; Galegher, Kraut, & Egido, 1990; Norman, 1988; Suchman, 1987) is examining the ways in which objects and graphic displays function to support collaborative mental work.

Shared objects and displays facilitate the process of referential anchoring— making sure that speakers and listeners understand a word or phrase in the same way. Sometimes shared referential anchoring is available without the physical presence of a common referent. If the participants in a conversation share a common history—if they have done something together, gone somewhere together, or know that they have common acquaintances, for example—they can refer to this shared past in a present conversation. To take a simple example, if a school class has gone to the zoo together, or if all members have witnessed a particular chemistry demonstration, it is possible to conduct a class science discussion differently than if there is no such shared past experience. For this reason, conversations inside a family or between intimates probably obey different rules for establishing common ground than do conversations among casual acquaintances. Krauss and Fussell (chapter 9) examine the ways in which individual speakers craft communications to fit assumptions about the social communities to which their listeners belong. They focus especially on a particular kind of social knowledge, interactants' assessments of each other's background knowledge and perspective. In a series of studies, the authors show that the ways in which people name and describe unfamiliar figures vary as a function of the expected listener. When the listener is a stranger, speakers shape their messages according to assumptions about the social category to which the listener belongs. Krauss and Fussell consider various possibilities for how knowledge of a listener's social category might guide assumptions about what the listener knows and suggest that people hold implicit theories about the distribution of knowledge that they apply in adapting their communications to their listeners.

CREATING COMMON CONCEPTIONS: THE SOURCES OF CULTURAL KNOWLEDGE

The idea that individuals' social categories might predict what they know is rooted in the assumption that members of social groups share common knowledge and conceptions about the world. How do these shared conceptions arise? How are they maintained over time and changing group membership? How are individual experiences coordinated to create group cultures? Questions of this kind have interested investigators from various disciplines, often with different underlying research agendas.

One issue of broad, recurring interest is the relative contribution of social transmission of knowledge versus individual knowledge construction in the formation of widely shared conceptions in a culture. As noted early in this chapter, the constructivist assumption in cognitive psychology focuses attention on how different people can come to know the same thing. Direct social influence is a simple, attractive answer to that question: People learn information and patterns of reasoning from one another, through either direct teaching or more informal cultural transmission mechanisms such as those considered by Lave (chapter 4) and Rogoff (chapter 16). But if individuals shared common processes of knowledge construction and if they were exposed to the same opportunities for knowledge construction (i.e., the same data), they would also arrive at common conceptions.

It seems likely that, for some kinds of shared knowledge, individually rooted processes may play a major role.

Boster (chapter 10) uses the distribution patterns of taxonomic knowledge in several disparate communities to illuminate the role of information availability in the formation of common conceptions. He shows that when high quality information is freely available—when "naked eye" observations are enough to form expert judgments—social transmission is not necessary to account for agreement among group members. A paradigmatic case is one in which categorizations are made entirely on the basis of observable physical properties of objects and everyone in a group is familiar with the same distribution of objects. Under such conditions, individuals agree on classifications without reference to patterns of social contact. One would predict that newcomers to the group, if given access to the same information as established group members, would join the "culture" on the basis of their independent information processing. Boster shows this process at work when novices in several domains of biological taxonomy make classification judgments similar to those of experts. In these cases, *cultural consensus* is a result of shared access to information and, presumably (although Boster does not make this point explicitly), of shared ways of interpreting information. Quite different in their effects on culture formation are conditions in which information is not freely available to all group members, either because exposure is limited to certain people or because culturally shared judgments are based on interpretations and theories and not only on direct observation of physical characteristics. Boster describes the first of these conditions, showing how, when knowledge availability is patchy (as for very rare species of plants), social transmission accounts for patterns of shared conceptions.

Gelman, Massey, and McManus (chapter 11) take up the question of individual contributions to the construction of shared conceptions from the other side—stressing not information availability but individuals' predispositions to attend to certain kinds of information. They examined the nature of learning in a children's museum, an environment structured to encourage parent–child interactions. Observing children and parents in the museum, Gelman, Massey, and McManus found that parents did not engage in much teaching, especially on topics they perceived as math- or science-related. If the museum observations reflect the extent of guidance that children generally receive from their parents, the authors argue, it would be difficult to account for preschool children's knowledge of number and quantity relations just on the basis of structured environmental input. Elaborating what they call a *constructivist theory of supporting environments*, Gelman, Massey, and McManus propose instead that learners determine which inputs in the environment are relevant to their cognitive growth, and that they make these choices on the basis of *skeletal knowledge structures* that lead them to search for particular patterns of information. Skeletal structures of this kind, they suggest, are part of the biological endowment of humans. These structures do not substitute for learning, but rather make learning possible by constraining and guiding attention so that, from among the many stimuli children encounter, they will select for attention those that support the formation of particular concepts. This means that common conceptions arise not just from common exposure to information but also from the fact that humans share common skeletal structures.

Much of what counts as knowledge goes well beyond the kinds of concepts whose construction is likely to be guided by skeletal structures or to be inferable from naked eye observations. The physical sciences, for example, consist of complex theoretical systems in which layers of interpretation condition what sense can be made of observations. When people are attempting to understand social systems, even more dependence on culturally patterned standards of interpretation is likely. Because interpretive systems vary substantially among cultural groups, a full account of shared social knowledge requires some kind of social transmission model of culture formation. Levine and Moreland (chapter 12) analyze the culture of work groups, examining especially what it takes for new members to become socialized into these cultures. Defining *culture* as the shared thoughts and customs of groups, they review a varied literature on the kinds of information that work groups share and the forms of behavior that mark group membership. Their review includes research on many kinds of groups: sports teams, legislatures, hospital employees, national park rangers, waitresses, strippers, cooks, aircrews, high steel ironworkers, electricians, machine toolers, folk performers, sailors, judges, policemen, prison guards, miners, and business managers. Their analysis stresses aspects of work knowledge and practice that fall outside the scope of officially described jobs, especially information about the group itself—its distinctiveness, its special codes, its informal status hierarchies and hidden communication networks, its unwritten standards of performance and conformance. In concluding their discussion, Levine and Moreland raise the question of the extent to which complete consonance of knowledge and perspective is optimal in work groups. Considering empirical research on group polarization, majority and minority influence, social loafing, and communication, they conclude that optimal distribution of knowledge in groups depends on the conditions in which the group works and the nature of the actions it must take.

COLLABORATING AT WORK

The reasons for society's preference for socially distributed, rather than individual, conditions of work are many. Sometimes the range of specific activities to be accomplished within a certain time is too great for any one individual. This can occur, for example, when several different systems must be simultaneously monitored and the information combined, or when a complex piece of machinery requires simultaneous adjustment of several parts to function properly. Multiple

11). The importance of individual cognitive processes in sociocognitive activity is a primary theme of several developmental psychologists' contributions to the volume. Their chapters look at both the role of social interaction in promoting individual cognitive development and the role of individual development in enabling effective interaction.

Social interaction as a stimulus for individual cognitive growth has become a prominent issue in developmental and educational research. Research inspired by Piaget has emphasized the role of contradiction, especially by peers, in promoting individual cognitive restructuring. An initially separate line of developmental research inspired by Vygotsky's views of cognitive socialization has focused more on collaborative cognitive activity as a source of development. In today's research it is often difficult to separate Piagetian from Vygotskian streams of influence. In this volume, two chapters explore the effects of specific forms of joint cognitive activity on individual learning, one focusing on the structure of interaction in a school classroom and the other on details of interaction in adult–child and child–child tutoring pairs.

Hatano and Inagaki (chapter 15) examine a particular form of class discussion and argument on science topics about which none of the participants was particularly knowledgeable at the outset. Learning thus resulted from their collective efforts to comprehend new information. The classes studied, in Japanese elementary schools, used a method of science instruction in which class members form groups initially committed to the same hypothesis. Pupils discuss and explain their choices to one another and, under the teacher's guidance, conduct experiments to confirm or deny hypotheses, after which additional "votes" choosing among the alternative hypotheses are taken. The formation of opinion groups creates a social environment in which partisanship—commitment to the group that shares one's initial hypothesis—motivates cognitive efforts to prove the correctness of one's own opinion and to challenge that of others. It is tempting to think of this in Wertsch's terms, as institutionalized or *organized multivocality* tempered by empirical checks on the validity of opinions. Hatano and Inagaki stress the dual social and epistemic motivation built into this form of classroom activity. The debate is energized by social (in this case, partisan) motivation. At the same time, the debate serves to make individuals aware of gaps and insufficiencies in their personal knowledge, which they try to correct. Even largely silent members, they claim, can participate in this process vicariously. Although social cognitive activity is essential to learning, Hatano and Inagaki insist that comprehension is, in the end, a private achievement.

Rogoff (chapter 16) shares Hatano and Inagaki's primary focus on individual learning. Studying children's acquisition of the cognitive skill of planning, she reintroduces the concept of apprenticeship but with a distinctly different emphasis from that of Lave. For Lave, apprentices learn without deliberate instruction, by participating in activities that are being conducted not for the sake of instruction, but of production. Rogoff ignores the production aspects of apprenticeship to focus on the instructional features of social interactions. In doing so, she shows that social interaction does not always advance individual learning; particular conditions and forms of interaction are required. Examining differences between adult and child tutors, she concludes that adults tend to guide the child partner through an overt process of planning, whereas child tutors, even when skilled in planning, often do the planning themselves and simply tell the partner what actions to carry out. The result is that the learner in most child–child dyads does not get to participate in the planning activity. It is as if the adults took teaching the child partner as a central goal of the shared activity, whereas the skilled peers took accomplishing the task as their main objective. Rogoff's results suggest that cognitive apprenticeships (cf. Collins, Brown, & Newman, 1989) may require social intents and organizations different in key respects from those effective in learning crafts and trades.

Rogoff found that even skillful tutoring did not always effectively produce learning. Her 4- and 5-year-old subjects appeared unable to benefit from guided participation in planning. The suggestion is that certain already developed individual cognitive capacities may be necessary for successful participation in particular forms of shared activity. This is the central theme of Brownell and Carriger's work (chapter 17). These authors examine collaboration between very young children, treating the ability to coordinate activity in play as a function of the cognitive capacities of the individual children. To study the collaboration of pairs of 12- to 30-month-olds (a period in which both language and sense of self as an independent causal agent are developing), Brownell and Carriger constructed a toy that children could operate only by coordinating their actions. Their hypothesis was that children's ability to coordinate activity deliberately is a function of their ability to represent others' behavior symbolically and, in particular, to attribute agency and intentionality to the other. To test this, aspects of performance during the collaborative session were examined in relation to the children's ability to differentiate self and other and to attribute independent agency to others. Clear age differences in ability to coordinate solutions on the experimental toy were apparent. For collaboration in a pair to occur, at least one of the children had to be able to represent the other as causing his or her own behavior. Thus, like Gelman et al. and Rogoff, these investigators show that the course of an interaction depends on what children bring to it.

This point is further highlighted in Damon's work (chapter 18), which offers an apologia for a continuing research focus on individuals and their (biologically grounded) development. Commenting on the concept of *situated cognition*, Damon expresses concern that too much emphasis on context and social constructionism will result in the loss of a valuable focus on individual development as both a contributor to and a result of social interactions. He also offers a normative expectation that individual abilities and, thus, capacities for particular forms of interaction, will develop in predictable ways with age. The key aspect of development to which Damon calls our attention is *progression*, or change with directionality. He takes issue with those, such as Lave, who appear to deny that certain kinds of knowledge and capacity are more advanced or valuable. Not surprisingly, given this view, Damon finds efforts such as Rogoff's to link the specific characteristics of social interactions with children's achievement of adult-valued cognitive capabilities more congenial. Analyzing several specific cases, however, he suggests it may not be so much *who* participates in an interaction (adult–child pairs vs. child–child pairs) as *how* they organize their joint activity that distinguishes interactions. All told, Damon offers a warning to psychologists: By focusing on social sharing, which tends to carry with it an interest in the context of behavior, they may lose sight of the individual over time.

SHARING COGNITION THROUGH THE MEDIUM OF CULTURE

Damon's championing of the individual points to what is almost certainly the major point of difference among contributors to this volume: the individual versus the group as primary object of attention and concern. The volume concludes with a wide-ranging discussion by Cole (chapter 19) that addresses this question directly. Noting that the word *share* can mean both *dividing* and *putting in common*, Cole suggests that chapter authors have, often implicitly, subscribed to different definitions of shared cognition. These definitions have consequences for the extent to which authors grapple with the multiple ways in which an effort to treat cognition as a social process constitutes a potentially fundamental challenge to the traditional analytic and methodological apparatus of psychology. It will not be surprising to those who have followed Cole's work to learn that he finds most interesting those lines of investigation that attempt to study cognition in its indigenous context of activity. He argues for the need to develop forms of study that treat neither the group nor the individual as the primary unit, but rather examine the ways in which cognitive and social activity unfold in a culturally mediated setting. Culture, for Cole, is the meeting point of the individual and the social. Culture, constituted of tools, artifacts, and ways of thought, is what carries the past history of a society into the present, thereby both enabling and constraining current thinking. Through the medium of culture, cognition is both divided—distributed—among individuals and held in common by them. But culture is itself an ill-defined concept. As Cole suggests, developing a psychologically useful theory of culture, along with rigorous methods for the systematic study of two or more interacting individuals, represents a major challenge for those who wish to understand socially shared cognition.

References

Amigues, R., Chevallard, Y., Johsua, S., Paour, J. L., & Schubauer-Leoni, M. L. (1988). *Le contrat didactique: Differentes approches* (Report No. 8, Interactions Didactiques). Geneva, Switzerland: University of Neuchatel.

Ashley, K. (1990). *Modeling legal argument: Reasoning with cases and hypotheticals.* Cambridge, MA: MIT Press.

Brown, J. S., Collins, A., & Duguid, P. (1989). Situated cognition and the culture of learning. *Educational Researcher, 18*(1), 32–42.

Brown, J. S., & Duguid, P. (1989, May). *Innovation in the workplace: A perspective on organizational learning.* Paper prepared for the Carnegie Mellon University Conference on Organizational Learning, Pittsburgh, PA.

Carey, S. (1985). *Conceptual change in childhood.* Cambridge, MA: MIT Press.

Chi, M. T. H. (1990). *Conceptual change across autological categories: Examples from learning and discovery in science.* Unpublished manuscript, University of Pittsburgh, Learning Research and Development Center.

Cicourel, A., Jennings, K. H., Jennings, S. H. M., Leiter, K. C. W., MacKay, R., Mehan, H., & Roth, D. R. (1974). *Language use and school performance.* New York: Academic Press.

Cole, M. (1985). The zone of proximal development: Where culture and cognition create each other. In J. V. Wertsch (Ed.), *Culture, communication, and cognition: Vygotskian perspectives* (pp. 146–161). Cambridge, England: Cambridge University Press.

Cole, M., Gay, J., Glick, J. A., & Sharp, D. W. (1971). *The cultural context of learning and thinking.* New York: Basic Books.

Collins, A., Brown, J. S., & Newman, S. E. (1989). Cognitive apprenticeship: Teaching the crafts of reading, writing, and mathematics. In L. B. Resnick (Ed.), *Knowing, learning, and instruction: Essays in honor of Robert Glaser* (pp. 453–494). Hillsdale, NJ: Erlbaum.

Doise, W., & Mugny, G. (1984). *The social development of the intellect.* Oxford, England: Pergamon Press.

Eckert, P. (1989). *Jocks and burnouts: Social categories and identity in high school.* New York: Teachers College Press.

Fish, S. E. (1980). *Is there a text in this class?: The authority of interpretive communities.* Cambridge, MA: Harvard University Press.

Galegher, J., Kraut, R. E., & Egido, C. (Eds.). (1990). *Intellectual teamwork: Social and technological foundations of cooperative work.* Hillsdale, NJ: Erlbaum.

Goodnow, J. J. (1976). The nature of intelligent behavior: Questions raised by cross-cultural studies. In L. B. Resnick (Ed.), *The nature of intelligence* (pp. 169–188). Hillsdale, NJ: Erlbaum.

Goody, E. N. (1989). Learning, apprenticeship, and the division of labor. In M. Coy (Ed.), *Apprenticeship: From theory to method and back again* (pp. 233–256). Albany: State University of New York Press.

Greeno, J. G. (1973). The structure of memory and the process of solving problems. In R. Solso (Ed.), *Contemporary issues in cognitive psychology: The Loyola Symposium* (pp. 103–133). Washington, DC: Holt, Rinehart & Winston.

Greeno, J. G. (1988). *Situations, mental models, and generative knowledge* (Report No. IRL88-0005). Palo Alto, CA: Institute for Research on Learning.

Grice, H. P. (1975). Logic and conversation. In P. Cole & J. L. Morgan (Eds.), *Syntax and semantics* (Vol. 3, pp. 225–242). New York: Seminar Press.

Grize, J.-B., & Pieraut-LeBonniec, G. (1983). *La contradiction: Essai sur les operations de la pensee.* Paris: Presses Universitaires de France.

CHAPTER 2

A CLASH OF CONVERSATIONAL WORLDS: INTERPRETING COGNITIVE DEVELOPMENT THROUGH COMMUNICATION

MICHAEL SIEGAL

According to Piaget (1970), young children are often unable to detect the invariant or concealed realities that underlie perceptual appearances. My aim in this chapter is to demonstrate that children may actually know a good deal about how these realities do not correspond to appearances, and that their lack of success with the many tasks that Piaget and others have used to support the existence of conceptual limitations during an early preoperational stage of cognitive development can be reinterpreted through an explanation that focuses on language. My proposal is that children are both sophisticated and limited users of rules of conversation that promote effective communication: sophisticated when it comes to the use of conversational rules in everyday, natural talk, but limited in specialized settings that require knowledge of the purpose intended by speakers who have put aside rules in the conventional use of language.

This research was supported by the National Health and Medical Research Council of Australia and by a University of Queensland Special Project Grant and International Collaborative Research Award.

Correspondence concerning this chapter should be addressed to Michael Siegal, Department of Psychology, University of Queensland, St. Lucia, Australia.

COMMUNICATION AND RULES OF CONVERSATION

When young children participate in everyday conversations, they often adjust their speech to suit the characteristics of the listener (Gelman & Shatz, 1977). They speak in less sophisticated ways to children younger than themselves and use more complicated forms of language when conversing with adults. Moreover, they are skilled in comprehending the motives of a speaker (Braine & Rumain, 1983). They assume that a speaker's messages will be cooperatively motivated by brevity, sincerity, relevance, and clarity, conventions of communication that have been noted by philosophers of language. These are rational, systematic rules that constrain conversations.

In his account of speech conventions, Grice (1975, p. 45) maintains that a Cooperative Principle underlies effective communication: "Make your conversational contribution such as is required, at the stage at which it occurs, by the accepted purpose or direction of the talk exchange in which you are engaged." To produce conversation in accordance with this principle, he lists four rules or maxims that may be described as the Maxims of (a) Quantity ("Speak no more or no less than is required"), (b) Quality ("Try to speak the truth and avoid falsehood"), (c) Relevance or Relation ("Be relevant and informative"), and (d) Manner ("Avoid obscurity and ambiguity"). These maxims can be called the *conversational rules.*[1]

In conversations between adults, it is mutually understood that the rules may sometimes be explicitly flouted to create what Grice has termed *conversational implicatures.* These nonconventional forms of language are used, for example, when the rules contradict each other (e.g., when being relevant and informative would violate the quantity rule to be brief and speak no more than is required), when irony is intended through an uninformative statement of the obvious, or when there is a politely motivated desire to ensure through repeated questioning that the listener understands. Even in adult conversations, however, the listener is apt to be misled if a rule is quietly broken.

In experimental settings, contrary to the relevance and quantity rules, experimenters may pose questions to children in which the answer is obvious or repeated. Unlike older children and adults, young children may not appreciate that the purpose of departing from these rules is to establish the children's understanding of concepts. They may inadvertently perceive an experimenter's well-meaning questions as uninformative and irrelevant. Moreover, contrary to the quality and manner rules, children may perceive questions as insincere and deceptive, or an experimenter may unjustifiably assume that children share with

---

[1]Although Grice's account has been highly influential, many commentators (e.g., Brown & Levinson, 1987; Cohen, 1971; Sperber & Wilson, 1986) have pointed to more complex issues (that will not be dealt with here) in the study of the pragmatic use of language.

adults the meaning of certain key words. Because children's conversational habits are based on an implicit understanding of the Cooperative Principle and the conventional use of conversational rules, in response to implicatures contained in unconventional forms of questioning, they may misinterpret the experimenter's purpose or use of language. They may respond incorrectly not because they do not know the answer but because the conversational worlds of adults and children clash. In some cases, communication may be jeopardized by children's perception that the experimenter is not even observing the basic principle that speakers cooperate with the listener.

Efforts have been made to investigate how children understand the nature and purpose of adults' questions. The results indicate that children can be inadvertently led to give answers that do not reflect the depth of their understanding, and that they have a greater knowledge of the realities underlying perceptual appearances than Piaget and others estimated.

PERCEPTION OF PURPOSE IN QUESTIONING: CONSERVATION OF NUMBER AS A STARTING POINT

Sixty years ago, Piaget (1929) wrote about the difficulties of questioning children by using a "clinical method." To diagnose their authentic reasoning abilities, his rule was to encourage "the flow of spontaneous tendencies," and he advocated that "every symptom" of the child's thought should be placed in its "mental context" (p. 4). Questions ideally should be asked in the manner and form of the spontaneous questions actually asked by children of the same age and younger. In efforts to avoid "systematic errors" inherent in the "pure experiment" in which children may give artificial responses, Piaget was particularly concerned with the effect of repeated questioning and lengthy interviewing. He sought to deal with this problem by presenting countersuggestions and by letting the child talk for a few minutes and later returning to the topic indirectly. He advocated that the interviewer probe the roots of the suspect answer and then ask the question in as many different ways as possible. But although he believed that "Suggestion may thus be avoided by means of patience and analysis," Piaget (1929, pp. 27–28) did concede a "much more serious difficulty," that of distinguishing from among the results of the examination the point to be regarded as the child's original contribution and that due to previous adult influences."

Piaget acknowledged but never clearly confronted this problem. In fact, a critical gulf in communication can occur even between adult speakers and listeners. Such a gulf is well shown in many humorous incidents, for example, in the Marx Brothers joke in which one man says to another, "Where can I get a hold of you?" and the response is, "I don't know. I'm ticklish all over!" Cases of misunderstanding a speaker's intent probably occur more frequently in communication with children. But these misunderstandings are also apt to be more subtle because children are less experienced in conversations. Compared with adults, children may be less likely to retort spontaneously in an effort to clarify a speaker's intent and to offer repairs for improving communication. Consequently, their misunderstanding of the purpose underlying questions may go unnoticed, and they may not reveal the depth of their knowledge.

Although Piaget advocated using countersuggestions to probe for certainty in children's answers, the children may not share the experimenter's implicature in violating the quantity rule—to test through repeated questioning whether they believe in their answer, irrespective of whether the opposite is maintained by their peers in general. Instead, they may extract meaning from their personal knowledge of others and strain to import their own relevance to the speaker's rule breaking. As Anne-Nelly Perret-Clermont has pointed out in chapter 3 of this volume, children's responses to suggestions such as "Another child gave me a different answer. Do you agree?" may be tacitly based on the presumed answer to the question "Is he a dumb or smart kid?", rather than referring to any child at all. Nevertheless, on the basis of conservation studies, Piaget often contended that young children center on the external perceptual aspects of transformations and ignore invariant features such as number. That is, in comparing the numbers of counters set out in parallel rows, they fail to take into account density as well as length and do not compensate by integrating information from two or more dimensions of a problem.

All the same, the issue of how children understand experimenters' questions has not gone unnoticed. In an incisive pair of studies, Rose and Blank (1974) tested the hypothesis that nonconservation of number is influenced by the language context and that repetition of the question (e.g., "Are there the same number in both rows, or does one row have more?") misleads children to change their answers and respond incorrectly. Asking only one question after the rows had been transformed produced more conservation responses in 6-year-olds compared with largely nonconservation responses in a standard two-question condition. This is similar to the effect we see in adult conversations where repeated questioning (e.g., "How are you?" Response: "OK." Repeated question: "How are you?") results in response switching or, perhaps in some cases, annoyance at having to repeat the answer. Yet Rose and Blank's findings have met with equivocal support in replication studies (e.g., Neilson, Dockrell, & McKechnie, 1983; Samuel & Bryant, 1984) and, in any event, were largely restricted to 6-year-olds' judgments of small numbers of items. To address this issue, we examined children's appreciation of repeated questioning in two conservation of number experiments with children aged 4 to 6 years (Siegal, Waters, & Dinwiddy, 1988).

A total of 180 children participated in Experiment 1. Within each age group, half were randomly assigned to a one-question condition and half to a standard two-question condition. The task involved comparing numbers in two rows of 20 counters that had been rearranged by the experimenter. As predicted, the children tested under the one-question condition gave significantly more conservation judgments (78% in all) than did those tested under the standard condition (23%).

In Experiment 2, we further examined the hypothesis that children interpret repeated questioning as requiring an inconsistent pattern of responses. Children were shown puppets who acted as subjects in videotaped conservation experiments and were asked to give causal attributions for the puppets' responses in one-question and two-question conditions. According to our theory, if children interpret a repeated request as a cue to change responses, they should give "external" attributions for puppets' conservation judgments in the standard two-question condition and more "internal" attributions for conservation responses or non-conservation responses in the one-question condition.

The 32 4- to 6-year-olds in this second experiment were initially alerted to the possibility that choices are made to please others by instructions based on Asch's (1958) series of conformity experiments, together with two practice requests for justifications. The experimenter first read a story such as the following, in which the characters were the same sex as the subject:

> Sally was playing with a few of her friends at kindergarten when the teacher came up to the children and showed them two blocks, one big and one small. The teacher asked each child to point to the biggest block. The first child pointed to the smaller block, and so did the others. Then it was Sally's turn. She pointed to the small block, too. Do you think that Sally pointed to the small block because (a) she really wanted to please the other children and be like them or because (b) she really thought that block was the biggest? (All the children chose *a*.)
>
> The teacher showed the same blocks to another group of children who were playing with Louise and asked them to point to the smallest block. The first child pointed to the big block, and so did the others. Then it was Louise's turn. She pointed to the other block instead. Do you think Louise pointed to the small block because (a) she wanted to please the other children or because (b) she really thought it was the smallest block? (All the children chose *b*.)
>
> So you see, sometimes people do things just to please others and sometimes they do things because they really think what they do is true.[2]

The children then viewed four videotaped segments depicting the responses of puppets on the conservation of number arrays used in the first study. The puppets were shown tested by an experimenter twice under one-question conditions and twice under standard conditions. For one segment in each condition, one

---

[2]From "Misleading Children: Causal Attributions for Inconsistency Under Repeated Questioning" by M. Siegal, L. J. Waters, & L. S. Dinwiddy, 1988, *Journal of Experimental Child Psychology*, 45, p. 445. Copyright 1988 by Academic Press. Reprinted by permission.

that can be approached by examining the interaction between the explicitness of children's knowledge and their conversational experience.

As Karmiloff-Smith (1986) suggests, it is useful to distinguish between knowledge that is consciously accessible (sometimes called *explicit* or *declarative knowledge*) and knowledge that can be implicitly represented in behavior (sometimes called *procedural knowledge*). For example, in language tasks, children can implicitly identify forms such as sentences, but they may not be able to respond to direct questions about these forms. Similarly, they may have a substantial implicit AR knowledge without possessing conscious access to the dual representational code that is necessary to respond to direct questions. Thus, if an experimenter's goal is to examine the early capacity for representation through direct questioning, some children may be unable to access their knowledge and may confuse appearance and reality. By contrast, they may demonstrate a procedural or implicit knowledge if the experimenter examines their understanding as a means of obtaining a clear-cut goal, such as procuring uncontaminated nutrients.

Yet experimenters may seek explicit, declarative knowledge from children using methods that require still further explicit knowledge. In communication with adults, young children may initially operate under a mental model that does not represent departures from conversational rules. As Johnson-Laird (1983) proposed, in making inferences, listeners typically imagine a state of affairs based on the meaning of the premises. They then formulate an informative conclusion that corresponds to this state and search for alternative models to test the validity of the conclusion. Young children's experience in communicating with adults often takes the form of a simple model: An *A* (adult) wants *B* (information). *B* can be obtained by asking *C* (child). The inference is simply that, by questioning *C* (and by *C* cooperatively supplying *B*), *A* acquires the desired *B*.

But what if this mental model is disturbed by repeated questioning on very similar tasks that contravene the quantity rule? Children may not construct a model based on an alternative state of affairs and an understanding of the implicature: *A* wants to be sure that *C* knows about *B*, and for this reason *A* uses prolonged techniques of questioning. Instead, they may operate on the basis of premises, such as that *A* believes that *B* can be found from *C* if *C* would change his or her mind, or that *A* was looking for a different *B* in the first place. Therefore, even if children have an explicit or declarative understanding of a problem, their knowledge may not be conveyed in response to techniques that require the construction of an alternative model of the task and the experimenter's intent.

According to Johnson-Laird (1983, pp. 126–145), there are both implicit and explicit inferential abilities in interpreting discourse. Implicit inferences are based on a single mental model that processes information rapidly. Explicit inferences are required when the single or default model does not work and alternative models must be sought. Nevertheless, the use of unconventional or unfamiliar language that requires the explicit construction of alternative mental models may conceal both an explicit and implicit knowledge of a subject area.

Of course there is more to cognitive development than the ability to share purposes and meanings in experimental contexts. Even if children do have this ability and possess an implicit representation that directs their attention to the relevant features of a problem, they may still lack the conceptual competence— the logico-mathematical knowledge and principles—to succeed fully. Only a skeletal understanding may be present. To ensure that a conceptual limitation in development is deep rather than superficial, it is necessary to rule out the interpretation of a clash between the conversational worlds of adults and children.

An approach that focuses on the language of the experiment harbors the possibility of discovering more capacity in early cognitive development than has often been envisioned. If this chapter has shown that conversational assumptions in forms of questioning must be made more explicit, it has achieved its purpose.

References

Asch, S. E. (1958). Effects of group pressure upon the modification and distortion of judgments. In E. E. Maccoby, T. M. Newcomb, & E. L. Hartley (Eds.), *Readings in social psychology* (3rd ed., pp. 174–183). New York: Holt.

Braine, M. D. S., & Rumain, B. (1983). Logical reasoning. In P. H. Mussen (Ed.), *Handbook of child psychology* (Vol. 3, pp. 263–340). New York: Wiley.

Brown, P., & Levinson, S. C. (1987). *Politeness: Some universals in language usage*. Cambridge, England: Cambridge University Press.

Cohen, L. J. (1971). Some remarks on Grice's views about the logical particles of natural language. In Y. Bar-Hillel (Ed.), *Pragmatics of natural languages* (pp. 50–68). Dordrecht, Holland: D. Reidel.

Fallon, A. E., Rozin, P., & Pliner, P. (1984). The child's conception of food rejections with special reference to disgust and contamination sensitivity. *Child Development, 55*, 566–575.

Flavell, J. H., Flavell, E. R., & Green, F. L. (1983). Development of the appearance–reality distinction. *Cognitive Psychology, 15*, 95–120.

Flavell, J. H., Green, F. L., & Flavell, E. R. (1986). Development of knowledge about the appearance–reality distinction. *Monographs of the Society for Research in Child Development, 51*(Serial No. 212).

Gelman, R., Meck, E., & Merkin, S. (1986). Young children's numerical competence. *Cognitive Development, 1*, 1–29.

Gelman, R., & Shatz, M. (1977). Appropriate speech adjustments: The operation of conversational constraints on talk to two-year-olds. In M. Lewis & L. A. Rosenblum (Eds.), *Interaction, conversation, and the development of language* (pp. 27–61). New York: Wiley.

Grice, H. P. (1975). Logic and conversation. In P. Cole & J. L. Morgan (Eds.), *Syntax and semantics, Vol 3: Speech acts* (pp. 41–58). New York: Academic Press.

Johnson-Laird, P. N. (1983). *Mental models*. Cambridge, MA: Harvard University Press.

Karmiloff-Smith, A. (1986). From meta-processes to conscious access: Evidence from children's metalinguistic and repair data. *Cognition, 23*, 95–147.

vergent responses that is the origin of the restructuring of the subject's thought. This is true even if the two divergent answers are equally wrong. This conflict is sociocognitive, not just cognitive, because the presence of another person obliges the subject to take into account the existence of a cognitive response different from his or her own. It is sociocognitive, not just social, in the sense that the confrontation's aim is not negotiating the participants' identities, their motivations, or any other affective or emotional aspect of the interaction, but only the understanding of the conceptual matters involved in the task.

Within the Piagetian theoretical framework, Inhelder, Sinclair, and Bovet (1974), as well as other authors, have stated that the source of progress lies in the cognitive conflict generated by the negative feedback to the child's response. Our research indicates that this feedback is always socially mediated. When confronted by negative feedback (i.e., a viewpoint different from his or her own), the child is faced with an objection to his or her mode of thinking. This objection can be presented directly to the child or through an experimental device designed for such a purpose. Our hypothesis is that the more direct the conflict that takes place in the social interaction, the more likely the interaction will trigger a cognitive restructuring.

But sociocognitive conflicts do not always result in developmental progress. At least two conditions must be fulfilled for progress to occur. One is that the subjects must have the necessary cognitive prerequisites to benefit from a given social interaction session. For example, for the conservation of number, only those nonconservers who can enumerate the tokens (count the number of tokens in the line) or who can place two sets of objects in one-to-one correspondence are likely to progress to the operatory stage after being confronted by a peer with an opposing viewpoint. Secondly, social confrontation is fruitful only if the gap between the partners' cognitive skills is not too wide (Doise & Mugny, 1984). That is, certain cognitive skills are needed for the child to benefit from the sociocognitive confrontation, which, in turn, strengthens his or her competencies.

These results can be integrated in an interactionist and constructivist model of cognitive development in which social and cognitive factors engender one another in a sequential order that reveals the progressive development of mental structures. New mental organizations make the subject capable of engaging in new social interactions, which, in turn, foster new mental organizations.

In formulating this integrative model of how cognitive and social processes interact to produce cognitive growth, a model that accounts for much of the results of the first generation studies, we are still left with a series of observations that cannot be explained by this model of development. We will now briefly present some results whose interpretation questions certain premises of this first model, notably the strong distinction we originally made between what is social and what is cognitive, and the idea of what is the content of development. We will see that cognition is not as autonomous a function as postulated initially but is the result of the individual's dependency on the communication constraints of the settings in which the individual grows and the patterns of intersubjectivity that the individual's partners invite him or her to establish (see Hutchins' chapter in this volume for a related analysis in adulthood).

Some facts remain unexplained

One unexplained fact that has been repeatedly observed is sex and social class differences in pretest performances that sometimes disappear by the posttest under certain types of experimental conditions (Nicolet, Grossen, & Perret-Clermont, 1988; Perret-Clermont, 1980; Perret-Clermont & Mugny, 1985; Perret-Clermont & Schubauer-Leoni, 1981). It seems that, given the opportunity to interact in certain social settings, lower-class subjects are likely to catch up (after a 10-minute experimental session) with their middle- and upper-class peers and eliminate the "developmental lag" (or "sociocultural handicap") indicated in their pretest performance. This result is not predicted by Piagetian theory, because Piaget's model sees development following a slow, integrative process in which maturation has an important role. It also casts doubt on the adequacy of such global concepts as developmental lag and sociocultural handicap to account for differences in cognitive developmental levels when these so-called handicaps can be eradicated by a brief confrontation with a peer. What is it, then, that actually changes in the subject's cognitive level? Is it his or her cognitive level of competence (i.e., operatory stage) or his or her understanding of the type of thinking that is expected to be displayed in this context?

A second unexplained observation is Lévy's (1981) finding that cognitive progress subsequent to certain social interactions occurs most often when the subject has been associated with the same adult experimenter for the three phases (pretest, experimental session, and posttest) of the research. The integrative model predicts the importance of confronting a point of view that is cognitively divergent but does not account for this role of the personal relationship with the experimenter.

A third unexplained observation, made by Doise, Dionnet, and Mugny (1978), as well as Donaldson (1978) and other researchers, is that the subject's performance level for a given operatory task can vary according to task or type of instruction given. (For a review of this debate in relation to Piagetian theory, see Light & Perret-Clermont, 1989.) To what extent do these tests assess the subject's operatory level? Or do they actually test a subject's communicative competence? Does the subject engage in individual reflection before answering the experimenter's questions, or does he or she rely on cues implicit in the adult discourse? Perhaps the child's cognitive performance is the result of interpretation of not only the cognitive dimensions of the task but its social meaning as well (see Goodnow's, 1990a, report on the role of the audience). We will address these questions in the discussion of our second generation studies. But let us first consider another approach to the interdependence of cognitive and social behaviors.

The Subject's Use of Social Resources for Cognitive Tasks

Autonomous cognitive activity or compliance?

In another series of first generation studies, Perret's (1977, 1978) explorations of subjects' social behavior on cognitive tasks pose similar questions about the identification of cognitive tasks and relevant behavior to accomplish them. Some tasks are of such a nature that the knowledge and skills required to perform them correctly go beyond individual reflection and activity with objects. This is most evident in the resolution of tasks using conventional or technological information. Many signs, rules, and notations rely on social consensus and cannot be invented or discovered by the individual alone. Like social norms and habits, they are made accessible to the individual by social transmission. Although the development of subjects' understanding of such a task or problem can be a function of their own intellectual competencies, they cannot acquire the cognitive resources needed to solve the problem without drawing on the knowledge of other people. Likewise, the child is active not only in exploring the physical environment and the consequences of his or her actions on it, but also in questioning the social environment and obtaining information from others (Berlyne, 1962; Bruner & Olson, 1973). Questioning can be a very adaptive behavior under certain circumstances and sometimes is the only means of finding a solution to a given task. But when is a subject who undertakes a complex task likely to use social resources to obtain the information needed?

The study of questioning behavior is particularly complex; many factors and processes explain why subjects do or do not ask for needed information. In her review of research on help-seeking behavior, Nelson-Le Gall (1985) argues for a reconceptualization of help seeking to consider primarily the adaptive and instrumental function of this behavior, which is seen as an achievement behavior. In this perspective Nelson-Le Gall (1985, Nelson-Le Gall & Jones, 1990) pays more attention to the learning and cognitive processes involved than to the social meaning of help seeking. She also shows that an approach focused on personal and sociocultural characteristics is not sufficient to account for the observed variability of this behavior.

Inspired by Robinson and Rackstraw's studies (1975) on pupils' questions and answers, Perret's overall goal was to study the interdependence of cognitive and social factors, looking specifically at the connections among the child's cognitive apprehension of a task, perception of the situation, expected social role, and social behavior.

Perret's observational studies of 8- to 11-year-old children's resolution of technical tasks (e.g., geometrical drawing or construction of a mobile or electrical circuit) were aimed at eliciting verbalization during task resolution to explore the connection between the subject's mode of problem solving and his or her questions.

When presenting the task to the subject, the experimenter always insisted on remaining available to the subject in case the child had questions, difficulties, or lack of information, hoping that the child would establish a dialogue concerning his or her resolution of the task. Results showed that the majority of subjects had difficulty establishing such dialogue during their task resolution and asked very few questions. To elicit subjects' questioning, the experimenter was obliged to repeat the instructions several times. This device worked for a few subjects, who increased their questions almost for the sake of asking questions and not as an aid to their problem solving.

Subjects' questions could be regrouped into two general categories according to the function of the given question. About half of the questions posed corresponded to the experimenter's expectations and were aimed at a better understanding of the task (e.g., concerning properties of the material, details about information given or terms used, or characteristics of the actions required). The other half were aimed at obtaining the experimenter's approval of the subjects' behavior, with children checking to see if their productions were accepted. Such children asked questions in search of feedback, wanting to be told what to do. By asking these questions, subjects test the adult's behavioral expectations and check their conformity to (supposed) social norms of adequacy. Contrary to what might be expected, these observations indicate that children's remarks and questions embedded in the adult–child dialogue do not reveal their autonomous cognitive activity but rather their attempts to comply with the sociocognitive demands of the adult as mediated by the given task.

In some tasks, Perret manipulated the information necessary for task resolution. For example, 6- to 10-year-old subjects were asked to make drawings from incomplete instructions or to build constructions from ambiguous schemas. Perret wanted to determine whether subjects would be aware of the incompleteness or ambiguity of the task instructions and, if so, whether they would ask the necessary questions. Results showed that subjects' behaviors varied with age. The youngest subjects did not notice the deficiency of the task instructions. They solved the task on their own without checking their solution against possible alternative solutions. Their questions did not refer to the ambiguity of the instructions. Robinson and Robinson (1976) observed that young children, in the case of communication difficulties, tended to blame the listener more often than the speaker and never analyzed the message itself. Perret's results could be interpreted as demonstrating the same tendency: Instead of focusing their attention on the task instructions, children tended to take responsibility for resolving the task as best they could without profiting from adult help or other social features that could facilitate their efforts.

Although the older subjects were aware of the ambiguities inherent in the task instructions, many of them tried to solve the task by themselves without asking for help. They used various cues to infer the missing information and reduce their uncertainty (without, however, checking to see if their inferences were correct). Other subjects did attempt to seek help from the experimenter, but fewer than half the questions these subjects asked concerned the information missing from the instructions. Instead, subjects were concerned with asking the adult about the "right" or "appropriate" thing to do. This "rightness" seemed to be more related to social approval than to the internal logic of the task.

More open questions

These observations show that research paradigms built on supposedly clear distinctions between what is social and what is cognitive will have an inherent weakness, because the causality of social and cognitive processes is, at the very least, circular and is perhaps even more complex (for a parallel discussion of the social nature of metacognitive processes, see Bell, 1985). The aim of the studies reported above was to identify the cognitive processes that permit the social activity of questioning. But these so-called cognitive processes do not apply only to understanding the task and the nature of the cognitive difficulties it presents (e.g., the need for supplementary information). They also include the simultaneous understanding of the social relationship established by the experimenter when presenting himself or herself and the task to the subject. The results of these studies have shown that the adult's signaling to the child that questions were welcome (and even desired) was not sufficient to trigger cognitive questioning. This observation leads us to wonder how the child interprets his or her role as subject in this situation. What does "solving the task" mean to the child? Does the child believe that displaying autonomous problem-solving behavior (even if the outcome is incorrect) is preferable to verbalizing and questioning the adult? Under what sociocognitive conditions do children feel they can legitimately draw on other people's knowledge as a resource for their own understanding?

Reflecting on these questions, we wondered about the school experience of these children. Does schooling cultivate (and if so, how?) the idea that the adult's presence is a resource that the pupil can use when faced with difficulty involving a complex task? How does instruction in schools promote (or discourage) children's reflexive and metacognitive capacities, their understanding of how to deal with ignorance, and their capacity to question others as well as themselves? And how do children think (and display their thinking) about specific objects, events, and notions and not only (or is it only?) about a supposed set of expectations in the adult's mind? This idea again raises the question of the content of development, which was our central concern in the second generation studies.

THE SOCIAL CONSTRUCTION OF MEANING: THE SECOND GENERATION STUDIES

The studies we have presented so far were based on (a) the premise that cognitive development is associated with information seeking and the growth of logical

competencies (and, in particular, of operatory structures) and (b) research paradigms that assume a disassociation of social and cognitive factors in order to study
how these factors impact on individual behavior. Results have shown the significant impact of social factors on cognitive behavior and call for a detailed examination of the exact processes whereby social interactions affect children's
understanding. Yet this interactionist and constructivist perspective cannot entirely
account for a series of observations showing that the modalities of the social
interaction, as well as the nature of the developing competencies, seem to depend
on the meaning that the social interaction conveys about the context and content
of the task. Operatory structures, in particular, do not seem to develop in a social
vacuum independently of the content of the problems through which they are
activated. Hence, we must study these social interactive contexts and take seriously
the matters dealt with in discourse.

This concern led us to conduct a second generation of studies in which the
"unit of analysis" (Wertsch & Sammarco, 1985) shifted. Up to this point, the
child's cognitive responses had been the object of our focus and had been seen
as related to social factors considered as independent variables. The unit of analysis
had been the individual's behavior. But another possible unit of analysis is one
that focuses not on the individual and his or her specific behaviors but on the
social interaction itself. Instead of examining the preconditions and consequences
of social interactions, we decided to observe the modalities of these encounters.
How is the relationship constructed? How is the task mutually constructed? How
do the interlocutors manage (or fail) to establish a common object of discourse?
Who regulates the dialogue, and is this regulation social or cognitive?

We will see that the circular causality between social and cognitive factors
that has been described is even more complex. Indeed, the cognitive activity of
the subject applies not only to his or her understanding of the logical features of
the task but also to the task's meaning within its context and to the understanding
of the social relationships that partners (experimenter or peers) establish around
this task. We will see that the perceived meaning of the social interactions, the
reasons for their occurrence, and the context in which they occur will affect the
way the subject considers the task, deals with it, and reflects and communicates
about it. Our studies focused on two different contexts: the setting of diagnostic
psychological tests and the context of teaching, learning, and assessment at school.

Operatory Structures and Context in Testing Situations

Experimental social history and prior experience

As mentioned earlier, when social factors are considered as independent variables,
researchers observe regularities that are difficult to explain, among them the
repeatedly found correlations between the sociological characteristics of subjects
(e.g., sex, social class, urban or rural environment) and their operatory level.

Before developing hypotheses on the possible mediators of these effects, it is important to make two epistemological points: (a) that correlations are not necessarily signs of causal relations; and (b) that, because differences always seem to favor urban upper- and middle-class subjects, an ethnocentric bias on the part of psychologists cannot be excluded. A critical question regarding these repeatedly observed sociological differences, then, is how this bias operates. This question calls for an integration of sociological and psychological accounts of cognitive development (Goodnow, 1990b).

To explore this question, we have started to consider systematically the social groups to which subjects belong. It appears that certain experimental conditions have a greater impact on subjects' task performance than do others only for certain social groups (Perret-Clermont & Schubauer-Leoni, 1981). For instance, in this research sample, the performances of lower-class girls differ from the rest of the population. They do better on the conservation of liquids test if it is presented to them in the classical manner as a comparison between the experimenter's glass and their own, but their performances drop when the task is staged so that the juice is to be divided between two identical dolls. This task staging has no effect for boys and middle-class children.

In another study, concerned with social marking, Nicolet noted that children from rural areas (especially farmers' children) perform better on the conservation of liquid test after playing a cooperative rather than a competitive game with a partner, and when a rule of equity of distribution of reward is applied to sharing the juice between partners. But this emphasis on equity has no effect for their urban contemporaries (Nicolet, Grossen, & Perret-Clermont, 1988). These results mean that the reported effects of task presentation and experimental instructions (Donaldson, 1978; Light & Perret-Clermont, 1989) on subjects' performance are likely to vary as a function of sociological parameters. They are also dependent on previous experimental procedures experienced by the subjects. For instance, we observed in the above mentioned study that those lower-class girls who performed poorly in the dolls condition did better after interacting with a peer during the experimental session. This was not the case for lower-class girls who observed an adult model during the experimental session. Likewise, in this experiment, group differences occurred as a function of the type of glass used in the conservation of liquid task, with girls performing better when they were given the wider glass than when they were given the thinner glass, perhaps because the latter gives nonconservers the illusion that they have received more juice (see also Rijsman, 1988).

How can we account for such varied results? We suggest that subjects derive meaning from the *experimental social history* that they have undergone (prior experiences and interpersonal relationships within the test and social interaction situations). In other words, there is no "dolls" or "glass" effect as such, but rather a complex interaction between the sociocognitive components of the experimental episode and the characteristics of the staging of the operatory notion that is presented to subjects by the task.

Establishing a common object of discourse and reflection

Results on the impact of the task presentation led us to initiate a series of studies focusing on children's perception of the testing situation itself to understand better what elements play a role in the elaboration of children's responses and what social knowledge is required to interpret adults' discourse and, hence, succeed at the task. Testing episodes were videotaped, and observations of the social interaction between tester and subject during the pretest revealed all sorts of cues by which an intersubjectivity is established between the two partners that will permit the subject to abstract, more or less successfully, the adult's object of discourse (Bell, Grossen, & Perret-Clermont, 1985; Grossen & Bell, 1988; Perret-Clermont & Brossard, 1985).

A basic observation corroborated by several of our studies is that the adult and the child do not always share the same perception of the situation. For instance, Grossen (1988) has observed numerous misunderstandings between tester and subject at the beginning of the conservation of liquids test when the subject is asked to equalize the contents of the two identical glasses. Some children spend a lot of time on this preliminary equalization, as if they understood this first demand as the major activity of the interview and not just a step in the establishment of the premise of equality necessary for the rest of the task. Nonconservers are more likely than others to misinterpret this first demand.

During the pretest, certain nonconservers suddenly become capable of giving conserving responses and correct justifications after the experimenter's conserving countersuggestion. That might be because the presentation of a different answer makes the subject aware of the nature of the question and cues him to the adult's expectations. If so, the child's response is not necessarily a reflection of any cognitive progress made during the testing interview, but rather a matter of understanding what the adult wants to talk about. Siegal (chapter 2 in this volume) presents evidence of the importance of these conversational conventions. Understanding these conventions is both a cognitive process and a matter of adequate socialization or acculturation (see Rogoff, 1982, p. 143) to the experimenter's conversational patterns.

A close look at video tapes and transcripts has made clear to us that, on the one hand, all subjects are not necessarily faced with identical tasks or procedures, even if procedures are rigorously standardized in the eyes of the tester. On the other hand, in practice, the psychologist has to go beyond a standardized testing script to make the subject's mode of thinking converge toward his or hers, using various sociocognitive strategies. This is similar to what Rogoff (chapter 16 in this volume; Rogoff & Gardner, 1984) describes in situations of guided participation; there is a building of an intersubjectivity in which nonverbal monitoring and adjustment are required on both sides. The subject must accept the interaction and enter into the game according to the adult's (normative) expectations if he or she wants to succeed on the test. We can observe a subject trying to decode the tacit assumptions of the adult concerning the definition of the situation, the expected roles, the focus of the discussion, and the taken-for-granted aspects of the interaction as the subject tries out answers and even tries to save face—all processes similar to those described by Levine and Moreland (this volume) in relation to the dynamics of a newcomer in a work group. In order to respond correctly to the conservation of liquids test, the child has to understand the requirement to abstract from, among other things, the perceptual evidence displayed (i.e., the dimensions of the glass, the level of the juice) and the social relationship of the partners (e.g., social rights due to age). Only under these conditions can the two partners discuss the abstract concept of the conservation of the quantities of liquid. In this negotiation of a common definition of the object of discourse, tester and subject are in an asymmetrical relationship in which the adult maintains control of the structure of the verbal exchange, giving the adult the power to define the object of discourse and the criteria of comprehension. Each testing interaction consists of social (and testing) routines, as well as individual strategies embedded in personal and relational experience taking place in a (more or less) staged and institutionalized situation that each partner interprets according to his or her own references.

The data just presented can also be read as illustrating that so-called individual testing is actually a complex social interaction in which the subject puts into play a wealth of social knowledge and skills, including the resolution of the task and the monitoring of the social interaction using interactive strategies. Is this the case only for psychological testing or does the display of scholastic competence rely on the same processes?

Scholastic Knowledge and Context in Testing Situations

Studying written formulations of addition problems (of the type $a + b - c = x$) by 7- to 9-year-olds, we have observed that pupils questioned by an experimenter within the classroom context tended to refer to mathematical notation used in school to represent mathematical operations and actions in their problem solving. However, when pupils were given the same task outside the classroom in a one-to-one interaction, their written solutions were more heterogeneous in nature, using natural language and illustrative drawings (Schubauer-Leoni & Perret-Clermont, 1980, 1985; Schubauer-Leoni, 1984, 1986b, 1986c). Varying the experimental settings revealed that subjects considered the $a + b - c = x$ type of notation canonic for classroom mathematics but used other notation (e.g., drawings or writing) more often to describe the same operation (i.e., dealing with flowers, candies, or dice) outside the classroom. Pupils produced the expected canonic notation only if they associated (through a series of cues) the testing situation with their classroom experience. In such situations, we observed guidance and mutual interpretation processes similar to those observed in Piagetian testing situations. It seems that, during the interaction with the adult, the child becomes acculturated to the type of answers expected from him or her in specific situations as a function of what is at stake in the encounter. The child tries to determine whether he or she is expected to display school learning, verbal competence, or a graphic and aesthetic performance. Often the child enters into a sort of guessing game to decode the experimenter's expectations and satisfy his or her demands. The subject undertakes this decoding in reference to previous experience, which is notably scholastic experience. The child also relies on his or her understanding of the type of relationship established between him- or herself and the adult; seldom does the child perceive the experimenter as a playmate. Usually children believe the experimenter occupies the dominant position in a hierarchical relationship and holds the criteria of definition and interpretation of the situation. Children often seem to give priority to a demonstration of their good will to comply.

Experimental sciences such as physics have long been aware of the artifactitious nature of any observational measurement: The instrument used partly creates the phenomena observed (or at least interferes with the data collected). Similarly, our research has made us aware, as psychologists, of the importance that characteristics of the testing situation itself have in generating behaviors that have been misleadingly considered a reflection of the cognitive characteristics of the individual subject but that actually mirror a particular testing relationship between the psychologist and subject. As a consequence, it is no longer possible to decide a priori if a competence is purely cognitive or also involves the social competence of displaying that behavior. Intelligence, then, can be considered as intrinsically a sociability. In other words, the cognitive competence of a subject can only be ''seen'' by someone who has the necessary cognitive and social skills to relate properly to that subject. This view provides an argument for abandoning a uniquely individualistic approach to the study of the development of intelligence.

The Construction of Context and Content in Teaching/ Learning Interactions

We have just examined how a subject's performance in testing situations results from interwoven processes linked to past and present cognitive and social experience. It should, therefore, be possible to observe within the schooling process how the growth of the cognitive resources of pupils is tightly interwoven with

& Schubauer-Leoni, 1989; Schubauer-Leoni, 1986a, 1986b). Teachers and pupils think of mathematical concepts, symbols, and problems within the specific context of their classroom activities. Cognitive processes and social regulations are so intricately interwoven in learning at school that it is difficult to separate them. It seems that, in these scholastic contexts (e.g., testing situations), the possibilities for children to display competencies depend on their interpretation of the situation, the task content, and the adult's discourse, as well as on what they perceive to be at stake in the interaction. The meaning is conveyed by the setting, the institutional framework in which the encounter takes place, the participants' dialogue and attitudes, their sense of social identity (as pointed out by Goodnow, 1990a), the objects manipulated, and the type of interpersonal relationship established. This meaning is not absolute. It is inferred and interpreted by the subject according to previous sociocognitive experience and the subject's goals in the interaction. The subject's initial interpretation is apt to be modified in the course of the interactions in response to the interlocutor's reactions.

CONCLUSION

Our research, initially aimed at studying the impact of social factors on cognitive performances, calls attention to the complex interdigitation of social and cognitive factors, whose causality is not simple. Our first generation research looked at the impact of social factors on cognitive development, and our results demonstrated the existence of causal relationships between cognitive development and social interaction. But this causality, first conceived in a rather mechanical mode, appeared to be more complex, with the construction of meaning interacting with the construction of logical reasoning, and both of these processes always being displayed within social interaction. This led us to reconsider exactly what is cognitive and what is social. For the second generation research, our object of analysis, therefore, had to shift from the individual and his or her cognitive performance to the social interaction in which this performance is produced. This shift of focus allows a description of the process of the social construction of responses: Social dimensions of the encounter contribute to its meaning, interact with the logical and formal aspects of the task in question, and even contribute to the definition of these aspects.

We have examined two specific contexts: testing situations and the school context of learning and assessment. An analysis of the modalities of social interactions observed in both contexts led us to conclude that competence depends on meanings socially constructed and shared within these situational contexts. In brief, what were traditionally considered intrapsychic logical processes are also social events with their past and present history within specific institutional and sociocultural contexts.

This does not mean that, given a "proper" situational context, any child can be capable of any performance at any time. Age trends have been reported; there is evidence for developmental acquisitions through varied personal and social experience. We have observed necessary sociocognitive prerequisites in order for a child to benefit from specific social interactions. The sociocultural context emphasizes the dimensions on which development is valued (Goodnow, 1990a; Damon, chapter 18 in this volume). In the microsituations of our observations, children obviously demonstrate efforts to converge toward the adult's expectations and task demands.

These progressive constructions of sociocognitive competencies are not purely endogenous phenomena located simply in the individual. They are artifacts of a chain of interlocutors' mutual expectations and adjustments in actions, verbalizations, and thoughts. These adjustments are sometimes asymmetrical between persons of unequal status and sometimes reciprocal between peers. For each person and for each group (e.g., experimental groups and classrooms, as well as family and scientific groups), these mutual adjustments have a history that contributes to the conferring of meaning on the present relationship in which the questioning and the display of competence take place (Hinde, Perret-Clermont, & Stevenson-Hinde, 1985; Perret-Clermont & Nicolet, 1988).

The perspective elaborated here opens the way for further research on the creation and transmission of meanings and knowledge in social interaction, the establishment of interpersonal relationships, the elaboration of intersubjectivity, and the construction of context. All these processes play an integral part in development, and their examination could contribute to a better understanding of the articulation of children's sociocognitive competencies in interaction. Intelligence can also be characterized as a form of sociability. A new question, therefore, arises: When and with whom does "logical reasoning" arise (i.e., when does reasoning develop on logical grounds and not on less rational ones)?

References

Bell, N. (1985). Quelques reflexions sur la métacognition [Some reflections on metacognition]. *Dossiers de Psychologie* (Tech. Rep. No. 25). Neuchâtel, Switzerland: University of Neuchâtel.

Bell, N., Grossen, M., Perret-Clermont, A.-N. (1985). Sociocognitive conflict and intellectual growth. In M. W. Berkowitz (Ed.), *Peer conflict and psychological growth* (pp. 41–54). San Francisco: Jossey-Bass.

Berlyne, D. (1962). Uncertainty and epistemic curiosity. *British Journal of Psychology*, *53*, 27–34.

Bruner, J., & Olson, D. (1973). Apprentissage par expérience directe et apprentissage par expérience mediatisée [Learning by direct experience and learning by mediated experience]. *Perspectives*, *3*(1) 21–42.

Doise, W., Dionnet, S., & Mugny, G. (1978). Conflit socio-cognitif, marquage social, et développement cognitif [Socio-cognitive conflict, social marking, and cognitive development]. *Cahiers de Psychologie, 21*, 231–243.

Doise, W., & Mugny, G. (1984). *The social development of the intellect.* Oxford, England: Pergamon Press.

Doise, M., Mugny, G., & Perret-Clermont, A.-N. (1975). Social interaction and the development of cognitive operations. *European Journal of Social Psychology, 5*, 367–383.

Donaldson, M. (1978). *Children's minds.* London: Fontana.

Goodnow, J. J. (1990a). The socialization of cognition: Acquiring cognitive values. In J. W. Stigler, R. A. Schweder, & G. Herdt (Eds.), *Cultural psychology: Essays on comparative human development* (pp. 259–286). Cambridge, England: Cambridge University Press.

Goodnow, J. J. (1990b). Using sociology to extend psychological accounts of cognitive development. *Human Development, 33*, 81–107.

Grossen, M. (1988). *La construction de l'intersubjectivité en situation de test* [The construction of intersubjectivity in the test situation]. Cousset, Switzerland: DelVal & Dossiers de Psychologie.

Grossen, M., & Bell, N. (1988). Définition de la situation de test et élaboration d'une notion logique [Definition of the test situation and elaboration of a logical idea]. In A.-N. Perret-Clermont & M. Nicolet (Eds.), *Interagir et connaître: Enjeux et régulations sociales dans le développement cognitif* (pp. 233–239). Cousset, Switzerland: DelVal.

Hinde, R., Perret-Clermont, A.-N., & Stevenson-Hinde, J. (Eds.). (1985). *Social relationships and cognitive development.* Oxford, England: Oxford University Press.

Inhelder, B., Sinclair, H., & Bovet, M. (1974). *Apprentissage et structures de la connaissance* [Learning and the development of cognition]. Paris: Presses Universitaires de France.

Jacquet, F., George, E., & Perret, J. F. (1988). *Connaissances mathematiques a l'ecole primaire. Fascicule 2: Collection exploration* [Mathematical knowledge in the primary school]. Bern, Switzerland: Lang.

Lévy, M. (1981). *La necessité sociale de depasser une situation conflictuelle générée par la présentation d'un modèle de solution de problème et par le questionnement d'un agent social* [The social necessity of overcoming a conflicted situation generated by the presentation of a model problem solution and questioning by a social agent]. Doctoral dissertation, University of Geneva, Geneva, Switzerland.

Light, P., & Perret-Clermont, A.-N. (1989). Social context effects in learning and testing. In A. Gallatey, D. Rogers, & J. A. Sloboda (Eds.), *Cognition and social worlds* (pp. 99–112). Oxford, England: Oxford University Press.

Mead, G. H. (1934). *Mind, self and society.* Chicago: University of Chicago Press.

Nelson-Le Gall, S. (1985). Help-seeking behavior in learning. In E. W. Gordon (Ed.), *Review of Research in Education: Vol. 12* (pp. 55–90). Washington, DC: American Educational Research Association.

Nelson-Le Gall, S., & Jones, E. (1990). Cognitive-motivational influences on the task-related help-seeking behavior of black children. *Child Development, 61*, 581–589.

Nicolet, M., Grossen, M., & Perret-Clermont, A.-N. (1988). Testons-nous des compétences cognitives? [Are we testing cognitive competencies?] *Revue Internationale de Psychologie Sociale, 1*, 71–91.

Perret, J. F. (1977). *Signification psychologique, épistémologique et intérêt pédagogique des conduits de recherche d'informations chez l'enfant: Mémoire* [The psychological and epistemological significance and the pedagogical interest of research on children's knowledge]. Geneva, Switzerland: University of Geneva.

Perret, J. F. (1978). Contribution à une psychologie cognitive de l'enfant en situation pédagogique [Contribution to a cognitive psychology of the child in a pedagogical situation]. Paper presented at the *Premier Congrès Portugais pour le Développement de l'Enfant*. Lisbon, Portugal.

Perret, J. F. (1985). *Comprendre l'écriture des nombres: Collection exploration* [To understand the writing of numbers]. Bern, Switzerland: Lang.

Perret, J. F. (1987). Pour quel apprentissage des mathematiques? [For what mathematics learning?] *European Journal of Psychology of Education, 2*(3), 247–260.

Perret, J. F. (1988a). *Connaissances mathématiques a l'école primaire. Fascicule introductif* [Mathematical knowledge in the primary school]. Bern, Switzerland: Lang.

Perret, J. F. (1988b). *Connaissances mathématiques a l'école primaire. Fascicule 3* [Mathematical knowledge in the primary school]. Bern, Switzerland: Lang.

Perret-Clermont, A.-N. (1980). *Social interaction and cognitive development in children.* New York: Academic Press.

Perret-Clermont, A.-N., & Brossard, A. (1985). On the interdigitation of social and cognitive processes. In R. A. Hinde, A.-N. Perret-Clermont, & J. Stevenson-Hinde (Eds.), *Social relationships and cognitive development* (pp. 309–327). Oxford: Oxford University Press.

Perret-Clermont, A.-N., & Mugny, G. (1985). En guise de conclusion: Effets sociologiques et processus didactiques [In conclusion: Sociological effects and didactic processes]. In G. Mugny (Ed.), *Psychologie sociale du développement cognitif* (pp. 251–261). Bern, Switzerland: Lang.

Perret-Clermont, A.-N., & Nicolet, M. (Eds.). (1988). *Interagir et connaître: Enjeux et régulations sociales dans le développement cognitif* [Interacting and knowing: Stakes and social regulations in cognitive development]. Cousset, Switzerland: DelVal.

Perret-Clermont, A.-N., & Schubauer-Leoni, M. L. (1981). Conflict and cooperation as opportunities for learning. In P. Robinson (Ed.), *Communication in development* (pp. 203–233). London: Academic Press.

Perret-Clermont, A.-N., & Schubauer-Leoni, M. L. (1989). *The social construction of meaning in math class interaction.* Paper presented at the UNESCO Sixth International Congress on Mathematical Education, Budapest, Hungary.

Piaget, J. (1950). *The psychology of intelligence.* New York: Harcourt Brace.

Piaget, J. (1965). *The moral judgment of the child.* New York: Free Press.

Piaget, J., & Szeminska, A. (1952). *The child's conception of number.* London: Routledge & Kegan Paul.

Resnick, L. B. (1987). Learning in school and out. *Educational Researcher, 16*, 13–20.

Rijsman, J. (1988). Partages et norme d'équité: Recherches sur le développement social de l'intelligence [Sharing and equity norms: Research on the social development of intelligence]. In A.-N. Perret-Clermont & M. Nicolet (Eds.), *Interagir et connaître: Enjeux et régulations sociales dans le développement cognitif* (pp. 123–137). Cousset, Switzerland: DelVal.

Robinson, E. J., & Robinson, W. P. (1976). The young child's understanding of communication. *Developmental Psychology, 12*, 328–333.

Robinson, W. P., & Rackstraw, S. J. (1975). *Questioning and answering of school children.* Sydney, Australia: Macquarie University.

Rogoff, B. (1982). Integrating context and cognitive development. In M. E. Lamb & A. L. Brown (Eds.), *Advances in developmental psychology* (Vol. 2, pp. 125–170). Hillsdale, NJ: Erlbaum.

Rogoff, B., & Gardner, W. (1984). Adult guidance of cognitive development. In B. Rogoff & J. Lave (Eds.), *Everyday cognition: Its development in social context* (pp. 95–116). Cambridge, MA: Harvard University Press.

Schubauer-Leoni, M. L. (1984). Formulations ecrites et resolutions de problemes additifs [Written formulations and solutions of additive problems]. *Interactions didactiques* (Tech. Rep. No. 5). Switzerland: University of Neuchâtel and University of Geneva.

Schubauer-Leoni, M. L. (1986a). *Maîtres-élèves-savoirs: Analyse psychosociale du jeu et des enjeux de la relation didactique* [Teachers, pupils, knowledge: A psycho-social analysis of the game and of the stakes of the didactic relationship]. Doctoral dissertation, University of Geneva, Geneva, Switzerland.

Schubauer-Leoni, M. L. (1986b). Le contrat didactique: Un cadre interprétatif pour comprendre les savoirs manifestés par les élèves en mathématique [The didactic contract: An interpretive framework for understanding the knowledge displayed by pupils in mathematics]. *Journal Européen de Psychologie de l'Education*, *1*(2), 139–153.

Schubauer-Leoni, M. L. (1986c). Le contrat didactique dans l'élaboration d'ecritures symboliques par des élèves de 8–9 ans [The didactic contract in the elaboration of symbolic notation by children of 8–9 years]. *Interactions didactiques* (Tech. Rep. No. 7). Switzerland: University of Neuchâtel and University of Geneva.

Schubauer-Leoni, M. L., & Perret-Clermont, A.-N. (1980). Interactions sociales et représentations symboliques dans le cadre de problèmes additifs [Social interaction and symbolic representations in the context of additive problems]. *Recherche en didactique des mathématiques*, *1*(3), 297–343.

Schubauer-Leoni, M. L., & Perret-Clermont, A.-N. (1985). Interactions sociales dans l'apprentissage de connaissances mathématiques chez l'enfant [Social interactions in children's mathematics problems]. In G. Mugny (Ed.), *Psychologie sociale du développement cognitif* (pp. 225–250). Bern, Switzerland: Lang.

Vygotsky, L. S. (1962). *Thought and language*. Cambridge, MA: MIT Press.

Wertsch, J. V., & Sammarco, J. G. (1985). Social precursors to individual cognitive functioning: The problem of units of analyses. In R. A. Hinde, A.-N. Perret-Clermont, & J. Stevenson-Hinde (Eds.), *Social relationships and cognitive development* (pp. 276–293). Oxford, England: Oxford University Press.

CHAPTER 4

SITUATING LEARNING IN COMMUNITIES OF PRACTICE

JEAN LAVE

INTRODUCTION

What would happen if a different eye, culturally and historically sensitized by an excursion through forms of apprenticeship in different parts of the world, were turned on specific contemporary cultural and historical features of learning processes as these are situated in communities of practice in the United States? Rather than turning to school-like activities for confirmation and guidance about the nature of learning, that gaze would reverse the perspective from which anthropologists look outward from their culture onto another. It would draw on what is known about learning in forms of apprenticeship in other cultures to consider learning in our own sociocultural, historically grounded world. Such a view invites a rethinking of the notion of learning, treating it as an emerging property of whole persons' legitimate peripheral participation in communities of practice. Such a view sees mind, culture, history, and the social world as interrelated processes that constitute each other, and intentionally

I would like to thank John Levine, Lauren Resnick, and Stephanie Teasley, the conveners of the Conference on Socially Shared Cognition, for the opportunity to participate in the conference and to prepare this chapter. Thanks to Paul Duguid, William Hanks, Lauren Resnick, Carol Stack, and Etienne Wenger for their critical and creative readings of the chapter.

Etienne Wenger and I developed this conception of learning in collaborative work. Learning as legitimate peripheral participation is described in detail in Lave and Wenger, 1991. Much of the argument of the present chapter has its roots in this collaboration.

blurs social scientists' divisions among component parts of persons, their activities, and the world. These strategies of inquiry—counterintuitive definitions of *learning*, reversed points of cultural view, and historical analysis of cognitive processes—are ways to move closer to an encompassing theory of persons-learning while exploring the implications of a more general theory of socially situated activity.

This attempt to rethink learning in social, cultural, and historical terms has developed in response to many of the same issues that have led to discussions of socially shared cognition in this volume. At the same time, I take issue with some work characterized in this way, for it either maintains overly simple boundaries between the individual (and thus the "cognitive") and some version of a world "out there," or turns to a radical constructivist view in which the world is (only) subjectively or intersubjectively constructed. Learning, it seems to me, is neither wholly subjective nor fully encompassed in social interaction, and it is not constituted separately from the social world (with its own structures and meanings) of which it is part. This recommends a decentered view of the locus and meaning of learning, in which learning is recognized as a social phenomenon constituted in the experienced, lived-in world, through legitimate peripheral participation in ongoing social practice; the process of changing knowledgeable skill is subsumed in processes of changing identity in and through membership in a community of practitioners; and mastery is an organizational, relational characteristic of communities of practice.

Anthropological studies of apprenticeship offer possible alternative cultural points of view on social processes of learning and inspiration for counterintuitive conceptualizations of such processes. Craft apprenticeship in West Africa and apprenticeship among Yucatec Mayan midwives, for example, are practices in which mastery comes about without didactic structuring and in such a fashion that knowledgeable skill is part of the construction of new identities of mastery in practice. Inquiring into the nature of such processes leads to questions about the sociocultural character of social re-production for both persons and communities of practice in contemporary American society. What are typical communities of practice? What and how do people learn as legitimate peripheral participants, and how is this arranged in the socially organized settings of everyday practice? What can we learn from examining contemporary social practice when it is conceived as a complex structure of interrelated processes of production and transformation of communities and participants?

Several peculiarities have emerged rather quickly in the pursuit of answers to these questions. There are highly valued forms of knowledgeable skill in this society for which learning is structured in apprentice-like forms. Furthermore, once one begins to think in terms of legitimate peripheral participation in communities of practice, many other forms of socially organized activity become salient as sites of learning (e.g., Alcoholics Anonymous, one of the examples in the discussion that follows). But if one turns to formal, explicit, salient educational sites (schooling being the primary one, but the workplace being characterized in similarly urgent terms), it is difficult to identify communities of practice, widespread mastery, and traditions of centripetal participation leading to changing identities of mastery. This is, of course, too broad a generalization to stand on its own. The point here is to sketch how a socially situated theory of learning reveals the problematic character of the social—institutional arrangements of schools and workplaces that are intended to bring about learning in the world in which we live.

Why is learning problematic in the modern world? One possible response to this question is suggested in the historical analysis of Marxist social theory concerning the alienated condition of contemporary life. In this late period of capitalism, widespread deep knowledgeability appears to be in short supply, especially in those settings that make the most self-conscious and vociferous demands for complex knowledgeable skill. Learning identities (in both senses) are embroiled in pervasive processes of commoditization. To commoditize labor, knowledge, and participation in communities of practice is to diminish possibilities for sustained development of identities of mastery. But if formally mandated forms of mastery are circumscribed, people, nonetheless, do learn and do come to have knowledgeably skilled identities of various sorts. Contemporary forms of learning often succeed in unmarked, unintended ways, and these forms of learning also require first recognition, then explanation. All these concerns indicate that we should not lose sight of the fact that institutional and individual successes and failures of learning are interdependent and are the product of the same historical processes.

In this chapter, I propose to consider learning not as a process of socially shared cognition that results in the end in the internalization of knowledge by individuals, but as a process of becoming a member of a sustained community of practice. Developing an identity as a member of a community and becoming knowledgeably skillful are part of the same process, with the former motivating, shaping, and giving meaning to the latter, which it subsumes. It is difficult to move from peripheral to full participation in today's world (including workplaces and schools), thereby developing knowledgeably skilled identities. This is because the processes by which we divide and sell labor, which are ubiquitous in our way of producing goods and services (including "knowledge"), truncate both the movement from peripheral to full participation and the scope of knowledgeable skill. Taken to an extreme, these processes separate identity from intended forms of knowledgeable practice. This view implies that learning and failure to learn are aspects of the same social–historical processes, and points to relationships between knowledgeability and identity as an important focus for research.

CULTURAL VIEWPOINTS AND THEORIES OF LEARNING

Theories of Situated Experience

It seems useful to introduce the concept of *situated activity* by attempting to clarify differences among its main theoretical variants. Indeed, the term has appeared recently with increasing frequency and with rising confusion about its meaning. Much of the confusion may stem from the assumption that situated activity is a single, unitary concept. However, situated activity is anything but a simple concept; it is a general theoretical perspective that generates interconnected theories of perception, cognition, language, learning, agency, the social world, and their interrelations. Furthermore, there appear to be at least three different genres of situated approaches.

Probably the most common approach is what might be called a *cognition plus* view. According to this view, researchers have for years analyzed the individual, internal business of cognitive processing, representations, memory, and problem solving, and cognitive theory should now attend to other factors as well. People process, represent, and remember in relation to each other and while located in a social world. Therefore, researchers should extend the scope of their intraindividual theory to include everyday activity and social interaction. For proponents of this view, social factors become conditions whose effects on individual cognition are then explored. But cognition, if seen as the result of social processes, is not itself the subject of reconceptualization in social terms. A proponent of this position is likely to argue that a person thinking alone in a forest is not engaged in social cognition.

The *interpretive* view locates situatedness in the use of language and/or social interaction. Interpretivists argue that we live in a pluralistic world composed of individuals who have perspectivally unique experience. This view stands in contrast to that of the first position, which postulates a fixed Cartesian external world in which words have fixed referential meaning and in which rational agents (e.g., "scientists" or "experts"), devoid (ideally) of feeling or interests, are engaged in linear communication of "information" without integral relations of power and control (Rommetveit, 1987). In the interpretive view, meaning is negotiated, the use of language is a social activity rather than a matter of individual transmission of information, and situated cognition is always interest-relative. Feelings and concerns are one important means by which situations are disambiguated and given structure, rather than being the source of distortions of rational thought. In this position there is no world independent of agents' construction of it—thus the emphasis on the constant negotiation and "reregistration" of "the situation." Situatedness here is not equated with physical locatedness in the world, in places, settings, or environments. It is not possible to walk into a situation.

Instead, language use and, thus, meaning are situated in interested, intersubjectively negotiated social interaction. This is different from the constraining physical view of context of most cognitivists.

Rommetveit proposes that the cognition plus and interpretive positions, heretofore disagreeing with each other adamantly, are converging. They are brought together, he argues, by cognitive scientists and artificial intelligence researchers who are adopting a hermeneutic view of situated meaning. The emphasis of several chapters in this volume on language and on socially shared cognition as negotiated meaning supports his proposal. But the two views of situated activity are also brought together by their thorough bracketing off of the social world as an object of study. Such compartmentalization, whether practical or theoretical in intent, has the effect of negating the possibility that subjects are fundamentally *constituted in* their relations with and activities in that world. This bracketing leads proponents of a third position, that of theories of social practice, to argue that the cognition plus and interpretive genres of situation theory are not really about situated activity because each offers only partial specification of key analytic units and questions needed to define situated activity.

The third view, which I will call *situated social practice* (and, where appropriate, *situated learning*), shares several tenets with the interpretive theory of situations. This theoretical view emphasizes the relational interdependency of agent and world, activity, meaning, cognition, learning, and knowing. It emphasizes the inherently socially negotiated quality of meaning and the interested, concerned character of the thought and action of persons engaged in activity. But, unlike the first two approaches, this view also claims that learning, thinking, and knowing are relations among people engaged in activity *in, with, and arising from the socially and culturally structured world*. This world is itself socially constituted. Thus, from this point of view, ''nature'' is as much socially generated as afternoon tea. And its generation, according to this perspective, takes place in dialectical relations between the social world and persons engaged in activity; together these produce and re-produce both world and persons in activity. Knowledge of the social world is always socially mediated and open-ended. Its meaning to given actors, its furnishings, and the relations of humans with and within it are produced, reproduced, and changed in the course of activity (which includes speech and thought, but cannot be reduced to one or the other). The idea of situatedness in theories of practice further differs from each of the other two approaches in insisting that cognition and communication, in and with the social world, are situated in the historical development of ongoing activity. Thus it is also a critical theory, because the social scientist's practice must be analyzed in the same historical, situated terms as any other practice under investigation. This third position situates learning in social practice in the lived-in world; the problem is to translate this view into a specific analytic approach to learning.

Learning as Legitimate Peripheral Participation: Yucatec Mayan Midwifery

Suppose there is not a strict boundary between the intra- and extracranial aspects of human experience, but rather reciprocal, recursive, and transformed partial incorporations of person and world in each other within in a complex field of relations between them. This assumption follows if we conceive of learners as whole persons, in activity within the world, and it leads to a distinctive description of learning: Legitimate peripheral participation offers a two-way bridge between the development of knowledgeable skill and identity—the production of persons— and the production and reproduction of communities of practice. Newcomers become oldtimers through a social process of increasingly centripetal participation, which depends on legitimate access to ongoing community practice. Newcomers develop a changing understanding of practice over time from improvised opportunities to participate peripherally in ongoing activities of the community. Knowledgeable skill is encompassed in the process of assuming an identity as a practitioner, of becoming a full participant, an oldtimer.

The terms used here—*oldtimers/newcomers*, *full participants*, *legitimate peripheral participants* (but not *teachers/pupils*, or *experts/novices*)—result from a search for a way to talk about social relations in which persons and practices change, re-produce, and transform each other. The terms *master* and *apprentice*, as they are used here, are not intended as a disguise for teacher–pupil relations: Masters usually do not have a direct, didactic impact on apprentices' learning activity, although they are often crucial in providing newcomers to a community with legitimate access to its practices.

Ethnographic studies of apprenticeship learning converge on a series of claims. This seems especially encouraging considering the diversity of forms of apprenticeship reported by anthropologists who have undertaken such research. Ethnographic studies in Mexico (Jordan, 1989), West Africa (Goody, 1982; Lave, 1983), and Hong Kong (Cooper, 1980), and accounts of craft apprenticeship in East Africa (King, 1977), among others, show that apprenticeship occurs in the context of a variety of forms of production (Goody, 1982). Processes of learning are given form in ongoing practice in ways in which teaching is not centrally implicated. Evaluation of apprentices' progress is intrinsic to their participation in ongoing work practices. Hence, apprenticeship usually involves no external tests and little praise or blame, progress being visible to the learner and others in the process of work itself. The organization of space and coordination among participants or, more generally, access for the apprentice to ongoing work and participation in that work are important conditions for learning.

Reanalysis of these cases as instances of learning through legitimate peripheral participation leads to somewhat different conclusions (Lave & Wenger,

1991). One difference of interpretation is particularly relevant here: The process of becoming a full practitioner through increasingly intense, interconnected, and "knowledgeably-skilled" participation, on the one hand, and the organization of processes of work, on the other hand, do not generally coincide at levels at which activity is intentionally organized. It follows that learners' perspectives on work will be different, and their comprehension of the practice will change across the process of learning. The changing relationship of newcomers to ongoing activity and to other practitioners—obviously much more complicated than there is space to discuss here—calls into question the assumption that modes of transmission of knowledge determine the level of generality of what oldtimers understand.

Attempts to compare schooling and apprenticeship have led to some notably converging analyses (e.g., Becker, 1972; see also Geer, 1972; Jordan, 1989; Lave & Wenger, 1991). Becker, for example, recognizes that learning-in-practice is a widely distributed and ubiquitous feature of contemporary life. He observes that apprentice learners are surrounded by the characteristic activities of their trade. Apprentices have the opportunity to see community practice in its complexity early on and have a broader idea of what it is about than just the particular tasks in which they are engaged or that are most easily observable. This appears to be central to processes of learning in apprenticeship. Becker goes on to suggest that, as a consequence of the accessibility of the full round of activities, the apprentice makes her or his own curriculum; apprenticeship thus provides an individualized and realistic learning setting.

Becker also argues that there are two grave difficulties that impede learning in apprenticeship. He believes apprenticeship is flawed in that teaching resources are scarce and must be recruited at the initiative of the individual apprentice. I disagree with this argument and will return to it shortly. The other difficulty has to do with structural constraints in work organizations on apprentices' access to the full range of activities of the job and, hence, to possibilities for truly mastering a trade. He draws on a compelling example, a study of butchers' apprentices in a union-sponsored combined trade school/on-the-job training program (Marshall, 1972). Marshall describes a seriously ineffective program, in which, among other things,

> The supermarket manager sees to it that his skilled journeymen can prepare
> a large volume of meat efficiently by specializing in short, repetitive tasks.
> He puts apprentices where they can work for him most efficiently, working
> at the meat wrapping machine. But the wrapping machine is in a different
> room from the cold room where the journeymen prepare cuts of meat.

In our terms, the butchers' apprentices are legitimate participants in the butchers' community of practice but do not have access as peripheral participants to the work of meatcutting. Economics, efficiency, control over the intensity and uniformity of labor, segregation of interrelated activities in space and time, the politics of knowledge control—among other characteristics of the organization of work—can diminish or enhance access, the curriculum, and the general understanding of on-the-job learners.

Forms of apprenticeship vary in the ways and in the degree to which they involve the exploitation of apprentices as sources of free or cheap labor. The institution of apprenticeship in European and American history has a deservedly ugly reputation as a mechanism for recruiting, controlling, and exploiting the labor of children and other newcomers. It is further implicated in the reproduction of structured inequalities of social class in those Western European countries where it is part of state educational systems today. In other historical circumstances (especially those in recent African history in which apprenticeship has been virtually ignored as an instrument of state policy, and where its local developments have a long history of their own), it appears not to have generated sufficiently inequitable power relations between apprentices and those with the economic and cultural capital to sponsor them to permit the growth of the exploitative practices often found where powerful mercantile and industrial forms of capitalist production dominate. Thus, the practices of indenturing, virtual slave labor, and exploitation of children characteristic of apprenticeship in some historical contexts are by no means true of all. The evidence from West Africa, Yucatan, and elsewhere strongly suggests that such exploitation is not a necessary integral aspect of the conditions for learning to labor through apprenticeship. At the same time, where apprenticeship is an exploitative form of labor, this is a characteristic of whatever learning is going on, not merely an exogenous or irrelevant "factor" in the learning setting.

Jordan (1989) has carried out extensive field research on Yucatec Mayan midwives whose apprenticeship is quite different—more effective and less exploitive—than that of the butchers in Marshall's study. These apprentices are peripheral participants, legitimate participants, and legitimately peripheral to the practice of midwifery. They have access to both broad knowledgeability about the practice of midwifery and to increasing participation in that practice. It is worth noting that it would be difficult to find evidence that teaching is the mode of knowledge "transmission" among the midwives. According to Jordan,

> Apprenticeship happens as a way of, and in the course of, daily life. It may not be recognized as a teaching effort at all. A Maya girl who eventually becomes a midwife most likely has a mother or grandmother who is a midwife, since midwifery is handed down in family lines. . . . Girls in such families, without being identified as apprentice midwives, absorb the essence of midwifery practice as well as specific knowledge about many procedures, simply in the process of growing up. They know what the life of a midwife is like (for example, that she needs to go out at all hours of the day or night), what kinds of stories the women and men who come to consult her tell, what kinds of herbs and other remedies need to be collected, and the like. As young children they might be sitting quietly in a corner as their mother administers a prenatal massage; they would hear sto-

ries of difficult cases, of miraculous outcomes, and the like. As they grow
older, they may be passing messages, running errands, getting needed supplies. A young girl might be present as her mother stops for a postpartum
visit after the daily shopping trip to the market. Eventually, after she has
had a child herself, she might come along to a birth, perhaps because her
ailing grandmother needs someone to walk with, and thus find herself
doing for the woman in labor what other women had done for her when
she gave birth; that is, she may take a turn . . . at supporting the laboring
woman. . . . Eventually, she may even administer prenatal massages to selected clients. At some point, she may decide that she actually wants to do
this kind of work. She then pays more attention, but only rarely does she
ask questions. Her mentor sees their association primarily as one that is of
some use to her ("Rosa already knows how to do a massage, so I can send
her if I am too busy"). As time goes on, the apprentice takes over more
and more of the work load, starting with the routine and tedious parts, and
ending with what is in Yucatan the culturally most significant, the birth of
the placenta.[1]

Jordan has described a situation in which learning is given structure and
shape through peripheral participation in ongoing activity. Learning activity is
improvised in practice; some of its goals are clear to learners early in the apprenticeship.

But these claims are subject to Becker's concern that lack of intentional
guidance and instruction makes learning difficult if not impossible. My disagreement with this point grows out of a recognition that there are resources other than
teaching through which newcomers grow into oldtimers' knowledge and skill.
These resources are to be found in at least two aspects of apprenticeship. One is
the existence of a broad view of what is to be learned from the very beginning.
Broad exposure to ongoing practice, such as that described for the midwives'
apprentices, is in effect a demonstration of the goals toward which newcomers
expect, and are expected, to move. The other is the notion that knowledge and
skill develop in the process—and as an integral part of the process—of becoming
like master practitioners within a community of practice. This more inclusive
process of generating identities is both a result of and motivation for participation.
It is through this process that common, shared, knowledgeable skill gets organized,
although no one specifically sets out to inculcate it uniformly into a group of
learners. It is rarely the case that individual apprentices must take the initiative
in getting someone to teach them in order to learn in circumstances where ongoing
everyday activity provides structuring resources for learning. Gradually increasing
participation in that practice, and a whole host of relations with the activities of

---

[1]From "Cosmopolitical Obstetrics: Some Insights From the Training of Traditional Midwives"
by B. Jordan, 1989, *Social Science and Medicine 28*(9), p. 932. Copyright 1989 by Pergamon Press.
Reprinted by permission.

more and less adept peers, also provide resources for learning. (I shall return shortly to the question of the availability of structuring resources for learning in contemporary places of work.)

In short, investigations of situated learning focus attention on ways in which the increasing participation of newcomers in ongoing practice shapes their gradual transformation into oldtimers. Newcomers furnished with comprehensive goals, an initial view of the whole, improvising within the multiply structured field of mature practice with near peers and exemplars of mature practice—these are characteristic of communities of practice that re-produce themselves successfully.

Identity in Participation: Alcoholics Anonymous

The description of Yucatec apprenticeship in midwifery provides a sense of how learning in practice takes place and what it means to move toward full participation in a community of practice. A more detailed view of the way in which the fashioning of identity is the means through which members become full participants, and how this subsumes the kind of knowledge and skill usually assumed to be the goal of newcomers' activity, may be found by analyzing the process of becoming a nondrinking alcoholic through Alcoholics Anonymous (AA).

It may seem unusual to characterize AA as a learning environment. But this characterization follows from the view of learning as legitimate peripheral participation in communities of practice. Indeed, analyzing communities of practice as sites of learning is one of the most useful characteristics of a theory of socially situated activity. AA, then, constitutes a community of practice, one in which newcomers gradually develop identities as nondrinking alcoholics. Cain (1991) argues that, in learning not to drink,

> The change these men and women have undergone is much more than a change in behavior. It is a transformation of their identities, from drinking non-alcoholics to non-drinking alcoholics, and it affects how they view and act in the world. . . . By "identity" I mean the way a person understands and views himself, and is viewed by others, a perception of self that is fairly constant. . . . (pp. 210, 212)

> As a cultural system, and one that no one is born into, all of the beliefs of AA must be learned. The propositions and interpretations of events and experiences, the appropriate behaviors and values of an AA alcoholic, and the appropriate placement of the alcoholic identity in the hierarchy of identities one holds must be learned. In short, the AA identity must be acquired, and its moral and aesthetic distinctions internalized. This cultural information is transmitted through the AA literature, and through talk in AA meetings and in one-to-one interactions. One important vehicle for this is the personal story. (p. 215)

New members of AA begin by attending meetings at which oldtimers give testimony about their drinking past and the course of the process of becoming sober. The contribution of an absolutely new member may be no more than one silent gesture—picking up a white chip at the end of the meeting to indicate the intention not to take a drink during the next 24 hours. Oldtimers may have told polished, hour-long stories, months and years in the making, of their lives as alcoholics. Cain argues that the main business of AA is the reconstruction of identity, through the process of construction of these life stories, and with them, the meaning of the teller's past and future action in the world.

An apprentice AA member attending several meetings a week spends that time in the company of near peers and adepts and, in the testimony at early meetings, has access to a comprehensive view of what the community is about. There are also clear models for constructing AA life stories in published accounts of drinkers' lives and in the storytelling performances of oldtimers. Goals are also made plain in the litany of the 12 Steps to sobriety, which guides the process of moving from peripheral to full participation in AA. Early on, newcomers learn to preface their contributions with the simple identifying statement "I'm an alcoholic" and, shortly, to introduce themselves and sketch the problems that brought them to AA. They begin by describing these events in non-AA terms. Their accounts are countered with exemplary stories by more experienced members who do not criticize or correct newcomers directly. Newcomers gradually generate a view that matches more closely the AA model, eventually producing skilled testimony in public meetings and gaining validation from others as they demonstrate appropriate understanding (Cain, 1991). The "12th Step" visit to an active drinker to try to persuade that person to become a newcomer in the organization initiates a new phase of participation, now as a recognized oldtimer.

There seem to be two kinds of meetings in AA, general meetings and discussion meetings. The latter tend to focus on a single aspect of what in the end will be a part of the reconstructed life story (perhaps one of the 12 Steps): "admitting you are powerless," "making amends," or "how to avoid the first drink" (Cain, 1991). These discussions have a dual purpose. Participants engage in the work of staying sober and, through this work, in the gradual construction of an identity. The notion of partial participation in segments of work that increase in complexity and scope (also a theme in Jordan's analysis) describes the changing form of participation in AA for newcomers as they gradually become oldtimers. In due course, those who move centripetally into full participation become increasingly good at not drinking, at making amends, at reconstructing their lives in terms of AA, at constructing AA stories, and at telling such stories—some of the knowledgeable skills subsumed in becoming a nondrinking alcoholic.

The Yucatec midwives' apprenticeship and Alcoholics Anonymous both seem straightforward in the sense that learners have access to the everyday activity involved in being and becoming members. There do not appear to be devastating structural barriers in the practice of midwifery or in belonging to AA that prevent newcomers from gradually becoming oldtimers themselves. Given that part of the activity an organization must engage in to survive is the organization of its own reproduction, structural barriers to learning cannot be the only relevant organizational forces at work. No rational organization can exempt the production of oldtimers from its agenda of crucial structural arrangements, and giving learners access to full participation is a condition for meeting this goal. Nonetheless, the ideas sketched here so far paint too clean and consistent a picture of learning activity, in several respects.

HISTORICAL ANALYSIS, COMMUNITIES, AND COGNITION

Communities of Practice and Processes of Learning

I began with the proposition that participation as members of a community of practice shapes newcomers' identities and in the process gives structure and meaning to knowledgeable skill. I have treated this process as a seamless whole. But there are ubiquitous structural discontinuities in learning processes. Learning in any setting is a complex business that to some extent involves irreducibly contradictory interests for the participants. This is as true of Yucatec midwifery and AA as of every other community of practice. The process of becoming a full practitioner in a community of practice involves two kinds of production: the production of continuity with, *and* the displacement of, the practice of oldtimers (Lave & Wenger, 1991). Newcomers and oldtimers are dependent on each other: newcomers in order to learn, and oldtimers in order to carry on the community of practice. At the same time, the success of both new and old members depends on the eventual replacement of oldtimers by newcomers-become-oldtimers themselves. The tensions this introduces into processes of learning are fundamental.

This proposition does not put an end to the relations of production of learning. The construction of practitioners' identities is a collective enterprise and is only partly a matter of an individual's sense of self, biography, and substance. The construction of identity is also a way of speaking of the community's constitution of itself through the activity of its practitioners. It further involves a recognition and validation by other participants of the changing practice of newcomers-become-oldtimers. Most of all, without participation with others, there may be no basis for lived identity. This conception of learning activity draws attention to the complex ways in which persons and communities of practice constitute themselves and each other.

Marxist sociologists have explored just such relations of incorporation between persons and communities of practice, viewed as processes of *subjectification* and *objectification*, and have tried to grapple with their particular character in contemporary society. Analysis begins with the most basic structural principles shaping this society. Persons, and their participation in communities of practice, are grounded in the contradiction associated with commoditization of production. The products of human labor are turned into commodities when they cease to be made for the value of their use in the lives of their makers and are produced in order to exchange them, to serve the interests and purposes of others without direct reference to the lives of their makers. As such, the results of labor are removed further and further from their common place in the lives of the laboring people who produce them in exchange for money in an anonymous global market, intensified still further when the *labor* that goes into making things suffers the same fate.

Commoditization places people between the pincers of two systematically interrelated aspects of the concept of alienation. One is the anthropomorphizing of objects as they become central forms of connectedness between people. The other is the objectification of persons as they take on exchange value as sources of labor power (e.g., an "A" student, wage labor "employees"). These concepts provide a useful focus for the present discussion because they pertain to a level of belief and action in the world at which participation, the fashioning of identity, and skillful knowledgeability are configured in practice. The first concept (fetishizing, anthropomorphizing) relfects the fact that, as a consequence of structuring relations among the *products* of human activity in terms of exchange value, we have come—mistakenly—to give objects (in all senses of that word) the properties of power, intention, and action that rightly belong only to whole human agents in communities. An anthropologist's (WMO) interview with the director of international advertising for Coca-Cola (MM) provides a vivid example of this phenomenon:

> WMO: There's a phrase that sometimes passes in the academic community—"Coca-colonization" of the world—which I'm sure you've heard before.
> MM: Yeah. I've heard it before. I don't think it's fair, really. Coca-Cola just happens to be the most successful of world brands, and people pick at it for that very reason. . . .
> WMO: Is it wrong or just that's how you feel?
> MM: It's wrong because *all the thing wants to do is to refresh you, and it is willing to understand your culture, to be meaningful to you and to be relevant to you. . . . I don't think that Coca-Cola projects. I think that Coca-Cola reflects.*
> WMO: Reflects in what sense?
> MM: A lifestyle, a civilization, a culture.
> WMO: Is it independent from that? It hasn't partly created that?

> MM: *Coca-Cola looks at it and then puts a mirror in front of*
> *you. Sometimes it puts a window in front of you that allows*
> *you to see how you'd like to be.*[2]

Not only have qualities of human agency been attributed to products such as Coca-Cola, but knowledgeable skill (e.g., expertise, IQ) has been endowed with separate and lively properties independent of the communities of which knowledge is a distributed, integral dimension.

The other aspect of alienation follows from the commoditization of labor through the selling and buying of the labor power of human beings (wage labor) who having sold their labor power, no longer turn their hands primarily to fashioning the solutions to their own needs. Alienation in this sense involves the idea of separation—of the abstraction or extraction of central forms of life participation (e.g., work, knowing, or doing something skillfully) from the human lives that really produce them, thus mistakenly giving human agents properties of objects. In particular, this implies that human activity becomes a means rather than an end in itself; people become hired *hands* or *employ-ees* rather than masters of their own productive activities.

These are powerful aspects of Western political economy and culture. They are relevant to a situated analysis of relations between the development of knowledgeable skill and the construction of identity, membership, and communities of practice, although, so far, I have treated membership and knowledgeability in unified terms as "mastery" or full participation. The conception of an oldtimer as a master practitioner does not reflect the ways in which the construction of identity and knowledgeable skill are characteristically shaped and misshapen when alienation—the effects of objectifying human beings and anthropomorphizing objects—prevails. Part of what gives the notion of mastery its seamless connotations is that it unites the identity of master with skilled knowledgeability. Apprenticeship thus seems to escape from the effects of commoditization. In the world today, however, much of human activity is based on the division of and selling of labor for a wage. Having a price has changed indelibly the common meaning of *labor*. The agent has little possibility of fashioning an identity that implies mastery, for commoditization of labor implies the detachment of the value of labor from the person. In such circumstances, the value of skill, transformed into an abstract labor power, is excised from the construction of personal identity. If becoming a master is not possible in such circumstances, the value accruing to knowledgeable skill when it is subsumed in the identity of mastery devolves elsewhere or disappears.

---

[2]From "The Airbrushing of Culture: An Insider Looks at Global Advertising" by W. O'Barr, 1989, *Public Culture*, 2(1), p. 15. Copyright 1989 by the Center for Transnational Cultural Studies. Reprinted by permission. Italics added.

This analysis places the concept of learning-in-practice in jeopardy. On the one hand, it appears that conditions for learning in contemporary society limit the possibility of mastery to just those forms of activity that continue to be associated with apprentice forms of learning—for example, in graduate programs in universities and in the practice of medicine, law, and the arts. On the other hand, I have argued that learning occurs under just the circumstances where the fashioning of identity and the gradual mastery of knowledgeable skill are part of an integral process of participation. How can this be?

The Workplace and School

In the contemporary world, both Yucatec midwifery and Alcoholics Anonymous lie outside the world of schooling, workplaces, and marketplaces (although they are not immune to their effects, e.g., Jordan, 1989). To take seriously the assumption that the contemporary social world can be described in the terms just proposed, involving the alienation of knowledgeable skill from the construction of identity, it might be useful to examine settings in which these effects are, arguably, most concentrated: contemporary workplaces and schools. Two principles emerge from this exercise, concerning relations between communities of practice on the one hand and the broader situatedness of such communities in a social formation as a whole on the other hand. The first principle is the prevalence of negatively valued identities (e.g., "We're just Loggers" or "We don't know *real* math"), and the second is the ad hoc, interstitial nature of communities of practice in which identities *are* formed and sustained knowledgeability is made possible.

Let us consider each principle in turn. First, the working out of relations of commodification and, thus, alienation shape experience and interpretations of experience and contribute to the creation of devalued or negatively valued identities. Commodification and alienation also contribute to the devaluation of *persons'* knowledgeable skill by comparison with the reified value of knowledge as a commodity. Second, structural constraints *on* (rather than within) communities of practice are important in the production of negative valuation of being and doing. That is, occupational and production-line specialization and other strategies for controlling—by dividing—work and workers narrow the possibilities for what may be learned (and, with them, the significance of membership) to an absurd minimum. The value of mastery in a community of practice diminishes if the process of centripetal participation is correspondingly limited or extinguished. The value of being an oldtimer may be reduced to whatever value there is in having existed in a given setting over a long period of time.

Where the scope of the ongoing activities of a community of practice is in close approximation to levels of human organization at which coherent, meaningful participation in activity is possible, as among the midwives and nondrinking alcoholics, conditions and resources for centripetal participation and eventual mastery are available. But there is a paradox here. It is exactly in those organizations in which control through the narrowing, trivialization, and decomposition of full participation is most common—in schools and workplaces—that learning is most often an institutional motive and yet, by the argument here, most likely to fail. On the other hand, conditions for learning flourish in the interstices of family life, in the participation of children in becoming normal adults (Fortes, 1938; Goody, 1989), in professions that have not yet been specialized out of intelligibility, in officially neglected areas of cultural production (e.g., Alcoholics Anonymous, rock music), in sports, and so on. And legitimate peripheral participation also has a place in sites of wage labor, although it follows from the argument about commodification that communities of practice are unlikely to exist there in formally defined ways.

Indeed, communities of practice in workplaces and schools are mostly ad hoc. In the workplace, people who are members of work groups in formal terms often form sustained but disjunctive communities of practice, as in the shop floor culture described by Willis (1977). These communities shape the ways in which work and play are produced, their meaning, and the skilled, stylized relations among oldtimers to which newcomers aspire—in short, forms of mastery. These communities of practice alone do not account for the organization of everyday activity in work settings, of course, but strongly shape the social practice of work, nonetheless.

Although the specific mechanisms are different, the decomposition of activity to the point of meaninglessness and the formation of informal communities of practice are to be found in schools as well as in the workplace. Standardization of curricula and examinations, evaluation through grading, the deskilling of teaching (Apple, 1979), relations between the decomposition of school knowledge by teachers and their control over students in classrooms (McNeil, 1986), and forms of student stratification and classification in schools all serve to reduce the meaning and even the possibility of engaging as a peripheral participant in knowledgeably skilled activity in the classroom. Furthermore, children form ad hoc communities of practice mostly outside the classroom (e.g., Willis, 1977). Becker (1972) hints at this when he says that children in school learn best what the school does not teach. "Burnouts" and "jocks" are more likely to exemplify mastery in a community of practice than are solid geometry students (Eckert, 1989). There are even interstitial communities of practice *in* classrooms, where, for example, newcomers generate distinctions between "real, valued knowledge" and what they themselves do, and consequently consider themselves inadequate even many (competent) years later (Lave, 1988).

In short, when official channels offer only possibilities to participate in institutionally mandated forms of commoditized activity, genuine participation, membership, and legitimate access to ongoing practice—of a practice considered worthy of the name—are rare. At the same time, schools and school-like workplace educational enterprises accord knowledgeable skill a reified existence, turning it into something to be "acquired" and its transmission into an institutional motive. This process generates pressures toward the trivializing decomposition of forms of activity. The result is a widespread generation of negative identities and mis-recognized or institutionally disapproved interstitial communities of practice.

Internalization and Learning Transfer: A Situated Critique

At this point, I would like to reconsider two fundamental questions in contemporary theorizing about learning. These questions are generally conceptualized in ways that suffer from the same overly simplistic character of my initial notion of mastery. *Internalization* is the cognition plus approach's answer to the question of how the social world and the individual come to have a good deal in common. This view of learning as ingestion (with teaching as feeding) is undergoing modification. This volume demonstrates the importance of social interaction, the joint construction of meaning, the distributed character of knowing, and, hence, the partial, transformed, situated nature of that which is taken in. But internalization might also be conceived of as the sum or, perhaps better, the structure of relations of subjectification and objectification of a human agent. According to this view, internalization must take historically and culturally specific forms. The transformations involved in these processes guarantee that a "straight pipe" metaphor of knowledge channeled into learners cannot be a reasonable way of characterizing that highly complex and problematic process.

Learning transfer is meant to explain how it is possible for there to be some general economy of knowledge so that humans are not chained to the particularities of literal existence. The vision of social existence implied by the notion of transfer, which accompanies equally colloquial notions of internalization treats life's situations as so many unconnected lily pads. This view reduces the organization of everyday practice to the question of how it is possible to hop from one lily pad to the next and still bring knowledge to bear on the fly, so to speak.

Two arguments have been developed that recommend against this vision of social life. The first is a very general proposition, reflected in anthropology's holistic approach (and in notions like that of a "social formation" or "social system"), that the structure of the social world as a whole is both constituted and reflected in the structures of its regions, institutions, and situations, so that they are neither isolated from one another nor composed of unconnected relations. The historical present addressed here offers an especially eloquent example: If communities of practice are located interstitially in institutional settings (both schools and workplaces) that prescribe their own versions of organization and proper newcomers become oldtimers, who thereby become the community of practice for the next newcomers, transforming their understanding as they transform their identities. Changed understanding is also forged (or not forged) in cycles of work, both long and short, and in relations of communities of practice to larger institutional orders. To understand all of this would be to understand the structure of transformations of knowledgeable skill and identity as well. Together, these questions recommend a close examination of ongoing social practice as the key to understanding situated learning.

References

Apple, M. (1979). *Ideology and curriculum*. London: Routledge and Kegan Paul.

Becker, H. (1972). A school is a lousy place to learn anything in. *American Behavioral Scientist, 16*, 85–105.

Cain, C. (1991). Personal stories: Identity acquisition and self-understanding in Alcoholics Anonymous. *Ethos, 19*(2), 210–254.

Cooper, E. (1980). *The wood-carvers of Hong Kong: Craft production in the world capitalist periphery*. Cambridge, England: Cambridge University Press.

Eckert, P. (1989). *Jocks and burnouts: Social categories and identity in high school*. New York: Teachers College Press.

Fortes, M. (1938). Social and psychological aspects of education in Taleland. Supplement to *Africa, 11*(4). London: Oxford University Press.

Geer, B. (Ed.). (1972). *Learning to work*. Beverly Hills: Sage Publications.

Goody, E. (Ed.). (1982). *From craft to industry: The ethnography of proto-industrial cloth production*. Cambridge, England: Cambridge University Press.

Goody, E. (1989). Learning and the division of labor. In M. Coy (Ed.), *Apprenticeship: From Theory to Method and Back Again*. Albany, NY: SUNY Press.

Jordan, B. (1989). Cosmopolitical obstetrics: Some insights from the training of traditional midwives. *Social Science and Medicine, 28*(9), 925–944.

King, K. (1977). *The African artisan: Education and the informal sector in Kenya*. New York: Teachers College Press.

Lave, J. (1983). *Tailored learning: Apprenticeship and everyday practice among craftsmen in West Africa*. Unpublished manuscript.

Lave, J. (1988). *Cognition in practice: Mind, mathematics and culture in everyday life*. Cambridge, England: Cambridge University Press.

Lave, J., & Wenger, E. (1991). *Situated learning: Legitimate peripheral participation*. Cambridge, England: Cambridge University Press.

Marshall, H. (1972). Structural constraints on learning: Butchers' apprentices. In B. Geer (Ed.), *Learning to work* (pp. 39–48). Beverly Hills, CA: Sage Publications.

McNeil, L. (1986). *Contradictions of control: School structure and school knowledge*. London: Routledge and Kegan Paul.

O'Barr, W. M. (1989). The airbrushing of culture: An insider looks at global advertising. *Public Culture, 2*(1), 1–19.

Rommetveit, R. (1987). Meaning, context and control: Convergent trends and controversial issues in current social science research on human cognition and communication. *Inquiry, 30*, 77–99.

Willis, P. (1977). *Learning to labour: How working class lads get working class jobs*. New York: Columbia University Press.

PART TWO

SOCIALLY CONSTRUCTED TOOLS OF REASONING

CHAPTER 5

A SOCIOCULTURAL APPROACH TO SOCIALLY SHARED COGNITION

JAMES V. WERTSCH

As Schegloff (see chapter 8 in this volume) has noted, psychologists' use of the term *socially shared cognition* triggers a set of resonances for sociologists, anthropologists, and representatives of other disciplines. In some cases, these resonances bear on issues that are readily understood and incorporated in existing paradigms of psychological inquiry, but in others, fundamental reformulation may be in order. Such reformulation often stems from presuppositions about the nature of the individual.

Psychological research is often grounded in the assumption that it is possible or even desirable to investigate the individual removed from his or her social or cultural context. This is sometimes done with the assumption that issues such as culture and social structure can be reduced to psychological phenomena when psychologists arrive at sufficiently powerful approaches; in other instances, the assumption is that cultural and social issues can be incorporated as additional variables once the basic forms of mental functioning in the individual have been isolated and understood. In either case the result has been the rise of theoretical constructs and units of analysis that make it next to impossible to incorporate the findings of the other social sciences into the discipline.

I take it to be the goal of this volume to explore ways in which social scientists from a variety of disciplines can find a way out of these impasses, and I shall seek

The writing of this chapter was assisted by the Spencer Foundation. The statements made and the views expressed are solely the responsibility of the author.

Correspondence concerning this chapter should be addressed to Dr. James V. Wertsch, Frances L. Hiatt School of Psychology, Clark University, Worcester, MA 01610-1477.

argued that attempts to unpack the nature of mental processes by analyzing only the static products of development will often result in failure. Instead of correctly identifying various aspects of these processes as emerging from the genetic transformation they have undergone, such attempts may be misled by the appearance of "fossilized" forms of behavior (Vygotsky, 1978).

Partly because of the practical tasks confronting him (cf. Wertsch & Youniss, 1987), Vygotsky focused most of his empirical research on the development of the individual, that is, on ontogenesis. However, the genetic method he envisioned applies to several other genetic domains as well, specifically, phylogenesis, sociocultural history, and microgenesis (Wertsch, 1985). He specifically rejected any recapitulationist parallels among the various domains he considered, arguing instead that each is governed by a unique set of explanatory principles (Vygotsky & Luria, 1930). In his view, what would ultimately be required is an account that specifies how the genetic forces in these domains are interrelated.

For Vygotsky, the main feature distinguishing ontogenesis from the two other domains that concerned him most—phylogenesis and sociocultural history— is that in ontogenesis multiple forces of development are simultaneously in operation. Specifically, he argued in the following paragraph that a *natural* and a *cultural* or *social* line of development interact to create the dynamics of change in ontogenesis:

> The growth of the normal child into civilization usually involves a fusion
> with the processes of organic maturation. Both planes of development—the
> natural and the cultural—coincide and mingle with one another. The two
> lines of change interpenetrate one another and essentially form a single line
> of sociobiological formation of the child's personality. (1960, p. 47)

As I have argued elsewhere (Wertsch, 1985), Vygotsky did not provide a concrete, detailed definition of these two lines of development. In particular, he was unclear about the natural line. Furthermore, his claim that the natural and cultural lines operate in isolation during early phases of ontogenesis is open to question, given recent research on infancy. However, some version of the dynamic that Vygotsky envisioned between the natural and cultural lines of development in ontogenesis is still a clear desideratum for developmental psychology, and one that has not been met adequately to date.

The Social Origins of Mental Functioning in the Individual

As was the case with other aspects of Vygotsky's writings, this theme was influenced by Marxist theory. The general claim at issue here is that in order to understand the individual it is necessary to understand the social relations in which the individual exists. Marx and Engels' (1959/1845) most succinct formulation of this claim can be found in their Sixth Thesis on Feuerbach, a thesis that surfaced in Vygotsky's writings as the assertion that "Humans' psychological nature represents the aggregate of internalized social relations that have become functions for the individual and form the individual's structure" (1981b, p. 164).

The task for Vygotsky here was to specify the social and individual processes involved. In carrying out this task, he followed his normal practice of integrating Marxist ideas with the ideas of other social scientists. For example, in the following passage, he borrowed from the French psychiatrist Janet (1926–27, 1928) to formulate his most general statement about the social origins of individual mental functioning, the "general genetic law of cultural development."

> Any function in the child's cultural development appears twice, or on two planes. First it appears on the social plane, and then on the psychological plane. First it appears between people as an interpsychological category, and then within the child as an intrapsychological category. This is equally true with regard to voluntary attention, logical memory, the formation of concepts, and the development of volition. . . . [I]t goes without saying that internalization transforms the process itself and changes its structure and functions. Social relations or relations among people genetically underlie all higher functions and their relationships. (1981b, p. 163)

The general genetic law of cultural development entails several claims that are not widely shared or even understood in contemporary psychology. First, this law makes a much stronger claim than simply that mental functioning in the individual derives from participation in social life. It argues that the specific structures and processes of intrapsychological functioning can be traced to their genetic precursors on the interpsychological plane. According to Vygotsky,

> [Higher mental functions'] composition, genetic structure, and means of action [i.e., forms of mediation]—in a word, their whole nature—is social. Even when we turn to mental [i.e., internal] processes, their nature remains quasisocial. In their private sphere, human beings retain the functions of social interactions. (1981b, p. 164)

This statement does not assume that higher mental functioning in the individual is a direct and simple copy of socially organized processes; the point Vygotsky made in his formulation of the general genetic law of cultural development about the transformations involved in internalization warns against any such view. However, it does mean that there is a close connection, grounded in genetic transitions, between the specific structures and processes of interpsychological and intrapsychological functioning. This, in turn, implies that different forms of interpsychological functioning give rise to related differences in the forms of intrapsychological functioning.

A second claim entailed in the general genetic law of cultural development concerns the definition of higher mental functions (e.g., thinking, voluntary attention, and logical memory). The definition involved here is quite different from interaction with nature. Furthermore, they are not inherited in the form of instincts or other innate predispositions. Instead, individuals have access to psychological tools by virtue of being part of a sociocultural milieu—that is, individuals "appropriate" (Leont'ev, 1959) such mediational means. This concept, coupled with the claim about how psychological tools reorganize human mental functioning, identifies a second way in which it can be said that "mind goes beyond the skin" in a Vygotskian approach. Instead of locating mental functioning in the individual in isolation, Vygotsky locates it in the individual functioning together with a mediational means.

A key to understanding Vygotsky's ideas about semiotic mediation is the "semiotic potentials" (Wertsch, 1985) that he saw in human language. His specific focus was on two such general potentials. On the one hand, he saw the potential for language to serve in a highly contextualized way. During early phases of ontogenesis, this involves ways in which language is tied to the "extralinguistic" context (Wertsch, 1985); later, speech comes to serve as its own context (a "linguistic" context), giving rise to phenomena, such as abbreviation, that characterize the structure of egocentric and inner speech. On the other hand, Vygotsky recognized the potential for language to function in decontextualized ways. In particular, his analysis of the emergence of "scientific" concepts is connected with the "decontextualization of mediational means" (Wertsch, 1985). This involves the process whereby linguistic expressions are lifted out of a context of communicative use and become objects of reflection and analysis. Examples of this process can be found in the practice of giving dictionary definitions of words. In this practice a word is treated as a sign type rather than a sign token; its definition is assumed to remain constant, regardless of any communicative context. This is specifically the kind of phenomenon that concerned Vygotsky in his account of "genuine" and scientific concepts.

These two general semiotic potentials are inherently linked to the other two themes that run throughout Vygotsky's writings. The highly contextualized potential is tied to the developmental processes involved in the transition from social speech (a form of interpsychological functioning) to egocentric and inner speech (forms of intrapsychological functioning). The move toward decontextualization is what underlay his genetic analysis of "complexes," "pseudoconcepts," and "genuine concepts," an analysis that views conceptual development in individuals as being inherently tied to their social environment.

A SOCIOCULTURAL APPROACH TO MIND: BEYOND VYGOTSKY

In its broadest formulation, the major goal of a Vygotskian approach is to create an analysis of mind that recognizes its historical, cultural, and institutional situatedness. In certain important respects, however, Vygotsky's empirical research did not meet this goal. The particular shortcoming on which I would like to focus here is that, when formulating his concrete empirical research, Vygotsky tended to equate social functioning with the interpsychological plane. That is, he tended to formulate his research so that social processes were understood in the first sense, but not the second sense of social phenomena outlined at the beginning of this chapter.

Near the end of his life, Vygotsky's writings reflected a growing awareness of this problem (see Wertsch, 1991). However, his empirical studies of the social origins of individual mental functioning were still limited primarily to the interpsychological plane of functioning. To transcend this limitation, it is necessary to expand on the fundamental theme of his approach, namely *semiotic mediation*. This theme lies at the core of any needed expansion, because it is semiotic mediation in a Vygotskian approach that serves to link the sociocultural setting with individual mental functioning. On the one hand, particular semiotic practices (e.g., using language in literacy activities) reflect and help constitute sociocultural settings; on the other hand, they shape the genesis of individual mental functioning (through the interpsychological plane).

I shall extend Vygotsky's approach by introducing some ideas from his contemporary, M. M. Bakhtin (1981, 1984; see also Voloshinov, 1973). Although there is no concrete evidence that Vygotsky and Bakhtin ever met, or even that either read the other's work, their approaches are grounded in quite similar sets of underlying assumptions. Instead of resulting in identical approaches, however, their similar roots lead to a great deal of complementarity. This is nowhere more evident than in connection with issues of semiotic mediation. Semiotic mediation was at the core of Vygotsky's analyses of human mental functioning, but it was only near the end of his life that he began to develop an account of it that could recognize some of the specific ways that mental functioning is socioculturally situated. Conversely, Bakhtin was not primarily interested in psychological issues, but he outlined a unique and powerful approach to semiotic mediation that has a wealth of implications for a psychology of socioculturally situated mental functioning.

Unlike many contemporary scholars of language who take as their object of analysis linguistic forms and semantic meaning abstracted from actual conditions of use, Bakhtin focused his analytic efforts on the *utterance* or "the *real unit* of speech communication" (Bakhtin, 1986, p. 71). His insistence on examining the utterance is similar to Soviet psychological theories of "activity" (e.g., Leont'ev, 1981) in that it focuses on actual, concrete action rather than on objects that can be derived from analytic abstraction. In this connection Bakhtin wrote,

> Speech can exist in reality only in the form of concrete utterances of individual speaking people, speech subjects. Speech is always cast in the form

of an utterance belonging to a particular speaking subject, and outside this
form it cannot exist. (1986, p. 71)

As Clark and Holquist (1984) have noted, this focus on utterance did not
mean that Bakhtin rejected the notion that there is constancy and systematicity
in language or speech. Instead, he viewed the utterance as the site at which
this constancy and systematicity enters into contact with unique, situated performance. Furthermore, the constancy and systematicity that he did see in
language was not limited to the types of phenomena linguists typically examine.
Although readily accepting the need to study "the specific object of linguistics,
something arrived at through a completely legitimate and necessary abstraction
from various aspects of the concrete life of the word" (1984, p. 181), Bakhtin
argued that *translinguistics* must create an alternative approach that would
incorporate a concern with how utterances and the voices producing them are
organized in sociocultural context. Bakhtin's comments indicate that translin-
gistics overlaps with the study of what today is called *pragmatics* or *discourse*,
but no easy definitions can be created using such contemporary terms because
of Bakhtin's grounding of translinguistics in a set of unique categories, especially voice and dialogicality.

In Bakhtin's account, the notion of utterance is inherently linked with
that of voice or the "speaking personality, the speaking consciousness" (Holquist
& Emerson, 1981, p. 434). This is so because an utterance can exist only by
being produced by a voice.[1] For Bakhtin, one of the major shortcomings of
linguistic (as opposed to translinguistic) analyses is that the units of analysis
(e.g., words, sentences) are abstracted from the concrete voices doing the
talking. The resulting units then "belong to nobody and are addressed to
nobody" (1986, p. 99). In Bakhtin's approach, the issue of how an utterance
belongs to a speaking voice as well as to others is a constant concern. It is
part of his more general observation that "Any utterance is a link in the chain
of speech communication" (1986, p. 84), an observation that, in turn, means
that "Utterances are not indifferent to one another, and are not self-sufficient;
they are aware of and mutually reflect one another" (1986, p. 91). Indeed,
this issue of how any utterance is inherently interrelated with others is at the
core of Bakhtin's approach. It is the issue that underlies the most fundamental
category in his approach—dialogicality.

Bakhtin's translinguistic analyses were grounded in the observation that
"The utterance is filled with *dialogic overtones*" (1986, p. 102). This basic
concern with dialogicality manifests itself in a variety of ways. For example, his

---

[1]Although Bakhtin was quite interested in phenomena such as intonation, his notion of voice
cannot be reduced to an analysis of vocal–auditory signals. It is more general, applying to written as
well as spoken communication, and conceived with the broader issues of a speaking subject's perspective, belief system, intention, and world view in mind.

approach to understanding, or what we would today term *comprehension*, is grounded in the idea that

> When the listener perceives and understands the meaning . . . of speech he simultaneously takes an active, responsive attitude toward it. He either agrees or disagrees with it . . . augments it, applies it, prepares for its execution, and so on. . . . Any understanding of live speech, a live utterance, is inherently responsive, although the degree of this activity varies extremely. Any understanding is imbued with response and necessarily elicits it in one form or another: the listener becomes the speaker. (1986, p. 68)

For Bakhtin, the notion of dialogue extended far beyond the process whereby one speaker's concrete utterances come into contact with utterances of another speaking consciousness (e.g., in face-to-face communication or in the process of understanding as outlined above). In addition to this "primordial dialogism of discourse" involving a dialogic orientation of one speaker's utterances to "others' utterances inside a *single* language" (1981, p. 275), Bakhtin concerned himself with other categories of dialogic orientation. Of particular importance for my purposes, he concerned himself with forms of dialogicality that emerge in connection with "social languages."

For Bakhtin, a social language is a way of speaking that is characteristic of a particular group in a particular sociocultural setting. Thus, he was concerned with the social languages of professions (e.g., lawyers or doctors), the social languages of different generations and genders, and so forth as they appear in concrete cultural and historical settings. Social languages differ from voices in that a type or category of voice, rather than an individual speaking personality, is involved. Such an analysis moves away from an exclusive focus on unique (i.e., unrepeatable) utterances to a focus on types or categories of utterances, but it continues to be grounded in the essential assumption that linguistic expressions cannot be understood if they are treated as if they belong to nobody.

A multitude of social languages typically exists within any single "national language" (e.g., Russian, French, or Thai). As examples of social languages, Bakhtin mentioned "social dialects, characteristic group behavior, professional jargons, generic languages, languages of generations and age groups, tendentious languages, languages of the authorities of various circles and of passing fashions, languages that serve the specific sociopolitical purposes of the day" (1981, p. 262).

In Bakhtin's view, speakers always use social languages in producing unique utterances, and these social languages shape what their individual voices can say. This process of producing unique utterances by speaking in social languages involves a specific kind of dialogicality or multivoicedness that Bakhtin termed *ventriloquation* (Bakhtin, 1981; Holquist, 1981), or the process whereby one voice speaks *through* another voice or voice type as found in a social language. According to Bakhtin,

> The word in language is half someone else's. It becomes "one's own"
> only when the speaker populates it with his own intention, his own accent,
> when he appropriates the word. . . . Prior to this moment of appropriation,
> the word does not exist in a neutral and impersonal language (it is not,
> after all, out of a dictionary that the speaker gets his words!), but rather it
> exists in other people's mouths, in other people's concrete contexts, serving
> other people's intentions: it is from there that one must take the word, and
> make it one's own. (1981, pp. 293–294)

One type of social language that Bakhtin examined in particular detail was the *speech genre*. In contrast to other types of social languages such as the social languages of generations, speech genres have a restricted and identifiable form. However, with any type of social language, speakers ventriloquate through speech genres and are thereby shaped in what they can say. This is so, even though speakers may be unaware of the process involved or even of the existence of speech genres. In Bakhtin's view,

> We speak only in definite speech genres, that is, all our utterances have
> definite and relatively stable typical *forms of construction of the whole*. Our
> repertoire of oral (and written) speech genres is rich. We use them confi-
> dently and skillfully *in practice*, and it is quite possible for us not even to
> suspect their existence *in theory*. Like Moliere's Monsieur Jourdain who,
> when speaking in prose, had no idea that was what he was doing, we speak
> in diverse genres without suspecting that they exist. (Bakhtin, 1986, p. 78)

The notion of ventriloquating through social languages has major implications for how one formulates an account of the socialization of cognitive skills and other aspects of mental functioning in a sociocultural approach to mind. Specifically, it suggests that, instead of defining mediational means in terms of linguistic units abstracted away from voices and communicative contexts, researchers should define these means in terms of phenomena that are by their very nature socioculturally situated. This occurs when one focuses on social languages. Because it is no more possible to produce an utterance without invoking a social language than it is to produce an utterance without invoking a national language, such as English, it follows that any communicative act is linked in a fundamental and concrete way to sociocultural context. Furthermore, in a Vygotskian approach, the inherent sociocultural situatedness of the mediational means used in interpsychological functioning entails that mental functioning in the individual is inherently tied to sociocultural setting as well.

The set of claims I have outlined from Bakhtin's writings is generally consistent with the overall approach Vygotsky envisioned. However, these claims suggest essential modifications and extensions of several of Vygotsky's concrete proposals. Specifically, Bakhtin's notion of a social language would seem to be a more appropriate unit of analysis than Vygotsky's account of word meaning for pursuing a sociocultural approach. This notion expands the horizon of social phenomena considered (i.e., from interpsychological to sociocultural), and it is not limited by the focus on literacy that characterizes much of Vygotsky's writings. In my view, Vygotsky's focus on word meaning, scientific concepts, and so forth reflects his overriding concern with the theoretical and practical issues that arise in a particular sociocultural setting—instruction in formal schooling. Bakhtin's writings suggest that discourse grounded in scientific concepts is only one of several social languages instead of some kind of general telos of development.

CHALLENGES FACING A SOCIOCULTURAL APPROACH TO MIND

There are obviously many tasks confronting those who wish to pursue a sociocultural approach to mind, and I shall touch on only three of them here. The key to all of these is the notion of a social language. The first essential step is to identify and characterize particular social languages. This is an extraordinarily challenging task, because most analyses in linguistics, sociolinguistics, semiotics, and other associated disciplines are not grounded in concepts similar to or even compatible with Bakhtin's account of dialogicality. To a large degree, social languages remain "invisible" to these analyses. An important start on this task can be found in the research of Heath (chapter 6 in this volume) on "eventcasts" and other genres. The speech forms Heath has identified are precisely the kinds of semiotic means that must be of concern to those interested in a sociocultural approach. Furthermore, the research of Krauss and Fussell (chapter 9 in this volume) bears on this issue in an interesting fashion, because they have identified some ways that the identity of particular kinds of speakers (i.e., voices) shapes how utterances are formulated and understood. In the case of social languages used in formal instructional settings, Heath (1986) has again made some major contributions.

   After making some headway on the issues of identifying and characterizing social languages, the next task confronting those concerned with the issues I have outlined is to specify how social languages reflect as well as create particular sociocultural settings. This task requires a grounding in issues that range far beyond the boundaries that typically define the activities of psychologists; that is, it is a task that can be realistically confronted only with a great deal of interdisciplinary cooperation. The ideas of social theorists and sociologists such as Bourdieu (1977, 1984) and Cicourel (1988, 1989) are relevant here.

   The writings of such figures can be quite useful when trying to understand some of the specific ways in which mental functioning is inherently tied to institutional practice through social languages. In particular, these ideas can serve as a corrective to the tendency to view forms of representation and mediation as if they were created solely for the purposes of psychological processes. Social languages typically emerge in response to cultural, institutional, and historical forces that may have little to do with what makes an efficient or appropriate mediational means from the perspective of psychological processes. This fact suggests a whole new venue of interdisciplinary collaboration.

The third essential step in this enterprise is to examine the processes whereby appropriating various social languages affects intrapsychological functioning. This is an issue that Minick and I have begun to map out in terms of Vygotsky's account of the zone of proximal development (Wertsch & Minick, 1990), but such analyses are still in their infancy. The general point here is that social languages are not simply transferred to some preexisting internal plane. Instead, mastering a social language is a process whereby psychological processes are *formed*. The social language itself is only one of the forces at work in such development, and its mastery occurs in a psychological system characterized by a host of other processes and demands. Just as social processes cannot be reduced to psychological processes, the latter cannot be reduced to the former.

My outline of a sociocultural approach to mind and of the challenges it raises by no means addresses all the questions that might be raised under the heading of socially shared cognition. However, it does provide a means for addressing a few central questions that must eventually be recognized by any attempt to create an account of this phenomenon. By harnessing notions such as dialogicality and social language, it provides a means for addressing the issue of how mental functioning is tied to the two levels of social organization outlined at the beginning of this chapter. Just as it was not enough for Vygotsky to equate social action with the interpsychological plane of functioning, it will not be enough for contemporary investigators to extend psychological accounts only to the level of dyadic or small group interaction. Cultural, historical, and social structural factors that have been at the core of so much of the research in other disciplines must be addressed in some way as well. This does not mean that all psychologists must become anthropologists, historians, or sociologists, but it does suggest the need to search for theoretical constructs and units of analysis that ensure a fundamental compatibility between the analyses conducted in psychology and other disciplines.

The key to formulating issues in such a way that this compatibility can exist is in the notion of mediation. I argued earlier that it is possible to understand the essence of Vygotsky's unique contribution only by understanding the role that mediational means played in his approach. I also argued that by incorporating some of Bakhtin's insights into the basic theoretical formulation provided by Vygotsky, it is possible to extend this formulation in some productive ways. Perhaps the most important implications of these theorists' writings today are that we need to formulate issues under the heading of socially shared cognition in such a way that concrete empirical studies can be conducted that do not reduce the inquiry to the exclusive language of a single discipline.

References

Bakhtin, M. M. (1981). *The dialogic imagination* (M. Holquist, Ed.; M. Holquist & C. Emerson, Trans.). Austin, TX: University of Texas Press.

Bakhtin, M. M. (1984). *Problems of Dostoevsky's poetics* (C. Emerson, Ed. and Trans.). Minneapolis: University of Minnesota Press.

Bakhtin, M. M. (1986). *Speech genres and other late essays* (C. Emerson & M. Holquist, Eds.; V. W. McGee, Trans.). Austin: University of Texas Press.

Berger, P. L., & Luckmann, T. (1966). *The social construction of reality: A treatise in the sociology of knowledge*. Garden City, NY: Anchor Books.

Bourdieu, P. (1977). *Outline of a theory of practice* (R. Nice, Trans.). Cambridge, England: Cambridge University Press.

Bourdieu, P. (1984). *Distinction: A social critique of the judgement of taste* (R. Nice, Trans.). Cambridge, MA: Harvard University Press.

Brown, A. L., & French, L. A. (1978). The zone of proximal development: Implications for intelligence testing in the year 2000. *Intelligence, 3*, 255–277.

Cicourel, A. (1988, November). *Aspects of formal and tacit knowledge in the collaborative organization of medical diagnostic reasoning*. Paper presented at the Workshop on Technology and Cooperative Work sponsored by Bell Communications Research, University of Arizona.

Cicourel, A. (1989, April). *Aspects of structural and processual theories of knowledge*. Paper presented at the Conference on the Social Theory of Pierre Bourdieu, Center for Psychosocial Studies, Chicago.

Clark, K., & Holquist, M. (1984). *M. M. Bakhtin: Life and works*. Cambridge, MA: Harvard University Press.

Cole, M. (1985). The zone of proximal development: Where culture and cognition create each other. In J. V. Wertsch (Ed.), *Culture, communication, and cognition: Vygotskian perspectives* (pp. 146–161). Cambridge, England: Cambridge University Press.

Giddens, A. (1984). Power, the dialectic of control and class structuration. In A. Giddens & G. Mackenzie (Eds.), *Social class and the division of labour: Essays in honour of Ilya Neustadt* (pp. 29–45). Cambridge, England: Cambridge University Press.

Heath, S. (1986). Sociocultural contexts of language development. In Bilingual Education Office, California State Department of Education (Ed.), *Beyond language: Social and cultural factors in schooling language minority students* (pp. 143–186). Los Angeles: Evaluation, Dissemination and Assessment Center, California State University, Los Angeles.

Holquist, M. (1981). The politics of representation. In S. Greenblatt (Ed.), *Allegory in representation: Selected papers from the English Institute* (pp. 163–183). Baltimore: Johns Hopkins University Press.

Holquist, M., & Emerson, C. (1981). Glossary. In M. M. Bakhtin, *The dialogic imagination* (M. Holquist, Ed.; M. Holquist & C. Emerson, Trans.). Austin, TX: University of Texas Press.

Janet, P. (1926–27). *La pensee interieure et ses troubles* [Inner thought and its problems]. Course given at the College de France.

Janet, P. (1928). *De l'angoisse a l'extase: Etudes sur les croyances et les sentiments: Vol. 2 Les sentiments fondamentaux* [From anguish to ecstasy: Studies in beliefs and feelings: Vol. 2. Basic feelings]. Paris: Librairie Felix Alcan.

Leont'ev, A. N. (1959). *Problemy razvitiya psikhiki* [Problems in the development of mind]. Moscow: Moscow University Press.

Leont'ev, A. N. (1981). The problem of activity in psychology. In J. V. Wertsch (Ed.), *The concept of activity in Soviet psychology* (pp. 37–71). Armonk, NY: M.E. Sharpe.

Marx, K., & Engels, F. (L. S. Feuer, Trans.). (1959). The German ideology. In L. S. Feuer (Ed.), *Marx and Engels: Basic writings on politics and philosophy.* Garden City, NY: Doubleday. (Original work published 1845)

Rogoff, B., & Wertsch, J. V. (Eds.). (1984). *Children's learning in the "zone of proximal development."* San Francisco: Jossey-Bass.

Tharp, R. G., & Gallimore, R. (1988). *Rousing minds to life: Teaching, learning, and schooling in social context.* Cambridge, England: Cambridge University Press.

Voloshinov, V. N. (1973). *Marxism and the philosophy of language* (L. Matejka & I. R. Titunik, Trans.). New York: Seminar Press.

Vygotsky, L. S. (1934). *Myshlenie i rech': Psikhologicheskie issledovaniya* [Thinking and speech: Psychological investigations]. Moscow and Leningrad: Gosudarstvennoe Sotsial'no-Ekonomicheskoe Izdatel'stvo.

Vygotsky, L. S. (1960). *Razvitie vysshykh psikhicheskikh functsii* [The development of higher mental functions]. Moscow: Izdatel'stvo Akademii Pedagogicheskikh Nauk.

Vygotsky, L. S. (1978). *Mind in society: The development of higher psychological processes* (M. Cole, V. John-Steiner, S. Scribner, & E. Souberman, Eds.). Cambridge, MA: Harvard University Press.

Vygotsky, L. S. (1981a). The instrumental method in psychology. In J. V. Wertsch (Ed.), *The concept of activity in Soviet psychology* (pp. 134–143). Armonk, NY: Sharpe.

Vygotsky, L. S. (1981b). The genesis of higher mental functions. In J. V. Wertsch (Ed.), *The concept of activity in Soviet psychology* (pp. 144–188). Armonk, NY: Sharpe.

Vygotsky, L. S., & Luria, A. R. (1930). *Etyudy po istorii povedeniya: Obez'yana, primitiv, rebenok* [Essays on the history of behavior: Ape, primitive, child]. Moscow and Leningrad: Gosudarstvennoe Izdatel'stvo.

Wertsch, J. V. (1985). *Vygotsky and the social formation of mind.* Cambridge, MA: Harvard University Press.

Wertsch, J. V. (1991). *Voices of the mind: A sociocultural approach to mediated action.* Cambridge, MA: Harvard University Press.

Wertsch, J. V., & Minick, N. (1990). Negotiating sense in the zone of proximal development. In M. Schwebel, C. A. Maher, & N. S. Fagley (Eds.), *Promoting cognitive growth over the life span* (pp. 71–88). Hillsdale, NJ: Erlbaum.

Wertsch, J. V., & Youniss, J. (1987). Contextualizing the investigator: The case of developmental psychology. *Human Development, 30,* 18–31.

CHAPTER 6

"IT'S ABOUT WINNING!" THE LANGUAGE OF KNOWLEDGE IN BASEBALL

SHIRLEY BRICE HEATH

Cartoonist Charles Schulz knows a lot about the world but not much about the language of young players on a baseball team. When Lucy taunts Charlie Brown about his pitching or batting and their conflict becomes a one-on-one confrontation, youngsters who play Little League baseball know that is not the way "real" baseball players talk to each other. Real teams talk not about losing but about winning; the dominant view is that the game will always get better and, as it does, so will the players. In their speech and actions, Little League baseball teams gear themselves to win.

This chapter will address the role of language—specifically problem-solving narratives—in the natural learning setting of Little League baseball. As part of a larger study of the language of youngsters engaged in activities sponsored by neighborhood-based organizations, these data came from the middle-class players and coach of a Little League baseball team in an urban area of northern California during the 1987–88 season.

The research reported here is part of the project "Language, Socialization, and Neighborhood-based Organizations," for which principal investigators Milbrey Wallin McLaughlin and Shirley Brice Heath were given funding by the Spencer Foundation. One goal of this project is to document linguistic practices in the everyday reasoning of youngsters in neighborhood organizations and to describe the political and social contexts that initiate, sustain, and alter their existence.

Mastery of roles for these boys thus followed from practice of skills and verbal manipulation (e.g., what-if scenes, secret language, and narratives of famous plays or players) of the possible frames or scenes that called forth particular roles.

ON THE FIELD

The team I studied was one of some 20 in a town of approximately 40,000 residents—most of whom live in households where one or more adults hold a professional position. The ethos of the town is one of an acceptance of education as a fundamental right and opportunity for honing skills and attitudes necessary for future career success. The town offers multiple types of neighborhood-based organizations, boasts more libraries per capita than any other city its size in California, and supports consistent news coverage of the athletic and artistic activities of its youth. The coach for Campos, the team studied here, was enrolled as a graduate student in business school after having completed a career in military aviation.

Players signed up for the team through the city recreation center, and youngsters in the same area of town ended up on one of 20 or more teams that practiced after school and on weekends near their neighborhoods. In mid-March, the coach of Campos sent the first of three newsletters to the players and their parents, telling them of his philosophy and of his choice to hold two "good two-hour practices" each week. The coach closed his first newsletter, which contained the practice schedule for the season, by advising the players to run on their "days off" to stay in shape. In a subsequent team letter, the coach thanked parents for their support and outlined his goals for the team. The players had heard these goals at their first practice: (a) to have a good time, (b) to learn and practice teamwork and sportsmanship, and (c) to learn a little more about the game of baseball. The coach emphasized the first two goals as most important and urged parents to let him know if their sons were not having fun or feeling part of the team. The team objective was "to win games as long as everyone is having a good time." The coach elaborated this point:

> Having a good time usually means being in the game. Most games go for five innings; only rarely does a . . . contest go all six innings. During a five-inning game with 13 players, the average playing time is under 3.5 innings. For a four-inning game, the average playing time is less than *3* innings. (coach's newsletter, April 28, 1988)

He then outlined in the newsletter his plan that all boys would play at least two innings, and that he would not start the nine strongest boys but would try to field a strong team throughout the scheduled six innings. Those boys who would play the most over the season would be those who responded to coaching, worked for the team, tried hard, and consistently exhibited good sportsmanship.

He urged some practice on their own, offering hints about ways the boys could practice in their home driveways. He closed the letter by requesting that parents "release" their sons to the team before the game and let them "do their own thing" without parental interference. The letter closed with the "Little League Pledge" from the official rule book: "I trust in God. I love my country and will respect its law. I will play fair and strive to win. But win or lose, I will always do my best" (coach's newsletter, April 28, 1988). The coach made the boys memorize the team's three goals and asked them to call these to mind at critical points during the season. He explained his premise in coaching to me in the following way: "Players and coach enter a fantasy world and pretend they are big-league players . . . players are not kids" (personal communication, December 27, 1988). His requests of the players were usually couched in terms of "How would they do this in the major leagues?" (personal communication, December 27, 1988). For example, this was the prompt that got the boys to tuck in their shirttails, accept questionable calls by umpires, and treat seriously the array of special signals the coach and players worked out.

The focus was on prototypes or generic categories of behavior for major league players, catchers, batters, and "good sports." The coach rarely called attention to specific features or behaviors that applied only to certain positions (e.g., catcher, pitcher, or shortstop). Because everyone on the team expected everyone else to succeed in hitting, throwing, and catching the ball and running fast, the lessons of practices applied to *all* players, not simply to those who might receive designation as *the* catcher, pitcher, or first baseman. In interviews, team members reflected their understanding of this approach by repeatedly naming "flexibility," "lots of action for everyone," and "creativity once you've got the basics" as the most appealing aspects of baseball.

The models or experts to whom the boys linked their own behaviors lay beyond the coach and the vagaries of team membership; they rested in the collective knowledge of team members as they read about baseball, watched games on television, or heard them on the radio. Frequent reminders made clear who the boys were: "We're professionals," "We're card-carrying members of a group," "We're all in it together." The coach and team kept a number of secrets from parents: special cheers, idiosyncratic terms, and hand and verbal signals to put certain strategies (e.g., bunting) into place during games. The coach and his players referred to balls that were easy to hit or easy to catch as "marshmallows." During games, the team and the coach would remind batters to "wait for a marshmallow." Frequent use of this and other terms (e.g., "dig" to refer to a low pitch) marked the inclusiveness of the team at games; neither their own parents nor members of the other team knew the meanings of the boys' cheers and technical terms.

The coach's self-portrayal emerged from a sense of what he was *not*: He made such statements as "Coaches must not see themselves as teachers," "Sports is not a schoolhouse," and "Don't teach about it, but play and learn." Experimentation and direct engagement with "basics of the game, and some of the fine points" set the foundation for "practical logic," deciding the "rationale," and "learning from each others' mistakes." The coach urged his players to "spectate knowingly" and estimated that 80% of his coaching time was spent in "stroking to establish a creditable authority and handing out baseballs and praise," whereas 20% of his time with the players went to reminding either individuals or the team as a whole that they were "not doing what they were capable of" and asking youngsters to show how they could improve (personal communication, December 27, 1988).

The coach warned the youngsters, "One thing I will not tolerate is quiet on the field." The boys cheered on their teammates before, during, and after the game. The coach used mistakes as models, sometimes asking the player who had made an error to replay verbally what he had done and to work with team members to figure out how the mistake occurred and which alternative approaches might have helped avoid the error. The coach called these "low-cost lessons," pointing out repeatedly that "bad days" happened, and when they did, the important move was to "go do something else and don't worry about it." The coach fostered a sense of participation in "the real thing" by using technical vocabulary (e.g., RBI for runs batted in, ERA for earned run average), approaching specifics of the game with an analysis of the physics of movement (e.g., predicting the course of grounders over rough terrain or the effect of a swing in which the bat hit just the top of the ball), and encouraging team members to reason through events in oral exchanges. The coach often reminded team members and parents alike of "streaks and slumps" in learning and urged the players to acknowledge the importance of "toughing out" certain "bad days" (personal communication, December 27, 1988).

Interviews with players, as well as observations of team activities and analyses of audiotapes and videotapes of practice and games, indicated that players saw nothing out of the ordinary in this coach's approach. Team members who had played on other teams identified only the order of practice as a distinguishing feature of different coaches with whom they had worked. During practice, when the coach called out for them to recapitulate verbally what they were doing, what they saw, or what went wrong, team members complied without indicating that this request was out of the ordinary. When he sometimes openly announced that he called for these analyses to see if the team was alert, the boys simply nodded and waited for the next play with his follow-up call for analysis. Interviews indicated that they viewed "looking out," "keeping track of what's going on," and "knowing how to figure strategies" as natural parts of team expectations. Team members, when asked why they participated in after-school activities such as Little League baseball, always responded with phrases such as "participation," "lots of activity," "you don't get bored," and "the promise of being able to do lots of things." But they also pointed out the importance of talk and the link of talk to action. One player contrasted classroom learning and baseball in the following manner:

> In baseball, they talk about stuff that more people, like don't know about. They talk about like, I know how to do things, but sometimes I don't know. Like, to be in the batter's box, one of the coaches told me to stand back a little more. Like I know how to do things, but not *how* to, so it's more fun to play baseball also because you are active, and there's fun to do baseball moving around and talk all the time. Like in school, you're quiet all the time. In baseball you can talk all you want.
>
> He taught us to get grounders, like, plant our feet down like this and move down. We wouldn't just be, like, just learning; he actually has us do that, and he actually gives us ground balls. Like in teaching, they just tell you how to do it. (Player Interview C, January, 1989)

This player's struggle with the meaning of "knowing *how* to do things" seems to indicate that the *talk*—the giving of a direct recommendation or rule—translated for him into improved play, as well as flexibility gained through individual experience with the most obvious parts of the game, such as running, batting, and catching.

Although the players saw no particular distinguishing features of this coach's approach, they were alert to distinctions between the language of coaching and that of teaching. When asked how they would compare their learning through athletic experiences with other kinds of learning, all made the immediate contrast with their school (and not with piano lessons, Sunday School, Hebrew School, or other out-of-school activities). They divided the talk of the coach into "pep talks" and "disciplinary talk." The former (which the boys estimated to be about 80% of the coach's speech) urged the boys to "do their best" and the latter talked about "what's been going wrong." This differentiation between the personalized nature of the coach's talk about improvement (e.g., through the use of personal pronouns such as *their*) and the depersonalized nature of talk about negative events and outcomes (e.g., through the use of impersonal pronouns such as *what*) also showed up in the actual use of pronouns during talks on the field. Pep talks abounded with personal pronouns and proper names; disciplinary talk centered on activities, events, and answers to queries like "*What* went wrong here?" or "*How* did that happen?"

NARRATIVES

Multi-turn talk during practice fell into two primary categories. The first centered on problem-solving narratives in which the coach and the boys cooperated to provide an "eventcast" of activities currently underway or projected to occur in the future. The second was a question-and-answer series focused on reflections, restatement of rules, and reanalysis of prior plays.

Eventcasts as Sociodramatic Play

Eventcasts constitute a genre of narratives that outline the features of an action either while it is underway or before it is to occur. The sequencing of the event gives the basic shape to these narratives. This feature is most evident in commentaries that accompany action in process; such commentaries are unscripted in that what is said depends on the unfolding of the actions in progress (Crystal & Davy, 1969). However, in addition to the sequencing of these actions, speakers interlace eventcasts with explication of specific features of roles, individual actors, and conditions of particular events within each episode (Heath, 1986). Perhaps the most widely familiar example of eventcast is sports announcer talk (SAT), the running commentary that radio and television announcers give of a game that is under way (Ferguson, 1983). As in the following examples, one or two sentences of SAT can trigger immediate recognition of this genre as distinctive from news reports, conversation, or even an after-game wrap-up:

1. Pitch to Rob
   one and one
   swing and pop-up foul

2. Tim on at second
   planning to get this one
   close one at third

3. Over at third is Bobby

4. Rob, *the guy who's always awake at practice*, heads out to center-field. . . .

5. One and one [one ball, one strike as "the count"]
   two for three [two hits, three times at bat as player's record]
   three to one [three runs, one run as score]

This register carries specific syntactic features such as those illustrated above: simplification (1 and 2—deletion of copula and sentence initial nominals); sentence inversions (3); heavy modifiers (4); and routines (5—ways of giving the count, keeping record of a player's batting, and reporting the score of the game).

For eventcasts to be interactive narratives, the boys and the coach had to be familiar with not only the syntax of SAT but also the technical vocabulary surrounding aspects of the game, from major league statistics (stats) to names of the catcher's equipment. When asked in interviews to name all the technical terms associated with baseball they could think of in four minutes, all the players named at least 45 such terms (e.g., outfield, plate, ERA). In addition, when asked to explain the meaning of the routines just listed in (5), the boys knew that the range of numbers possible in the first two of the three items was limited. For example, because the number of balls (four) and of strikes (three) for one turn at bat is set, a call of "five and four" is not possible.

During practice, the coach used SAT in a modified eventcast or *bid for sociodramatic play* that set a problem within a narrative of unfolding actions. He laid out a situation that led the boys to imagine the particular scene or series of events that formed the context for their next actions. After the play, the coach initially asked the boys to analyze what occurred, and if they did not respond fully, he set up a *conditional (if-then) statement* in which he identified and analyzed a key move. He often added a brief *rule restatement*, which was then followed by a *conditional extender*—an if-then claim about some particular condition that extended the context for thinking about the applicability of the rule. The following two examples illustrate parts of this technique:

1. *Bid for sociodramatic play*
   Okay, now there's a runner on second, Randy. He thinks this is going over the fence, and he's rounding the bags, but he didn't tag out. High towering fly. Tim's got it, let's nail him.
   [Coach then hits a high fly to Randy.]
   Ohhhh. [Randy misses the ball. After the miss, several players and a volunteer parent offer their analyses. The coach waits and then says:]

2. *Set-up for conditional statement*
   Here again, Randy, the most important thing. If you backed up two steps and got off the bag, [then] you could have grabbed that ball and made the play.

3. *Rule restatement*
   The most important thing is to get the ball and then go after the play. You usually have time.

4. *Conditional extender*
   Or [if you don't have time to get back to the bag, then] you might even be able to tag him coming in, coming back to the bag.

For actions demonstrated, as well as actions that might be called for in hypothesized plays, the coach offered eventcasts during the play ("Randy's there on first now, and the batter gets a marshmallow. . . .") or modally marked scenarios ("He would have been there on first, and what would the player on second be doing, where would he be?").

During demonstration of exercises, the coach verbally scripted his actions as he demonstrated. As indicated in the following two examples, his comments are of two types: reasons for particular actions and the context of when and how he learned about a particular exercise, warm-up drill, or strategy:

1. Let's try one more warm-up drill, so we're really ready for grounders. Remember this one? [demonstrates exercise] You used to be good at

that one, right? [demonstrates as he talks] Take each hand and reach
around behind the leg and touch the heel of the other, of the opposite
foot.

2. That's one I learned in Europe. Soccer players use it over there, and it's
really good for the gelatin. Okay, let's try a few grounders.

Much of the coach's talk with the boys focused on what he retained from his
earlier devotion to baseball and to following the games with regularity now. The
boys imitated this talk, as well as the commitment to using sources of knowledge
about the game other than those immediately at hand in their own practices. One
player summarized his learning about baseball outside of practice as follows:

> In baseball season, I look at the paper every day. I watch, like, the high-
> lights on the news, listen to the radio, and I hear different stuff, like what
> other players are doing and that lets me know, like, that's a new thing for
> me. I always keep learning new things about baseball, and it makes me do
> the same things on the field. (Player Interview C, January, 1989)

After games or practice, on occasions when the team would go out for pizza, the
boys talked minimally about their own games, but primarily about what was
happening in the major leagues.

The give-and-take, back-and-forth nature of reasoning, arguing, and making
a point on and off the field illustrate the dialogical nature of the discourse. The
coach assumes an audience of listeners who share his situation and orientation to
action and who recognize that talk about baseball is dominant and valid in this
context. Within this large frame, the coach gives cues to the boys to bring into
place certain scenarios in which players take on certain roles, execute particular
actions, and may meet with several outcomes. The coach constantly models verbal
explication of the features of these scenarios by setting up problem-solving narratives as conditionals.

A brief digression is necessary here on conditionals and their examination
within the context of natural logic, which assumes that, within daily discourse,
every assertion is not proved and that action plays a major role in daily discourse
(Grize, 1982). Conditional constructions allow interlocutors to make inferences
that try out various alternatives on the "small-scale model" of external reality
that individuals carry around in their heads. Speakers and listeners must imagine
connections across situations and bring knowledge of past events to bear on a
projected scenario (Ferguson, Reilly, ter Meulen, & Traugott, 1986).

Conditionals can carry low hypotheticality and future time reference (e.g.,
"If he comes tomorrow, we should talk about that," said by one member of a
committee about another member known to be consistent in committee attendance).
They may also carry high hypotheticality with no time reference and be counterfactual; conditionals of this variety tell us much about inferencing and some of
the cognitive prerequisites or combinations of such prerequisites to the acquisition

of conditionals (Bowerman, 1986). Counterfactual conditionals depend on variations of shared bodies of prior knowledge or expertise distributed among interlocutors. For example, if one member of the parent committee trying to raise funds for a camping trip for Little Leaguers says, "If we only had millionaires with open pockets on our board, then we'd have no worries," listeners are assumed to understand that such persons would not only donate funds but would also help raise funds from their associates. In addition, such a statement may be generated with the hope that some board members may have some ideas of ways to bring wealthy and influential members to the board. Such conditionals are highly hypothetical and carry no reference to a specific future time.

In addition, conditionals tell us much about the marking of topic (Haiman, 1978) and the pragmatics of correcting and controlling what is to be talked about (as well as offering a guide to action) within an atmosphere of collaboration and collegiality. It is common within a heated discussion of real events for a speaker to deflect the heat by introducing a call to pretend. Such calls acknowledge analogy making, comparison, and the freeing of participants from what is often the tangle of current real events. The meanings of counterfactuals depend on participants carrying out semantic interpretations within a known state of affairs or context. The imminence or immediate state of affairs that makes the conditional possible need not be stated. For example, an adult observing a child about to reach out to take a package of gum in a grocery store can assert, "I'll pinch you." The adult need not say, "In this public place, objects do not belong to you, and therefore, you may not touch such objects with the intention of taking them into your possession. If you try to do so, you will be punished." The observable context, plus prior norms of behavior and cause-and-effect events in the adult–child relationship, enables the child to interpret the "I'll pinch you" statement as a conditional meaning, "If you touch the gum, I'll pinch you."

Bids for sociodramatic play provide one category of conditional that depends heavily on assumptions about members bringing a prior body of knowledge to bear on current activities. Sociodramatic play is characterized by six play elements: verbal communication, make-believe with regard to objects, imitative role play, persistence, interactions between two or more players, and make-believe in regard to actions and situations (Smilansky, 1968). Invitations to such play come if participants agree that all have had some shared experiences or will quickly learn certain prototypical features from others in the sociodramatic play. For example, a group of children cannot play "doctor" without the assumption that all the children have had experiences with doctors or will follow the "experts" in playing such scenes. In addition, these discourse contexts also assume generalized real-world knowledge (e.g., an object dropped from the table will fall), as well as an immediate surrounding context in which sociodramatic play is appropriate (i.e., relationships obtain between interlocutors so that one or more can issue the call for sociodramatic play; Akatsuka, 1986).

Sociodramatic play presents, then, a special situation for conditionality in that it is made possible by a meta-awareness on the part of all participants that the call for the play is a call for pretense or imagination. Although both children and adults will sometimes introduce invitations to pretense by specific lexical markers, such as *suppose*, *let's pretend*, or *imagine*, it is more often the case that sociodramatic play is initiated simply by an announcement of counterfactual conditions (e.g., "Man on second, top of the eighth inning . . ." said during practice drill on grounders). Within some cultures, conditionals make up a large part of the everyday world of young children's language input (Heath, 1983). Some middle-class, literate, school-oriented families surround their children with make-believe stories or "let's pretend" occasions in which conditionals serve discourse functions.[1] Bids for sociodramatic play are essentially unchallengeable (Givon, 1982); interlocutors are assumed to have to agree to play word games, tell stories, or pretend in animated play.

Within the Little League team already described, sociodramatic play—within the ongoing play of the drama of the full season—allows the players to achieve mastery, to contrast, illustrate, and explore options. It asserts nonliteral, untrue, counterfactual conditions of the current limited world and makes possible many other worlds (Bruner, 1986). Rules for the logic of pretense go into effect once the participants recognize what is at work. Gregory Bateson has told us that social play is possible only if the participants are capable of metacommunication, of signaling that a counterfactual is at work (Bateson, 1972). The frame of play not only makes the assertions counterfactual, but it also transforms roles within the situations and orchestrates a collaborative process. For the interaction to be successful, all interlocutors or participants in the scene must take the perspective that play is "on." Thus, participants' constant attention is necessary, because the shifts between what is real and what is not real can come at any moment.

Those who have studied play in various cultures around the world have repeatedly documented the learning value of sociodramatic play—or, indeed, of play in general. Although the primary function of play is regarded as enjoyment, its secondary function has long been characterized as mastery (Kuczaj, 1982).

---

[1]It is important to note that current shifting dynamics of family life within the American middle class, as well as among families in poverty, force youngsters to take on independent responsibilities of decision making much earlier than was the case before the 1950s. Thus, opportunities for role-play through word games and make-believe have greatly diminished in the leisure activities of families across classes. An increasing percentage of households today lack members who play the traditional roles of mother, father, or extended family members (Wallerstein & Blakeslee, 1989). The context for language socialization of these children is not that of adults in sustained and highly redundant play routines. Occasions for sustained talk and face-to-face interactions outside immediate decision making or conflict resolution have become increasingly unavailable for both middle-class and working-class children (Csikszentmihalyi & Larson, 1984; Heath, 1990). Sustained opportunities for the "mutual tuning-in" (Schutz, 1951) upon which linguistic and metalinguistic awareness rest would seem to occur for children of the middle and teenage years much more with their peers and adults in neighborhood-based activities than with adults in the home.

Language play as pattern-practice and drill is well known to linguists (Ferguson & Macken, 1983; Weir, 1962). Anthropologists have acknowledged the powerful role that nonordinary language play has in some communities where teasing, gibberish rhymes, and pretend games promote role-shifting, the acquisition of new genres, and cooperative discourse. The analysis of these routines points out the synchronicity of these encounters and their interdependence with judgments about role relationships and suspension of customary conventions of interactions (Abrahams, 1964; Dundes, Leach, & Ozkok, 1970; Schieffelin & Ochs, 1986).

Sociodramatic play provides a frame with conditions for problem solving that all interlocutors must acknowledge as a *causal* environment that will bring about certain effects or results. The coach characterized the efforts of the entire team, including his own, as being within the "good time" of "a fantasy world" (see team goals, team objective, and coach's premise stated earlier). He shaped and reshaped this world and allowed it to expand greatly the types of reasoning, inferencing, and action taking practiced by the boys. He marked, and encouraged the boys to mark, what they were learning from the shifts made possible in their sociodramatic plays by asking them specific sets of questions as follow-ups or lead-ins to plays. To their conditional world, the coach added rules that he then followed up with more conditionals that would lead team members to expand their understanding of various contexts that could shape outcomes of applications of rules (see "setup for conditional statement," outlined previously).

Questions of Knowing

During practice, the coach asked the players questions that called for three types of narrative responses covering past events: (a) *reflections*—options and think-aloud analyses of certain plays or scenes; (b) *rule recounts*—recitations of rules that applied in the situation just witnessed; and (c) *recites*—say-aloud scripts of what either he or they would be thinking or saying to themselves during certain types of plays.

Reflections

The boys expected analysis as part of their practice. The coach sometimes made explicit the fact that he would call for the analysis of a play, a particular move, or a segment of practice drills. He would call out to specific players by name: "Randy, what did you think of that one [grounder]?" "Rob, do you know why you got that one?" Often, after a sociodramatic play, he would ask the boys to analyze what had taken place within the action elicited from the set-up of the situation. The boys would collectively offer views on what occurred, and the coach would restate and supplement their comments. When players did not answer direct questions, the coach also used completion techniques to elicit their reflections, such as, "And you want to do what?" [No answer]. "And you aim for the _____?" (with marked rising intonation). The coach would wait until one or more boys finished his sentence and then restate what he saw as the possible reflection of the player, ending with a request for confirmation ("Right?").

In addition, the coach often asked vague questions that one or more boys would answer. He would then follow up with additional queries or substitutes for specific parts of their answers, sometimes offering "wrong" interpretations or restatements that provoked further clarification from the players. This strategy tested the attention of other players, who could protest if the boy being questioned did not catch the fact that the coach had given a wrong interpretation or had misstated a rule. This strategy is illustrated in the following example:

Coach:	What about a fly ball?
Player:	You, you have, you have your glove, you have your glove a couple inches from your face, and you're looking up at a position semiperpendicular to the ground, and you have your feet a little bit, about like grounder wise, planted apart steadily, so you can move back, forth, and around.
Coach:	You gotta be able to move. What about your legs? Stiff and straight, right?
Player:	No.
Coach:	No?
Player:	They're, they're ready to move.
Coach:	Which is how?
Player:	Bend the knees.
Coach:	Bend those knees, right?
Player:	Right.

Rule recounts
Simple rules, often repeated, marked much of the talk between coach and players. Throughout the season, the coach asked the boys to restate their team goals and the Little League pledge. He also gave them several sets of rules for particular situations on the field. The following exchange over rules illustrates talk about rules during fielding practice:

> What are the three rules? Do you remember? [shouts from various parts of the field] That's right. First you get the ball, then you get set, and then you get rid of it. [Several boys shout out the three rules before the coach yells out again] That's right, get the ball, get set, and then get rid of it.
>
> And if you're real close to the bag, how do you throw it? [boys shout various answers, including "underhand"] Underhand, that's right. Why? [boys again shout various answers] That's right, make it easy for him to catch.

Restatements of rules after the first few practices were collaborative, with players from all over the field shouting parts, and the coach closing off by recapping in simple form the full run-through of all rules recited by the boys. The calls for such rules may be divided into direct questions (first exchange) and conditionals (second exchange).

Recites

In addition to general rules for specific broad achievement goals (e.g., catching, hitting, or fielding), the coach elicited from each boy direct recitation of what the coach would say and what the player would be thinking or saying to himself during his performance within certain roles. The coach would ask, for example, "What do I say when I want to see that position?" Of a player at bat during practice, he would ask, "What did you do right on that one?", "What are you going to tell yourself?", or "You really launched into that one. Was your shoulder down?"

To test how such efforts carried over into the boys' abilities to think about how they internally monitored their actions, I involved some of the boys in stimulated recall by showing them segments of a videotape of a championship game and asking each player involved in certain key plays to say aloud what he might have been thinking at particular moments of play. One player, up for his second bat during the game, offered this analysis:

> I'm thinking, I'm one for one. I don't want to make any mistakes. Just
> calm down and put the bat on the ball, and go for two for two. I like
> having a good percentage up at the plate. When I see pitches that I like to
> hit, I swing harder. (Player Interview C, January, 1989)

Direct speech or self-talk (e.g., the "Just calm down . . . two for two" segment) occurred frequently in such recites of past performances, as did expressions of the boys' sense of assessment of their activities by counts (two and two) and records (one for one).

The coach's questions that asked for reflections, rule recounts, and recites had the effect of personalizing the boys' strategies, approaches, and knowledge about the game. To these personalizing queries, the coach added personification of both equipment and player moves. For example, the coach often referred to the bat (and not the batter) as "really lazy." He used diminutives to describe particular moves that led to errors: "Your step is just a little bit too short" (rather than "You aren't taking big steps to get out there"). When the boys made mistakes during practice, he often offered them conditionals granting personal agentry in his analysis of their moves: "Sandy, don't screen 'em, *if you can*—that's OK *if you wanna* catch 'em, but screening 'em can make it tough. *If you're gonna go for it*, go all the way." Such offers of personal agentry often preceded general conditionals that contained impersonal second person pronouns.

SETTING A LEARNER FRAME

Several features of Little League life made possible the conditions that led to the language uses and reflective practice the boys demonstrated. The pervasive ethos of the team was one of a fantasy of major league play and of problem solving within the overarching conditional (i.e., if you want your team to succeed—or the play/drama to go well—you must first take on the job of improving your own learning). In general, competition among players on the team did not become an issue, because opportunities to play various roles rotated during practice, and the public reflections on what and how certain players were doing led to a consensual perspective on which boys would play key positions during games. Team members recognized that their primary goal was to demonstrate and analyze various skills necessary for all players (e.g., batting, catching flies and grounders, knowing types of pitches and appropriate occasions for their uses).

Key conditions for the team's "guided participation" (Rogoff, 1986, 1989) included the legitimation of differences, focus on monitoring, and integrative praxis. Each of these supported the problem-solving narratives of conditionality and the collaborative and highly interactive questioning I have examined. These verbally reinforced displays of skills and knowledge depended on nonverbal supports that came from the boys' attending, observing, and participating throughout practices and the games, as well as adding to their knowledge of baseball through sources available outside team activities.

Legitimation of Differences

Players learned from the first day of practice, and through written materials from the coach, that they were in the business of valuing differences. If a boy was small, that did not mean he could not be a strong hitter; if a boy was overweight, that did not mean he could not be a fast runner. The coach expected and called attention to variations in pitching, sliding, and running styles—and even to variations in degrees of knowledge of the small-print rulings for Little League games. Some boys studied the rules and talked with their fathers and the coach about specific rules that applied to Little League or that offered guidance on interpreting umpires' judgments. Others chose to alternate batting as a right-hander or left-hander, to deviate from expected styles of pitching, or to make the most of the lack of balance between their talents (e.g., boys who did not have the highest batting averages were sometimes best known as fast runners).

To keep the valuing of differences from getting out of hand and undermining team achievement, boys had to be situationally sensitive in their criteria of justification for differences. They could not be different just for the sake of difference; they had to be sensitive in their planning and competent in oral explanations if called on to explain changes in their behaviors. Moreover, such differences kept categories flowing: The weakest outfielder of the early season could move to catcher by mid-season; the smallest player who lagged behind all the other players in running time and batting power could become the team's strategist. The coach and players called attention to these differences often, both during practices and in interviews.

Monitoring

Team players expected to be ready to offer verbal evidence of their close attention to what was going on around them and to what others were doing. The consistent attention to monitoring by all members kept individuals from becoming isolated and spread positive evaluations as well as descriptive analyses of moves and actions across all team members. Monitoring was a consistent public activity; it held little value as a private indulgence. The coach stressed that "Bad days happen to us all," and that neither individual worry and shame nor small-group ostracizing of individual players for mistakes should happen.

Positive public monitoring was highly personalized. During practice, the coach prefaced approximately 65% of his questions with vocatives (e.g., "*Roddy*, what were you doing right in that catch?"). Players openly talked about their changes of pace and expertise through the season and their relative weaknesses and strengths. The coach guided them verbally in their observation and analysis of nearly every element of practice and games, recapitulating strategies and running through the effects of change in one element of a context on other elements (e.g., "What could have happened, Sam, if Rob had bunted? What about the man on second?"). Together, players and coach pondered aloud their performance as a team, as well as the contributions of various members to the team effort on particular days. The universal sin was "goofing off" (e.g., being a "hotdog"), and in interviews players volunteered various causes for such behavior (e.g., being tired, feeling lazy, having a long weekend, watching too much TV, or "being a couch potato"). Teammate approval worked as a strong form of social control, as did the coach's invoking of the major league image for the team. Disciplinary talk by the coach focused on the impending penalty or jeopardy to the group as a whole caused by individuals who goofed off.

Several other verbal strategies put a positive frame on monitoring within both practices and games. Less than 1% of the coach's utterances during practice marked behaviors or players with negative linguistic forms. To express negative valuations, the coach used certain terms of disapproval (e.g., *hot dog*), asked the team to make sounds to show what they thought when someone missed a ball because he was clowning or not paying attention, and issued general negative directives ("Don't go for the low ones"). When a player had a bad time at bat or missed several catches in sequence, the coach usually offered no assessment but asked a question that called for one of the kinds of responses discussed above. Another tactic was to choose one positive feature of a player's behavior and announce it, leaving aside any verbal elaboration of the error: "Okay, you had your glove out there, that was good" (said to a player who had just missed a throw to first base).

In games as well as practices, neither team members nor the coach designated plays or decisions as negative. Groans and moans expressed disappointment without direct articulation of assessments. In contrast to the almost constant use of extended sequences of interactive talk between coaches and players during practice, relatively short utterances (an average of three words) were used during games, such as "There you go," "Elbow up," "Hey, Mike, beautiful," "Come on, Ryan," "Go, Buddy," "Awesome, Joe," "You like that?" "Wait for a marshmallow," "Swing it away," "Way to watch," "You got it," or "Let's hear it." Of the approximately 3,600 utterances by the coach and players recorded during a nine-inning game when their team was at bat, the only instance of a negative was a shout by the coach for a positive play. He yelled to a player rounding third base toward home plate, "Don't stop."

Integrative Praxis

The team's learning environment was highly integrative. For both players and coach, the fundamental integration came in bringing play and work together. But several other integrative features marked the team's life. Theory and practice came together in the players' constant redistribution of their knowledge of particular poses, moves, and strategies during practice. Theories met practice in the different styles and levels of mastery of individual players, and the application of particular theories to specific players and plays received consistent attention from coach and team members. In addition, the world inside the team met with that outside the team through the underlying team directive to collect information from sources outside team life such as major league games or *Sports Illustrated* stories. The practice of mathematical routines came together with abstract representations of individual achievement as the boys considered mathematical and graphic portrayals of their achievements over the course of the season.

This integration in several forms rested squarely on the view team members seemed to have of themselves as decision-making "professionals" who wanted to be like and act like their models in the major leagues. Any matter of debate about the team resolved itself in the rhetorical question, "How would they do this in the major leagues?" Thus, the knowledge base for answering this question depended on the boys' observing, reading, and listening to sources beyond the immediate team. The general assumption of both the coach and players was that players would learn what it meant to be the best by watching and studying the experts—those reported in the newspaper and on radio and television—as well as more local sources, such as fathers, older players, and neighbors. Team members consulted various types of sources during the season to gain knowledge, receive guided practice, check on decisions or calls during games, or validate particular rules and regulations specific to Little League. Some sources were highly interactive and depended on direct participation (e.g., after-school pitching practice with fathers or neighborhood friends); others (e.g., watching games on television) took place in isolation or with friends and family members who confirmed hunches or tested the general acceptability of theories developed in Little League play.

Stats—published statistics on major league teams present and past—played a major role in characterizations of the game and of self for several team members. They talked easily about certain mathematical portrayals of games, and several of them had some sense of how their play through the season translated into stats.

On the field, all the boys practiced mathematical routines, such as rounding, estimating, and averaging, and they heard talk about concepts from geometry generally covered in fifth- and sixth-grade mathematics (Stenmark, Thompson, & Cossey, 1986). Some of the boys went further than others by working with their fathers to keep game statistics and flow charts. The results of these assessments were common knowledge among the players, although the comparative results of individuals' averages were never discussed during practice or used privately with certain players to goad them to better performance. Instead, the major portion of think-aloud reflections focused on individuals improving their own performance through attention, analysis, and practice.

Although the aura of "learning to be like the experts" hung over the team, none of the members claimed that they wanted to play in the major leagues or grow up to become a professional ballplayer. Those interviewed said that, aside from giving them time to be with their friends, playing ball allowed them to get "the basics" and to be creative with these basics. They expected practice sessions to be devoted to learning about elements of certain types of action in the game and to assume a certain independently gained level of knowledge on their part. They often used their own knowledge of cases—of players, plays, and games—to ask questions, make a point, or challenge other players' analyses of certain plays.

CONCLUSION

There are several questions to ask about the language of knowing in baseball: Does it work? What kinds of results does it produce? Do the boys know any more than they did before the season started? At the opening of the season, the Little League team studied here was near the bottom of the league—a group of inexperienced newcomers. At the end of the season, they were the champions of their area's Little League teams. It was not feasible to control and test for their preknowledge and postknowledge of baseball vocabulary and discourse genres (e.g., SAT), rules of Little League play, or understanding of mathematical concepts and perceptions of sources relevant to the game. We can only infer from their team's climb in the league, as well as from self-reports and demonstrations in interviews and stimulated recall sessions, that the goals and strategies of their learning context facilitated their achievements and attitudes.

But more important than these informal indications of results is the illustration within the Little League activities of several contextual features positively regarded in recent research on learning. Within the season, the boys participated intensely in apprenticeship with an expert (John-Steiner, 1986), self-monitoring and reflective practice (Palincsar & Brown, 1984), guided participation (Rogoff, 1989), and socially shared negotiation of knowledge and action (Hutchins, 1986). Moreover, the reasoning used in Little League activities supports many of the arguments given by those who support "natural logic" and the study of reasoning within everyday discourse (Grize, 1982; Toulmin, 1958). The high density of both action and verbal explication per unit of time in practices set argumentation within constant test situations. The boys knew that silent monitoring was to accompany their actions; thus, dialogue—both in thought and in oral expression— marked their practices. The coach's modeling and the interactive discourse of team members modeled the necessary steps to prepare for successful dialogue: (a) evoke a frame or scheme for the topic or problem to be addressed, (b) consider potential replies to utterances (acknowledging the differential expectation attached to questions vs. statements), and (c) formulate a counter discourse (Grize, 1982).

The primary kind of discourse in which the boys engaged—sociodramatic play—and the conditionality statements and calls for reflection that followed this discourse rested on a meta-awareness of the talk of theory-in-action. The cooperative principle behind their talk was the assumption of a stance of "reflective awareness" that carried the value of giving a sense of "deliberate control" (Vygotsky, 1987).

Translated into laymen's terms, many of these contextual features in support of learning appear in parents' recommendations about Little League team management: "Get the kids to help each other," "Let them know when they're doing something right," "Make it fun—take the negative out of it," "Get someone [as coach] who knows what he's doing." However, parents rarely give such recommendations for learning in schools. Those interviewed about this Little League team said they held these principles as necessary for after-school activities *because* they did not expect any of these features to mark classroom life or school learning.

Yet, in the late 1980s, the metaphor of teaching as coaching gained popular attention. A major education reform movement, "essential schools," promoted the coach–player relationship and team collaboration in classroom learning (Sizer, 1984). The vast majority of research on coaching, however, has focused on the one-to-one nature of the interaction and emphasized how individuals acquire complex skills in certain types of naturalistic settings (e.g., Fry, 1987; Romano, 1987, on writing conferences as coaching).

The case presented here of a Little League team and its coach illustrates the following coaching practices between a single instructor and a group of players or learners:

- ☑ Learners assume prototypical identities as professionals who must handle all basics or key activities (e.g., catching, hitting) in a sustained dramatic ritual with codified impersonal rules and local personalized rules.
- ☑ The learning task has a seasonal span and a goal of the best possible performance in each presentation, because individual games or performances add up and help determine the season's outcome.
- ☑ Within problem-solving narratives of sociodramatic play, the coach calls on learners to analyze hypothetical episodes within each play and to consider how varying single features of these episodes can potentially create different outcomes.
- ☑ Exercises and practice assume the fundamental sequence of basic activities plus "creativity"; aside from accepting team rules and certain activities as essential to the drama, no emphasis is given to learning X before Y.
- ☑ Learners *reflect* and *recite* to demonstrate their attention to their own participation in activities; the coach illustrates components of each activity by simple rule sets and by calling attention to individuals' fulfillment of certain rules.

Central to the task of coaching many learners at the same time is acceptance of the value of differences among learners. A team cannot expect to have all members at the same level of ability in the same complex skills. Instead, the potential for division of labor within the full-season drama depends on varying levels of performance in each niche; however, the general upgrading of performance for each individual rests in the social control potential of having knowledge about separate tasks shared and distributed among all members. Added to the general distribution of knowledge is the shared value of monitoring self and others and living within a context of learning through conditionalities, which result in social control and group improvement through individual achievement.

Within pedagogical theory, scholars recommend behaviors, attitudes, and structural changes to make individuals and institutions reshape themselves into players who have a volunteer mentality and who want to improve themselves and their team and keep on learning. *Motivation* is the pedagogical term that often enters discussions of such reshapings. The understanding of what makes individuals take up different tasks with varying degrees of involvement and volunteerism can derive much from current philosophical work that enables us to link intention with the ideal coordination of theory and evidence (Wilson, 1989) and to consider the relative value of certain judgments or reasons under varying circumstances. The practice of making distinctions between theory and evidence helps explain actions with particular "intentional sets" that result from the intersection of roles, rules, and situations (Altieri, 1981). Psychologists who examine reasoning in everyday experience indicate that knowledge structures are induced from ordinary experience as "pragmatic reasoning schemas" (Cheng & Holyoak, 1985). Moreover, the explication of such schemas allows individuals to revise these schemas on the basis of variations of context or functions and to make inferences about their "contingency values" (Smith, 1988).

This chapter (and the project of which it is a part) reveals how structured voluntary learning (e.g., that of Little League teams) involves youngsters in self-revising and reflection and promotes individual achievement through collaboration. The best summative characterization of what happens in such groups may well be the constitution of a *normative community*. Historians, social scientists, artists, and philosophers have in the past decade given intense attention to the elements and qualities of community within American life and the dissonance between the quest for community and the ideal of individualism in American life (Bellah, Madsen, Sullivan, Swidler, & Tipton, 1985). Aside from the intention of longevity and permanence and the expectation of stable spatial connections traditionally linked with communal association, neighborhood teams carry many other features of communities, including interaction and mutual dependence, expressive ties through numerous symbol systems, mutual and common sentiments, shared beliefs, and an ethic of individual responsibility to the communal life (Nisbet, 1953; Scherer, 1972). These features help shape individual identity, lead to an acceptance of group standards, offer a sense of place through identification with the group, and ensure a sense of "winning" through solidarity and mutual support. Knowledge building and awareness of the interdependence of knowing and acting rest on some degree of intentionality to link play and work for productive individual and team outcomes.

References

Abrahams, R. (1964). *Deep down in the jungle: Negro narrative folklore from the streets of Philadelphia*. Chicago: Aldine.

Akatsuka, N. (1986). Conditionals are discourse-bound. In E. C. Traugott, A. ter Meulen, J. S. Reilly, & C. A. Ferguson (Eds.), *On conditionals* (pp. 333–352). Cambridge, England: Cambridge University Press.

Altieri, C. (1981). *Act & quality: A theory of literary meaning and humanistic understanding*. Amherst, MA: University of Massachusetts Press.

Bateson, G. (1956). The message "This is play." In B. Schaffner (Ed.), *Group processes: Transactions of the Second Conference* (pp. 145–242). New York: Josiah Macy, Jr. Foundation.

Bateson, G. (1972). *Steps to an ecology of mind*. New York: Ballantine.

Bellah, R. N., Madsen, R., Sullivan, W. M., Swidler, A., & Tipton, S. M. (1985). *Habits of the heart: Individualism and commitment in American life*. Berkeley, CA: University of California Press.

Bowerman, M. (1986). First steps in acquiring conditionals. In E. C. Traugott, A. ter Meulen, J. S. Reilly, & C. A. Ferguson (Eds.), *On conditionals* (pp. 285–308). Cambridge, England: Cambridge University Press.

Bruner, J. (1986). *Actual minds, possible worlds*. Cambridge, MA: Harvard University Press.

Cheng, P. W., & Holyoak, K. J. (1985). Pragmatic reasoning schemas. *Cognitive Psychology, 17*, 391–416.

Crystal, D., & Davy, D. (1969). The language of unscripted commentary. In D. Crystal & D. Davy (Eds.), *Investigating English style* (pp. 125–146). Bloomington: Indiana University Press.

Csikszentmihalyi, M., & Larson, R. (1984). *Being adolescent: Conflict and growth in the teenage years*. New York: Basic Books.

Dundes, A., Leach, J. W., & Ozkok, B. (1970). The strategy of Turkish boys' verbal dueling rhymes. *Journal of American Folklore, 83*, 325–349.

Ferguson, C. A. (1983). Sports announcer talk: Syntactic aspects of register variation. *Language in Society, 12*, 153–172.

Ferguson, C. A., & Macken, M. (1983). The role of play in phonological development. In K. E. Nelson (Ed.), *Children's language* (Vol. 4, pp. 231–254). Hillsdale, NJ: Erlbaum.

Ferguson, C. A., Reilly, J. S., ter Meulen, A., & Traugott, E. (1986). Overview. In E. C. Traugott, A. ter Meulen, J. S. Reilly, & C. A. Ferguson (Eds.), *On conditionals* (pp. 3–20). Cambridge, England: Cambridge University Press.

Fine, G. A. (1987). *With the boys*. Chicago: University of Chicago Press.

Fry, D. (1987). *The coaching writer*. St. Petersburg, FL: Poynter Institute.

Givon, T. (1982). Logic vs. pragmatics, with human language as the referee: Toward an empirically viable epistemology. *Journal of Pragmatics, 6*, 81–133.

Goffman, E. (1974). *Frame Analysis: An essay on the organization of experience*. New York: Harper and Row.

Grize, J.-B. (1982). *De la logique a l'argumentation* [From logic to argumentation]. Geneve: Librairie Droz.

Haiman, J. (1978). Conditionals are topics. *Language, 54*, 564–589.

Heath, S. B. (1983). A lot of talk about nothing. *Language Arts, 60*(8), 999–1007.

Heath, S. B. (1986). Sociocultural contexts of language development. In Bilingual Education Office, California State Department of Education (Ed.), *Beyond language: Social and cultural factors in schooling language minority students* (pp. 143–186). Los Angeles: California State University.

Heath, S. B. (1990). The children of Trackton's children: Spoken and written language in social change. In J. W. Stigler, R. A. Shweder, & G. S. Herdt (Eds.), *Cultural psychology: The Chicago symposia on human development* (pp. 496–519). Cambridge, England: Cambridge University Press.

Hedegaard, M. (1986). Two approaches to thinking and knowledge acquisition. *The Quarterly Newsletter of the Laboratory of Comparative Human Cognition, 8*(2), 58–63.

Hutchins, E. (1986). Mediation and automatization. *Quarterly Newsletter of the Laboratory of Comparative Human Cognition, 8*(2), 47–58.

John-Steiner, V. (1986). *Notebooks of the mind.* Albuquerque: University of New Mexico Press.

Kuczaj, S. (1982). Language play and language acquisition. *Advances in Child Development and Behavior, 17,* 198–232.

Nisbet, R. (1953). *The quest for community: A study in the ethics of order and freedom.* New York: Oxford University Press.

Palincsar, A. S., & Brown, A. L. (1984). Reciprocal teaching of comprehension-fostering and comprehension-monitoring activities. *Cognition and Instruction, 1*(2), 117–175.

Rogoff, B. (1986). Adult assistance of children's learning. In T. E. Raphael, (Ed.), *The contexts of school-based literacy* (pp. 27–40). New York: Random House.

Rogoff, B. (1989). *Apprentices in thinking: Children's guided participation in culture.* New York: Oxford University Press.

Romano, T. (1987). *Clearing the way: Working with teenage writers.* Portsmouth, NH: Heinemann.

Scherer, J. (1972). *Contemporary community: Sociological illusion or reality?* London: Tavistock.

Schieffelin, B. B., & Ochs, E. (Eds.). (1986). *Language socialization across cultures.* Cambridge, England: Cambridge University Press.

Schutz, A. (1951). Making music together: A study in social relationship. *Social Research, 18*(1), 76–97.

Shore, B. (1989, May). *The American pastime: Ritual baseball.* Paper presented at Center for Advanced Study in Behavioral Sciences, Stanford University, Stanford, CA.

Sizer, T. (1984). *Horace's compromise.* Boston: Houghton-Mifflin.

Smilansky, S. (1968). *The effects of sociodramatic play on disadvantaged preschool children.* New York: Wiley.

Smith, B. H. (1988). *Contingencies of value.* Cambridge, MA: Harvard University Press.

Stenmark, J. K., Thompson, V., & Cossey, R. (1986). *Family math.* Berkeley, CA: Lawrence Hall of Science.

Toulmin, S. E. (1958). *The uses of argument.* Cambridge, England: Cambridge University Press.

Vygotsky, L. S. (1987). *Thinking and speech.* (N. Minick, Trans.). New York: Plenum.

Wallerstein, J., & Blakeslee, S. (1989). *Second chances: Men, women and children a decade after divorce.* New York: Ticknor & Fields.

Weir, R. (1962). *Language in the crib.* The Hague: Mouton.

Wertsch, J. V. (Ed.). (1985). *Culture, communication and cognition: Vygotskian perspectives.* Cambridge, England: Cambridge University Press.

Wilson, G. M. (1989). *The intentionality of human action* (rev. ed.). Stanford, CA: Stanford University Press.

PART THREE

COORDINATING COGNITION: LINGUISTIC TOOLS AND SOCIAL KNOWLEDGE

CHAPTER 7

GROUNDING IN COMMUNICATION

HERBERT H. CLARK AND SUSAN E. BRENNAN

GROUNDING

It takes two people working together to play a duet, shake hands, play chess, waltz, teach, or make love. To succeed, the two of them have to coordinate both the content and process of what they are doing. Alan and Barbara, on the piano, must come to play the same Mozart duet. This is coordination of content. They must also synchronize their entrances and exits, coordinate how loudly to play forte and pianissimo, and otherwise adjust to each other's tempo and dynamics. This is coordination of process. They cannot even begin to coordinate on content without assuming a vast amount of shared information or common ground—that is, mutual knowledge, mutual beliefs, and mutual assumptions (Clark & Carlson, 1982; Clark & Marshall, 1981; Lewis, 1969; Schelling, 1960). And to coordinate on process, they need to update their common ground moment by moment. All collective actions are built on common ground and its accumulation.

We thank many colleagues for discussion of the issues we take up here. The research was supported in part by National Science Foundation Grant BNS 83-20284 and a National Science Foundation Graduate Fellowship.

Correspondence concerning this chapter should be addressed to Herbert H. Clark, Department of Psychology, Jordan Hall, Building 420, Stanford University, Stanford, CA 94305-2130, or Susan E. Brennan, Department of Psychology, State University of New York at Stony Brook, Stony Brook NY 11794-2500.

Communication, of course, is a collective activity of the first order. When Alan speaks to Barbara, he must do more than merely plan and issue utterances, and she must do more than just listen and understand. They have to coordinate on content (Grice, 1975, 1978). When Alan refers to "my dogs," the two of them must reach the mutual belief that he is referring to his feet. They must also coordinate on process. Speech is evanescent, and so Alan must try to speak only when he thinks Barbara is attending to, hearing, and trying to understand what he is saying, and she must guide him by giving him evidence that she is doing just this. Accomplishing this, once again, requires the two of them to keep track of their common ground and its moment-by-moment changes.

In communication, common ground cannot be properly updated without a process we shall call *grounding* (see Clark & Schaefer, 1987, 1989; Clark & Wilkes-Gibbs, 1986; Isaacs & Clark, 1987). In conversation, for example, the participants try to establish that what has been said has been understood. In our terminology, they try to ground what has been said—that is, make it part of their common ground. But how they do this changes a great deal from one situation to the next. Grounding takes one shape in face-to-face conversation but another in personal letters. It takes one shape in casual gossip but another in calls to directory assistance.

Grounding is so basic to communication—indeed, to all collective actions—that it is important to understand how it works. In this chapter we take up two main factors that shape it. One is *purpose*—what the two people are trying to accomplish in their communication. The other is the *medium* of communication—the techniques available in the medium for accomplishing that purpose, and what it costs to use them. We begin by briefly describing grounding as it appears in casual face-to-face conversation. We then consider how it gets shaped by other purposes and in other media.

Grounding in Conversation

What does it take to contribute to conversation? Suppose Alan utters to Barbara, "Do you and your husband have a car?" In the standard view of speech acts (e.g., Bach & Harnish, 1979; Searle, 1969), what Alan has done is *ask* Barbara whether she and her husband have a car, and, in this way, he has carried the conversation forward. But this isn't quite right. Consider this actual exchange:[1]

---

[1] All examples, except those marked otherwise, come from the so-called London-Lund corpus (Svartvik & Quirk, 1980). We retain the following symbols from the London-Lund notation: "." for a brief pause (of one light syllable); "–" for a unit pause (of one stress unit or foot); "," for the end of a tone unit, which we mark only if it comes mid-turn; "(laughs)" or single parenthesis for contextual comments; "((words))" or double parentheses for incomprehensible words; and "*yes*" or asterisks for paired instances of simultaneous talk.

Alan:	Now, - um, do you and your husband have a j- car
Barbara:	- have a car?
Alan:	Yeah
Barbara:	No -

Even though Alan has uttered "Do you and your husband have a car?", he hasn't managed to ask Barbara whether she and her husband have a car. We know this because Barbara indicates, with "- have a car?", that she hasn't understood him.[2] Only after Alan has answered her query (with "yeah") and she is willing to answer the original question ("no -") do the two of them apparently believe he has succeeded. So asking a question requires more than uttering an interrogative sentence. It must also be established that the respondent has understood what the questioner meant.

Of course, understanding can never be perfect. We assume that the criterion people try to reach in conversation is as follows (Clark & Schaefer, 1989; Clark & Wilkes-Gibbs, 1986): The contributor and his or her partners mutually believe that the partners have understood what the contributor meant to a criterion sufficient for current purposes. This is called the *grounding criterion*. Technically, then, grounding is the collective process by which the participants try to reach this mutual belief. To see some of the forms grounding takes in conversation, let us consider the process of contributing to conversation. Here we will follow a model proposed by Clark and Schaefer (1989) that was founded on a long tradition of work on turns and repairs by Sacks, Schegloff, Jefferson, and others (e.g., Sacks, Schegloff, & Jefferson, 1974; Schegloff, Jefferson, & Sacks, 1977; Schegloff, 1982).

Contributing to Conversation

Most contributions to conversation begin with the potential contributor presenting an utterance to his or her partner. In our example, Alan presents Barbara with the utterance, "Now, - um do you and your husband have a j- car." Why does he present it? Because he wants Barbara to hear it, register it, and understand what he means by it. But he cannot know whether he has succeeded unless she provides evidence of her understanding. In our example, indeed, she provides evidence that she has *not* understood him yet. It is only after the exchange, "- have a car?" and "yeah," that she gives positive evidence of understanding by initiating the answer "no." So contributing to conversation generally divides into two phases:

---

[2]Actually, the word *ask* is ambiguous between "utter an interrogative sentence" and "succeed in getting the addressee to recognize that you want certain information." Note that you can say, "Ken asked Julia 'Are you coming' but failed to ask her whether she was coming because she couldn't hear him." We will use *ask* in the second sense.

Presentation phase: A presents utterance u for B to consider. He does so on the assumption that, if B gives evidence e or stronger, he can believe that she understands what he means by u.

Acceptance phase: B accepts utterance u by giving evidence e that she believes she understands what A means by u. She does so on the assumption that, once A registers that evidence, he will also believe that she understands.

It takes both phases for a contribution to be complete.

The presentation phase can become very complicated. One way is by self-repairs. In our example, Alan doesn't present the pristine utterance, "Do you and your husband have a car," but rather the messier, "now, - um do you and your husband have a j- car." He expects Barbara to see, for example, that "j-" isn't part of the sentence he is ultimately committed to. Establishing what he is and is not ultimately committed to is no easy task. Another complication is embedding. The presentation itself can contain distinct contributions each with its own presentation and acceptance phases (we will see examples of embedding later in this chapter).

Grounding becomes most evident in the acceptance phase. By the end of A's presentation of some utterance u, the partner B may believe she is in one of these states for all or part of u:

State 0:   B didn't notice that A uttered any u.
State 1:   B noticed that A uttered some u (but wasn't in state 2).
State 2:   B correctly heard u (but wasn't in state 3).
State 3:   B understood what A meant by u.

In our example, Barbara apparently thinks she is in state 3 for the first part of Alan's presentation but in state 2 for the final phrase. Because she wants to be in state 3 for the entire presentation, she needs to clear up her understanding of the final phrase. This is what leads her to initiate the *side sequence* (Jefferson, 1972) or *insertion sequence* (Schegloff, 1972) with "- have a car?" All of this is part of the acceptance phase, and so Alan's contribution divides up this way:

Presentation phase:
        Alan: Now, - um do you and your husband have a j-car
Acceptance phase:
        Barbara: - have a car?
        Alan: Yeah

Actually, the acceptance phase only gets completed when Barbara initiates the answer "no" and Alan accepts it as the evidence he needs.

The acceptance phase may also contain embedded contributions. Barbara's "- have a car?" is the presentation phase of a contribution that is wholly contained within the acceptance phase of the main contribution. It is accepted when Alan says "yeah," which is itself a presentation with its own acceptance (see Clark & Schaefer, 1987). So contributions often emerge in hierarchies. They may contain contributions embedded within both their presentation and their acceptance phases.

There is an essential difference, therefore, between merely uttering some words—a presentation—and doing what one intends to do by uttering them—a contribution. When you say to a friend, "I want you to meet Mr. Jones," it isn't guaranteed that you have succeeded in introducing him to Mr. Jones. His hearing aid may have been off. He may have misheard you. Or he may have misunderstood you, as Chico did Groucho in this exchange:

> Groucho: Ravelli, I want you to meet Mr. Jones.
> Chico: Awright, where should I meet him?

Even without Chico around, grounding is essential.

Evidence in Grounding

Once we utter something in a conversation, one might suppose, all we need to look for is *negative evidence*—evidence that we have been misheard or misunderstood. If we find some, we repair the problem, but if we don't, we assume, by default, that we have been understood. This is, indeed, what is explicitly or tacitly assumed in many accounts of language use (e.g., Grosz & Sidner, 1986; Litman & Allen, 1987; Stalnaker, 1978). When Barbara says "- have a car?" she is giving Alan negative evidence and a clue to what she has misunderstood. But if negative evidence is all we looked for, we would often accept information we had little justification for accepting. In fact, people ordinarily reach for a higher criterion. As the contribution model says, people ultimately seek *positive evidence* of understanding. Let us look at the three most common forms of positive evidence and see how they work.

First, *acknowledgments* are the most obvious form of positive evidence. By acknowledgments we mean much of what has been called *back-channel responses*. These include continuers such as *uh huh, yeah*, and the British *m* (Schegloff, 1982), as in the following example:

> B: Um well I ha((dn't)) done any English at *all,*
> A: *((1 syll))*
> B: You know, since O-level.
> A: Yea .
> B: And I went to some second year seminars, where there are only about half a dozen people,
> A: *m*
> B: *and* they discussed what ((a)) word was,
> A: **m**
> B: **and -** what's a sentence, that's *ev*en more difficult.

A: *yeah* yeah -
       (and so on)

Continuers are used by partners, according to Schegloff, to signal that they are passing up the opportunity to initiate a repair on the turn so far and, by implication, that they think they have understood the turn so far. Acknowledgments also include assessments, such as *gosh, really,* and *good God* (see Goodwin, 1986), and gestures such as head nods that have much the same force as continuers (see Goodwin, 1981). Acknowledgments are generally produced without the speaker taking a turn at talk.

A second, common form of positive evidence is the initiation of the *relevant next turn.* Consider this exchange:

A: Did you know mother had been drinking -
B: I don't think, mother had been drinking at all .

Suppose A is trying to ask B a question. If B understands it, she can be expected to answer it in her next turn. Questions and answers form what are called *adjacency pairs,* and once the first part of an adjacency pair is on the floor, the second part is conditionally relevant as the next turn (Schegloff & Sacks, 1973). So A looks for B to provide not just any utterance, but an answer to his question. If B's utterance is appropriate as an answer, as in our example, it is also evidence that she has understood A's question. If it is not appropriate, it is evidence that she has not understood A's question, as caricatured here:

Miss Dimple: Where can I get a hold of you?
       Chico: I don't know, lady. You see, I'm very ticklish.
Miss Dimple: I mean, where do you live?
       Chico: I live with my brother.

Chico's answer gives Miss Dimple evidence that he has misunderstood her question, and that leads to the correction in her following turn (for an authentic, spontaneous example, see Clark & Schaefer, 1989). So B may initiate the next turn as positive evidence of her understanding, but A will not take it that way unless it shows her understanding to be correct.

What makes a next turn appropriate or relevant? That isn't difficult to decide for the second part of an adjacency pair—the answer to a question, the response to a request, or the acceptance of an invitation. It also isn't difficult to decide for most other next turns. Conversation generally divides into coherent sections that have identifiable entries, bodies, and exits (see, e.g., Schegloff & Sacks, 1973). These sections are devoted to one or another social process, such as making plans or exchanging information. Most turns are designed to carry that process forward and give evidence about the speaker's understanding of the previous step in the process. As Sacks et al. (1974, p. 728) noted, "Regularly, then, a turn's talk will display its speaker's understanding of a prior turn's talk, or whatever other talk it marks itself as directed to.'' Initiating the relevant next turn is ordinarily an excellent piece of positive evidence.

Requiring positive evidence of understanding seems to lead to an infinite regress. The problem is this: When B says "uh huh" or "you're there all day" in response to A's presentation, she herself is making a presentation. Now her presentation, being more words, requires positive evidence of understanding from A, which requires him to give more words. But his words constitute another presentation that she must accept with more words, and so on ad infinitum. If every presentation were accepted with positive evidence in the form of words, the process would spin out to infinity. Empirically, it is easy to show that people do not take an infinite number of words to contribute to a conversation. How, then, *do* they do it?

There is no infinite regress in the contribution model because some forms of evidence, such as the relevant next turn and continued attention (our next form of evidence), do not have separate presentations. A relevant next turn provides positive evidence of understanding of the presentation phase it follows, but it does so by initiating the next contribution without a break. So although the acceptance process can spin out for many turns, it usually ends with the partner initiating a relevant next turn. Take the following example, in which A is presenting a book identification number:

> A: F .six two
> B: F six two
> A: Yes
> B: Thanks very much

The first presentation is accepted with a repetition, the repetition with an acknowledgment, and the acknowledgment with a thanks, which is the next contribution at the level of original contribution.

The third and most basic form of positive evidence is *continued attention*. In conversation people monitor what their partners are doing moment by moment— in particular, what they are attending to. If Alan presented an utterance while Barbara wasn't paying attention, he could hardly assume that she was understanding him. She must show that she is paying attention, and one way is through eye gaze. Suppose she is looking away from Alan. As Goodwin (1981) has shown, Alan can try to capture her gaze—and also, presumably, her attention—by starting an utterance. Just as she begins turning to him, he will start the utterance over again. Or he can start an utterance, pause until she starts turning, and then go on with the utterance. Speakers have many ways of getting a partner's attention.

Positive evidence of understanding comes with attention that is unbroken or undisturbed. Alan has reason to believe Barbara is following him as long as she continues to attend in the expected way. Whenever she turns to listen to someone else, looks puzzled, or hangs up the telephone, Alan has reason to believe that he has lost her. She is no longer hearing or understanding to criterion. Ordinarily, that will push him into taking corrective action.

Least Collaborative Effort

People apparently don't like to work any harder than they have to, and in language use this truism has been embodied in several principles of least effort. The traditional version exhorts the speaker: Don't expend any more effort than you need to get your addressees to understand you with as little effort. Grice (1975) expressed this idea in terms of two maxims: *Quantity*—Make your contribution as informative as is required for the current purpose of the exchange, but do not make your contribution more informative than is required—and *Manner*—Be brief (avoid unnecessary prolixity). According to both versions, speakers are supposed to create what we will call *proper utterances*, ones they believe will be readily and fully understood by their addressees.

The principle of least effort, however, assumes flawless presentations and trouble-free acceptances. It does not allow for grounding and, therefore, cannot do justice to what really happens in conversations. Here are just three problems with this principle (Clark & Wilkes-Gibbs, 1986).

1. *Time pressure*. Speakers appear to limit the time and effort they allow for planning and issuing each utterance, and that often leads them to issue improper utterances. They may utter a sentence or phrase, discover it to be inadequate, and then amend it, as in "Number 7's the goofy guy that's falling over—with his leg kicked up." They may start a phrase, think better of it, and start a different phrase, as in "We must ha- we're big enough to stand on our own feet now." They may create patently improper parts of utterances, such as *what's his name* in "If he puts it into the diplomatic bag, as um - what's his name, Micky Cohn did, . then it's not so bad." They may invite their interlocutors to complete their utterances, as in this exchange (Wilkes-Gibbs, 1986):

> A: That tree has, uh, uh
> B: Tentworms.
> A: Yeah.
> B: Yeah.

If all these speakers had taken the time and effort needed, they could have produced proper utterances—flawless performances. They didn't. The principle of least effort says that they should have.

2. *Errors*. Speakers often issue improper utterances because they make errors and have to repair them, as in Alan's "now, - um do you and your husband have a j- car?" If Alan had taken more time and effort, he could have avoided errors and dysfluencies. Why didn't he?

3. *Ignorance*. Speakers sometimes realize they just don't know enough about their interlocutor to design a proper utterance, so they are forced to issue an improper utterance instead. Take the person who was trying to identify an abstract figure that resembled an ice skater (Clark & Wilkes-Gibbs, 1986), who said, "Um, the next one's the person ice skating that has two arms?" Why the question intonation, or what Sacks and Schegloff (1979) have called a *try marker*? With it the speaker was indicating that he was not sure that his definite description "the person ice skating that has two arms" was adequate to pick out the right figure. He was asking his partner whether it was adequate and, if it was not, inviting an alternative description. Here, no matter how hard the speaker tried, he might not have managed a proper utterance. So why did he do what he did?

The principle of least effort, it has been argued, must therefore be replaced with the following principle (Clark & Wilkes-Gibbs, 1986):

> *The principle of least collaborative effort*: In conversation, the participants try to minimize their collaborative effort—the work that both do from the initiation of each contribution to its mutual acceptance.

Such a principle helps account for many phenomena. Consider repairs. As Schegloff et al. (1977) noted, speakers have two strong preferences about repairs: (a) They prefer to repair their own utterances rather than let their interlocutors do it, and (b) they prefer to initiate their own repairs rather than let their interlocutors prompt them to do it. Although these two preferences have many causes, the upshot is that they minimize collaborative effort. As for preference 1, it generally takes less effort for the speaker than for an interlocutor to make a repair. An interlocutor will usually need extra turns, and he or she has to get the speaker to accept the repair anyway. As for preference 2, it usually takes less effort for the speaker than for an interlocutor to initiate a repair. The interlocutor will generally create extra turns in doing so, whereas the speaker will not. Every extra turn adds to collaborative effort.

Also, speakers often realize that it will take more collaborative effort to design a proper utterance than to design an improper utterance and enlist their addressees' help. Speakers, for example, can present a provisional utterance and add try markers to ask for confirmation. They can present a difficult utterance in installments and check for understanding after each installment (as we will describe later). They can invite addressees to complete an utterance they are having trouble with. And they have many other collaborative techniques at their disposal. The principle of least collaborative effort is essential for a full account of face-to-face conversation.

GROUNDING CHANGES WITH PURPOSE

People in conversation generally try to establish collective purposes (Grice, 1975). If they are planning a party, that may be their overall collective purpose. In each section of the conversation, their purpose might be to complete pieces of that plan, and in each subsection it would be even more specific. Other times their overall purpose might be to get acquainted, swap gossip, or instruct and learn. Grounding should change with these purposes. If addressees are to understand what the speaker meant "to a criterion sufficient for current purposes," then the criterion should change as their collective purposes change. So, too, should the techniques they exploit. Techniques should change, for example, with the content of the conversation—with what needs to be understood. Indeed, specialized techniques have evolved for grounding different types of content. We will illustrate with two types of content—references and verbatim content.

Grounding References

Many conversations focus on objects and their identities; when they do, it becomes crucial to identify the objects quickly and securely. Conversations like these arise, for example, when an expert is teaching a novice how to build things, and the two of them refer again and again to pieces of the construction. They arise in court when lawyers and witnesses try to establish the identities of persons, places, and things. They also arise in tasks in which people have to arrange figures, post cards, blocks, color chips, or other such objects. In psychology, an entire industry has been built on this type of task patterned after Krauss and Weinheimer's (1964, 1966, 1967) original referential communication task. Yet conversations like these are common enough in real life.

The purpose of interest here is to establish *referential identity*—that is, the mutual belief that the addressees have correctly identified a referent. There are several common techniques for establishing this.

1. *Alternative descriptions.* When speakers refer to objects, they typically use one or more referring expressions—a definite or indefinite description, proper noun, demonstrative, or pronoun. One way their partners can demonstrate that they have identified the referent or can check on its identity is by presenting an alternative description, as in this interchange:

A: Well, that young gentleman from - ((the park)) .
B: Joe Joe Wright you mean? - - *(- - laughs)*
A: *yes, (laughs) yes*
B: ((God)), I thought it was old Joe Wright who(('d)) walked
      in at first

A describes a referent as "that young gentleman from the park"; B gives evidence of having identified the man by offering an alternative description; he adds the question intonation to get confirmation of that description; and A accepts that description. This technique is common whenever referential identity is at stake (e.g., Clark & Wilkes-Gibbs, 1986; Isaacs & Clark, 1987).

2. *Indicative gestures.* When a speaker refers to a nearby object, the partners can give positive evidence that they have identified it by pointing, looking, or touching. In this example, S had been handed a photograph of a flower patch (Clark, Schreuder, & Buttrick, 1983):

> B: How would you describe the color of this flower?
> S: You mean this one [pointing]?
> B: Yes.
> S: It's off yellow.

S confirmed the referent of B's "this flower" by pointing.

3. *Referential installments.* It is often important to establish the identity of a referent before saying something about it. The reason is simple. Until the referent has been properly identified, the rest of the utterance will be difficult, if not impossible, to understand. The speaker can secure the reference by treating it as an installment of the utterance to be confirmed separately. Take this exchange between an expert and a novice assembling a pump (Cohen, 1984):

> S: Take the spout—the little one that looks like the end of an
>   oil can—
> J: Okay.
> S: and put that on the opening in the other large tube. With
>   the round top.

In the first line, S presents "the spout—the little one that looks like the end of an oil can" and then pauses for evidence that J has identified the referent. He goes on only when that installment has been grounded.

In English, there is a specialized construction for just this purpose called *left-dislocation.* It is traditionally illustrated with invented examples such as *Your dog he just bit me.* This example begins with a "left dislocated" noun phrase, *your dog,* followed by a full sentence with a pronoun, *he,* referring to the same object. In genuine conversation, left-dislocation rarely looks like this. A more typical example is this second exchange from S and J:

> S: Okay now, the small blue cap we talked about before?
> J: Yeah.
> S: Put that over the hole on the side of that tube—
> J: Yeah.
> S: —that is nearest to the top, or nearest to the red handle.

As Geluykens (1988) has shown, 29% of the left dislocated noun phrases in the London-Lund corpus (Svartvik & Quirk, 1980) are followed by an intervening move from the interlocutor (either a continuer or something more extensive), as in our example. Another 52% are followed by a pause during which the partner could have nodded acceptance. Left-dislocation may have evolved for just this specialized purpose—grounding references separately.

4. *Trial references.* Speakers can also initiate the grounding process for a reference in mid-utterance. When speakers find themselves about to present a name or description that they are not sure is entirely correct or comprehensible, they can present it with a *try marker* followed by a slight pause, and get their partners to confirm or correct it before completing the presentation. Consider this example:

> A: So I wrote off to . Bill, . uh who ((had)) presumably dis-
> appeared by this time, certainly, a man called Annegra?
> B: Yeah, Allegra.
> A: Allegra, uh replied, . uh and I . put . two other people
> [continues].

A apparently wants to assert, "A man called Annegra replied, and I . . .''. But being uncertain about the name *Annegra*, he presents it with a try marker. B confirms, with "yeah," that she knows who he is referring to, but then corrects the name to *Allegra*. A accepts the correction by re-presenting *Allegra* and continuing. The entire correction is made swiftly and efficiently.

There are other techniques adapted for this purpose, but the four we have mentioned give an idea of their range and specialization.

Grounding Verbatim Content

Sometimes it is important to register the verbatim content of what is said. When a friend tells you a telephone number, you do more than listen for the gist of it. You try to get it verbatim so that you can copy it down or rehearse it until you dial the number. The same goes for names, addresses, book titles, credit card numbers, bank accounts, dollar amounts, and library call numbers. These are specialized situations, and specialized grounding techniques have evolved for them. Here are a few:

1. *Verbatim displays.* When customers call directory enquiries for a tele-phone number, they often confirm the number they are given with a verbatim display, as in this British example (Clark & Schaefer, 1987):

> O: It's Cambridge 12345
> C: 12345
> O: That's right.
> C: Thank you very much.

C confirms the number that O has presented him by repeating it verbatim, "12345." In the British calls studied by Clark and Schaefer (1987), customers responded to the operators' number presentations with verbatim displays over

70% of the time. Operators, in turn, often responded to the customers' presentations of names, towns, and street addresses with verbatim displays.

2. *Installments.* When speakers present a lot of information to be registered verbatim, they generally cut it up into bite-sized chunks, or installments, and receive verbatim displays on each installment, as in this example:

A: Ah, what ((are you)) now, *where*
C: *yes* forty-nine Skipton Place
A: Forty-one
C: Nine . nine
A: Forty-nine, Skipton Place,
C: W one .
A: Skipton Place, . W one, ((so)) Mr D Challam
C: Yes
A: Forty-nine Skipton Place, W one,
C: Yes
A: Right oh.

C divides his address into repeatable chunks, and A gives a verbatim display for each. Speakers seem able to divide most types of information into such chunks. They do it spontaneously, for example, for recipes presented over the telephone (Goldberg, 1975).

Dividing a presentation into repeatable installments is based on the tacit recognition that people have limited immediate memory spans. Even the telephone company recognizes this and divides telephone numbers into conventional installments of three or four digits in size. In the calls to directory enquiries studied by Clark and Schaefer (1987), British operators always divided numbers of seven or more digits into their conventional groupings.

3. *Spelling.* For many words, getting the verbatim content right means getting the spelling right. So contributors often spell out critical words, as in the following:

A: The name is Iain, . I A I N .
C: m
A: Lathom-Meadows, that's L A T, . H O M, . hyphen, - Meadows,
C: Yes .

Or they have other tricks for getting the spelling right, as illustrated here:

B: And my name, is James Persian-Omo, that's Persian like the carpet
C: Yes
B: Hyphen, . Omo like the detergent, O M O
C: Yeah.

Other times, it is the partners who do the spelling as they confirm a name.

On occasion, two partners in conversation will set different criteria, one stricter than the other. Imagine a father instructing a 5-year-old son on how to play a game or work a machine. The son may think he understands an instruction while the father still has serious doubts. The father may go on testing for understanding long after the son thinks he needs to.

To summarize, specialized techniques have evolved for grounding special pieces of conversation. When it is critical that a reference be well established, people will use techniques that are custom designed for that purpose. When it is the verbatim content that is crucial, they will use other techniques. In this way, grounding changes with the current purpose.

GROUNDING CHANGES WITH THE MEDIUM

By the principle of least collaborative effort, people should try to ground with as little combined effort as needed. But what takes effort changes dramatically with the communication medium. The techniques available in one medium may not be available in another, and even when a technique is available, it may cost more in one medium than in the other. Our prediction is straightforward: People should ground with those techniques available in a medium that lead to the least collaborative effort.

Consider the acknowledgment *okay*. In face-to-face or telephone conversations, it can be timed precisely so that it constitutes evidence of understanding and not an interruption. In keyboard teleconferencing—when people communicate over keyboards and screens—it is difficult to time an acknowledgment precisely, and trying to do so may interrupt the other typist. So the cost of an acknowledgment is higher in this medium.

Media come in a great variety, and new ones are being introduced every year. Think of the telegraph, videotape, picturephone, express mail, fax machines, electronic bulletin boards, and little yellow post-it notes. Here we will consider a sample of two-way personal media: face-to-face conversation, the telephone, video teleconferencing, keyboard teleconferencing, answering machines, electronic mail (email), and personal letters. For now we will put aside such one-way, broadcastable media as books, newspapers, television, and radio. Some personal media have been compared experimentally (see, for example, Ochsman & Chapanis, 1974), but most of these studies identify and describe differences without a theoretical framework for explaining them. We propose to set them in a framework that will account for many of their differences.

Constraints on Grounding

Personal media vary on many dimensions that affect grounding. Here are eight constraints that a medium may impose on communication between two people, A and B.

1. *Copresence: A and B share the same physical environment.* In face-to-face conversation, the participants are usually in the same surroundings and can readily see and hear what each other is doing and looking at. In other media there is no such possibility.

2. *Visibility: A and B are visible to each other.* In face-to-face conversation, the participants can see each other, and in other media they cannot. They may also be able to see each other, as in video teleconferencing, without being able to see what each other is doing or looking at.

3. *Audibility: A and B communicate by speaking.* Face to face, on the telephone, and with some kinds of teleconferencing, participants can hear each other and take note of timing and intonation. In other media they cannot. An answering machine preserves intonation, but only some aspects of utterance timing.

4. *Cotemporality: B receives at roughly the same time as A produces.* In most conversations, an utterance is produced just about when it is received and understood, without delay. In media such as letters and electronic mail, this is not the case.

5. *Simultaneity: A and B can send and receive at once and simultaneously.* Sometimes messages can be conveyed and received by both parties at once, as when a hearer smiles during a speaker's utterance. Simultaneous utterances are also allowed, for example, in the keyboard teleconferencing program called *talk*, where what both parties type appears letter by letter in two distinct halves of the screen. Other media are cotemporal but not simultaneous, such as the kind of keyboard teleconferencing that transmits characters only after the typist hits a carriage return.

6. *Sequentiality: A's and B's turns cannot get out of sequence.* In face-to-face conversation, turns ordinarily form a sequence that does not include intervening turns from different conversations with other people. With email, answering machines, and letters, a message and its reply may be separated by any number of irrelevant messages or activities; interruptions do not have the same force.

7. *Reviewability: B can review A's messages.* Speech fades quickly, but in media such as email, letters, and recorded messages, an utterance stays behind as an artifact that can be reviewed later by either of the partners—or even by a third party. In keyboard teleconferencing, the last few utterances stay visible on the screen for awhile.

8. *Revisability: A can revise messages for B.* Some media, such as letters and email, allow a participant to revise an utterance privately before sending it to a partner. In face-to-face and telephone conversations, most self-repairs must be done publicly. Some kinds of keyboard teleconferencing fall in between; what a person types appears on the partner's screen only after every carriage return, rather than letter by letter.

Table 1

SEVEN MEDIA AND THEIR ASSOCIATED CONSTRAINTS

Medium	Constraints
Face-to-face	Copresence, visibility, audibility, cotemporality, simultaneity, sequentiality
Telephone	Audibility, cotemporality, simultaneity, sequentiality
Video teleconference	Visibility, audibility, cotemporality, simultaneity, sequentiality
Terminal teleconference	Cotemporality, sequentiality, reviewability
Answering machines	Audibility, reviewability
Electronic mail	Reviewability, revisability
Letters	Reviewability, revisability

There are other differences across media, but these are among the most important for grounding. Table 1 characterizes seven personal media by these constraints.

Costs of Grounding

When a medium lacks one of these characteristics, it generally forces people to use alternative grounding techniques. It does so because the costs of the various techniques of grounding change. We will describe eleven costs that change. The first two, formulation and production costs, are paid by the speaker. The next two, reception and understanding costs, are paid by the addressee. The rest are paid by both. We emphasize that these costs are not independent of each other.

Formulation costs
It costs time and effort to formulate and reformulate utterances. It costs more to plan complicated than simple utterances, more to retrieve uncommon than common words, and more to create descriptions for unfamiliar than familiar objects. It costs more to formulate perfect than imperfect utterances. As we will see, these costs are often traded off for others, depending on the medium.

Production costs
The act of producing an utterance itself has a cost that varies from medium to medium. It takes little effort (for most of us) to speak or gesture, more effort to type on a computer keyboard or typewriter, and the most effort (for many of us,

anyway) to write by hand. Speaking is swift, typing is slower, and handwriting is slowest. These costs are traded off for other costs as well. People are willing to use more words talking than in typewriting to accomplish a goal, and the faster people are at typing, the more words they are willing to use.

Reception costs

Listening is generally easy, and reading harder, although it may be easier to read than to listen to complicated instructions or abstract arguments. It also costs to have to wait while the speaker produces a turn. This wait takes its toll in keyboard conversations when addressees must suffer as they watch an utterance appear letter by letter with painstaking backspacing to repair misspellings.

Understanding costs

It is also more costly for people to understand certain words, constructions, and concepts than others, regardless of the medium. The costs can be compounded when contextual clues are missing. Email, for example, is neither cotemporal nor sequential. That makes understanding harder because the addressee has to imagine appropriate contexts for both the sender and the message, and to remember what the message is in response to, even when the ''subject'' field of the message is filled in.

Start-up costs

This is the cost of starting up a new discourse. It is the cost of getting B initially to notice that A has uttered something and to accept that he or she has been addressed. Start-up costs are minimal face to face, where A need only get B's attention and speak. They are a bit higher when A must get to a telephone, look up a number, dial it, and determine that the answerer is B. They are often higher yet in email. First, A has to get access to the right software and hardware, find the right email address, and start the message. Second, the message may not reach the addressee if the channel is unreliable or the address has typos in it. Third, depending on the system, the sender may or may not be notified of its delivery. And finally, once the message is delivered, there is no guarantee that the addressee will read it right away. There are similar start-up costs in writing letters.

Delay costs

These are the costs of delaying an utterance in order to plan, revise, and execute it more carefully. In face-to-face conversation, as in all cotemporal and simultaneous media, these costs are high because of the way delays, even brief delays, are interpreted. When speakers leave too long a gap before starting a turn, they may be misheard as dropping out of the conversation or as implying other more damaging things. And when they leave too long a pause in the middle of a turn, they may be misheard as having finished their turn. With the pressure to minimize both midturn pauses and preturn gaps, speakers are often forced to utter words they may have to revise or to let their addressees help them out. Even when it is clear that a delay is due to the speaker's production difficulty, it costs the addressees to wait. In media without cotemporality—such as email and personal letters— delays that would be crippling in conversation are not even noticeable, and so their costs are nil. But in cotemporal media, the cost of a delay can be high: When the drugged Juliet failed to respond, Romeo did himself in.

Delay costs often trade off with formulation costs. In writing letters, we can take our time planning and revising each sentence. Computerized text editing has made this even easier. But in face-to-face and telephone conversations, where delay costs are high, we have to formulate utterances quickly. That forces us to use simpler constructions and to be satisfied with less than perfect utterances. The other media lie between these two extremes.

Asynchrony costs
In conversation, people time their utterances with great precision (Jefferson, 1973). They can begin an utterance precisely at the completion of the prior speaker's turn. They can time acknowledgments to mark what it is they are acknowledging. They can interrupt a particular word to show agreement or disagreement on some aspect of it. In media without copresence, visibility, audibility, or simultaneity, timing is much less precise, and without cotemporality, it is altogether impossible. So grounding techniques that rely on precision of timing should go up in cost when production and reception are asynchronous.

Speaker change costs
In conversation the general rule is, "Two people can speak at the same time only for short periods or about limited content." The rule is usually simplified to "One speaker at a time" (see Sacks et al., 1974), and it tends to hold for other media as well. But the cost of changing speakers varies with the medium. In face-to-face conversation it is low. The participants find it easy to arrange for one speaker to stop and another to start. There are regular rules for turn taking in which the points of possible change in speakers are frequent, easily marked, and readily recognized, and the changes can be instantaneous. Also, the costs of simultaneous speech, at least for short intervals and limited content, are minor. The participants usually continue to understand without disruption.

The cost of changing speakers is higher in media with fewer cues for changes in turns. Costs are quite high, for example, in keyboard teleconferencing, where the points of speaker change are not as easily marked or readily recognized. These points may need to be marked by a convention such as the use of "o" (for "over"), a device that is also used by airplane pilots and citizens' band radio operators, when only one party can be heard at a time. Speaker change costs are greater still in letters, answering machines, and email, where it may take much work for one participant to stop and another to start up. Changing the speaker in these media is a little like starting up a communication from scratch. One effect of high speaker change costs is that people try to do more within a turn.

Display costs
In face-to-face conversation, it is easy to point to, nod at, or present an object for our interlocutors. It is also easy to gaze at our interlocutors to show them we are attending, to monitor their facial expressions, or to pick them out as addressees. In media without copresence, gestures cost a lot, are severely limited, or are out of the question. In video teleconferencing, we can use only a limited range of gestures, and we cannot always look at someone as a way of designating "you." Showing pictures is possible with media such as video, fax machines, and letters.

Fault costs
There are costs associated with producing an utterance fault, that is, any mistake or missaying. Some faults lead to failures in understanding, and failures in one utterance are likely to undermine the next one. The costs of these faults increase with the gravity of the failures. Other faults make the speaker look foolish, illiterate, or impolite, so they also have their costs. The cost of most faults trades off with what it costs to repair them (our next category) or to prevent them in the first place. To avoid paying fault costs, speakers may elect to pay more in formulation costs. But it depends on the medium. In conversation, a hearer may expect faults from a speaker because the production of speech is so spontaneous. In email, faults are not as easily justified, because the sender has already had a chance to revise them, and because the damage done is not as easily repaired.

Repair costs
Some repairs take little time or effort; others take a lot, and still others are impossible to make. Because faults tend to snowball, speakers should want to repair them as quickly as possible. In audible conversation, as we noted earlier, speakers prefer to initiate and make their own repairs, and there is evidence that they interrupt themselves and make these repairs just as soon as they detect a fault (Levelt, 1983). These preferences tend to minimize the cost of a repair. Self-corrections take fewer words and turns than do repairs by others, and so do repairs initiated by oneself rather than by others. These preferences also help minimize the cost of faults: They tend to remove a fault from the floor as quickly as possible. In media that are not cotemporal, repairs initiated or made by others become very costly indeed, so speakers will try hard to avoid relying on others to repair misunderstandings. It is less costly for them to revise what they say before sending it. Another way to minimize repair costs may be to change to a different medium to make the repair.

Cost Tradeoffs

People manage to communicate effectively by all the media we have mentioned, but that does not mean that they do so in the same way in each medium. The way people proceed reflects the costs they incur. Recall the intermediate states 0 to 3 mentioned earlier for face-to-face conversation: (0) A and B failing to establish any connection yet, (1) A getting B's attention, (2) B perceiving A's utterance correctly, and (3) B understanding what A meant. There are costs to getting to each state, and in some media the states are quite distinct. In media that are not cotemporal, there is the additional problem that A does not have immediate evidence as to which of these states B is in with respect to A's utterance. In a medium such as email, B's lack of response can be highly ambiguous. Did she not get the message, did she get it and not read it, did she read it and choose not to respond, did she not understand it, or what? A does not know whether B is in state 0, 1, 2, or 3.

Once we assume that people need to ground what they say and that they trade off on the costs of grounding, we can account for some of the differences in language use across media. Consider a study reported by Cohen (1984) in which tutors instructed students on assembling a pump. Their communication was either by telephone or by keyboard. Over the telephone, tutors would first get students to identify an object, and only when they had confirmed its identification did they ask students to do something with it.

> S: Uh, now there's a little plastic blue cap.
> J: Yep.
> S: Put that on the top hole in the cylinder you just worked with.

In contrast, in keyboard conversations, tutors would identify an object and instruct students what to do with it all in a single turn.

> K: Next, take the blue cap that has the pink thing on it and screw it to the blue piece you just screwed on.

That is, there were many more separate requests for identification over the telephone than in keyboard conversations. According to Cohen, "Speakers attempt to achieve more detailed goals in giving instructions than do users of keyboards" (Cohen, 1984, p. 97).

But why? The principle of least effort suggests a reason: The two media have different profiles of grounding costs. Over the telephone, it doesn't cost much to produce an utterance or change speakers. On a keyboard, it costs much more. So to minimize these costs, tutors and students on a keyboard might seek and provide evidence after larger constituents; that is, they should try to do more within each turn than they would over the telephone. This prediction would account for the difference Cohen describes between the two media. In addition, repairs are more costly over the keyboard; if tutors and students are aware of this, they might formulate their utterances more carefully. But because delay costs can be just as high over the keyboard as on the telephone, and speaker change costs are higher, there are likely to be more misunderstandings over a keyboard, and repairs will take more collaborative effort. The differences among these and other media can be explained by the techniques participants choose for grounding. They balance the perceived costs for formulation, production, reception, understanding, start-up, delay, timing, speaker change, display, faults, and repair.

Medium and Purpose Interact

Grounding techniques depend on both purpose and medium, and these sometimes interact. Face-to-face conversations appear to be preferred for reprimanding, whereas telephone conversations or letters may be preferred for refusing an unreasonable request (Furnham, 1982). In a study of working groups, face-to-face conversation was preferred for negotiating and reaching consensus, whereas email was preferred for coordinating schedules, assigning tasks, and making progress reports (Finholt, Sproull, & Kiesler, 1990).

    These preferences can be explained in terms of the costs associated with each medium relative to the participants' purposes. Sometimes the participants want a reviewable record of a conversation—as for schedules, task assignments, and progress reports; and other times they do not. Sometimes speakers want to get a hearer's full attention, and sometimes they want to avoid interrupting. Sometimes people want their reactions to be seen, as in negotiating and reaching consensus, and sometimes they do not. Which medium is best for which purpose, then, depends on the form grounding takes in a medium and whether that serves the participants' purposes.

    Finally, as more participants join the conversation and the medium must support the work of a whole group, costs and tradeoffs shift. Start-up costs may be greater. Reception costs will increase if a hearer must put effort into identifying who is speaking or writing. Fault costs and repair costs will be higher when a group is involved. Any medium that supports cooperative work can be evaluated in terms of the techniques it allows for grounding.

CONCLUSION

Grounding is essential to communication. Once we have formulated a message, we must do more than just send it off. We need to assure ourselves that it has been understood as we intended it to be. Otherwise, we have little assurance that the discourse we are taking part in will proceed in an orderly way. For whatever we say, our goal is to reach the grounding criterion: that we and our addressees mutually believe that they have understood what we meant well enough for current purposes. This is the process we have called *grounding*.

The techniques we use for grounding change both with purpose and with medium. Special techniques have evolved, for example, for grounding references to objects and for grounding the verbatim content of what is said. Grounding techniques also change with the medium. In the framework we have offered, media differ in the costs they impose on such actions as delaying speech, starting up a turn, changing speakers, making errors, and repairing errors. In grounding what we say, we try to minimize effort for us and our partners. Ordinarily, this means paying as few of these costs as possible.

The lesson is that communication is a collective activity. It requires the coordinated action of all the participants. Grounding is crucial for keeping that coordination on track.

References

Bach, K., & Harnish, R. M. (1979). *Linguistic communication and speech acts.* Cambridge, MA: MIT Press.

Clark, H. H., & Carlson, T. (1982). Hearers and speech acts. *Language, 58*(2), 332–373.

Clark, H. H., & Marshall, C. R. (1981). Definite reference and mutual knowledge. In A. K. Joshi, B. L. Webber, & I. A. Sag (Eds.), *Elements of discourse understanding* (pp. 10–63). Cambridge, England: Cambridge University Press.

Clark, H. H., & Schaefer, E. F. (1987). Collaborating on contributions to conversations. *Language and Cognitive Processes, 2*(1), 19–41.

Clark, H. H., & Schaefer, E. F. (1989). Contributing to discourse. *Cognitive Science, 13,* 259–294.

Clark, H. H., Schreuder, R., & Buttrick, S. (1983). Common ground and the understanding of demonstrative reference. *Journal of Verbal Learning and Verbal Behavior, 22,* 1–39.

Clark, H. H., & Wilkes-Gibbs, D. (1986). Referring as a collaborative process. *Cognition, 22,* 1–39.

Cohen, P. R. (1984). The pragmatics of referring and the modality of communication. *Computational Linguistics, 10*(2), 97–146.

Finholt, T., Sproull, L., & Kiesler, S. (1990). Communication and performance in ad hoc task groups. In J. Galegher, R. Kraut, & C. Egido (Eds.), *Intellectual teamwork: Social and technological foundations of cooperative work* (pp. 291–326). Hillsdale, NJ: Erlbaum.

Furnham, A. (1982). The message, the context, and the medium. *Language and Communication, 2,* 33–47.

Geluykens, R. (1988). The interactional nature of referent-introduction. *Papers from the 24th Regional Meeting, Chicago Linguistic Society,* 141–154.

Goldberg, C. (1975). A system for the transfer of instructions in natural settings. *Semiotica, 14,* 269–296.

Goodwin, C. (1981). *Conversational organization: Interaction between speakers and hearers.* New York: Academic Press.

Goodwin, C. (1986). Between and within: Alternative sequential treatments of continuers and assessments. *Human Studies, 9*, 205–217.

Grice, H. P. (1975). Logic and conversation. In P. Cole & J. L. Morgan (Eds.), *Syntax and semantics, Volume 3: Speech acts* (pp. 225–242). New York: Seminar Press.

Grice, H. P. (1978). Some further notes on logic and conversation. In P. Cole (Ed.), *Syntax and semantics, volume 9: Pragmatics* (pp. 113–128). New York: Academic Press.

Grosz, B. J., & Sidner, C. L. (1986). Attention, intentions, and the structure of discourse. *Computational Linguistics, 12*, 175–204.

Isaacs, E. A., & Clark, H. H. (1987). References in conversation between experts and novices. *Journal of Experimental Psychology, 116*, 26–37.

Jefferson, G. (1972). Side sequences. In D. Sudnow (Ed.), *Studies in social interaction* (pp. 294–338). New York: Free Press.

Jefferson, G. (1973). A case of precision timing in ordinary conversation: Overlapped tag-positioned address terms in closing sequences. *Semiotica, 9*, 47–96.

Krauss, R. M., & Weinheimer, S. (1964). Changes in reference phases as a function of frequency of usage in social interaction: A preliminary study. *Psychonomic Study, 1*, 113–114.

Krauss, R. M., & Weinheimer, S. (1966). Concurrent feedback, confirmation, and the encoding of referents in verbal communication. *Journal of Personality and Social Psychology, 4*, 343–346.

Krauss, R. M., & Weinheimer, S. (1967). Effect of referent similarity and communication mode on verbal encoding. *Journal of Verbal Learning and Verbal Behavior, 6*, 359–363.

Levelt, W. J. M. (1983). Monitoring and self-repair in speech. *Cognition, 14*, 41–104.

Lewis, D. K. (1969). *Convention: A philosophical study*. Cambridge, MA: Harvard University Press.

Litman, D. J., & Allen, J. F. (1987). A plan recognition model for subdialogues in conversation. *Cognitive Science, 11*, 163–200.

Ochsman, R. B., & Chapanis, A. (1974). The effects of 10 communication modes on the behavior of teams during cooperative problem-solving. *International Journal of Man–Machine Studies, 6*, 579–619.

Sacks, H., & Schegloff, E. A. (1979). Two preferences in the organization of reference to persons in conversation and their interaction. In G. Psathas (Ed.), *Everyday language: Studies in ethnomethodology* (pp. 15–21). New York: Irvington.

Sacks, H., Schegloff, E. A., & Jefferson, G. (1974). A simplest systematics for the organization of turn-taking in conversation. *Language, 50*, 696–735.

Schegloff, E. A. (1972). Notes on a conversational practice: Formulating place. In D. Sudnow (Ed.), *Studies in social interaction* (pp. 75–119). New York: Free Press.

Schegloff, E. A. (1982). Discourse as an interactional achievement: Some uses of "uh huh" and other things that come between sentences. In D. Tannen (Ed.), *Analyzing discourse: Text and talk. Georgetown University Roundtable on Languages and Linguistics 1981* (pp. 71–93). Washington, DC: Georgetown University Press.

Schegloff, E. A., Jefferson, G., & Sacks, H. (1977). The preference for self-correction in the organization of repair in conversation. *Language, 53*, 361–382.

Schegloff, E. A., & Sacks, H. (1973). Opening up closings. *Semiotica, 8*, 289–327.

Schelling, T. C. (1960). *The strategy of conflict*. Oxford: Oxford University Press.

Searle, J. R. (1969). *Speech acts*. Cambridge, England: Cambridge University Press.

Stalnaker, R. C. (1978). Assertion. In P. Cole (Ed.), *Syntax and semantics, Volume 9: Pragmatics* (pp. 315–332). New York: Academic Press.

Svartvik, J., & Quirk, R. (Eds.). (1980). *A corpus of English conversation*. Lund, Sweden: Gleerup.

Wilkes-Gibbs, D. (1986). *Collaborative processes of language use in conversation*. Unpublished doctoral dissertation, Stanford University, Stanford, CA.

CHAPTER 8

CONVERSATION ANALYSIS AND SOCIALLY SHARED COGNITION

EMANUEL A. SCHEGLOFF

OVERVIEW

In this effort to develop an appreciation of how the social analysis of conversation relates to socially shared cognition, I will proceed in three stages.

First, it seems appropriate in a volume organized, sponsored, and supported by psychologists, and composed for the most part of contributions by psychologists, to indicate some of the resonances that the term *socially shared cognition* sets off for a sociologist, if only to provide some background for the different approach I take. This introduction will of necessity be limited to a sketch of some of the relevant intellectual background, so boldly drawn as to verge on caricature, but will focus on the relevance of a preoccupation with the *procedural* sense of— and basis for—"social sharedness," and with talk-in-interaction as a strategic setting in which to study social sharedness.

In a second stage, I will outline briefly a few basic components of that approach to talk-in-interaction that represents the narrower usage of the term *conversation analysis*, and identify a number of distinct areas in which this approach has explicated ideas that would fall under—or might expand the scope of the study of—socially shared cognition. In the course of this account, I will

My thanks go to Paul Drew and John Heritage, as well as to the editors of the volume, for thoughtful comments that have helped me clarify parts of the text, in places with a special concern for a readership composed primarily of psychologists.

150

introduce several central elements of the organization of talk-in-interaction that conversation analysis has focused on and that appear to have multifaceted relevance for the interface between interaction and cognition. I will particularly address the organizations of turn-taking and of repair, one of which provides the arena for the somewhat more detailed undertaking that follows.

In the third stage, I will examine a few aspects of that component of the organization of repair that furnishes what I call "the last structurally provided defense of intersubjectivity in conversation." By this phrase, I allude to the relevance for participants in interaction of "intersubjectivity"—the maintenance of a *world* (including the developing course of the interaction itself) mutually understood by the participants as some *same* world. I mean to underscore as well that there are structures operating to organize ordinary talk-in-interaction, that these structures engender opportunities to detect and repair problems in the achievement and maintenance of intersubjectivity, and that these opportunities and their use are describable. I will describe two variant forms that efforts to repair problems of intersubjectivity can take. In the present context, I take this topic to be a centrally relevant aspect of socially shared cognition.

HISTORICAL ECHOES OF SOCIALLY SHARED COGNITION

It is important to note the shift from terms such as *common culture* or *shared knowledge* to *socially shared cognition*. The former terms were part of an analytic and theoretical orientation in anthropology and sociology that, in the modern pantheon at least, can be traced back to Durkheim (1951/1897, 1915). There is not the space here to describe the vicissitudes of that theoretic stance in Western sociology over the last 50 years or so. Suffice it to say that it reached the peak of its influence in the social theory of Talcott Parsons (see, for example, 1937, 1951), for whom the "common values" that Durkheim had foregrounded served as the very glue of the social order. And, although Parsons himself paid virtually no attention to the epistemic thrust of Durkheim's concerns, vernacular or commonsense knowledge, insofar as it was itself informed and infiltrated by common values, was part of that same glue.

This theoretical stance came under severe pressure from a number of directions during and after the 1960s. Only one of these critiques will concern us here—that developed by Harold Garfinkel under the rubric *ethnomethodology*.

In a series of studies (collected in Garfinkel, 1967) prompted in the first instance by confronting the work of Parsons with the most sociologically relevant strands of phenomenology (cf. Heritage, 1984a for a lucid account of the theoretical lineages and interactions here), Garfinkel asked what exactly might be intended by such notions as "common" or "shared" knowledge. In the days when computers were still UNIVACs, Garfinkel viewed as untenable that notion of common or shared knowledge that was more or less equal to the claim that separate memory drums had identical contents. When even the sense of ordinary words and very simple sentences could be shown not to engender identical explications when presented to different persons, when those explications themselves had to be reconciled to provide them a "sense of equivalence," and when *those* reconciliations in turn required such reconciliation, the notion of "common culture" or "shared knowledge" as composed of same substantive components—whether norms or propositions—held by different persons became increasingly difficult to defend.

Instead, what seemed programmatically promising to Garfinkel was a *procedural* sense of common or shared, a set of practices by which actions and stances could be predicated on and displayed as oriented to "knowledge held in common"—knowledge that might thereby be reconfirmed, modified, and expanded. Garfinkel's term *ethnomethodology*—with its explicit preoccupation with the procedures by which commonsense knowledge is acquired, confirmed, revised—can be partially understood by reference to this matrix of concerns.

Much subsequent work touching on these and related matters—whether prompted by Garfinkel's concerns or by others'—has developed in recent years under various rubrics that reflect the changing concerns and professional identities of those doing the theorizing. In the title for this volume (and the conference on which it reports), the replacement of *culture* and *knowledge* with *cognition* seems to track the shift from the concerns of anthropology, classical epistemology, sociological theory, and the sociology of knowledge to those of psychology, cognitive science, and artificial intelligence. And the specification of *common* or *shared* as "*socially* shared" may reflect a concern with the *processes* of sharing and its embeddedness in the context of social situations. It suits my purposes to assume this concern because this chapter focuses on the embeddedness, the inextricable intertwinedness, of cognition and interaction. In my own work, I have explored this connection through the study of talk-in-interaction, specifically conversation. It may be useful to provide some background about this domain of inquiry.

BACKGROUND ON CONVERSATION ANALYSIS

Among the various lines of inquiry ultimately concerned with talk-in-interaction[1]— whether termed *sociolinguistics, pragmatics, discourse analysis, interpersonal*

---

[1] I use the term *talk-in-interaction* in what follows both to avoid the common understanding of "conversation" as "chitchat" or "small talk," and to reserve the term *conversation* for that unmodified organization of talk-in-interaction that is systematically transformed in the realization of other "speech-exchange systems" (Sacks et al., 1974) such as courtroom proceedings, debates, interviews of various sorts, ceremonies, lectures, and psychotherapy. The general term *talk-in-interaction* is used to include exactly what the term names—talk in interaction.

communication, or some other disciplinary label, an insistence on repeated and close analysis of recorded mundane scenes of ordinary interaction and detailed transcripts of them has served as a methodological hallmark of the work known as *conversation analysis* (CA). (For overviews, see Levinson, 1983, and Heritage, 1984a; for recent collections of representative work, see Atkinson & Heritage, 1984; Boden & Zimmerman, in press; Button, Drew, & Heritage, 1986; Button & Lee, 1987; Heritage & Drew, in press; and Maynard, 1987, 1988.)

Work of this type has had a number of general concerns. One of these has been to enrich our capacity to analyze ordinary conversational interaction in a way that can account for the actual course that particular episodes of interaction take and that can capture the orientation of the participants to it. Another has been to develop a systematic explication of the recurrent and stable practices of talking in interaction that participants in ordinary talk-in-interaction employ to talk and to understand what is going on. Indeed, these concerns have gone hand in hand, one test of the adequacy of a description of some practice being its capacity to yield convincing analysis of singular episodes of conversation, and one result of incisive single case analysis being the formulation of recurrent practices of talking.

A substantial body of work in CA can be appreciated for its bearing on the interface between cognition and interaction. Much CA work brings general concerns with the *methodical* underpinnings (the *how*) of ordinary shared knowledge and skilled practice to a defined focus in the conduct of everyday interaction, accessible to empirical inquiry. Practices of conduct in ordinary interaction can be examined for the ways in which they furnish or embody procedures by which a sense of a world known in common is reinforced and implemented. Several different domains of research in CA are relevant to this topic, one of which I will develop in greater detail.

But before focusing on several specific themes in CA work that engage a concern with socially shared cognition, it is important to make explicit a fundamental theme embodied in this work that often seems to be missing from cognitivist concerns.

On the Interactive Foundations of the Cognitive

This theme is that the domain of social action and interaction outside the cognitive apparatus—whether conceived of as mind or brain, as hardware, software, or wetware—is not a structureless medium that merely transmits messages, knowledge, information, or behavior that are planned and processed inside the skull, with no further ado. Rather, the world of interaction has its own structures and constraints. Its shape not only bears on the fate of acts, messages, and utterances once they are enacted by persons. It also enters into the very composition, design, and structuring of conduct and is part and parcel of whatever processes—cognitive or otherwise—are germane to the conception and constitution of acts, messages, or utterances in the first instance.

The very things that it occurs to speakers to express, their implementation in certain linguistic forms, and the opportunity to articulate them in sound with determinate and coordinate body movements—such as gesture, posture, and facial expression—are constrained and shaped by the structures by which talk-in-interaction is organized. And whether such utterances are heard or claimed to be heard, and how they are understood or misunderstood are also in substantial measure shaped by those organizations of talk-in-interaction.

However, it should not be thought that these organizations—of turn taking,[2] of the coherence of sequences of successive utterances, or of whole occasions of talk—merely give social shape to cognitive outcomes produced by autonomous cognitive processes and expressed by autonomously structured linguistic resources. As I hope will be apparent from the data presented and discussed below, the structures of interaction penetrate into the very warp of these apparently autonomous domains. On reflection, it is not implausible for this to be the case.

In many respects, of course, the fundamental or primordial scene of social life is that of direct interaction between members of a social species, typically ones who are physically copresent. For humans, talking in interaction appears to be a distinctive form of this primary constituent of social life, and ordinary conversation is very likely the basic form of organization for talk-in-interaction. Conversational interaction may be thought of as a form of social organization through which most, if not all, the major institutions of societies—the economy, the polity, the family, and the reproduction and socialization of the population—get their work done. And it surely appears to be the basic and primordial environment for the use and the development of natural language.

Therefore, it should hardly surprise us if some of the most fundamental features of natural language are shaped in accordance with their home environment in copresent interaction, as adaptations to it, or as part of its very warp and weft (cf. Schegloff, 1989a).

For example, if the basic natural environment for sentences is in turns at talk in conversation, we should take seriously the possibility that aspects of their structure (e.g., their grammatical structure) are to be understood as adaptations to that environment. In view of the thoroughly interactional character of the organization of turn taking in conversation (Sacks, Schegloff, & Jefferson, 1974),

---

[2]By *turn taking* I refer to the systematic allocation of opportunities to talk and the systematic regulation of the size of those opportunities. Psychologists may be more familiar with accounts of turn taking whose domain is differently formulated, such as Jaffe and Feldstein (1970) or Duncan (1974a, 1974b) and Duncan and Fiske (1977), but I am relying on the account in Sacks et al., 1974.

the grammatical structures of language should in the first instance be understood as at least partially shaped by interactional considerations (Schegloff, 1979).

There is another respect in which what might be thought to be intrinsic properties of natural language are partially the product of its fundamental situatedness in interactional contexts. The organization of conversation, and more generally of talk-in-interaction, includes among its generic components (those apparently relevant and in play when talk is in progress or even incipient, the latter making it potentially relevant to interaction beyond talk) an element that we call the *organization of repair* (Schegloff, Jefferson, & Sacks, 1977). This is an organized set of practices by which parties to talk-in-interaction can address problems in speaking, hearing, and understanding the talk.

The presence of such an organization in virtually all talk-in-interaction allows natural language to be constructed differently than might otherwise have been the case. Given that hearers have resources available for addressing problems in understanding, should they arise, the resources of natural language need not, for example, be unambiguous. They need not have invariant mappings of signs or symbols and their signifieds. They need not have a syntax that assigns only a single interpretation to a given expression. They need not be limited to literal usage, but may be used in idiomatic, metaphoric, and other nonliteral tropes.

Talk-in-interaction, then, is interactive quite apart from its contextuality (by reference to which it is virtually always responsive or prosposive) and its collaborativeness (in the sense that whatever gets done is a joint achievement of speakers and their interlocutors). Those senses aside, the kinds of language components from which it is fashioned—sounds, words, and sentences—have the character they do and are formed the way they are in part because they are designed to inhabit an environment in which the apparatus of repair is available and in which, accordingly, flexible arrangements can be permitted.[3]

In like manner, our articulatory apparatus and our practices of articulation and hearing may have developed the way they did in part because repair is available to catch such problems in speaking and hearing as may arise. Similar considerations apply to other aspects of natural language.

Thematic Relations Between CA and Socially Shared Cognition

Before continuing the discussion of the domain of repair, it is important to touch on several other, quite different areas of conversation-analytic work that may be

---

[3]This stands in contrast to discourse domains such as science and logic in which such "flexible arrangements" (it is claimed) cannot be permitted, and whose building blocks must, therefore, be of a different character, as in so-called artificial or formal languages.

of interest to persons drawn to this general theme. Inadequate as these overly brief accounts will be, they may nonetheless point those interested in socially shared cognition from a psychological perspective toward work they are not familiar with that may be of substantial interest.

One such area of inquiry is concerned with forms of reference (most extensively examined for person reference by Sacks, 1972a, 1972b, but also for place reference by Schegloff, 1972) and their organization and deployment. One important line of research concerns the ways in which the organization of categorical terms of reference for persons (what Sacks termed *membership categorization devices*) organizes a broad scope of commonsense knowledge about persons (Sacks, 1972a, 1972b, in press). Another line of work focuses on how some reference terms for persons invoke, mask, or presume the absence of shared knowledge—what has been called *recognitional reference* (Sacks & Schegloff, 1979). The last of these lines of work transmutes the socially shared feature from being the researcher's characterization of the knowledge to being that of the interactants (Sacks & Schegloff, 1979).

An offshoot of Sacks' work on the membership categorization devices concerns some telling areas in which categories of person and the commonsense knowledge organized by reference to them are *not* shared (1979). There are, for example, terms used to identify sets of persons that are not used by those persons themselves. Such categories may be said to be owned and administered by dominant groups vis-a-vis others. There are numerous historical and ethnographic reports of such occurrences, but Sacks points to the recurrent invention or cooptation of categories such as *hotrodder*, *surfer*, *beatnik*, *flapper*, *punker* by *adolescents* or *teenagers*. The latter two terms are owned and administered by adults, who define conditions of applicability and what is known about members of the category, with the members of the category themselves having little or no control over the deployment of the terms. The former sets of categories (which Sacks terms *revolutionary categories*) come to be administered by their incumbents, who define conditions of membership and proper belonging, generally to the uncertain dismay of the "straight" society. This work points to a whole area of a sociology of cognition not currently envisioned by the cognitive sciences.

Another domain of work is concerned with the ways in which the types of activities that utterance types can do (utterance types such as "question" or "announcement") implicate shared knowledge. Thus, announcement-formatted talk, when it delivers what is taken to be already shared knowledge, can be understood by its recipients to be doing some other activity. Or, formulating some previously ongoing talk for a newly arrived interactant in a way that accommodates what the newcomer is taken to know about can serve to invite the newcomer to join the talk (Sacks, in press; Schegloff, 1989b).

Another line of CA work bearing on the cognition–interaction interface concerns how participants in talk-in-interaction can take up stances toward their own knowledge states or that of a speaker, for example through the use of particles such as *oh* (Heritage, 1984b). *Oh* can claim a change in the speaker's state, but its utterance enacts an interactional stance and does not necessarily reflect a cognitive event. By discriminating these two quite different, but not always distinguished, domains, researchers can better explicate the empirical relationship between them.

A last direction of work to be mentioned here focuses on how an orientation to the distribution of knowledge among speakers and potential recipients or audience (both where the knowledge is shared and where it is not) can enter into the very constitution and design of utterances, as well as the deployment of bodies, in interaction (Goodwin, 1979, 1980, 1981).

In the remainder of this chapter, however, I want to take a different approach and explore how the organization of repair in talk-in-interaction affects the intersection of cognition and interaction, not as it bears on the character of language per se, but as it enters into the conduct of particular episodes of talk-in-interaction.

THE DEFENSE OF INTERSUBJECTIVITY

Socially shared cognition is nowhere more important than in the course of direct interaction between persons. The very coherence and viability of the course of such interaction, jointly produced by the participants through a series of moves in a series of moments that are each built in some coherent fashion with respect to what went before, depends on some considerable degree of shared understanding of what has gone before, both proximately and distally, and what alternative courses of action lie ahead. Such intersubjectivity is not always untroubled.

A Brief Introduction to the Organization of Repair

Of the various aspects of the organization of talk-in-interaction that contribute to the sustaining of socially shared cognition, one that is specialized for the task is called the *organization of repair*. This is an organization of practices of talk and other conduct by which participants can deal with problems or troubles in speaking, hearing, or understanding the talk. Such practices can be instituted at various places in the talk, but past work (Schegloff et al., 1977) has indicated that these places are properly thought of by their relationship to the source of the trouble. Using this organizing principle and a metric composed of turns at talk, it appears that virtually all efforts to deal with such problems in the talk, including problems in shared understanding, are initiated either in the turn in which the trouble or potential trouble occurs (as when a speaker stops to clarify a potential ambiguity before or just after finishing that turn at talk), in the next turn by some other

participant (a recipient for whom it may be relevant to respond), or in the following
turn by the speaker of the trouble source—what we can refer to as *third position
repair*.

The sequential basis for third position repair can be very briefly sketched.
In turns at talk in ordinary conversation, speakers ordinarily address themselves
to prior talk and, most commonly, to immediately preceding talk. In doing so,
speakers reveal aspects of their understanding of the prior talk to which their
own is addressed. And in doing so, speakers can reveal to speakers of the prior
talk understanding that the latter find problematic, that is, *mis*understandings.
When this occurs, speakers of the misunderstood talk can undertake to repair
the misunderstanding, and this can thus constitute third position repair, repair
after an interlocutor's response (second position) has revealed trouble in understanding an earlier turn (the *repairable* in the first position). The ordinary
sequential organization of conversation thus provides for displays of mutual
understanding and problems therein, one running basis for the cultivation and
grounding of intersubjectivity.

Third position repair may be thought of as the last systematically provided
opportunity to catch (among other problems) divergent understandings that embody
breakdowns of intersubjectivity, that is, trouble in socially shared cognition of
the talk and conduct in the interaction.[4]

It turns out that third position repairs have a highly recurrent format built
of a very limited set of types of components. Detailed presentation of this
format and the deployment of its components is not possible in the compass
of this chapter (cf. Schegloff, in press-a). However, I offer several exemplars
below to serve as a point of departure. What I wish to do in this chapter is
present two *variant* forms. These are clearly instances of third position repair
as we otherwise formulate and deal with it, but they are fashioned differently
by their speakers.

The Canonical Format for Third Position Repair

The recurrent form of third position repair should be grossly recognizable from
the following four instances:[5]

    1. GTS 1:37

a→ D: Well that's a little different from last week.

b→ L: heh heh heh Yeah. We were in hysterics last week.

---

[4]As I am using the term, *repair* is not addressed to all divergences of understanding, but only
to ones presented by the production and uptake of the talk itself.

[5]There are components not exemplified here, but the four instances presented embody the most
essential features. See Appendix to this chapter for an explanation of the transcript notation conventions.

c→ D: No, I mean Al.
    L: Oh. He . . .

2. FD IV:66

a→ A: Now what was that house number you said ˌyou were-
    B: ⌐No phone. No.
    A: Sir?
b→ B: No phone at all.
c→ A: No I mean the uh house number, ˌy-
    B: ⌐Thirdy eight oh one?
    A: Thirdy eight oh <u>one</u>.

3. CDHQ I:52

a→ A: Which one::s are closed, an' which ones are open.
b→ Z: Most of 'em. This, this,ˌthis, this ((pointing to map))
c→ A: ⌐I 'on't mean on the shelters,
c→   I mean on the roads.
    Z: Oh!

4. SPC, 74

    G: Well what did Miss Jevon say when you spoke to her.
    C: She said she would be glad to talk to you and she would be waiting for your call.
    G: Boy, it was some wait. Everyone else in that clinic has been just wonderful to me. Both the Diabetic Clinic and the Psychiatric Clinic. It's just that woman.
a→ C: Well, what are you going to do, Mr. Greenberg.
b→ G: Well that's true. When you are a charity patient, when you are a beggar,
b→   you can't do anything about it, you just have to take what's handed out
b→   to you, and-
c→ C: No, I mean about yourself. What are you going to do for yourself. . . .

I hope that it is clear in each of these cases that the third position repair turns (marked by the *c* arrows) are addressed to repairing some trouble in understanding a prior utterance by the same speaker (marked by the *a* arrows), trouble revealed by an intervening turn by another (marked by the *b* arrows).

What is striking is that the highly recurrent format of the third position repairs appears to be one that is used when troubles in understanding arise across two quite different types of understanding trouble—claimed misunder-

standing of the reference of some element of the trouble-source turn (as in the
first three instances) and (as in the fourth instance) trouble in assessing the
sequential implicativeness (the action upshot) of the trouble-source turn (Schegloff, 1987). In general the organization of repair appears to be independent of
the organization and source of trouble being addressed. However, in the materials to be examined below, when other than the aforementioned types of
understanding troubles are being addressed—when the trouble is of hearing,
of memory, of modality (e.g., between a serious utterance and a joke), or of
sequential implementation—then it appears that the different source and type
of trouble prompts a differently constructed instrument with which to accomplish it.

In referring here to *instruments*, I mean to underscore that the forms of
talk involved are devices used to accomplish an undertaking—here, the resolution of some problem in understanding. We will examine two such different
types of instruments, two of the variant forms that third position repair can
take (each of which requires some explication of the interactional context in
which it occurs).

Let me note in advance that the two fragments of interaction to be discussed below bear on intersubjectivity—or socially shared cognition—in multiple ways. One way is in the misunderstanding and repair contained in them.
But in each of these cases, that which is misunderstood *itself* concerns socially
shared cognition—what is or is not known in common. In one case, the issue
is whether the two participants already share certain knowledge; in the other,
it is whether the participants share an understanding of what exactly one of
them is doing in the talk.

Third Position Repair With Memory Trouble

In the first fragment, M and N are two women roommates in their late 20s in Los
Angeles in the mid-1970s,[6] and Stuart (N's boyfriend) has been living on the East
Coast. N has talked to Stuart earlier on the telephone.

5. M and N, 1

M: What' Stuart have to say.
N: Didn' I tell you?
a→ M: No::,
N: He's <u>coming</u>

[6]Formulating persons and settings in the manner used in the text is analytically problematic in
a variety of ways, as sketched in Schegloff (in press-b). Because I have not supplied the relevant
analytic warrant for the characterizations in the text, the account is informal, at best.

b→ M: Oh that's right
   N: |Yeah he's <u>coming</u> he's <u>coming</u>.
b→ M: Oh that's right, |he's going to Berkeley
   N: |Yes.

The utterances marked with the *b* arrows are correcting M's earlier turn, "no," at the *a* arrow, a self-correction touched off by the intervening turn by N, "He's coming."

M's first turn in this sequence is heard (and designed) as an initial inquiry about the conversation with Stuart and as an incidental one. That is, the formulation as "have to say" does not appear designed to solicit some particular news that M has reason to think might have emerged in N's conversation with Stuart (as in "What did he/Stuart say?" or a question asking specifically about the anticipated news). M's inquiry is tantamount to asking whether anything reportable occurred.

It could be proposed that if anything reportable had occurred it would have been reported. However, it appears that members of this culture treat some occurrences and some news as of such strength as to warrant (with respect to a particular potential recipient) initiating a topic/sequence or even a conversation to report them, whereas other occurrences and news, although reportable in response to an inquiry that warrants their telling, are not of such strength as to warrant telling on one's own initiative (again, with relation to a particular recipient). Hence, a query such as M's here can be produced so as to license a telling of the latter sort, and to provide a sequential position in which it can be properly told.

Note that N's response is compatible with this account. She does not in the first instance answer the question. There *is* an answer; Stuart *did* have something to say, and in fact, what there is to tell is rather more than the minimum qualifying as a tellable in response to an inquiry. The outcome of the earlier conversation with Stuart was considered significant enough to warrant N's initiating a telling without waiting for an eliciting inquiry. That is, there was news, and N told M about it, or thinks she did. That news has already been shared, and N assumes M already knows it. That M apparently does not remember it is itself potentially a noticeable fact about the relationship between M and N, as it would have been if N had not conveyed news of this magnitude to M on her own initiative (i.e., without being asked).

Hence, if N has any doubt that she did already tell M, there is some point in displaying that she treated their relationship as one in which this news would have prompted an earlier, self-initiated telling. If it should turn out that she has not told N, it is because she "failed to carry through an intention," not because she doesn't think M a proper recipient of news to which she accords the status she is about to display. The shared character of this knowledge is, then, itself a matter of concern.

In any case, the fact that N believes she has already told M the news makes problematic a response to the current inquiry. N "knows" that M already knows the news, and there are constraints on telling a recipient something the speaker supposes (or ought to suppose) the recipient already knows. Therefore, she does not simply offer a straightforward response to the inquiry.

N's "Didn' I tell you?", then, projects news. On the one hand, it serves as a prompt to M to retrieve some news that N has recently told her and then to retract the question, and suggests the order of object M should be searching for—something that would have been grounds for her initiating a telling to M. On the other hand, this question can serve as a "pre-telling," one that marks what is to be told as sufficiently worthy of telling as to have been told without benefit of inquiry. Accordingly, it projects or augurs big news.

Note, then, that the alternative response types to this yes–no type question are not simply *yes* and *no*. A yes-class response, for which the question is markedly constructed to display a preference, should be realized not by a *yes* answer, but by some self-repair, some touched-off memory by M that she *had* been told and some demonstration of what she remembers the news to be. A no-class response, on the other hand, should be realized by a *no* answer, to be followed by the telling by N, which would be responsive to the question by M that initiated this sequence.

If "Didn I tell you?" projects "big news," how big is "big"? Whatever magnitude of news N's pre-telling orients M to, M overshoots and overlooks the news that N had, in fact, conveyed to her (that the boyfriend is relocating to the West Coast), news that M will show she remembers a moment later by adding it to N's preannouncement. At first, however, she does not recall being told news from the previous N–Stuart conversation, and she responds accordingly, "no," whereupon N provides the response to the initially proffered inquiry: "He's *coming*." With this utterance, a well-formed sequence is completed—a question–answer pair with a question–answer insertion expanding it (Schegloff, 1972).

But the delivery of the news touches off in M the recollection that she has indeed been told this before, and in response she undertakes to repair her earlier answer to "Didn' I tell you?" "Oh that's right" is, of course, not a verification that "He's coming," but a confirmation that N had, in fact, told her, and M follows that up with a demonstration that she has more of the information than N has reannounced here; she adds to it a detail from the earlier telling as evidence that she does, in fact, remember. (For a fuller treatment of "Oh that's right" as a form of utterance for doing this interactional job, see Heritage, 1984b.)

Note that M's "Oh that's right" turn repairs her own prior turn, and not only expresses a belated recognition that she had been told the news before, but also articulates the form of utterance that ought properly to have occurred in its place. To "Didn' I tell you," M might properly have responded, "Oh that's right" (as well as "he's going to Berkeley").

This utterance is a third position repair as that term has been applied to other, differently appearing, segments of talk. The same speaker's prior utterance is what is in need of repair. And the relevance of repair has been occasioned by the intervening turn by an interlocutor; it is by virtue of what the interlocutor says in the intervening turn that the repair is undertaken and addresses the job that it does.

Note that the intervening turn does not itself address the problem. After M denies having been told what Stuart had to say, N does not try to correct her, to jog her memory to reverse her answer. N's ensuing talk displays an acceptance of M's claim and does an appropriate next turn in light of it. It is that appropriate next turn's *occasioning* of the repair, rather than itself *initiating* it, that embodies a distinct path by which the parties come to a shared understanding of the situation and marks this as an instance of third position repair.

The form that the repair takes, however, is different in this case from that of vast majority of third position repairs. In most such repairs, the problem is a misunderstanding by the second speaker of something in the trouble-source turn, a misunderstanding that is addressed in the turn following the one that displays it. And the format of most third position repairs is designed for the major exigencies of that type of problem. In this instance, however, the problem is not misunder- standing by interlocutor.

In the first instance, the question that M asks displays a wrong grasp of the speaker's own circumstances. The issue here is precisely socially shared knowledge and what *is* shared by the interlocutors. The two questions with which this sequence starts go directly to this matter. The first, in inquiring, disclaims knowledge; the second, in inquiring, means to remind its recipient that the inquired-after is already known and known in common. What gets repaired is the response to that inquiry, and the repair reverses the response in light of the intervening turn. As noted, it replaces the wrong response with the right one.

It is perhaps worth remarking that this repair is done at all, that M acknowl- edges that she *had* been told the news and had forgotten it. For news of this importance, and to her roommate, this may be a not inconsequential forgetting and acknowledgment. M could, alternatively, re-receive the news on its redelivery as if she were hearing it for the first time. Then, to "He's *coming*," she might have responded, "Oh how *marvelous!*" We note, then, that what is being ac- complished here is not only passing on the information about Stuart, but also keeping straight the record about N's memory, about N's assessment of the status of the news vis-a-vis the status of her relationship with M, about M's memory and the place of N's telling of her news in the personal "economy" of M's current affairs and relationships. This interactional and cognitive "bookkeeping" overrides whatever might have been gained by a bland re-receipt of the news. (That participants do sometimes rerun a sequence for "another first time" has been shown with other recorded interactions.)[7]

Third Position Repair With Unit Trouble

Sometimes the problem addressed by repair concerns a lack of shared understanding of the discourse unit being built, its boundaries, and the appropriate place and manner in which to respond to it. Here again, third position repair may take a form different from the canonical one. The following excerpt is taken from a telephone call to a radio talk show in New York City in the mid-1960s.

6.   BC Gray, 74-75

B: This is in reference to a call, that was made about a month ago.
A: Yessir?
B: A woman called, uh sayin she uh signed a contract for huh son who is- who was a minuh.
A: Mm hm,
B: And she claims inna contract, there were things given, and then taken away, in small writing.
     ((pause))
A: Mm hm
B: Uh, now meanwhile, about a month ehh no about two weeks before she made the call I read in, I read or either heard-uh I either read or hoid onna television, where the judge, hadda case like this.

---

[7]I might mention that not all cases in which a speaker reverses a previous utterance, such as a previous answer, take this form. First of all, some of them take the form of fourth position repairs; this happens particularly when the originating question was misunderstood (Schegloff, 1988). But there are also third position repair treatments of such "wrong" answers. For example:

O: And this is a-this is the junior high school you went to?
J: Uh huh.
O: Uh oh::: how was it.
J: I didn't go there.
O: Oh
J: I thought you meant Sam go there.
O: Sam went there.

Here, "I didn't go there" replaces and repairs the same speaker's "uh huh" as an answer to the question, and the repair is prompted by the intervening follow-up question. But as the ensuing diagnostic utterance makes clear, this was based on a misunderstanding of the initial question, and this sequence is thus an alternative to fourth position repair. Instead of, J: "Oh you mean me"; O: "yeah"; J: "I didn't go there," we get a third position repair plus a diagnostic utterance. In the instance treated in the text, however, the problem was in the speaker not *remembering*, rather than misunderstanding, and the repair takes a quite different form.

A: Mh hm,

B: And he got disgusted an' he says "I"—he's sick of these cases where they give things in big writing, an' take 'em, an' take 'em away in small writing.

A: Mmhm,

B: An' 'e claimed the contract void.

A: Mhhm?

→ B: Uh what I mean is it c'd help this woman that called. You know uh, that's the reason I <u>called</u>.

A few paragraphs will be necessary to sketch the sequential structure by which this talk is shaped by its participants, a sequential structure that provides both the context for and the substance of the problem in understanding that is addressed.

After the initial exchanges in the opening of the conversation, the caller launched into the talk reproduced here in the sequential position at which first topics (in this setting, typically the *only* topics) are introduced, ordinarily designed and heard as the reason for the call (Sacks, in press; Schegloff, 1986). The topic in this instance is built from the outset as a telling, as a sort of story. It is, in any case, designed to comprise more than one of the units out of which turns are ordinarily built, units (such as clauses and sentences) on whose possible completion an interlocutor may (and sometimes *must*) properly begin a next turn (Sacks, 1974; Sacks et al., 1974).

One way an interlocutor can cooperate with such a conversational undertaking is to withhold full turns at talk at the places where they might otherwise be initiated and, instead, provide little tokens that display an appreciation that an extended turn at talk is still under way, is not yet complete, has not presented problems of hearing or understanding that recipient will now raise, and that the speaker should continue with the unit in progress (hence these interpolations may be called *continuers*; see Schegloff, 1982).

For story telling, when recipients agree to such a partial transformation of the ordinarily operative turn-taking organization, the locus of monitoring for the possible end of the current speaker's talking shifts from these "turn constructional units" (e.g., clauses, sentences, some phrases; Sacks et al., 1974) to the story as a unit. Recipients then monitor for the arrival of that type of element in the telling that the speaker's precharacterization of the story may have projected as its point (Sacks, 1974). In other (i.e., nonstory) types of extended units as well, recipients monitor the extended discourse unit for the point at which it will have reached the embodiment of a sequentially relevant unit, given the context, and at which they may or should enter the talk with a sequentially appropriate next turn.

In the case at hand, the radio personality has understood that some such extended unit has been launched, and at a series of what might otherwise be possible completions of the speaker's turn, he indicates his grasp that the talk is not over (and his willingness to let it go on) by providing a series of these continuers, albeit in at least one case after a bit of delay. (Note that, in that case, the caller does not continue until his interlocutor eventually provides a continuer.)

We have here, then, a case of socially shared cognition in a most practical, indeed, pragmatic sense, and a procedural one as well. The cognition concerns the project in which these participants are engaged, an engagement that is at every point constituted by and renewed *as a project*, by their acting appropriately on that understanding.

The trouble arises here over the understanding of when the caller's talk has been brought to a recognizable and sequentially implicative conclusion. In brief, at a point at which the caller thinks he is done, his recipient does not perceive that he is done. Without here providing a detailed explication, this divergence can be roughly characterized along the following lines.

On the one hand, the talk is designed to do "ending a story," with the report of a recognizable final action in a course of action by one of the characters being reported in the story (Sacks, 1972b): A judge makes a disposition of a case. But in this instance, "story completion" is not tantamount to "extended turn completion" for its recipient, in part because the story has been premarked as having some bearing on another conversation previously broadcast. Although the story may have been brought to a recognizable possible completion, its bearing on the previous caller's problem has apparently not been adequately displayed for its recipient, and the project being pursued in this extended turn is accordingly not recognized as being possibly complete. And so the recipient (the host) utters another continuer.

This continuer, of course, displays to the caller that some failure of understanding has occurred. It should be noted that, in such a case, a continuer (even though it is, in effect, passing the opportunity for a full turn at talk and is, in that sense, semantically vacuous) can serve to display its speaker's misunderstanding of the ongoing talk in some respects, here with respect to its sequential status (cf. Schegloff 1982, pp. 91–92, Note 16). But the misunderstanding here does not concern the substance of the talk, either its lexico–semantic–topical reference or its action–pragmatic upshot. It concerns instead the procedural infrastructure of the talk, the organization of turns and their components, out of which the talk is built.

This contrast is, to a considerable degree, an artificial one, for it is by recognizing that a turn has been built to be complete that a recipient may gauge what it is being used to do. And, in failing to grasp what action some unit of talk is doing, and that that action has in effect been completed, a recipient can fail to see that the turn has been designedly completed. The latter is the case in the present instance. Still, this is a different type of misunderstanding from the problem in grasping the sequential implicativeness of an utterance explored elsewhere

(Schegloff, 1984, 1987), where utterances designed to do one action are instead understood to be doing another.

The form that the repair takes is also different from the form it takes in more reference- or upshot-implicated misunderstandings. In effect, the caller here provides the grounding of the story in the intended action of "help[ing] this woman that called" (last line of the excerpt). But he does this not as a simple continuation or conclusion of his telling; by framing it with "What I mean is . . ." he does it in the manner of a repair, as a re-take on what he has been doing in the preceding talk. He then recompletes the unit by formulating its sequential–functional status in the talk. In formulating it as the reason for the call, he, in effect, brings it (again) to a conclusion.

Here, as in the first "variant" examined earlier, a speaker is prompted to undertake some reparative operation on his or her preceding talk by virtue of a problem revealed by the intervening talk of an interlocutor. Although in this instance the problem is one of understanding, that problem is not in understanding some reference in the talk or the action implication of a turn, but the sequential status of the talk through which whatever is being done is accomplished, the constituting structure of the talk. And this appears to prompt a variant form for the repair.

Format Variation

In these two cases, we have noted that different forms of the turn that does third position repair seem fitted to different types of trouble being addressed. But these instances, each a singular display of its trouble type, are not alone as exemplars of this point. It may be noted as well that, when the problem involves a mistaking of joke for a serious utterance, or vice versa, or when the trouble is one in which an interlocutor has misheard rather than misunderstood, the form that the repair initiation and solution take may be different again. At the same time, all kinds of potential discriminations between different types of misunderstanding, for example, between misunderstandings of reference and of sequential implicativeness (Schegloff, 1987), appear not to engender a differentiation in the device used to deal with them.

REVIEW AND CONCLUSION

Built into the very organization by which opportunities to talk are allocated to participants in ordinary conversation is a related "understanding–display" device (Sacks et al., 1974). The consequence is that speakers almost necessarily reveal their understanding of that to which their talk is addressed, whether that is prior talk, other conduct, or events and occurrences "scenic" to the interaction. When an utterance is addressed to prior talk, its speaker reveals some understanding of that prior talk, an understanding that the speaker of that prior talk may treat as problematic. In the immediate aftermath of such problem-revealing utterances, there is a structurally provided opportunity to deal with and repair the problem of understanding. Insofar as shared understanding by the coparticipants in conversation of the import or upshot of an utterance is part of what would be meant by *intersubjectivity*, and this, in turn, is part of what would be meant by *socially shared cognition*, this discussion has been addressed to one socially central locus of socially shared cognition. It is central in that it is an inescapable element of any ordinary interaction of which talk is a part, and this is where a good part of the society's work—including the socialization and "encognizing" of the young—occurs.

The specific theme of the preceding discussion has been the following. Although in general the organization of repair is *not* sensitive to the type of problem being addressed, in the case of third position repair, we do appear to find variant forms of the repair utterance fitted to particular variant types of the source of the problem, although other types of gross differentiation are not so marked.

The underlying conception behind this discussion stresses an orientation to an organization of activities, of conduct, and of the practices by which activities and conduct are produced and ordered. This conception departs sharply from the cognitive apparatus as the focus of inquiry, and it may be useful to end with a comment on this divergence of perspective between the idiom common in cognitive science and that of conversation analysis.

Various sources have imparted to the Western cultural and intellectual tradition a decidedly individualistic and psychologistic cast. In Western tradition, it is the single, embodied, minded individual who constitutes the autonomous reality. Organized aggregations—whether of persons or of activities—tend to be treated as derivative, transient, and contingent. They are something to be added on, after basic understandings are anchored in individual-based reality. It has accordingly seemed appropriate in the cognitive sciences to study cognition in the splendid isolation of the individual mind or brain, and to reserve the social aspect for later supplementary consideration.

I have not explicitly stated, but have meant to suggest, that such a stance may be deeply misconceived, because our understanding of the world and of one another is posed as a problem, and resolved as an achievement, in an inescapably social and interactional context—both with tools forged in the workshops of interaction and in settings in which we are answerable to our fellows. Interaction and talk-in-interaction are structured environments for action and cognition, and they shape both the constitution of the actions and utterances needing to be "cognized" and the contingencies for solving them. To bring the study of cognition explicitly into the arena of the social is to bring it home again.

References

Atkinson, J. M., & Heritage, J. C. (Eds.). (1984). *Structures of social action: Studies in conversation analysis*. Cambridge, England: Cambridge University Press.
Boden, D., & Zimmerman, D. H. (Eds.). (in press). *Talk and social structure*. Cambridge: Polity Press.
Button, G., Drew, P., & Heritage, J. (Eds.). (1986). Interaction and language use [Special Issue]. *Human Studies, 9*(2–3).
Button, G., & Lee, J. R. E. (Eds.). (1987). *Talk and social organisation*. Clevedon: Multilingual Matters.
Duncan, S. (1974a). Some signals and rules for taking speaking turns in conversations. In S. Weitz (Ed.), *Non-verbal communication* (pp. 298–311). New York: Oxford University Press.
Duncan, S. (1974b). On the structure of speaker–auditor interaction during speaking turns. *Language in Society, 2*, 161–180.
Duncan, S., & Fiske, D. W. (1977). *Face to face interaction: Research, methods and theory*. New York: Wiley.
Durkheim, E. (1915). *The elementary forms of the religious life*. London: George Allen & Unwin Ltd.
Durkheim, E. (1951). *Suicide: A study in sociology*. (J. A. Spaulding & G. Simpson, Trans.). Glencoe, IL: The Free Press. (Original work published 1897)
Garfinkel, H. (1967). *Studies in ethnomethodology*. Englewood Cliffs, NJ: Prentice-Hall.
Goodwin, C. (1979). The interactive construction of a sentence in natural conversation. In G. Psathas (Ed.), *Everyday language: Studies in ethnomethodology* (pp. 97–121). New York: Irvington.
Goodwin, C. (1980). Restarts, pauses and the achievement of a state of mutual gaze at turn beginning. *Sociological Inquiry, 50*(3/4), 272–302.
Goodwin, C. (1981). *Conversational organisation: Interaction between speakers and hearers*. New York: Academic Press.
Heritage, J. (1984a). *Garfinkel and ethnomethodology*. New York: Polity Press.
Heritage, J. (1984b). A change of state token and aspects of its sequential placement. In J. M. Atkinson & J. C. Heritage (Eds.), *Structures of social action: Studies in conversational analysis* (pp. 299–345). Cambridge, England: Cambridge University-Press.
Heritage, J., & Drew, P. (in press) *Talk at work*. Cambridge, England: Cambridge University Press.
Jaffe, J., & Feldstein, S. (1970). *Rhythms of dialogue*. New York: Academic Press.
Levinson, S. C. (1983). *Pragmatics*. Cambridge, England: Cambridge University Press.
Maynard, D. (Ed.). (1987). Language and social interaction [Special Issue]. *Social Psychology Quarterly, 50*(2).
Maynard, D. (Ed.). (1988). Language, interaction and social problems [Special Issue]. *Social Problems, 35*(4).
Parsons, T. (1937). *The structure of social action*. New York: McGraw-Hill.
Parsons, T. (1951). *The social system*. Glencoe, IL: The Free Press.
Sacks, H. (1972a). An initial investigation of the usability of conversational data for doing sociology. In D. N. Sudnow (Ed.), *Studies in social interaction* (pp. 31–74). New York: Free Press.
Sacks, H. (1972b). On the analyzability of stories by children. In J. J. Gumperz & D. Hymes (Eds.), *Directions in sociolinguistics* (pp. 325–345). New York: Holt, Rinehart and Winston.

Sacks, H. (1974). An analysis of the course of a joke's telling in conversation. In R. Bauman & J. Sherzer (Eds.), *Explorations in the ethnography of speaking* (pp. 337–353). Cambridge, England: Cambridge University Press.

Sacks, H. (1979). Hotrodder: a revolutionary category. In G. Psathas (Ed.), *Everyday language: Studies in ethnomethodology* (pp. 7–14). New York: Irvington.

Sacks, H. (in press). *Lectures on conversation (1964–1972)*. Oxford: Basil Blackwell.

Sacks, H., & Schegloff, E. A. (1979). Two preferences in the organisation of reference to persons in conversation and their interaction. In G. Psathas (Ed.), *Everyday language: Studies in ethnomethodology* (pp. 15–21). New York: Irvington.

Sacks, H., Schegloff, E. A., & Jefferson, G. (1974). A simplest systematics for the organisation of turn-taking for conversation. *Language, 50*, 696–735.

Schegloff, E. A. (1972). Notes on conversational practice: Formulating place. In D. N. Sudnow (Ed.), *Studies in social interaction* (pp. 75–119). New York: Free Press.

Schegloff, E. A. (1979). The relevance of repair to syntax-for-conversation. In T. Givon (Ed.), *Syntax and semantics, Volume 12: Discourse and syntax* (pp. 261–286). New York: Academic Press.

Schegloff, E. A. (1982). Discourse as an interactional achievement: Some uses of "uh huh" and other things that come between sentences. In D. Tannen (Ed.), *Analyzing discourse, text and talk* (pp. 71–93). Washington DC: Georgetown University Roundtable on Languages and Linguistics, Georgetown University Press.

Schegloff, E. A. (1984). On some questions and ambiguities in conversation. In J. M. Atkinson & J. Heritage (Eds.), *Structures of social action* (pp. 28–52). Cambridge, England: Cambridge University Press.

Schegloff, E. A. (1986). The routine as achievement. *Human Studies, 9*(2/3), 111–152.

Schegloff, E. A. (1987). Some sources of misunderstanding in talk-in-interaction. *Linguistics, 25*, 201–218.

Schegloff, E. A. (1988). Presequences and indirection: Applying speech act theory to ordinary conversation. *Journal of Pragmatics, 12*, 55–62.

Schegloff, E.A. (1989a). Reflections on language, development and the interactional character of talk-in-interaction. In M. Bornstein & J. S. Bruner (Eds.), *Interaction in human development* (pp. 139–153). New York: Erlbaum.

Schegloff, E. A. (1989b). Harvey Sacks' lectures on conversation: The 1964–65 lectures— An introduction/memoir. *Human Studies, 12*, 185–209.

Schegloff, E. A. (in press-a). Repair after next turn: The last structurally provided defense of intersubjectivity in conversation. *American Journal of Sociology.*

Schegloff, E. A. (in press-b). Reflections on talk and social structure. In D. Boden & D. Zimmerman (Eds.), *Talk and social structure.* Cambridge: Polity Press.

Schegloff, E. A., Jefferson, G., & Sacks, H. (1977). The preference for self correction in the organisation of repair in conversation. *Language, 53*, 361–382.

APPENDIX

A brief guide to a few of the conventions employed in the transcripts may help the reader in what appears a more forbidding undertaking than it actually is. Some effort is made to have the spelling of the words roughly indicate the manner of their production, and there is often, therefore, a departure from normal spelling. Otherwise:

$\rightarrow$ Arrows in the margin point to the lines of transcript relevant to the point being made in the text.

( )   Empty parentheses indicate talk too obscure to transcribe. Letters inside such parentheses indicate the transcriber's best try at what is being said.

[ ]   Interlocking left-brackets indicate where overlapping talk begins; interlocking right-brackets indicate where overlapping talk ends.

((points))   Words in double parentheses indicate comments about the talk, not transcriptions of it.

(0.8)   Numbers in parentheses indicate periods of silence, in tenths of a second.

: : :   Colons indicate a lengthening of the sound just preceding them, proportional to the number of colons.

-         A hyphen indicates an abrupt cut-off or self-interruptions of the sound in progress indicated by the preceding letter(s).

He says   Underlining indicates stress or emphasis.

A fuller glossary of notational conventions can be found in Sacks et al., 1974, and in Atkinson and Heritage, 1984, pp. ix–xvii.

CHAPTER 9

CONSTRUCTING SHARED COMMUNICATIVE ENVIRONMENTS

ROBERT M. KRAUSS AND SUSAN R. FUSSELL

INTRODUCTION

Communication is generally understood to require a foundation of knowledge and terminology that participants take to be *shared*—that is, assumed by each partic- ipant to be known by each of the other participants. One way of characterizing this body of shared information is in terms of what Clark and his colleagues (Clark, 1985; Clark & Carlson, 1982; Clark & Marshall, 1981) have called *common ground* or *mutual knowledge*—the information, beliefs, attitudes, and so on that participants share, know they share, and know that all other participants know they share, and so on ad infinitum. Although theorists differ as to the precise nature of this shared knowledge base (Johnson-Laird, 1982; Sperber & Wilson, 1986), there is no disagreement with the general proposition that communicators must formulate a "shared communicative environment" in which their talk will be comprehensible.

In this chapter we will focus on the question of how communicators construct such common frameworks. We contend that communicators are seldom able to define their shared communicative environment with anything approaching cer- tainty. As a result, such constructions are of necessity tentative and probabilistic, resembling hypotheses that participants continuously modify and reformulate on the basis of additional evidence. Because there are no simple mechanisms for identifying common ground, speakers and hearers may form different hypotheses using different sources of information. On some occasions, a message itself will be sufficient to induce the necessary common ground (Rommetveit, 1974); at other times, the discrepancies between a speaker's and an addressee's perspectives may be so great as to preclude understanding. We will use the terms *common ground* and *mutual knowledge* to refer to these hypotheses about what is shared and (at least partially) known to be shared between oneself and one's interlocutors.

The degree of difficulty participants will experience in constructing a shared communicative environment will be determined in part by the kinds of relevant information they have about their fellow interlocutors. Although many different types of social knowledge may be involved in the creation of shared communicative environments (e.g., participants' plans, attitudes, social relationships; Clark, 1985; Krauss & Fussell, 1990), in this chapter we will focus on interactants' assessments of one another's background knowledge and perspectives. In the absence of direct information about what others know or do not know, communicators must try to infer what is *mutually* known. With people about whom one has little information, these inferences may, of necessity, be remote. To speak understandably and to understand what others are saying, a communicator must make a great many assumptions about what other participants do and do not know, and about the assumptions they are likely to make about what others know. To a substantial degree, the ability to communicate effectively is dependent on the correctness of these assumptions. In this chapter we will review research on referential communication that bears on the processes of constructing and using shared communicative environments in communication, and discuss some issues this research raises.

SOURCES OF INFORMATION FOR COMMON GROUND HYPOTHESES

We believe that communicators use two interrelated sources of evidence to construct hypotheses about the contents of their shared communicative environments: prior beliefs and expectations about others, and feedback that derives from the dynamics of interaction.

Prior Beliefs and Expectations About Others

One source of information about what is shared is the communicator's prior knowledge and beliefs about what others know. These suppositions may come from a variety of sources that vary along a continuum of directness of knowledge, and the strength or confidence with which they are held may depend on the basis from which they are derived. At one end of the continuum is the direct personal knowledge we have of particular individuals. If, for instance, John tells Mary that he attended a Yankee game and was elated by their come-from-behind win in the 12th inning, this information would be part of the common ground between John and Mary. Of course, it is not necessary to state something explicitly in order for it to be mutually known. If John and Mary had attended the game together, and Mary had noticed John's elation (and both were aware she had noticed it), they could assume that this information was part of their common ground.[1]

Other inferences about shared knowledge derive from less direct sources. From direct knowledge about others' habitual behaviors, speakers may extrapolate to specific events that have a high probability of being a basis for common ground. If John and Mary (mutually) know that John is an ardent Yankee fan who watches all the team's games, and Mary has seen a particular game, then she may assume that the contents of that game are part of their shared communicative environment.[2]

At the other end of the continuum is information that derives not from direct knowledge of specific individuals, but from knowledge of the social categories to which those individuals can be assigned. Each individual is a member of a number of social categories, and category membership can be an accurate predictor of what the individual is likely to know. So, for example, it is reasonable to assume that a person belonging to the occupational category "New York City taxi driver" knows that, with a few exceptions, the even-numbered streets in Manhattan are one-way eastbound and the odd-numbered streets are one-way westbound. Such assumptions may be wrong—there exist New York taxi drivers whose knowledge of local geography barely goes beyond "The Bronx is up and the Battery's down"—but they nevertheless provide some basis for assuming that shared knowledge exists. How good a basis they provide depends, in part, on how confidently the person can be assigned to membership in the category and on how well developed one's expectations for category-based knowledge are.

Interactional Dynamics

A second source of evidence for common ground hypotheses comes from the dynamics of the interaction process itself. One way of characterizing this source

---

[1]Clark and Marshall (1981) proposed the *physical copresence heuristic*: Two people are mutually copresent if they *mutually know* that they both were somewhere—that is, each knows both that the other was there and that the other knows that, and so on ad infinitum. Obviously not all aspects of an event at which two people were copresent can reasonably be assumed to be mutually known, only those that are above some threshold of salience. Differences between communicators' interests may lead them to focus on different aspects of the shared context. Thus, assumptions of common ground based on physical copresence must be mediated by assumptions about one's interlocutors, and these assumptions must frequently go beyond the minimal ones Clark and Marshall suggested (that one's partners are rational, attentive, and so on) to consider their interests, motives, and other characteristics that will affect how they perceive the shared environment.

[2]Notice that John should not make the same assumption until he hears Mary talk about the game, because up to that point he does not know that she has seen it.

is in terms of what Clark and Marshall call the *linguistic copresence heuristic* (Clark & Marshall, 1981). In the course of a conversation, anything said at time T can be assumed to be mutually known at time $T + 1$.[3] In this way, individual knowledge becomes part of the shared communicative environment. However, the linguistic copresence heuristic fails to capture the dynamism and flexibility of human communication that account for much of its effectiveness. It portrays the process as one in which participants alternate in producing discrete messages, interacting much like correspondents using electronic mail. However, conversation (and similar interactive forms) permits communicators to formulate messages that are tightly linked to the immediate knowledge and perspectives of the individual participants, because it affords the participants moment-to-moment information on each other's understanding.

One of the devices by which this is accomplished is what Yngve and others have called messages transmitted in the back channel (Yngve, 1970). The brief vocalizations, head nods and shakes, and facial expressions produced by the participant who at that moment is nominally in the role of listener are a rich source of information about the state of the common ground. Such information permits the formulation of messages that are extremely efficient because they are based on a reasonably precise assessment of the hearer's current knowledge and understanding.

In the sections that follow, we will first examine research that focuses primarily on the effects of our first source of hypotheses about shared knowledge—prior knowledge, beliefs, and inferences about others—on message production and comprehension; following that, we will examine studies that reveal how interactional dynamics affect the construction of shared communicative environments. We will then discuss the nature and source of a priori suppositions about others in greater detail. In the final section, we will outline some ways we would expect these two sources of knowledge to interact in the construction of shared communicative environments and note some issues for future research.

---

[3] As with the other heuristics Clark and Marshall described, some measure of qualification is in order. Surely it is not the case that one expects his or her conversational partner to remember everything that was said in the course of a long conversation, but just how to characterize in a formal way what it is and is not reasonable to expect another to remember is not a simple job. More important, what must be shared is the interpretation of utterances, not the literal strings of words themselves. As Krauss has argued elsewhere (1987), listener's interpretations can be characterized as "meaning hypotheses," that is, as tentative understandings constructed from the evidence at hand. These hypotheses are not static entities but are modified, sometimes radically (cf. Fox, 1987), in light of new evidence or further reflection. Thus, the process of constructing shared communicative environments through the *linguistic copresence heuristic* must be mediated by one's assumptions about specific interlocutors (e.g., how they have interpreted a given utterance or how likely they are to remember it) to an even greater extent than use of the physical copresence heuristic (see footnote 1).

Suppositions About Others

What evidence is there to indicate that communicators do indeed take the informational status of a listener into account when they formulate messages? We have done several studies that speak to this point.

Self and others

The common ground we share with ourselves is both more extensive and more certainly known than the common ground we share with others, and this fact should be reflected in the messages we construct for ourselves and others.[4] We investigated this issue in an experiment (Fussell & Krauss, 1989a) in which undergraduates named a set of "nonsense figures" such as those in Figure 1. Because these figures have no well-established conventionalized names, in communicating them a speaker must pay careful attention to the common ground he or she shares with the message recipient. In the experiment, subjects formulated messages about the figures under one of two conditions. Half of our subjects were asked to name or describe each figure in a way that would enable the subject himself or herself, at some later time, to pick the designated figure out of a large array of figures; we called this the Nonsocial Naming Condition. The remainder of our subjects were instructed to name or describe each figure in a way that would enable some other undergraduate to select the designated figure; we called this the Social Naming Condition. About two weeks later, all subjects returned to the laboratory and tried to match each of a large number of names and descriptions to the figure that had elicited it. One third of the names were those the subject had given two weeks earlier; we call these Own Names. Another third were Social Names, that is, those of another subject from the Social Naming Condition. The remaining third were Nonsocial Names, those of another subject from the Nonsocial Naming Condition.

The results of the experiment are shown on the right side of Figure 2. We take as our criterion of communication effectiveness the accuracy with which a message permits a receiver to select the designated figure. It will be seen that the most effective messages were ones whose source was the subject

---

[4] It may seem odd to think of common ground as potentially problematic in messages directed to oneself, but such communications rely on common ground in the same way as do communications directed to others. In formulating messages for oneself, one must project one's own mental state at some later time. It is not an uncommon experience to be unable to make sense of a note written to oneself, which, at the time it was written, seemed transparently clear. Such incidents suggest that the correspondence between current and future states of mind can be less than perfect. Experimental evidence that we edit responses to stimuli in order to make them communicative to ourselves is provided by Danks (1970), who found that subjects naming nonsense figures for themselves to remember later give different responses from those who simply free associate to the stimuli.

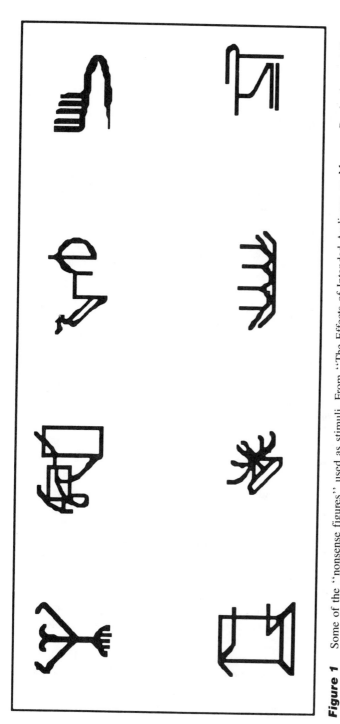

Figure 1 Some of the "nonsense figures" used as stimuli. From "The Effects of Intended Audience on Message Production and Comprehension: Reference in a Common Ground Framework" by S. R. Fussell and R. M. Krauss, 1989, *Journal of Experimental Social Psychology*, *25*, p. 206. Copyright 1989 by Academic Press. Reprinted by permission.

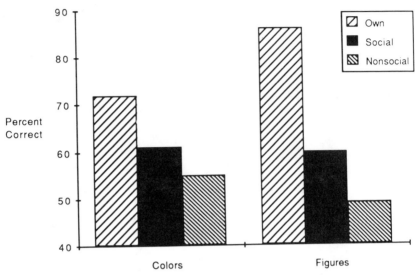

Figure 2   Recognition accuracy based on Own, Social, and Nonsocial messages. Data from " 'Inner Speech' and 'External Speech': Characteristics and Communication Effectiveness of Socially and Nonsocially Encoded Messages" by R. M. Krauss, P. S. Vivekananthan, and S. Weinheimer, 1968. *Journal of Personality and Social Psychology, 9*, p. 297. Copyright 1968 by the American Psychological Association. Adapted by permission. From "The Effects of Intended Audience on Message Production and Comprehension: Reference in a Common Ground Framework" by S. R. Fussell and R. M. Krauss, 1989, *Journal of Experimental Social Psychology, 25*, p. 209. Copyright 1989 by Academic Press. Reprinted by permission.

himself or herself. However, among messages whose source was another person, those produced in the Social Naming Condition communicated more effectively than did those intended for the source himself or herself (i. e., messages produced in the Nonsocial Naming Condition). In formulating messages for themselves, our subjects were able to use the extensive common ground available by employing arcane or idiosyncratic knowledge that one could not reasonably assume another person would have available, and to exploit perspectives that one could not reliably expect another person to take. Also shown in Figure 2 are the results of an earlier experiment (Krauss, Vivekananthan, & Weinheimer, 1968) using the same design, in which color chips were used as stimuli. The results for recognition accuracy in the two experiments closely parallel each other.

A lexical analysis of social and nonsocial messages yields some insight into the differences in language responsible for the differences in recognition accuracy. Nonsocial messages were less than half as long as Social messages, and they were considerably less stereotyped and more diverse lexically. For each subject, we computed two indexes of lexical diversity: a type-token ratio[5] and a uniqueness score (i.e., the proportion of words in a subject's messages that were not found in any other subjects' messages). On both indexes, Nonsocial messages were significantly more diverse than Social messages.

We hypothesized that these lexical differences resulted from different strategies adopted by subjects who generated messages in the two conditions. There appeared to be three ways our subjects went about characterizing the nonsense figure stimuli. One way was to describe them analytically, in terms of their geometric elements—as a collection of lines, arcs, angles, and so forth. A second way was to describe them in terms of the objects or images they suggest, for example, a "Picasso nude" or a "skinny crayfish." We call the former type of characterization a *literal description* and the latter kind a *figurative description*. A third strategy, which seemed neither literal nor figurative, was to characterize a figure in terms of a familiar symbol, specifically a number or a letter of the alphabet. We called this a *symbol description.*[6] We coded each of our describers' messages for the type of description it contained.

As one would expect, figurative messages tended to be shorter than literal ones (it takes fewer words to say what something looks like than to list its geometrical elements and describe their spatial arrangement), and this was true for both social and nonsocial describers. As Figure 3 shows, symbol descriptions, which contain both literal and figurative elements, fell midway in length between those two types of messages. The geometric elements that make up a literal description can reasonably be assumed to be familiar to virtually all college students and, hence, part of their shared communicative environment. Figurative descriptions, however, can be problematic. Although they are efficient where common ground exists, if the addressee is unfamiliar with the object the stimulus is being likened to, or cannot see how the figure resembles it, communication will fail. Hence, we would expect social describers to rely more heavily on literal descriptions and less heavily on figurative descriptions in comparison with nonsocial describers. As Figure 4 shows, although the preponderance of messages in both conditions is figurative, social describers produce more literal descriptions and fewer figurative descriptions than nonsocial describers. The proportion of symbol descriptions is just about identical in the two conditions.

To examine the relationship between common ground and communicative effectiveness, we categorized each figurative description in terms of the primary

---

[5]A type-token ratio is the number of different words in a speaker's messages (types) divided by the total number of words (tokens).

[6]The symbol descriptions were quite diverse in form and probably do not represent a distinctive naming strategy. Some were holistic ("capital G" to describe a whole figure), whereas others were rather analytic ("E, backward 4, and angle"). One reason for using the symbol description category is that it reduces the heterogeneity of the other two categories.

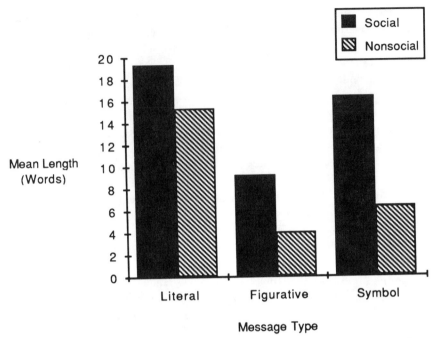

Figure 3   Mean description length by message type and describing condition. From "The Effects of Intended Audience on Message Production and Comprehension: Reference in a Common Ground Framework" by S. R. Fussell and R. M. Krauss, 1989, *Journal of Experimental Social Psychology*, *25*, p. 211. Copyright 1989 by Academic Press. Adapted by permission.

concept or image it used (typically the head noun) and then divided our messages into those in which the primary concept was *shared* (i.e., occurred in seven or more descriptions of a given stimulus) and those in which it was *idiosyncratic* (i.e., occurred in fewer than seven descriptions). This enabled us to examine the relationship between message type and communication effectiveness, with the figurative descriptions divided into those whose primary concept was shared or idiosyncratic. Recognition accuracy for subjects using their own descriptions was about the same for the two message types (regardless of whether they were in the social or nonsocial describing condition). However, accuracy of performance using the descriptions of others did depend on message type. The data are shown in Figure 5. Subjects were most accurate using literal descriptions, next most accurate with figurative descriptions (with the the shared and idiosyncratic categories combined), and least accurate with symbol descriptions. But for figurative messages, the accuracy resulting from shared and idiosyncratic descriptions differs markedly. Shared figurative descriptions are about as good as literal descriptions, whereas the idiosyncratic figurative descriptions are considerably worse than literal ones. Note also that the shared figurative descriptions generated in the nonsocial naming

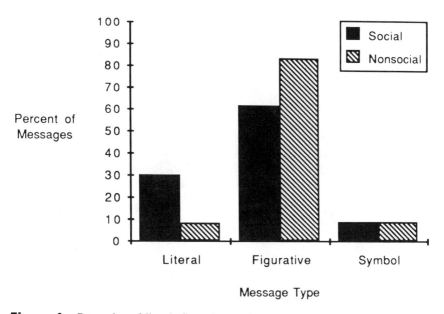

Figure 4   Proportion of literal, figurative, and symbol-based descriptions in the two describing conditions. From "The Effects of Intended Audience on Message Production and Comprehension: Reference in a Common Ground Framework" by S. R. Fussell and R. M. Krauss, 1989, *Journal of Experimental Social Psychology*, *25*, p. 212. Copyright 1989 by Academic Press. Reprinted by permission.

condition elicit the same percentage of correct identifications as those generated in the social naming condition.

These results fit nicely with an interpretation in terms of common ground. An idiosyncratic figurative description reflects a perspective on a stimulus figure voiced by one, and only one, subject. It seems reasonable to assume that at least some proportion of these descriptions reflects a miscalculation of the contents of the shared communicative environment—believing that others would view the figure from the same perspective as the subject himself or herself did. Of course, this is precisely the circumstance under which we would expect to find poor communication, and that is indeed where we find it.

Friends versus strangers

The distinction between *self* and *other* is rather rudimentary. We wondered whether it could be shown that people differentiate between message recipients when neither recipient is the self. Using the same experimental paradigm, we recruited pairs of subjects who identified themselves as friends (Fussell & Krauss, 1989b). Then we had each subject label the nonsense figures so that his or her friend could identify them. About two weeks later, we had all our subjects return and try to

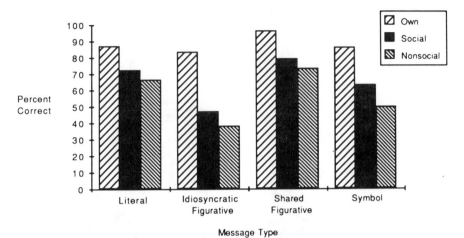

Figure 5   Identification accuracy from Self, Other–Social, and Other–Nonsocial messages for four message types. From "The Effects of Intended Audience on Message Production and Comprehension: Reference in a Common Ground Framework" by S. R. Fussell and R. M. Krauss, 1989, *Journal of Experimental Social Psychology*, *25*, p. 214. Copyright 1989 by Academic Press. Reprinted by permission.

identify the nonsense figures on the basis of three types of names: the names that the subject had generated (Own Names), the names the subject's friend had generated (Friend's Names), and the names that a randomly selected other subject had generated for his or her friend (Stranger's Names). As Figure 6 illustrates, the three types of names produced differences in how accurately a receiver could identify the nonsense figures. As in the previous experiments, subjects were most accurate using names they themselves had generated. But, in using names formulated by some other person, they were more accurate using names formulated specifically for them (i.e., Friend's Names) than they were using names formulated for some other person (i.e., Stranger's Names). Although the margin of difference between the Friend's and Stranger's Names conditions is small—only about five percent—it is reliable statistically.

These results provide stronger support for the common ground hypothesis than the relatively narrow margin of difference between the Friend and Stranger conditions would lead one to conclude, because the experimental situation was one that would minimize the likelihood of finding such differences. Our subject population was quite homogeneous and shared considerable background knowledge; all were undergraduates enrolled in the same introductory psychology course. Theoretically, the common ground between two randomly selected subjects would be considerable. In addition, most of the "friendships" in our study were of recent vintage and relatively superficial; some of our subjects did not even know their "friend's" last name. Few of our pairs were true intimates. That we should have

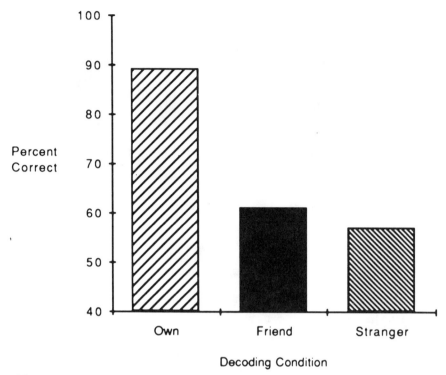

Decoding Condition

Figure 6   Identification accuracy for Own, Friend's, and Stranger's names. From "Understanding Friends and Strangers: The Effects of Audience Design on Message Comprehension" by S. R. Fussell and R. M. Krauss, 1989, *European Journal of Social Psychology*, *19*, p. 515.

found *any* differences under such unfavorable circumstances underscores our subjects' skill in exploiting the common ground that existed between themselves and their addressee. In an experiment in which subjects were true intimates (for example, married couples) or in which there was substantial diversity in background knowledge (for example, subjects from different cultural backgrounds), we would expect to find considerably larger differences. Similarly, in situations that accentuate privately shared knowledge or restrict the use of community common ground (Clark & Schaefer, 1987), messages addressed to a friend should be much better understood by that friend than by others.

Common ground and category membership
In communicating with friends, people are likely to have direct and detailed knowledge of the information they share with their intended recipient. But people frequently communicate with individuals whom they have never met before, and about whom they know only that they are members of certain communities or

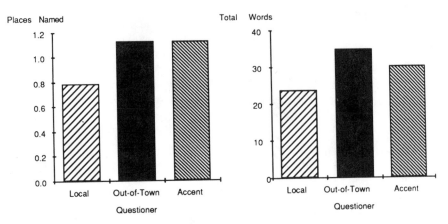

Figure 7   Number of words in response and number of places named as function of questioner condition. *Manipulating the Amount of Information Obtained From a Person Giving Directions* by D. Kingsbury, 1968, Unpublished honors thesis, Harvard University, Cambridge, MA.

social categories. Is there any evidence that senders make differentiations among receivers when all they have available is knowledge of the recipient's community membership? A field experiment by Douglas Kingsbury (1968) suggests that they do. Kingsbury stopped randomly selected male pedestrians in downtown Boston and asked for directions to Jordan Marsh, a well-known local department store about six blocks away. To a third of the people he stopped, he said, "Can you tell me how to get to Jordan Marsh?" To another third, he prefaced his question with "I'm from out of town." To the remaining third, he asked the unprefaced question but used what he called a rural Missouri accent. He covertly tape-recorded their responses.

Kingsbury transcribed these responses and performed a variety of analyses on them. We will discuss only two: the total number of words in the respondent's directions and the number of places en route to the destination referred to by the respondent. As shown in Figure 7, when Kingsbury prefaced his question with "I'm from out of town," he received longer and more detailed responses than he did to the unprefaced question. In a sense, this is not particularly surprising. By the maxim of relevance, when Kingsbury prefaced his question by stating that he was from out of town, he was implicitly indicating something about the information he lacked.[7] What is more surprising is that the rural Missouri accent—exotic even in cosmopolitan Boston—produced results quite similar to the explicit statement. It seems reasonable to assume that respondents assigned the questioner to a category of persons who lack certain kinds of local information, and that they inferred this from his speech.

---

[7]For example, one would not say, "I'm from out of town. Can you tell me what time it is?"

The studies reviewed in this section suggest that prior knowledge or suppositions about others' characteristics, whether from category membership or from more direct personal knowledge, are incorporated into communicators' hypotheses about what is mutually known and, thus, what should be explicitly stated in their messages. Even when the target is some vague "other person," the speaker must make *some* assumptions about what that person knows. The assumptions may be general (e.g., that the recipient will know the referent of the word *indigo* or will not know what an inductorium looks like), but without some such assumptions the speaker would have no reason for differentiating between messages for his or her own use and messages directed at another person.

Interactional Dynamics

Most of the research discussed thus far has not involved interaction between speaker and addressee. As a result, communicators' hypotheses about what was shared knowledge derived mainly from our first type of evidence—prior knowledge or beliefs about the addressee. However, participants in conversation (and similar interactive forms) can participate in the formulation of another speaker's utterance: They can ask questions, paraphrase, or seek clarification. Moreover, work by Kraut and his colleagues (Kraut & Lewis, 1984; Kraut, Lewis, & Swezey, 1982) and Duncan and Fiske (1977) suggests that participants in face-to-face interaction routinely use a signaling system whose function it is to enable the interacting parties to coordinate with respect to meaning. These aspects of conversational exchanges allow interactants to construct their shared communicative environments on a moment-to-moment basis. As a result, the meanings of utterances are more appropriately thought of as a joint product arrived at collaboratively by the participants than as a property of messages encoded by the speaker and decoded by the listener (Clark & Wilkes-Gibbs, 1986; Krauss, 1986, 1987).

The evolution of referring expressions

The process by which descriptions of innominate objects are transformed into referring expressions illustrates some of the dynamic factors involved in the development of common ground (Carroll, 1985). Imagine that two people have to communicate on a series of occasions about nonsense figures that have no names and that do not bear a close resemblance to anything in particular. Typically, on successive references, a name for the nonsense figure evolves in a reasonably orderly way. The process is illustrated in Figure 8. On their first reference to one of these stimuli, most people use a long, rather unwieldy referring expression that is more like a description than a name. Over the course of successive references, this phrase typically is shortened to one or two words. Often the referring expression that the pair finally settles on is not one that, by itself, would evoke the

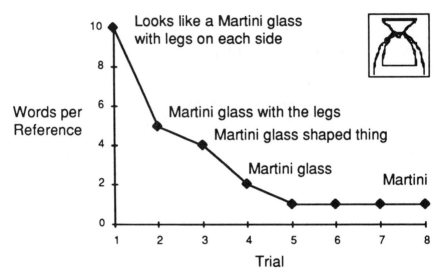

Figure 8   Illustration of shortening of referring expression over successive references.

stimulus. Its use presumes the mutual knowledge that has accrued over the course of its development. In the example shown in Figure 8, it is unlikely that *Martini*, by itself, would direct an uninitiated listener to the correct figure.

Krauss and Weinheimer (1964) hypothesized that this process of shortening was heavily dependent on back-channel responses transmitted by the receiver. Without the information contained in such responses, a sender could not confidently assume the receiver would be able to understand the message and, to prevent errors, would maintain a relatively high level of redundancy. In effect, the back-channel responses serve to establish what is and is not in common ground. If this hypothesis is correct, reducing the amount of back-channel information should affect the rate at which the sender shortens the referring expressions for the nonsense figures. Krauss and Weinheimer designed an experiment that compared the performance of dyads using bidirectional circuits (on which the receiver as well as the sender could transmit) with that of dyads using unidirectional circuits (on which only the sender could transmit). Curves representing the average number of words in the first, second, and subsequent references to the figures in the two experimental conditions are shown in Figure 9. Preventing the sender from receiving back-channel responses produced a flatter curve than did making such responses available to the sender (Krauss & Weinheimer, 1966). That is, in the absence of back-channel responses, the names used to refer to the stimuli were shortened at a much slower rate.

It seems clear that a speaker's ability to formulate efficient messages is critically dependent on information about the receiver's understanding. In the

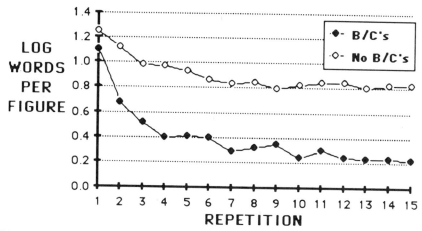

Figure 9 Change in length of referring expression as function of availability of back-channel responses. B/Cs = Back-channel responses. From "Concurrent Feedback, Confirmation and the Encoding of Referents in Verbal Communication" by R. M. Krauss and S. Weinheimer, 1966, *Journal of Personality and Social Psychology*, *4*, pp. 343–346. Copyright 1966 by the American Psychological Association. Adapted by permission.

absence of such information, the sender cannot confidently assume that the message is being correctly understood and, in an apparent effort to avoid misunderstanding, transmits messages that are highly redundant.

Effects of listener responses on message content

Kraut and his associates have examined in greater detail some of the mechanisms by which listener responses affect the semantic content of a speaker's messages. Their work has the additional advantage of having used an experimental situation that is more similar to natural conversation than the referential communication tasks used in the work discussed earlier. In one study (Kraut & Lewis, 1984), they examined how back-channel responses affected clause-to-clause relationships in the speech of people responding to questions about their personal history and opinions asked by either an active listener (who provided normal feedback) or a passive listener (who was instructed to inhibit back-channel and other responses). Using a scheme based on the analysis of rhetorical predicates (Grimes, 1975), Kraut and Lewis classified each clause in terms of its relationship to preceding clauses. They found that speakers were more likely to paraphrase or give consequences, alternatives, or limitations to previous information when addressing an active (as opposed to a passive) listener; in contrast, they were more likely to elaborate on previous information when addressing a passive listener.

In a second study, speakers narrated the plot of a cowboy movie they had just seen to a listener, who then took a set of objective tests to determine the extent of his or her knowledge of the movie (Kraut et al., 1982). Listeners were either allowed to respond to the speaker in a normal fashion or were restricted to back-channel communication. For each listener there was a yoked control (an "eavesdropper") who heard everything the speaker said but was unable to interact with him or her. On a variety of measures, it was shown that both listeners and eavesdroppers understood better when the listener provided more feedback (even when content was equated). Furthermore, feedback enabled speakers to tailor their descriptions to the specialized needs of the listeners: Listeners' knowledge of the movie's plot was superior to that of eavesdroppers, despite the fact that both had access to the same information. Similar results are reported by Schober & Clark (1989).

The Source and Nature of Prior Suppositions About Others

The studies discussed above have focused on the effects of perceived knowledge (either from general intuitions about another student or one's friends, or through the interactional construction of common ground) on message form. We have not, however, addressed the perspective-taking process in detail. Characterizing exactly what is assumed known and why is important in understanding how shared communicative environments are created. Although these issues arise both for prior expectations about knowledge and for the interpretation of interactional feedback, we will focus here on prior suppositions about what others know.

One approach to these issues is provided by Clark and Marshall's (1981) "community co-membership" heuristic: Communicators may identify their shared group memberships, from which they can infer that the body of knowledge common to this group membership is mutually known. Of course, it is not essential that participants have identical reasons for knowing something. One person might be able to identify the Chrysler Building because she is a longtime New York City resident, another, because he is an expert on urban architecture. As long as the participants can classify each other as New Yorker and architectural expert, and both (mutually) acknowledge these categorizations as being reasonable bases for recognizing the Chrysler Building, they can assume it is part of their shared communicative environment.[8] These different bases of knowing, however, may lead to different predictions about how likely each person is to possess related information, for example, about a frequently encountered but architecturally undistinguished New York City building.

---

[8]Clark and Marshall might argue that what serves as the grounds for assuming mutual knowledge in this case is the communicators' membership in a higher level category: people who know that both New Yorkers and architects can identify the Chrysler building. Although this is true, it skirts the issue of how individuals use category memberships to generate predictions about what is known.

Even if we assume for the moment that the task of identifying conversationally relevant category memberships is unproblematic (but see the discussion below), several questions arise. How, for instance, does a speaker who believes that an addressee is a member of a particular social category establish the boundaries of that person's category-related knowledge? It seems reasonable to expect a member of the category "New Yorker" to know the location of such landmarks as the Empire State Building or St. Patrick's Cathedral and less certain that the person is familiar with such arcane attractions as the Soldier's and Sailor's Monument or the Museum of Colored Glass and Light. Although some boundaries may be rooted in experience (i.e., one's previous success or failure in requesting directions from New Yorkers), in most cases the relationship between knowledge and category membership is indirect (i.e., based on suppositions about the typical behaviors and interests of category members and their effects on what might be known).

The nature of a particular category may affect the sorts of inferences that can be drawn from membership in it, as well as the confidence one has in such inferences. Some categories may be well-developed structures from which clear-cut inferences can be made (e.g., "Doctors know physiology"); others may be ad hoc groupings developed for specific purposes (e.g., "co-workers who live near my home" may become relevant when one's car has broken down; Barsalou, 1983; Murphy & Medin, 1985). Inferences from a particular category membership to knowledge may also be qualified by other characteristics (e.g., interests, habits) or group memberships of the person. For instance, other things being equal, a middle-aged Manhattanite might be thought more likely than a younger one to know the location of the Museum of Colored Glass and Light, simply because of longer experience in the city, whereas the younger person might be presumed more likely to know the location of CBGB (a night club catering to young people with avant-garde tastes) because of age-related interests.

We have suggested that determining what knowledge is shared from a person's personal characteristics and category memberships is not always a straightforward matter and may require substantial inferential work on the part of the assessor. There may be many potential sources of information that may vary in how directly they bear on what is known. On a particular occasion of language use, of course, communicators are unlikely to consider every piece of relevant evidence; instead, situational factors such as the topic of conversation or the location of the interaction are likely to shape what evidence is used to establish common ground. And the conclusions reached about the likelihood that something is or is not known will often be tentative hypotheses to be tested in the course of interaction, rather than simple yes or no decisions. To understand how people create shared communicative environments, we need to know when and how the different sources of information about others' knowledge are used to determine what those others know.

We propose that the process of determining what is mutually known is guided, in part, by communicators' implicit theories about the social distribution of knowledge. As with other forms of social reasoning, people may use a variety of knowledge structures (e.g., schemata, stereotypes, or inference heuristics) when estimating what others know (see, for example, Fiske & Taylor, 1984; Markus & Zajonc, 1985).[9] Such structures facilitate the task of drawing inferences, but they may also induce systematic errors or biases (e.g., Kahneman, Slovic, & Tversky, 1982; Nisbett & Ross, 1980) and, consequently, errors in the calculation of what is mutually known. For example, use of the "availability heuristic" (Tversky & Kahneman, 1973) may be one reason subjects in the noninteractive communication tasks reviewed above frequently used idiosyncratic and relatively noncommunicative figurative expressions: The high availability of their own perspective led them to overestimate the degree to which it would be shared by others. Similarly, the ease with which people can think of their own labels for things (e.g., computer files and recipes) may account for their insensitivity to intersubjective diversity in labeling such items (Furnas, Landauer, Gomez, & Dumais, 1987). More generally, speakers may be liable to the "false consensus" bias— the assumption that others are more similar to themselves than is actually the case (Ross, Greene, & House, 1977).[10]

Social Categories and Knowledge Judgments

In our more recent research, we have been investigating the nature and accuracy of these lay theories of the distribution of knowledge. To examine the use of gender category membership as a basis for knowledge inferences, we (Fussell, 1990; Fussell & Krauss, 1991) had 50 subjects estimate the percentages of male students and female students who could correctly identify the objects in pictures of a variety of everyday items. The depicted entities fell into eight categories hypothesized in advance to be differentially familiar to male and female students (e.g., tools, kitchen utensils). We asked subjects to provide either the name of each item if they knew it or a "feeling of knowing" (i.e., an estimate of the likelihood they would recall it later or recognize it if they heard or saw it) if they did not.

---

[9]Curiously, although social psychologists have put considerable energy into the study of subjects' inferences of personality and emotional traits from behavioral or category information, rarely have they addressed the mechanisms by which shared knowledge, beliefs, or perspectives might be inferred.

[10]The possibility of *false consensus* bias leads to an interesting problem for the investigation of social aspects of language production, namely, how to discriminate situations in which language is not tailored to the addressee from situations in which it is, but the addressee is erroneously presumed to have the same knowledge as the speaker. The latter assumption would lead to language that is indeed tailored to the addressee but is indistinguishable from that tailored for oneself. As we argue in the text, one way to tackle this problem is to independently assess communicators' beliefs about their addressees' knowledge.

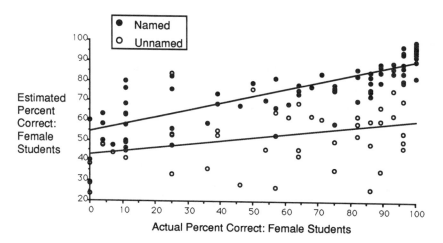

Figure 10   Actual percentage of correct identifications by female targets plotted against mean estimated proportion of correct identifications by female target. (○ represents mean judgments by subjects who know the name of an object; ● represents mean judgments by subjects who do not know the name of an object. The line intercepting the origin represents the unit line. The other two lines represent the best fit to the data for subjects who know the name [top] and subjects who do not know the name [bottom].) From ''Perspective-taking in communication: Representations of others' knowledge in reference'' by R. M. Krauss and S. R. Fussell, in press, *Social Cognition*. Copyright by Guilford Press. Reprinted by permission. Data derived from *The Coordination of Knowledge in Communication: People's Assumptions About Others' Knowledge and Their Effects on Referential Communication* by S. R. Fussell, 1990, Unpublished doctoral dissertation, Columbia University, New York, NY.

Sensitivity

The overall correlations between average estimates of the percentages who could identify the item and the actual percentages of correct identifications in the sample were quite high ($r = .73$ for male targets, .81 for female targets). Although these correlations are consistent with the proposition that subjects are sensitive to others' knowledge, they could also be the result of a strong false consensus bias: If all subjects who could identify a given picture assumed everyone else could identify it, and all who could not identify a picture assumed no one could identify it, the correlation between the mean identifiability rating for each picture and the proportion in the population who could identify the item in the picture would be perfect.

Evidence that this is not the case is displayed in Figure 10, in which the actual percentage of subjects who knew each item's name is plotted against the estimated percentage of subjects who would know it. The closed circles represent mean estimates by subjects who did not know the item's name ("unknowledgeable subjects") and the open circles represent mean estimates by subjects who did know the name ("knowledgeable subjects").[11] Knowledgeable subjects show a high degree of sensitivity to level of knowledge in the target populations (rs = .76 and .83 for male and female targets, respectively). In contrast, subjects who did not know an item's name were considerably less accurate in their estimates of how many undergraduates would know that name (both $rs \cong$ .4). This pattern of results also holds for individual subjects across items: The mean correlation between estimated and actual percentage correct was .53 and .58 for male and female targets, respectively, for those observations for which an individual knew the name, and zero-order for those observations in which the subject was un-knowledgeable.

Bias

Despite their sensitivity to differences in degree of knowledge in the student population, subjects who know an item's name might be biased in the direction of their own knowledge (Nickerson, Baddeley, & Freeman, 1987). If we compare subjects' estimates to the line intersecting the origin in Figure 10, which represents the unit line, it is clear that our subjects do not simply overestimate or underestimate all values. (Circles that lie below the unit line are underestimates; those that lie above the unit line are overestimates.) Even for items that are seldom correctly identified, estimates from subjects who themselves know the name are above .50. Thus, although knowledgeable subjects are aware that certain items are less likely to be known than others, they, like the unknowledgeable subjects, substantially overestimate the proportion of people who know the names of the lesser-known items.

Effects of category memberships on knowledge judgments

The estimates for male and female targets are, for the most part, very similar, although each plot is fitted best by the estimates for that gender. To examine whether subjects made different estimates for male and female targets, we plotted the mean difference between subjects' estimates for each sex against the actual

---

[11]Although we have labeled these groups *knowledgeable subjects* and *unknowledgeable subjects*, these names refer to estimates made by subjects who did and did not know the item's name, rather than to an individual's overall level of expertise. Hence, a given subject might be knowledgeable on one item and unknowledgeable on the next. In this analysis, we excluded from the unknowledgeable category instances in which the wrong name was given, because subjects who thought an item was something else might have quite different estimates of how many people would know that item. However, those who provided no name may also have had different notions about what sort of thing the target was, and this may be one reason for the heterogeneity of their estimates. Because results for male and female targets were essentially the same in terms of overall pattern, we have shown the results for the female targets only.

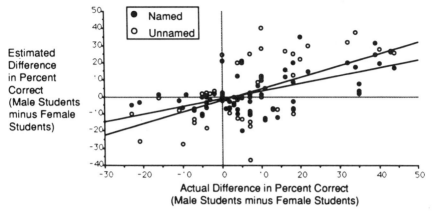

Figure 11   Percentage of correct identifications by male students minus percentage of
correct identifications by female students plotted against mean difference
between estimates for male and female students. (○ represents mean judgments by subjects who know the name of an object; ● represents mean
judgments by subjects who do not know the name of an object.) From
"Perspective-taking in communication: Representations of others' knowledge in reference" by R. M. Krauss and S. R. Fussell, in press, *Social
Cognition*. Copyright by Guilford Press. Reprinted by permission. Data
derived from *The Coordination of Knowledge in Communication: People's
Assumptions About Others' Knowledge and Their Effects on Referential
Communication* by S. R. Fussell, 1990, Unpublished doctoral dissertation,
Columbia University, New York, NY.

difference in proportions correct (see Figure 11). We have again plotted the values
separately for knowledgeable and unknowledgeable subjects. Both groups of subjects appear to be sensitive to gender differences in item knowledge ($rs = .61$
and .57 for knowledgeable and unknowledgeable subjects, respectively) and, as
the zero intercept indicates, their judgments do not appear to be biased toward
one or the other sex. Thus, although subjects who do not know what something
is called are poor judges of the relative proportion of people who know the name
of that item, as a group they nonetheless appear to be sensitive to gender differences
in knowledge. However, individual subjects varied greatly in this respect. Individual correlations for knowledgeable subjects ranged from .04 to .73, with a
mean of .44, and for unknowledgeable subjects from $-.21$ to .72, with a mean
of .36.[12]

The results of this experiment demonstrate that subjects can make reasonably
accurate estimates of the proportions of category members who will be able to
name various objects, but that their estimates are somewhat biased by their own

---

[12]Some subjects stated that they believed the real purpose of the experiment was to study
stereotyping and did not want to appear to be sexist by giving different responses for male and female
students. We would expect the correlations for these subjects to be low.

level of knowledge. In two other experiments (Fussell, 1990; Fussell & Krauss, 1990; 1991) we have obtained similar results using New York City landmarks and pictures of public figures. However, as we have reported elsewhere (Fussell, 1990; Fussell; & Krauss, 1991), although such judgments have significant effects on the creation of referring expressions in conversation, these effects appear to be attenuated when feedback from the listener is available.

FURTHER ISSUES

The research that we have reviewed (and other studies we have not considered here) both supports the notion that speakers and listeners create a shared communicative context by coordinating their knowledge, perspective, and other information, and yields some insight into the process by which this coordination is accomplished. Yet there is much about this process that we do not understand. In this section, we will address what we see as three of the central issues and domains for further work: (a) how communicators assess their communicationally relevant attributes or category memberships; (b) how prior beliefs and interactional dynamics interact in the construction of mutual cognitive environments; and (c) how the mode of communication affects the construction of shared communicative environments.

Assessing Relevant Attributes or Category Memberships

In the study of knowledge assessments described above, subjects made estimates of expertise using membership categories we provided to them, which may or may not be the same as those they make naturally in the course of everyday interaction. Understanding how shared communicative environments are established depends on an understanding of how such categorizations are made during conversations, and, particularly, how this process is affected by situational factors. The process is much more complicated than it may initially appear. A fundamental question concerns how communicators go about identifying one another's membership categories or attributes. Kingsbury's experiment suggests that speakers use their addressee's dialect as a cue to group membership and from this assumption infer what the addressees are likely to know. It seems reasonable to suppose that such features as dress and manner serve similar functions (Krauss & Glucksberg, 1977), but we are a long way from understanding the details of how this process works. It is also unclear how speakers and hearers determine those attributes or community memberships that are relevant to the construction of the shared communicative environment in a particular situation. Any addressee can be classified in various ways and at different levels of categorization. A particular individual might be categorized as an American, a male, a lawyer, a sports enthusiast, and so on. Despite the impressive body of social psychological research on social stereotypes and categories, there are surprisingly few data on people's natural categorization schemes—how they spontaneously group others for purposes of making inferences. Such data are essential to an understanding of how the addressee's communicationally relevant characteristics are assessed.

In many communicative contexts, speakers have a variety of information about addressees from a number of different sources, and some of this information may have inconsistent or contradictory implications for what is common ground. Personal attributes, for example, may modify or change category-based expectations; other things being equal, a well-dressed, formal-mannered male undergraduate might be assumed to know less about cars than a scruffy, casual one. More generally, we need to know how information about an individual's personal properties and his or her social category memberships are taken into account in the making of knowledge attributions. And, because an individual's multiple category memberships may have different (and even contradictory) implications for what he or she knows, we need to understand the combinatorial heuristics people employ in such situations.

Interaction Between Prior Beliefs and Interactional Dynamics

One might conclude from the organization of this chapter that communicators use prior beliefs and suppositions when they communicate in noninteractive contexts, and use interactionally provided evidence in conversation, but we do not believe this to be the case. Rather, we propose that in interactive contexts speakers and hearers use a combination of these two sources of information in constructing common ground hypotheses. There is a dynamic relationship between prior suppositions and interactionally provided evidence: Expectations guide the elicitation and interpretation of feedback and, at the same time, feedback leads to modifications of prior beliefs.

How prior expectations shape the elicitation and interpretation of feedback

We can identify several points at which knowledge attributions might play an important role in shaping interaction.

First, when and where feedback is elicited may be guided by a speaker's theories of what is likely to be known. Several authors (Auer, 1984; Clark & Wilkes-Gibbs, 1986; Sacks & Schegloff, 1979) have noted that communicators in interactive contexts have available a variety of referential strategies to deal with addressee knowledge that falls between fully knowledgeable and unknowledgeable. For instance, speakers may end a description with a "try-marker" (Sacks & Schegloff, 1979)—a rising terminal intonation used with a declarative sentence—to indicate that the speaker is unsure of the listener's ability to identify the referent. Because these additional referring strategies invoke the listener's participation, they reduce the share of the burden for successful communication that falls on the speaker. Nevertheless, such forms of reference require complex social inference processes to be used appropriately, in the same way that standard noninteractional forms do. For instance, overt side sequences, or segments devoted to establishing that some bit of information is mutually known, may reduce the difficulty of inferring what the listener knows, but they also run the risk of disrupting the interaction—for example, by implying that the listener is less knowledgeable than he or she actually is. Someone at a psycholinguistics conference who asked a colleague "What sort of research do you do?" would find a response that began "Do you know what a transformational grammar is?" to be offputting. The types of feedback speakers attempt to elicit, and the points in the discourse at which they attempt to elicit them, should be influenced by prior theories of the social distribution of knowledge.

Second, suppositions about a partner's expertise may form the context in which his or her responses are interpreted. Much feedback in conversation is ambiguous: Simple back-channels such as "uh-uh" or "umm" can have multiple and contradictory functions (e.g., attention vs. agreement; mishearing vs. lack of comprehension), and speakers must draw on social knowledge to interpret these listener responses and modify their messages appropriately. Social knowledge is similarly required to understand overt questions, comments, and other sources of feedback, such as the addressee's subsequent acts or remarks. For instance, what is taken as the criterion that a message has been adequately understood (cf. Clark & Wilkes-Gibbs, 1986) may depend on the speaker's a priori expectation that it will or will not be understood. When the listener is expected to have little knowledge of the referent, greater evidence of comprehension may be required.

Experience can modify the content or use of theories

During the course of interaction, each participant's apparent understandings and failures to understand the partner's messages provide feedback about the appropriateness of the assumptions on which these messages are based. For messages that incorporate category-based assumptions about what is known, this feedback can be interpreted in at least two general ways. It may be understood as an indication that the initial attribution of knowledge to category was in error—that such knowledge is not, in fact, characteristic of members of that category. If this conclusion is reached, feedback from the current interaction should affect one's theory of how category and knowledge are related and would be reflected in future communication with other members of the same social category.

Alternatively, it may be concluded that the coparticipant is an atypical member of the category or perhaps was misclassified and is not a member at all (Schegloff, 1972). The available evidence suggests that communicators are surprisingly adept at using feedback to modify their social categorizations. For example, Isaacs and Clark (1987) found that speakers who did not know in advance how knowledgeable their addressees were about New York City quickly adapted their messages to the listener's expertise, presumably by the familiarity the listener's responses demonstrated.

General theories or intuitions about what sorts of knowledge are likely to co-occur, and of the relative likelihoods of knowing various things within a given domain, may affect what a speaker assumes the addressee knows from the preceding discourse, including the success or failure of earlier attempts at reference. An addressee who earlier proved unable to identify the Empire State Building would probably be assumed to be unable to identify St. Patrick's Cathedral, regardless of how identifiable to the public in general that building might be.

The Effect of the Domain of Communication

As Volosinov (1986; see also Fish, 1980; Nystrand, 1986) has argued, coordination of perspective is important for even the most distant text. Nevertheless, different types of communication arrangements (e.g., messages transmitted face-to-face vs. those transmitted over the telephone; spoken vs. written messages) can affect the process of constructing shared communicative environments in several ways (Clark & Brennan, this volume; Krauss & Fussell, 1990; Rutter, 1987). First, different modes of communication may limit or alter the type of information one has about one's addressee and, consequently, the sorts of prior suppositions one can make. In electronic mail systems, for example, physical appearance, accent, and other information frequently used to assign individuals to social categories are (usually) limited or absent, and one must use other resources, such as message content, to make these assessments. Second, the amount and quality of feedback and the ease with which it can be obtained may vary substantially among different modes of communication. These differences may affect communicators' relative reliance on prior suppositions and current responses. The feedback intensiveness of such interactive forms as conversation may reduce the participants' need to construct utterances that are certain to be communicative; when misunderstandings occur, there is ample opportunity for correction and repair (Schegloff, 1979). At the same time, the "real-time" nature of the processing required in interaction may reduce participants' opportunities to engage in social reasoning. As a result, speakers and hearers may rely heavily on simple heuristics that lead them to make erroneous assumptions. In noninteractive contexts, communicators may spend more time considering the addressee's point of view.

CONCLUSION

In this chapter, we have argued that coordinated communication requires interlocutors to create and use a shared body of knowledge, beliefs, and so forth as the basis for their talk. In our view, this shared communicative environment is, at any moment, a tentative hypothesis constructed by communicators from two somewhat different types of social knowledge: their theories or intuitions about the addressee's beliefs, background knowledge, and so forth, and their knowledge of interactional rules and such conversational resources as verbal and nonverbal feedback. The extent to which one or the other source is relied on varies with the nature and modality of the communication, the point within the dialogue that is under observation, and so on. These two sources of information are not, of course, entirely distinct, but rather interact with one another as well as with the continuously evolving formulation of common ground.

References

Auer, J. C. P. (1984). Referential problems in conversation. *Journal of Pragmatics, 8,* 627–648.

Barsalou, L. (1983). Ad hoc categories. *Memory and Cognition, 11,* 211–227.

Carroll, J. M. (1985). *What's in a name?* New York: Freeman.

Clark, H. H. (1985). Language use and language users. In G. Lindzey & E. Aronson (Eds.), *Handbook of social psychology* (pp. 179–231). New York: Random House.

Clark, H. H., & Carlson, T. B. (1982). Speech acts and hearers' beliefs. In N. V. Smith (Ed.), *Mutual knowledge* (pp. 1–36). New York: Academic Press.

Clark, H. H., & Marshall, C. R. (1981). Definite reference and mutual knowledge. In A. K. Joshi, B. L. Webber & I. A. Sag (Eds.), *Elements of discourse understanding* (pp. 10–63). Cambridge, England: Cambridge University Press.

Clark, H. H., & Schaefer, E. F. (1987). Concealing one's meaning from overhearers. *Journal of Memory and Language, 26,* 209–225.

Clark, H. H., & Wilkes-Gibbs, D. (1986). Referring as a collaborative process. *Cognition, 22,* 1–39.

Danks, J. H. (1970). Encoding of novel figures for communication and memory. *Cognitive Psychology, 1,* 179–191.

Duncan, S., & Fiske, D. (1977). *Face-to-face interaction: Research, methods, and theory.* Hillsdale, NJ: Erlbaum.

Fish, S. (1980). *Is there a text in this class? The authority of interpretive communities.* Cambridge, MA: Harvard University Press.

Fiske, S. T., & Taylor, S. E. (1984). *Social cognition.* New York: Random House.

Fox, B. (1987). Interactional reconstruction in real-time language processing. *Cognitive Science, 11,* 365–387.

Furnas, G. W., Landauer, T. K., Gomez, L. M., & Dumais, S. T. (1987). The vocabulary problem in human-system communication. *Communications of the ACM, 30,* 964–971.

Fussell, S. R. (1990). *The coordination of knowledge in communication: People's assumptions about others' knowledge and their effects on referential communication.* Unpublished doctoral dissertation, Columbia University, New York, NY.

Fussell, S. R., & Krauss, R. M. (1989a). The effects of intended audience on message production and comprehension: Reference in a common ground framework. *Journal of Experimental Social Psychology, 25,* 203–219.

Fussell, S. R., & Krauss, R. M. (1989b). Understanding friends and strangers: The effects of audience design on message comprehension. *European Journal of Social Psychology, 19*, 509–526.

Fussell, S. R., & Krauss, R. M. (1990). *Accuracy and bias in estimates of others' knowledge.* Manuscript submitted for publication.

Fussell, S. R., & Krauss, R. M. (1991). *Coordination of knowledge in communication: Effects of speakers' assumptions about what others know.* Manuscript submitted for publication.

Grimes, J. (1975). *The thread of discourse.* The Hague: Mouton.

Isaacs, E. A., & Clark, H. H. (1987). References in conversation between experts and novices. *Journal of Experimental Psychology: General, 116*, 26–37.

Johnson-Laird, P. (1982). Mutual ignorance: Comments on Clark and Carlson's paper. In N. V. Smith (Ed.), *Mutual knowledge* (pp. 40–45). New York: Academic Press.

Kahneman, D., Slovic, P., & Tversky, A. (1982). *Judgment under uncertainty: Heuristics and biases.* Cambridge, England: Cambridge University Press.

Kingsbury, D. (1968). *Manipulating the amount of information obtained from a person giving directions.* Unpublished honors thesis, Harvard University, Cambridge, MA.

Krauss, R. M. (1986). Cognition and communication: A social psychological perspective. *Psychological Journal (USSR), 7*, 37–49.

Krauss, R. M. (1987). The role of the listener: Addressee influences on message formulation. *Journal of Language and Social Psychology, 6*, 81–97.

Krauss, R. M., & Fussell, S. R. (1990). Mutual knowledge and communicative effectiveness. In J. Galegher, R. E. Kraut, & C. Egido (Eds.), *Intellectual teamwork: Social and technical bases of collaborative work.* Hillsdale, NJ: Erlbaum.

Krauss, R. M. & Fussell, S. R. (in press). Perspective-taking in communication. Representations of others' knowledge in reference. *Social Cognition.*

Krauss, R. M., & Glucksberg, S. (1977). Social and nonsocial speech. *Scientific American, 236*, 100–105.

Krauss, R. M., & Weinheimer, S. (1964). Changes in the length of reference phrases as a function of social interaction: A preliminary study. *Psychonomic Science, 1*, 113–114.

Krauss, R. M., & Weinheimer, S. (1966). Concurrent feedback, confirmation and the encoding of referents in verbal communication. *Journal of Personality and Social Psychology, 4*, 343–346.

Krauss, R. M., Vivekananthan, P. S., & Weinheimer, S. (1968). "Inner speech" and "external speech": Characteristics and communication effectiveness of socially and nonsocially encoded messages. *Journal of Personality and Social Psychology, 9*, 295–300.

Kraut, R. E., & Lewis, S. H. (1984). Feedback and the coordination of conversation. In H. Sypher & J. Applegate (Eds.), *Communication by children and adults: Social cognitive and strategic processes* (pp. 231–260). Beverley Hills, CA: Sage.

Kraut, R. E., Lewis, S. H., & Swezey, L. (1982). Listener responsiveness and the coordination of conversation. *Journal of Personality and Social Psychology, 43*, 718–731.

Markus, H., & Zajonc, R. B. (1985). The cognitive perspective in social psychology. In G. Lindzey & E. Aronson (Eds.), *The handbook of social psychology* (pp. 137–230). New York: Random House.

Murphy, G. L., & Medin, D. L. (1985). The role of theories in conceptual coherence. *Psychological Review, 92*, 289–316.

Nickerson, R. S., Baddeley, A., & Freeman, B. (1987). Are people's estimates of what other people know influenced by what they themselves know? *Acta Psychologica, 64*, 245–259.

Nisbett, R., & Ross, L. C. (1980). *Human inference: Strategies and shortcomings of social judgment*. Englewood Cliffs, NJ: Prentice-Hall.

Nystrand, M. (1986). *The structure of written communication. Studies in reciprocity between writers and readers*. Orlando, FL: Academic Press.

Rommetveit, R. (1974). *On message structure: A framework for the study of language and communication*. New York: Wiley.

Ross, L., Greene, D., & House, P. (1977). The false consensus phenomenon: An attributional bias in self-perception and social perception processes. *Journal of Experimental Social Psychology*, *13*, 279–301.

Rutter, D. (1987). *Communicating by telephone*. Oxford: Pergamon Press.

Sacks, H., & Schegloff, E. (1979). Two preferences in the organization of reference to persons in conversation and their interaction. In G. Psathas (Ed.), *Everyday language: Studies in ethnomethodology* (pp. 15–21). New York: Irvington.

Schegloff, E. A. (1972). Notes on a conversational practice: Formulating place. In D. Sudnow (Ed.), *Studies in social interaction* (pp. 75–119). New York: Free Press.

Schegloff, E. A. (1979). The relevance of repair to syntax-for-conversation. In T. Givon (Ed.), *Syntax and semantics 12: Discourse and syntax* (pp. 261–286). New York: Academic Press.

Schober, M. F., & Clark, H. H. (1989). Understanding by addressees and overhearers. *Cognitive Psychology*, *21*, 211–232.

Sperber, D., & Wilson, D. (1986). *Relevance: Communication and cognition*. Cambridge, MA: Harvard University Press.

Tversky, A., & Kahneman, D. (1973). Availability: A heuristic for judging frequency and probability. *Cognitive Psychology*, *5*, 207–232.

Volosinov, V. N. (1986). *Marxism and the philosophy of language*. Cambridge, MA: Harvard University Press.

Yngve, V. H. (1970). On getting a word in edgewise. *Papers from the sixth regional meeting of the Chicago Linguistics Society*. Chicago: Chicago Linguistics Society.

PART FOUR

CREATING COMMON CONCEPTIONS: THE SOURCES OF CULTURAL KNOWLEDGE

CHAPTER 10

THE INFORMATION ECONOMY MODEL APPLIED TO BIOLOGICAL SIMILARITY JUDGMENT

JAMES S. BOSTER

One way cognitive anthropologists discover how cognition is socially shared is through examining how the product of cognition, knowledge, comes to have a patterned social distribution. The strategy is to study the process by examining its consequences. The process of socially shared cognition comprises the collective struggles of individuals to learn, interpret, and understand their world. In building their representations of the world, individuals learn both from what they directly experience and from what others teach them. Because they vary in their experiences and in their goals in interpreting experience, individuals vary in their understandings. Thus the consequence of the process of socially shared cognition is a patterned distribution of cultural knowledge through a community. We can use this pattern to make inferences about how people learn. The task is like that of economics: Instead of charting the pattern of the production, distribution, and consumption

I would like to acknowledge gratefully the collaboration of Carolyn Mervis and Kathy Johnson in the Amherst mammal data (the project was Johnson's undergraduate honors thesis project); Isaias Bello Perez for his help in collecting the Tlaxcalan mammal data; Jeffrey Johnson for sharing the data from the fish project; Michelene Chi for allowing me to analyze the data from her dinosaur projects; Brent Berlin and John O'Neill for collecting the Aguaruna and Huambisa bird identification data; John O'Neill for providing the scientific determinations of all specimens used in the Kentucky bird studies, as well as a successive pile sort of the birds himself; and Penny Beile for her assistance in the Kentucky bird study. I would also like to thank Leslie Clark, John Levine, Lauren Resnick, John Roberts, A. Kimball Romney, and Sara Sturdevant for their helpful comments.

of wealth, one attempts to describe and explain how information is acquired, transmitted, and used. On the basis of this analogy, I have borrowed Roberts' term *information economy* (1964) to label the model I have been developing to describe and explain the social distribution of knowledge. This chapter has two objectives: to provide a preliminary sketch of the model and to illustrate how it applies to the interpretation of several recent studies of biological similarity judgment.

THE INFORMATION ECONOMY MODEL

The information economy model (IEM) can be summarized as follows: Because culture is learned, both the degree of sharing and the pattern of sharing cultural knowledge reflect the quantity, quality, and distribution of individuals' opportunities to learn. The character and distribution of learning opportunities are, in turn, determined by the characteristics of the learners, the nature of the knowledge domain, and the ways in which the domain is learned.

Learning Opportunities and Intracultural Variation

The IEM proposes that the degree of agreement individuals can reach about a domain is largely determined by the quantity and quality of available information about the domain, whereas the "patchiness" of the social distribution of cultural knowledge is determined primarily by the patchiness of learning opportunities. Just as the degree of sharing of cultural knowledge[1] ranges from the universal to the idiosyncratic, so learning opportunities may be either ubiquitous or rare, and may vary in quality. Similarly, just as the pattern of sharing of cultural knowledge ranges from even to patchy distributions across individuals, so may learning opportunities vary from being potentially available to all to being available to only a subset of individuals. By a patchy distribution of information across individuals, I mean one in which clusters of individuals share clumps of information not shared by others.

Quantity and Quality of Information

The world is by turns a straightforward and a confusing place: Domains vary in the quantity and quality of information available about them. At one end of the

---

[1]Here I am restricting use of the term *cultural knowledge* to propositions that members of the community would regard as matters of fact, cases in which one's beliefs are not significantly affected by one's calculation of self-interest. Matters of opinion, such as political dispute, are excluded from the range of beliefs treated by the model. Extension of the model to matters of opinion is an important concern to be addressed in future work.

continuum are domains for which good quality information is freely available and there is a high degree of coherence and redundancy in the information. For such domains, learning will be easy, average individual knowledge great, and agreement between individuals high. Even in the early stages of learning the domain, novices should recognize the same underlying pattern of similarities among the items as do experts. For example, novices sort birds similarly to the way experts do, presumably because the basis for judgment is readily available by inspecting the birds (Boster, 1987). In this case, the coherence of the information is a consequence of the intercorrelation of relevant and irrelevant attributes. If attributes in a domain are strongly correlated, even if an individual chooses to attend to attributes that generally are considered irrelevant, he or she is likely to find the same pattern of similarities as do other individuals, because the attribute attended to is often correlated with the attributes generally considered relevant (but see Boster & D'Andrade, 1989). At the other end of the continuum are domains for which information is of poor quality, difficult to obtain, incoherent, or inconsistent. For such domains, learning will be difficult, average individual knowledge low, and overall agreement weak. During the early stages of learning, novices are considerably less likely to recognize the same pattern of similarities as do experts. In this type of domain, if a novice chooses to attend to irrelevant attributions, these are unlikely to be strongly correlated with the attributes that experts consider relevant. For example, it is relatively difficult without specialized equipment to monitor one's own blood pressure and to figure out the factors that raise or lower it; hence, there is a large gulf between folk and expert models of blood pressure (Garro, 1988).

Distribution of Opportunities to Learn the Domain

Although the quantity and quality of learning opportunities determine the overall level of sharing of knowledge, the relative evenness of the distribution of opportunities to learn the domain determines the social distribution of knowledge. At one end of a continuum are domains in which the opportunities to learn are equally available to members of the community. These are the domains considered by the *cultural consensus* model (Romney, Weller, & Batchelder, 1986). This model asserts that, if individuals share a common culture, give their answers independently, and have competences that are constant over all questions, the expected agreement between any pair of individuals is simply the product of their competences, when *competence* refers to an individual's degree of agreement with the culturally defined standard or "truth." For example, if Mary knows the truth 90% of the time and John knows the truth 80% of the time, they are expected to agree about (.9 × .8) or 72% of the time. As discussed below, variation in competence should be interpretable as the outcome of differences in the individuals' access to information about the domain and their motivation and skills in accumulating and organizing that information.

At the other end of this continuum are domains for which opportunities to learn are more patchily distributed, both across individuals and across items in the domain. The cultural consensus model will fit not as well (or not at all) in such domains because there are likely to be many subsets of individuals who agree with each other more often than would be expected given the product of their competences. These subsets are composed of individuals who have shared opportunities to learn, either because they share direct observation of rare phenomena or because they communicate information through the social network.

Because the social transmission of information is a common source of the patchiness of learning opportunities, one can understand the difference between even and patchy learning opportunities as a contrast between psychological and social models of the distribution of cultural knowledge. The cultural consensus model is a psychological (or individual-based) model of knowledge distribution, because it explains the pattern of agreement among individuals in terms of their intrinsic competences. Thus, it applies to situations in which one need not know the pattern of social connections among individuals to predict their agreement. These are cases in which the domain information is relatively freely and evenly available to all and the only factors that determine the pattern of agreement are the individuals' abilities and motivations to learn. Of course, there are many cases in which individuals do share much more knowledge with each other than they would be expected to share given their pattern of agreement with others; spouses, collaborators, and other intimates often share large chunks of common understanding that others do not. One can explain the high agreement between these intimates in terms of their social relationship, not their individual competences.

My use of the cultural consensus model to reanalyze data on variation in Aguaruna Jivaro manioc identification (Boster, 1986b) illustrates the contrast between even and patchy domains. (The Aguaruna Jivaro are an Amerindian group living on the rim of the Amazon basin in Northern Peru; manioc [*Manihot esculenta*], a starchy root crop, is the mainstay of their diet.) In this case, the degree of fit to the cultural consensus model depended on the rarity of the manioc varieties. When common varieties were identified, virtually all the agreement between informants could be attributed to their general cultural knowledge, because learning opportunities were fairly evenly distributed and available to all. When rarer varieties were identified, however, the deviations from the general cultural consensus were significant. The pairs of women who agreed with each other more than would be expected given their general knowledge of manioc were typically closely related kinswomen (e.g., mothers and daughters or sisters). Here, because learning opportunities are patchy, kinswomen agree with each other because they learn from one another, sharing numerous privileged opportunities to agree on names for the rarer varieties.

Explanations of Variation

By describing the pattern of intracultural variation as a consequence of the quantity, quality, and distribution of learning opportunities, the problem of explaining the distribution of knowledge in a community is transformed into one of explaining the distribution of learning opportunities. The next step is to relate the character and distribution of learning opportunities to the ways in which *individuals learn about the world*. The subject, verb, and object of the last clause (*individuals, learn, world*) indicate three complementary tactics in explaining variation. To explain variation one must ask: (a) Who does the learning? (b) How do they learn? and (c) What do they learn about?

Who does the learning?

Both the inherent characteristics of individual learners and the interrelationships among these individuals may help explain the pattern of variation among them. By *inherent characteristics*, I mean those factors that globally affect individuals' chances, abilities, and motivations to learn. The outcome of this set of factors is the individual's cultural competence (Romney, Weller, & Batchelder, 1986) because these factors influence how closely an individual agrees with the cultural standard. Motivation may stem from the individual's response to expectations created by his or her social role (e.g., occupation, sex role, kin relationships, voluntary associations), whereas chances to learn may stem from the individual's age and experiences. For example, in the case of Aguaruna manioc identification described above, women generally know more about manioc than do men because women are the principal cultivators of the society; women are thus provided the motive and chance to learn more about manioc because of their social role. Learning can be viewed as an interaction between individuals and an information source, and, therefore, constraints on an individual's chances to learn may stem from characteristics of either the individual or the information source. Thus, an individual with greater talent or motivation to learn than another can be treated as having access to more and better information. Hence, I use the phrase *opportunities to learn* to refer to the cumulative result of an individual's motivation, talent, and luck.

Although the inherent characteristics of individuals affect the quantity and quality of information available to them, the pattern of relationships between individuals affects the distribution of learning opportunities. For example, if cultural information is transmitted through a social network, adjacent individuals in the network would be expected to agree more with each other than with more distant individuals. If the distribution of opportunities to learn has an extremely patchy distribution, one would expect the amount of knowledge shared by randomly chosen pairs of individuals to be shaped largely by their social relationship

rather than by their general cultural knowledge. This is illustrated by the Aguaruna's identification of rare manioc varieties. Because the rare varieties were
cultivated by only a few women, usually only they and their close associates (e.g.,
daughters or sisters) had ample opportunities to visit the gardens and learn to
recognize the variety. Thus, social relationships were a far more important de-
terminant of agreement on the rare varieties than on the common ones.

How do people learn?

As indicated earlier, one can relate the character and distribution of learning
opportunities to modes of acquiring knowledge. There are various ways in which
individuals acquire knowledge, including direct observation of the world, verbal
transmission of information, and inference from other things they know. The
relative importance of these modes of learning depends on the sources of structure
in experience that give rise to shared understanding. The sources of structure vary
in the degree to which they are available to individuals independently of one
another. The following sources of structure are listed from low to high levels of
social mediation. The first source of structure is that inherent in the natural world
(e.g., the succession of the seasons and passages of planets, the form of plants,
and the behavior of animals). The second source of structure is that imposed on
human experience by our characteristics as perceiving, thinking, and feeling beings
(e.g., the physiology of perception, the character of the human mind, and the
nature of human emotions and drives). A third source stems from interaction with
an environment structured by deliberate human action (e.g., the layout of cities
and supermarkets and the forms of artifacts). A fourth source is regularities in
human social interaction (e.g., patterns of dominance and submission, of solidarity
and conflict, of deviance and conformity). Finally, the most socially mediated
source of structure in experience is the social transmission of information through
a symbol system (e.g., oral or written language).

Most conceptions of culture have focused almost entirely on this last source
of structure as the source of cultural knowledge. This is understandable. Of all
the sources of structure in experience, the social transmission of information is
most likely to produce a pattern of interindividual variation that reflects individuals'
affiliations in distinct social groups. In other words, social transmission of information most readily leads to systematic cultural differences among social groups.
If one were only interested in ferreting out and documenting cultural differences
among social groups, it would be appropriate to define culture so that the mode
of learning cultural knowledge is limited to social transmission. The problem with
this approach is that it is difficult to isolate rigorously learning through social
transmission from learning through other sources. Although it is natural to emphasize social transmission of knowledge as the basis of culturally specific un-

derstandings of the world, it should not be done to the exclusion of other possible sources of structure in experience.

Nature of domains

The next step in explaining patterns of intracultural variation is to relate modes of learning (i.e., direct observation, verbal transmission, and inference) and the sources of structure in experience to the objective nature of domains and the organization of cultural knowledge. The objective nature of a domain affects both the quality and the distribution of individuals' opportunities to learn about the domain. Domains vary from being directly observable and primarily defined on morphological attributes (e.g., biological organisms) to being directly observable and defined (by experts) primarily on functional attributes (e.g., artifacts), being observable only through their effects or symptoms (e.g., disease), and being essentially unobservable (e.g., spirits). Instances of categories in directly observable domains are likely to be recognized on the basis of family resemblances to prototypical members of the category (cf. Rosch & Mervis, 1976). In such domains, one would expect greater variability in attribute description than in item identification. Conversely, categories in indirectly observable domains or unobservable domains are likely to be learned primarily from other people's verbal descriptions and to be defined on the basis of the presence of a set of verbalizable attributes. In such domains, one would expect greater variability in item identification than in attribute description (cf. Frake, 1961). Furthermore, because such domains are learned primarily through verbal communication, the pattern of interindividual agreement should strongly reflect the pattern of social relations among the individuals. Thus, domains vary in the ways in which individuals typically learn about them. To the extent that a domain is learned through direct experience, the pattern of interindividual agreement should reflect the distribution of opportunities to experience various instances of the categories. On the other hand, to the extent learning comes through verbal transmission, the pattern of agreement should reflect the social distribution of knowledge and the social communication network. Regardless of the way in which the domain is learned, learning opportunities may be either evenly distributed or patchily distributed. However, information acquired through direct experience should generally be more evenly distributed than information dependent on verbal transmission or inferences from other knowledge.

One can also distinguish among several different kinds of domain information: (a) information about the morphological attributes of objects that allow them to be recognized as instances of particular categories; (b) information about the names of the categories at various hierarchical levels; (c) information about nonmorphological attributes (e.g., function and behavior) that can be learned only through sustained observation or from other people; (d) connotative meaning, or appropriate affect toward category; and (e) information about relationships to other categories (e.g., category inclusion and contrast, causal relations, and part–whole relations). Just as domains may vary in the way people typically learn about them, these types of domain information differ in their accessibility and their order of acquisition. Although the exact order of acquisition is unknown, knowledge of morphological attributes should generally be the most accessible and should be learned before the other types of knowledge.

STUDIES OF BIOLOGICAL SIMILARITY JUDGMENT

To illustrate the application of the IEM, I will use it in the balance of this chapter to interpret the results of several recent studies of biological similarity judgment. Again, the IEM proposes that patterns of agreement among individuals depend on the availability of learning opportunities. It interprets instances of high agreement or consensus on a domain as resulting from the free availability of good quality domain information to all members of the community. This raises two related questions: (a) How is knowledge socially distributed within a group when the knowledge is not limited to that particular group? and (b) What is the pattern of intracultural variation in domains characterized by strong crosscultural universals?

Cultural universals represent cases in which independent groups of people have come to common understandings of the world. By and large, these commonalties are not mysterious. After all, human beings are members of the same species, live in the same real world (although in radically different social and natural environments), and confront many of the same problems in getting along in that world. It is, therefore, not surprising that independent human groups sometimes make common inferences from common experience. However, one expects these cultural universals only in domains with a sufficiently strong, salient, and unambiguous structure in experience. According to the IEM, if the structure in experience were sufficiently strong to allow independent human groups to come to a shared understanding, that structure should be strong and freely available enough to allow individual members of the same social group to reach a consensus. In other words, the patterns of intracultural variation in domains characterized by strong crosscultural universals should show high degrees of fit to the cultural consensus model and high levels of individual competence. (Conversely, if the domain structure is not sufficiently strong and salient to allow consensus within a community, cross-cultural agreement on the domain is unlikely.)

One of the better documented cases of crosscultural universals is in folk biological classification. At least four different types of universals have been described in this domain: (a) universals in the structure of folk taxonomic systems (Berlin, Breedlove, & Raven, 1973); (b) universals in mapping of categories onto biological species (Berlin, 1973; Hunn, 1975); (c) universals in judgments of similarities among organisms (Boster, Berlin, & O'Neill, 1986; Boster, 1987); and (d) universals in choice of attributes of organisms (Boster & D'Andrade, 1989).

My own work has been directed toward documenting the last two types of universals. Boster, Berlin, and O'Neill (1986) established that Jivaroans and scientific ornithologists agree in their recognition of patterns of resemblance among a collection of South American bird specimens. Subsequently, I showed that this result is not limited to people with long experience with the birds; ornithologically naive college students substantially agreed with the Jivaroans and the scientists in judging the similarities among the same bird specimens (Boster, 1987). Finally, D'Andrade and I (1989) have argued that crosscultural agreement in biological classification is the outcome of a pan-human perceptual strategy that selects those characteristics of a collection of organisms that yield the most informative classification. In other words, crosscultural commonality has its source in the nature of individual cognition.

The final portion of this chapter will focus on a comparison of crosscultural and intracultural variation in biological similarity judgment. Biological similarity judgment readily lends itself to an examination of intracultural variation. In contrast to the first two types of universals described earlier, one can study biological similarity judgment without assuming that everyone agrees, and one can elicit similarity judgments from informants who lack an explicit linguistic classification scheme for the organisms or even from those who have never seen the organisms before. Given that the opportunities to learn biological domains are relatively freely available to all observers, one would expect high levels of agreement and a high degree of fit to the cultural consensus model, according to the IEM.

Each of the studies reviewed here elicited similarity judgments from informants using concrete (as opposed to verbal) stimuli representing different biological domains: mammals, dinosaurs, fish, and birds. Three distinct methods of eliciting similarity judgments were used in these studies: triad test, free pile sort (FPS), and the successive pile sort (SPS).[2] Different tasks elicited different amounts

---

[2] In the triad task, informants were presented with three stimuli at a time and were asked to judge which of the three was the most different from the other two. Lambda two balanced-incomplete-block designs were used in which each pair of stimuli only occurred twice in the set of triads (Burton & Nerlove, 1976). This greatly reduced the number of triads presented to informants; for 25 items, a complete design has 2,300 triads, whereas a lambda two design has only 200 triads. An informant's judgment of the similarity of each pair of stimuli was assessed by counting the number of triads (0, 1, or 2) in which the pair was judged most similar in the triad. In the free pile sort, informants were presented with a collection of stimuli and were asked to sort them into piles according to which they thought were most similar to one another. Informants were instructed to form as many piles as they wished and to base their judgments of similarity on any characteristic they chose. An informant's judgment of the similarity of each pair of stimuli was assessed by noting whether the informant had placed the pair in the same pile (1) or not (0). The successive pile sort began by asking informants to place the stimuli into piles as they would in an ordinary free pile sort. Then, the informant was asked to merge the most similar pair of piles. The informant continued to merge piles until all piles of stimuli were merged. Next, the informant's initial piles were restored, and informants were asked to split the pile they thought was most heterogeneous into two subpiles. The informant continued to split piles until all stimuli were separated. An informant's judgment of the similarity of each pair of stimuli was assessed by counting the rank order in which they were split apart.

of information from each informant, with the successive pile sort eliciting the most and the free pile sort the least. The studies generally compared different groups of informants, including groups of domain experts and novices, different age groups (7-year-olds, 10-year-olds, and adults), different cultural groups (e.g., Jivaro, Tlaxcalan, and U.S.), different regional groups (North Carolina, Texas, and Florida), or some combination of these.

Data Analysis

For each study, a correlation matrix was produced by correlating the similarity matrices derived from informants' responses. This interinformant correlation matrix was then assessed for its fit to the cultural consensus model (Romney, Weller, & Batchelder, 1986).[3] Minimum residual factor analysis was used to check whether an interinformant correlation matrix fits the model. If it does, there should be a single factor solution so that there are no negative scores on the first factor, and the first latent root (the largest eigenvalue) should be large compared with all other latent roots. In other words, the pattern of correlations among individual informants should be entirely due to the extent to which each knows the common (culturally relative) "truth." In its application to the results of these studies, a fit to the cultural consensus model would indicate that there is an overall agreement on the pattern of similarity among the organisms. The cultural consensus model also allows the estimation of individual knowledge levels from interinformant agreement: If an interinformant correlation matrix fits the model, one is justified in using the informants' scores on the first factor of the minimum residual factor analysis as an estimate of the informants' cultural competences. The competences of the diverse informant groups can then be compared. In addition, each informant's similarity judgments are correlated with aggregate similarity judgments based on either his or her own group's or another informant group's judgments. Each informant's similarity matrix is also correlated with the matrix of *taxonomic distances* (Boster, Berlin, & O'Neill, 1986) among the specimens. This measure is calculated by counting the nodes one has to ascend in the scientific taxonomic tree to arrive at one that includes both species. Because biological systematists base their reconstructions of phylogeny primarily on the sharing of morphological characters,

---

[3]The application of the cultural consensus model to similarity judgment data represents an extension of the method beyond the scope of the *formal process model* developed by Romney, Weller, and Batchelder (1986), because the original model applies only to dichotomous data. When Romney, Batchelder, and Weller (1987) and Weller (1987) generalized the consensus model to accommodate rank order and interval scale data, respectively, they referred to these extensions as *data models* to distinguish them from the more fully developed formal process model. My use of the consensus model to analyze interinformant correlations on similarity judgments would also be termed a data model and was suggested to me by Romney.

Table 1

DIMENSIONS OF DIFFERENCE AMONG THE STUDIES

Location	Domain	Method	N of stimuli	Nature of stimuli	Scientific authority
Amherst & Tlaxcala	Mammals	Triad test	25	Line drawings	Eisenberg (1981)
Pennsylvania	Dinosaurs	FPS	20	Color plates	Lambert (1983)
South East (United States)	Fish	FPS	43	Line drawings	Nelson (1984)
Kentucky & Amazonas, Peru	Birds	FPS	40 × 2	Prepared specimens	Meyer Deschaensee (1970)
Kentucky & Amazonas, Peru	Birds	SPS	15 × 2	Prepared specimens	Meyer Deschaensee (1970)

Note: FPS = free pile sort; SPS = successive pile sort.

taxonomic distance is an easily computed proxy measure of the similarities of form among species. Pearson correlation is used here as a measure of similarity among alternative classifications rather than as an inferential statistic.

Description of the Studies

There were several dimensions of difference among the studies. First, there was variation in the type of similarity judgment task performed (i.e., triad test, free pile sort, or successive pile sort). Second, there were different kinds of contrasts among the subgroups of informants examined in each study, including expertise, age, region of the country, and society. A third dimension of difference among the studies involved the nature (and the number) of stimulus items; organisms were variously represented by line drawings, color plates, and stuffed specimens. These various stimulus materials differed in their realism and complexity. A fourth dimension of difference involved the class of organisms used; these included mammals, reptiles (dinosaurs), birds, and fish. Table 1 summarizes these differences among the studies.

In the mammal study, 25 color drawings of mammals were used as stimuli in a triad test. The informants were 20 Amherst adults, 20 Amherst 10-year-olds, 20 Amherst 7-year-olds, 20 Tlaxcalan (Mexican) mature adults (ages 43 to 71), and 20 Tlaxcalan young adults (ages 20 to 45). For further details of the Amherst mammal study, see Johnson (1988) and Johnson, Mervis, and Boster (1988).

In the dinosaur study, 20 color plates of dinosaurs were used as stimuli in a free pile sort. The informants were 15 dinosaur novices, 8 intermediates, and 15 dinosaur experts, ages 4 to 7. Further details of the design of the study are given in Chi and Koeske (1983), Gobbo and Chi (1986), and Chi, Hutchinson, and Robin (1989).

In the fish study, 43 line drawings of salt water fish species were used as stimuli in a free pile sort. The informants were 15 East Florida expert fishermen, 15 West Florida expert fishermen, 15 Texas expert fishermen, 15 North Carolina expert fishermen, and 15 North Carolina novice fishermen. For further details, see Boster and Johnson (1989).

The bird study consisted of two separate experiments. In the first, two sets of 40 stuffed specimens of South American birds (40 nonpasserine and 40 passerine species) were used as stimuli in a free pile sort. The informants were 37 University of Kentucky ornithologically naive undergraduates who had been screened to ensure that they had no formal training in zoology and no familiarity with these South American birds. In addition, results of identification tasks with the birds among the Aguaruna and Huambisa Jivaro (Berlin, Boster, & O'Neill, 1981; Boster, Berlin, & O'Neill, 1986) were used to generate similarity matrices among the birds. In the second experiment, two sets of 15 stuffed specimens of South American birds (15 nonpasserine and 15 passerine species) were used as stimuli in a successive pile sort. These subsets of the birds used in the first experiment were chosen so that each had the same underlying taxonomic structure as the other. The informants were 45 University of Kentucky ornithologically naive undergraduates. Again, the results of identification tasks with the birds among the Aguaruna and Huambisa Jivaro (Berlin, Boster, & O'Neill, 1981; Boster, Berlin, & O'Neill, 1986), as well as the results of free pile sort experiments, were used to generate similarity matrices among the subsets of the birds. See Boster (1987) for additional details.

Results

The first result was that, in all five studies, the interinformant correlation matrices appeared to fit the cultural consensus model. As shown in Table 2, for all studies the ratio of the first to second eigenvalue was high (range = 4.2 to 14.3), and there were no strongly negative scores on the first factor. (The lowest value in any of the studies was − .02, effectively zero.) This indicates that, in all five studies, there was a good deal of agreement on biological similarity judgment, and any subgroup differentiation did not obscure that overall consensus. This fit

Table 2

FIT TO THE CULTURAL CONSENSUS MODEL

Study	First Eigen-value	Second Eigen-value	Ratio of Eigen-values	Lowest first factor score
Mammals triad				
Amherst	23.38	3.30	7.08	.26
Tlaxcala	7.27	1.52	4.78	.02
Both	28.93	3.99	7.25	.00
Dinosaurs FPS				
All data	15.10	2.54	5.94	−.02
No pairs	14.64	1.71	8.56	.37
Fish FPS	12.15	2.63	4.60	.06
Birds FPS				
Nonpasserine	17.45	1.22	14.30	.17
Passerine	7.30	1.75	4.17	.11
Birds SPS				
Nonpasserine	29.58	2.27	13.03	.33
Passerine	18.34	2.09	8.78	.04

Note: FPS = free pile sort; SPS = successive pile sort.

justified the use of the first factor score as a measure of the agreement of each informant with other informants or informants' competence (Romney, Weller, & Batchelder, 1986).

Second, the relationship between expertise and competence (as just defined) was variable. Most applications of the cultural consensus model have documented cases in which experts have significantly higher competence than novices; that is, they agree more than novices (Boster, 1985; D'Andrade, 1987; Garro, 1986; Romney, Weller, & Batchelder, 1986). In at least one of the studies reviewed here, however, experts did not have higher competences in similarity judgment than novices (Table 3, Part C, Fish, $t = .71$, $p > .05$). In two other studies, judgment about the relationship between expertise and competence depended on how the data were treated. In the dinosaur study, if informants making only two piles were eliminated (Table 3, Part B, No Pairs), there was a significant difference between novices and experts ($t = 2.11$, $p < .05$). If all the data were included (Table 3, Part B, All Data), however, there was no significant difference between

Table 3

COMPETENCE ESTIMATES AND CORRELATIONS WITH TAXONOMIC MODEL

Study	Competence		r[a]		
	M	SD	M	SD	n
Mammals triad					
Amherst (AM)					
7-year-olds	.61	.12	.23	.08	20
10-year-olds	.63	.13	.26	.10	20
Adults	.59	.14	.31	.14	20
Tlaxcala (TL)					
Young adults	.37	.21	.13	.11	20
Mature adults	.38	.21	.16	.13	20
AM and TL					
7-year-olds	.61	.12	.23	.08	20
10-year-olds	.63	.13	.26	.10	20
AM adults	.58	.14	.31	.14	20
TL young adults	.32	.19	.13	.11	20
TL mature adults	.35	.20	.16	.13	20
Dinosaurs FPS					
All data					
Novices	.55	.28	.41	.18	15
Intermediates	.61	.23	.50	.27	8
Experts	.54	.36	.42	.25	15
No pairs					
Novices	.62	.22	.45	.17	13
Intermediates	.71	.11	.60	.22	6
Experts	.80	.17	.58	.13	9
Fish FPS					
Novice	.36	.11	.24	.09	15
All experts	.39	.13	.16	.08	60
EF experts	.42	.11	.18	.06	15
WF experts	.39	.10	.16	.08	15
TX experts	.35	.17	.15	.11	15
NC experts	.39	.12	.17	.08	15

Table 3 (continued)

| Study | Competence | | r^a | | |
	M	SD	M	SD	n
Birds FPS					
Nonpasserine	.67	.15	.49	.11	37
Passerine	.43	.13	.20	.06	37
Birds SPS					
Nonpasserine	.80	.12	.73	.14	45
Passerine	.61	.19	.28	.12	45

Note: FPS = free pile sort; SPS = successive pile sort; EF = East Florida fishermen; WF = West Florida fishermen; TX = Texas fishermen; and NC = North Carolina fishermen.
[a]r = Correlation between informants' responses and the taxonomic model.

the novices and experts ($t = .06$, $p > .05$).[4] Similarly, in the mammal study, if Tlaxcalan informants were treated as novices in triad judgments of world mammals vis-a-vis Amherst informants (Table 3, Part A), there were significant differences between the novices and experts ($t = 8.49$, $p < .001$). However, in the mammal study, if the Amherst 7- and 10-year-olds were treated as novices in triad judgments of world mammals vis-a-vis adults (Table 3, Part A), there were no significant differences in competence by expertise ($F = .54$, $p > .05$).

In those cases in which one group (nominally experts) had significantly higher competences than another (nominally novices), they generally also had significantly higher correlations to the taxonomic model (Table 3, Part A, Mammals, Amherst vs. Tlaxcala, $t = 5.20$, $p < .001$; Table 3, Part B, Dinosaurs, No Pairs, $t = 1.96$, $p < .05$ if treated as a one-tailed test). The reverse was not true; the novices in the fish study were closer to the taxonomic model than the expert fishermen ($t = 3.07$, $p < .01$) (Boster & Johnson, 1989).

---

[4]The inclusion of extreme lumpers also worsens the fit of the dinosaur FPS data to the cultural consensus model. If the responses of informants making only two piles are removed, the fit to the cultural consensus model is substantially improved (Table 2, Part B, No Pairs). The lumper–splitter problem is a major drawback of using results of the free pile sort to assess individual differences. Boorman and Arabie (1972; Arabie & Boorman, 1973) have shown that often the pattern of individual variation on the free pile sort is swamped by differences between such lumpers and splitters. They concluded that free pile sort is useless for making inferences about individual differences. However, some recent studies (Boster, Johnson, & Weller, 1987; Boster & Johnson, 1989) have suggested a qualification of their finding: For those domains offering various possible levels of making splits among stimuli, individual differences in pile sorting will probably only reflect differences in aesthetic preferences for the number of piles. However, for those domains with a salient cutpoint (analogous to Berlin's notion of the generic or Rosch's notion of the basic level object), the differences among individuals' responses are more likely to be independent of the lumper–splitter contrast. For example, when the extreme lumpers are removed from the dinosaur sample, there is negligible residual correlation between lumping and competence ($r = .03$). Nevertheless, the lumper-splitter problem is a major reason for preferring the successive pile sort to the free pile sort.

Table 4

RELATIONSHIP BETWEEN COMPETENCE AND CORRELATION WITH THE
TAXONOMIC MODEL

Study	Mean r and SDs between INs' responses and the TM		r between aggreate of INs' responses and the TM	r between competence and INs' approach to TM
	M	SD		
Mammals triad				
Amherst	.27	.11	.43	.66
Tlaxcala	.14	.12	.39	.80
Both	.22	.13	.44	.81
Dinosaurs FPS				
All data	.43	.22	.75	.88
No pairs	.52	.18	.73	.80
Fish FPS	.18	.09	.46	.41
Birds FPS				
Nonpasserine	.49	.11	.71	.91
Passerine	.20	.06	.45	.73
Birds SPS				
Nonpasserine	.73	.14	.91	.92
Passerine	.28	.12	.46	.64

Note: TM = taxonomic model; INs = informants; FPS = free pile sort; and SPS = successive pile sort.

The third result, shown in Table 4, was that in all cases the correlation of the aggregate of informant responses to the taxonomic model was higher than the mean individual correlation to the taxonomic model. In other words, the aggregated similarity judgments are always closer to the scientific system of classification than is the average individual.

Fourth, also shown in Table 4, competence tended to be highly correlated with approach to the taxonomic model. That is, the higher an informant's agreement with other informants, the closer his or her similarity judgments will be to the scientific classification of the organisms. It would appear that often the scientific classification is close to what the target informants aim at in making their similarity judgments.

Fifth, from the crosscultural studies (mammals and birds), it appeared that competence is correlated not only with approach to the taxonomic model but also

Table 5

CORRELATION BETWEEN COMPETENCE AND APPROACH TO ALTERNATIVE
STANDARDS: MAMMAL TRIAD STUDY ALTERNATIVE STANDARDS

Informants	Taxonomic model	Adults	Amherst 10-year-olds	7-year-olds	Tlaxcala Mature adults	Young adults
Amherst	.66	.70	.97	.89	.73	.90
Tlaxcalan	.80	.86	.93	.94	.92	.96

with approach to aggregate structures derived from the responses of other groups
of informants. For example, Tables 5 and 6 show the correlations between competence and various possible aggregate standards for the mammal and bird studies.
It can be seen that competence strongly correlates with approach to all of the
standards: The more one agrees with the members of one's own group in biological
similarity judgment, the more likely one will agree with members of culturally
different groups.

Finally, in the crosscultural studies, aggregates tended to be closer than
individuals were; the level of intracultural variation was much larger than the level
of crosscultural variation. It appears that all groups of informants are aiming at
similar targets; the aggregates are much more tightly clustered around the shared
target than are the individuals. This is illustrated in Figure 1. The figure shows
a multidimensional scaling of the intercorrelations among Tlaxcalan adult and
Amherst 7-year-old informants' responses to the mammal triad task, along with
various aggregate structures. The aggregates (in caps) are clustered tightly in the

Table 6

CORRELATION BETWEEN COMPETENCE AND APPROACH TO ALTERNATIVE
STANDARDS: BIRD FPS AND SPS STUDIES

Subtasks	Taxonomic model	Aguaruna Jivaro	Huambisa Jivaro	FPS aggregate
	Bird FPS study alternative standards			
Nonpasserines	.91	.70	.73	
Passerines	.73	.71	.89	
	Bird SPS study alternative standards			
Nonpasserines	.92	.72	.82	.92
Passerines	.64	.78	.94	.94

Note: The Aguaruna Jivaro and Huambisa Jivaro aggregate structures were derived from an analysis
of their ''confusion'' in a bird identification task (Berlin, Boster, & O'Neill, 1981; Boster, Berlin,
& O'Neill, 1986). FPS = free pile sort; SPS = successive pile sort.

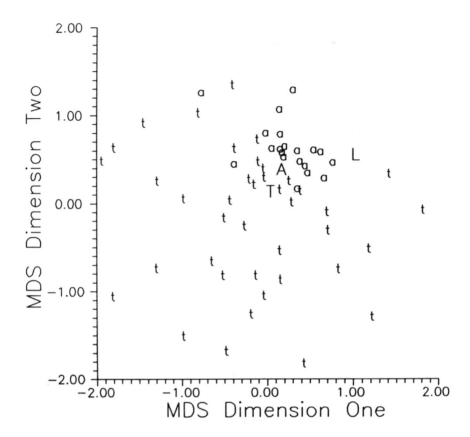

Figure 1   Multidimensional scaling of triad similiarity judgments among mammals.
a = Individual Amherst 7-year-olds; t = Individual Tlaxcala adults; A =
Aggregate of Amherst information; T = Aggregate of Tlaxcala informants;
L = Linnaean taxonomic model.

center of the space; the individual informants (in lower case) are scattered more
widely. Subject groups may differ slightly in their targets but mainly vary in their
degree of scatter around the shared targets.

   If informant groups share a common target but differ in their degree of
approach to it, certain interesting anomalies may result. For example, the Amherst
informants were closer on average to the Tlaxcalan aggregate than the Tlaxcalans
were (Table 7).

   Both the Amherst and the Tlaxcalan informants were aiming at similar
targets (the aggregate structures are highly correlated), but the Amherst subjects
converged much more tightly than the Tlaxcalans, and by approaching their
own consensus they also approached the Tlaxcalan one. This is also illustrated

Table 7

MEANS AND STANDARD DEVIATIONS WITH ALTERNATIVE STANDARDS
FOR MAMMAL TRIAD

| Informants | TM | | Amherst subjects | | | | | | Tlaxcala subjects | | | |
| | | | Adults | | Age 10 | | Age 7 | | Mature adults | | Young adults | |
	M	SD	M	SD	M	SD	M	SD	M	SD	M	SD
Amherst	.27	.11	.57	.13	.60	.13	.59	.14	.46	.11	.47	.12
Tlaxcala	.14	.12	.27	.17	.30	.18	.30	.19	.37	.19	.36	.18
t	5.20		9.81		9.88		8.90		2.96		3.85	

Note: TM = taxonomic model. All differences were significant at the .01 level.

in Figure 1, which shows that the Amherst 7-year-olds were more tightly clustered around all aggregates (including the Tlaxcalan one) than the Tlaxcalan informants were.

Discussion

The results of these studies of biological similarity judgment closely corresponded to what would be expected, given the IEM, in a domain in which learning opportunities are of relatively high quality and are relatively freely available to all observers. To review, the patterns of variation among informants showed a high degree of fit to Romney, Weller, and Batchelder's (1986) cultural consensus model: Expertise sometimes (but not always) leads to higher competence, aggregate structures are more highly correlated than individuals are, and competence correlates with approach to all informant groups' aggregate structures.

The correlation of individual competence with approach to the aggregate is a feature of those domains that fit the cultural consensus model and, more generally, an outcome of averaging noisy measures of the same phenomenon. Epstein (1979) noted, "When measures of behavior are averaged over an increasing number of events, stability coefficients increase to high levels for all kinds of data, including objective behavior, self-ratings, and ratings by others. . . ." One would expect that, when populations of individuals are aiming at the same target, aggregates will more stably and reliably hit the target than will individuals.

These patterns of intracultural and crosscultural variation in biological similarity judgment appear similar to the pattern described by Berlin and Kay (1969) in discussing the focal points of basic color categories. Berlin and Kay found that, for a given basic color category, there was much higher agreement on the focal chip across aggregates from different societies than there was among informants within a single society. In other words, there was large within-group variation and little between-group variation.

Color, like biological organisms, is another example of a domain in which there is a strong structure in experience that is not dependent on social transmission of information: We learn the best examples of color categories from our lateral geniculate nuclei (Kay & McDaniel, 1976) not through ostensive definition. This strong structure, shared by different human groups by virtue of their common phylogeny, forms the target around which individuals vary. Individuals may vary at how well they approximate the target, but aggregates of individuals will tend to cancel out the "noise" and reinforce the "signal." Because of this shared structure, it is possible to construct tasks in which individuals recapitulate the evolutionary development of color lexicons (Boster, 1986a); crosscultural universals in color classification can be explained by shared cognitive strategies used by individuals.

Of course, the source of structure in biological similarity judgment is in the world, not in the brain, and so the results of an investigation of biological similarity judgment are much more dependent on factors other than the inherent structure in the domain, such as the amount of individuals' experience with the organisms, the other kinds of knowledge they have about them, the representativeness or realism of the stimulus materials, and the design of the similarity judgment task. The inherent structure in biological domains appears robust enough to emerge relatively clearly in all these studies, but it is not as tidy a picture as in the case of color.

The contrast between experts and novices illustrates the effect that prior experience can have on the performance of the task. One might say that, for experts, the stimuli were treated as a "sign"; the specimen or stimulus item "refers" to a category with which the expert has other rich experience (e.g., photographs of fish for recreational fishermen, specimens of birds for Aguaruna and Huambisa hunters, pictures of dinosaurs for avid 7-year-olds). For novices with little previous experience or knowledge of the domain, the same stimulus item is a token only of a vague superordinate category, (e.g., South American bird specimens or salt water fish for ornithologically and icthyologically naive college students). The novices are much more dependent on the structure inherent in the stimulus item itself to guide their judgments than are the experts.

If the other experience that experts have of the domain largely reinforces the judgments one would make on morphological grounds (as represented in the stimuli), one would expect experts to agree much more highly—both with each other and with the scientific classification—than novices. This appeared to be the case in the Amherst (Johnson, Mervis, & Boster, 1988) and Tlaxcala mammal experiments. It seems that, by the time a middle-class Amherst child is seven, he or she has been exposed through picture books, television, or trips to the zoo to sufficient examples of giraffes, gorillas, and chipmunks to judge similarities among mammals more or less along the lines that his or her parents would. It seems likely that the Tlaxcalan corn farmers, in addition to potentially having greater difficulty with the experimental task itself, had not had nearly as much exposure to these world mammals and so had a much harder time supplying for the interpretation of the pictures the proper scale and other attributes of the animals. Thus the Tlaxcalans tended to judge *bear* and *beaver* as similar because both were represented as roundish and black. If the task were performed with a stimulus set of mammals local to the Tlaxcalans, I am confident that this picture would be substantially changed.

In contrast, if the experts' other experience leads to sorting on alternative criteria, experts would not be expected to agree highly either with each other or with the scientific classification. This appeared to be the case in the fish study. Boster and Johnson (1989) showed that the novices sorted fish solely according to morphological features of the fish, whereas experts relied about equally on morphological and functional or behavioral information. Consequently, novices approached the scientific classification of fish more closely than expert fishermen.

Chi's dinosaur work (1983) provides an interesting intermediate case. Many (6 out 15) of Chi's dinosaur experts chose to divide the dinosaurs into two piles on the behavioral criteria of plant eating and meat eating. These examples of extreme lumping were not well correlated with either the aggregate responses or the taxonomic model. However, if we eliminate from consideration those informants who only made two piles and hunt for higher competence and correlation with the taxonomic model on the part of Chi's experts, we find it.

CONCLUSIONS

This chapter presents a sketch of the Information Economy Model and an illustration of its application to the interpretation of five recent studies of biological similarity judgment. Consistent with the expectations of the IEM, I found that (a) the patterns of variation among informants showed a high degree of fit to Romney, Weller, and Batchelder's (1986) cultural consensus model; (b) expertise sometimes, but not always, led to higher competence; (c) aggregate structures were more highly correlated than individuals were; and (d) competence correlated with approach to all informant groups' aggregate structures.

These results suggest that, when learning opportunities are freely available, culturally diverse groups of informants can converge on a single consensus; they can agree (share *culture*) without the benefit of social information transmission. It is ironic that the cultural consensus model may work best when information is not culturally transmitted, when individuals agree by virtue of their independent insights into the task rather than by virtue of their social contacts.

Experience and expertise, however, can make a difference. It is as though the phenomenal world is sometimes available at different levels; one picture presents itself without close study, another after long experience. The existence of differences between experts and novices depends on the amount of difference between these two pictures. If what experts learn reinforces the judgments one would make on the basis of morphological criteria, experts will agree more than novices. If expertise leads to acquisition of numerous alternate bases of judgment, the truth can set the experts free, and they will have responses to the similarity judgment task that are as variable as novices' responses.

References

Arabie, P., & Boorman, S. A. (1973). Multidimensional scaling of measures of distances between partitions. *Journal of Mathematical Psychology, 10*, 148–203.

Berlin, B. (1973). Folk systematics in relation to biological classification and nomenclature. *Annual Review of Ecology and Systematics, 4*, 259–271.

Berlin, B., Boster, J., & O'Neill, J. P. (1981). The perceptual bases of ethnobiological classification: Evidence from Aguaruna Jívaro ornithology. *Journal of Ethnobiology, 1*(1), 95–108.

Berlin, B., Breedlove, D., & Raven, P. (1973). General principles of classification and nomenclature in folk biology. *American Anthropologist, 75*, 214–242.

Berlin, B., & Kay, P. (1969). *Basic color terms: Their universality and evolution.* Berkeley: University of California Press.

Boorman, S. A., & Arabie, P. (1972). Structural measures and the method of sorting. In R. N. Shepard, A. K. Romney, & S. B. Nerlove (Eds.), *Multidimensional scaling: Theory and applications in the behavioral sciences* (Vol. 1, pp. 225–249). New York: Seminar Press.

Boster, J. (1985). Requiem for the omniscient informant: There's life in the old girl yet. In J. Dougherty (Ed.), *Directions in cognitive anthropology* (pp. 177–197). Urbana: University of Illinois Press.

Boster, J. (1986a). Can individuals recapitulate the evolutionary development of color lexicons? *Ethnology, 25*(1), 61–74.

Boster, J. (1986b). Exchange of varieties and information between Aguaruna manioc cultivators. *American Anthropologist, 88*(2), 429–436.

Boster, J. (1987). Agreement between biological classification systems is not dependent on cultural transmission. *American Anthropologist, 89*(4), 914–920.

Boster, J., Berlin, B., & O'Neill, J. P. (1986). The correspondence of Jivaroan to scientific ornithology. *American Anthropologist, 88*(3), 569–583.

Boster, J., & D'Andrade, R. G. (1989). Natural and human sources of cross-cultural agreement in ornithological classification. *American Anthropologist, 91*(1), 132–142.

Boster, J., & Johnson, J. C. (1989). Form or function: A comparison of expert and novice judgments of similarity among fish. *American Anthropologist, 91*(4), 866–889.

Boster, J., Johnson, J. C., & Weller, S. (1987). Social position and shared knowledge: Actors' perceptions of status, role, and social structure. *Social Networks, 9*, 375–387.

Burton, M., & Nerlove, S. B. (1976). Balanced designs for triad tests: Two examples from English. *Social Science Research, 5*, 247–267.

Chi, M. T. H., Hutchinson, J., & Robin, A. (1989). How inferences about novel domain-related concepts can be constrained by structured knowledge. *Merrill-Palmer Quarterly, 35*(1), 27–62.

Chi, M. T., & Koeske, R. (1983). Network representation of a child's dinosaur knowledge. *Developmental Psychology, 19*, 29–39.

D'Andrade, R. G. (1987). Modal responses and cultural expertise. *American Behavioral Scientist, 31*(2), 194–202.

Eisenberg, J. F. (1981). *The mammalian radiations: An analysis in trends in evolution, adaptation, and behavior.* Chicago: University of Chicago Press.

Epstein, S. (1979). The stability of behavior: I. On predicting most of the people much of the time. *Journal of Personality and Social Psychology, 37*(7), 1097–1126.

Frake, C. (1961). The diagnosis of disease among the Subanun of Mindanao. *American Anthropologist, 63*, 113–132.

Garro, L. (1986). Intracultural variation in folk medical knowledge: A comparison between curers and non-curers. *American Anthropologist, 88*(2), 351–370.

Garro, L. (1988). Explaining high blood pressure: Variation in knowledge about illness. *American Ethnologist, 15*(1), 98–119.

Gobbo, C., & Chi, M. T. (1986). How knowledge is structured and used by expert and novice children. *Cognitive Development, 1*, 221–237.

Hunn, E. S. (1975). A measure of the degree of correspondence of folk to scientific biological classification. *American Ethnologist, 2*, 309–327.

Johnson, K. (1988). *Developmental changes in the structure of the mammal domain.* Honors thesis, University of Massachusetts, Amherst.

Johnson, K., Mervis, C., & Boster, J. (1988). *Developmental changes in the structure of the mammal domain.* Unpublished manuscript.

Kay, P., & McDaniel, C. K. (1976). The linguistic significance of the meanings of basic color terms. *Language, 54*, 610–646.

Lambert, D. (1983). *A field guide to dinosaurs.* New York: Avon.

Meyer DeSchaensee, R. (1970). *A guide to the birds of South America.* Wynnewood, PA: Livingston Publishing Company.

Nelson, J. S. (1984). *Fishes of the world* (2nd ed.). New York: Wiley.

Roberts, J. (1964). The self-management of cultures. In W. H. Goodenough (Ed.), *Explorations in cultural anthropology* (pp. 433–454). New York: McGraw Hill.

Romney, A. K., Weller, S. C., & Batchelder, W. H. (1986). Culture as consensus: A theory of culture and informant accuracy. *American Anthropologist, 88*, 313–338.

Romney, A. K., Batchelder, W. H., & Weller, S. C. (1987). Recent applications of cultural consensus theory. *American Behavioral Scientist, 31*(2), 163–177.

Rosch, E., & Mervis, C. (1976). Family resemblances: Studies in the internal structure of categories. *Cognitive Psychology, 7*, 573–605.

Weller, S. C. (1987). Shared knowledge, intracultural variation, and knowledge aggregation. *American Behavioral Scientist, 31*(2), 178–193.

CHAPTER 11

CHARACTERIZING SUPPORTING ENVIRONMENTS FOR COGNITIVE DEVELOPMENT: LESSONS FROM CHILDREN IN A MUSEUM

ROCHEL GELMAN, CHRISTINE M. MASSEY, AND MARY McMANUS

INTRODUCTION

There can be no doubt about it: Cognitive development must take place in the context of supporting environments, be these of the social, cultural, or natural world. But how should we characterize these environments? The standard account—that the more frequently novices are offered or exposed to inputs that we want them to learn about, the more likely they are to learn about them—runs into trouble as soon as we acknowledge that the young are active participants in their own cognitive development. Under this assumption, what counts as relevant is governed as much by what the young bring to the situation as by what we think.

Partial support for this work came from a Commonwealth of Pennsylvania Grant for Cognitive Science to the University of Pennsylvania. Other sources of support were National Science Foundation Grant BNS 85–19575 and BNS 89–16220 and William Smith Term Chair funds to Rochel Gelman. We thank Edward Zigler for helping us procure a Smith Richardson Foundation Grant for the Please Touch Museum.

We are grateful to Portia Sperr, Nancy Kolb, and the design and educational staff at the Please Touch Museum for their insight and cooperation. We thank Melissa Cohen, David Dryer, William Kriebel, Kathleen Letizia, and Susanne Martin for their assistance in data collection. Special thanks go to Steve Guberman and our editors, who gave us extensive feedback on a previous draft of this paper, and to Aravind Joshi and Betty Meck for their continuing support of our efforts.

Put differently, if we allow learners to contribute to the definition of relevant inputs, we no longer control the definition of relevance. Consequently, it follows that *"learner" and "teacher" need not share the same interpretation of a given input.* And young learners do not necessarily agree with our judgment that the same input is being offered on two different occasions. In short, a constructivist theory of mind forces us to reconsider both the nature of relevant inputs and the role of frequency in a constructivist theory of supporting environments.

Our efforts to create museum environments that foster informal learning about mathematics and physics underscore the above points. A comparison of our exhibits with others at the same museum offers clues as to how the young can both be served by knowledgeable others—either adults or peers—and actively select and define what they view as relevant inputs.

WANTED: A CONSTRUCTIVIST THEORY OF SUPPORTING ENVIRONMENTS

Within the Empiricist tradition, there is one criterion for what counts as relevant data for a concept: The sources of that concept must be traceable back to sensory inputs. Social and physical stimuli do not differ in principle. If it turns out that social stimuli are more effective, this is because they are more readily sensed, offer richer bundles of sensory inputs, and/or are more likely to meet the requirements of the laws of association, but not because they are social per se.

Locke concluded that the blind could not learn visual concepts or terms because they cannot detect the sensations generated by the presumed relevant source, a skilled knower and speaker pointing to pertinent novel objects and actions. It turns out that the facts do not square with our Lockean intuitions. Landau and Gleitman (1985) report that acquisition of syntax, early vocabulary, and the functional uses of language in congenitally blind children can be remarkably like the acquisition of the same abilities in normal, sighted children. For example, Kelli, one of their young subjects, would hold up an object when told to "Let Mommy see the car" and hide an object when told to "Make it so Mommy can't see the car." She also turned around when asked to "Let me see your back," but not when asked to "Let me see your front." Kelli surely had to learn the meaning of *see*; she was not born knowing the English correspondence to this particular sound, anymore than a Spanish child is born knowing that *sí* means *yes*.

Structures of Mind Look for Structured Patterns of Input

The Landau and Gleitman data are reinforced by findings that deaf children do learn to produce and comprehend language if they are allowed to reveal this capacity through their hands (Newport, 1980). What kinds of supporting inputs serve learning in these cases? They have to be structured patterns of data, as opposed to punctate sensations, patterns that can be characterized with reference to grammatical categories. For example, Landau and Gleitman (1985) show that even minimal knowledge of syntactic patterns can begin to render unfamiliar verbs meaningful. Young children can use their nascent knowledge of syntax to find inputs that feed further development of their language. See Pinker (1989) for more on this point.

Within a constructivist framework, the foregoing can be recast as follows: Young learners are sometimes more expert than are knowledgeable individuals at defining supporting environments for learning. Despite their novice status as knowers of the target language, they are "experts" on the nature of the relevant inputs for language learning because they bring structured knowledge to the flow of speech (or hand patterns) they encounter. Such knowledge, no matter how skeletal, serves to focus attention on the class of inputs that share structural characteristics with it. The environment still must provide these data if children are to learn. Because adults are fluent users of the language, they cannot help but provide the necessary linguistic environment for children acquiring language, but adults need not know what is relevant for language learning, nor need they work at "teaching" the language.

The proposal that young language learners can make guesses as to which inputs are relevant, allowing that they have nascent structures of knowledge, is related to our contention that initial domain-specific skeletal principles serve cognitive development. Given the child's active tendencies to apply whatever structures are available, no matter how skeletal or devoid of flesh these might be, these structures can still serve to start children down paths of learning that adults, too, pursued as children. As a result, although our young start out knowing almost nothing, they have reason to traverse some common paths of learning. Additionally, these skeletal structures serve as memory organizing files, making it possible to keep learned bits together in memory before they are understood to be related. See Gelman (1990) for further development of these rational–constructivist ideas.

Matters Piagetian

The idea that children are sometimes "experts" on the nature of relevant inputs is consistent with Piagetian theory, wherein children are assumed to be actively involved in seeking out and even generating data that nourish the development of their cognitive schema. Karmiloff-Smith and her colleagues (e.g., Karmiloff-Smith & Inhelder, 1974–1975) detailed the way children's tendencies to apply their implicit "theories" lead them to explore problem spaces and generate, on their own, conditions for further learning. Note that this kind of view of the environment does not assign a special role to social supports for cognitive development. It does not matter whether children find intellectual nourishment in their physical, social, or own mental world, as long as they find some suitable nourishments to assimilate to the cognitive structures they possess. Piaget would insist that whatever inputs children use as nourishing supports for their conceptual development must be characterized in structural terms.

Piaget had little to say about the relationship among social, physical, mental, and cultural supports for cognitive development. And he denied that language, as opposed to other representational formats, has a special status as a medium of thought development (Furth, 1966). In fact, the notion that the content of a domain influences the degree to which children will master it is, in a way, inconsistent with Piaget's theory, which holds that development involves the acquisition of general logical structures of mind—ones that apply across a wide range of disparate tasks and domains. But there is considerable evidence that different domains of knowledge are not all equal in form. We cannot assume that relevant inputs for cognitive development are best characterized in logical terms. Still, Piaget did suggest that peer interactions might function best to engender development, possibly because a peer is more likely to share related assumptions about the key features of an environment at a given point in development.

Matters Vygotskian

Vygotsky, and those who share a commitment to his and his colleagues' views on development, also grant the child an active role in cognitive development (e.g., Saxe, Guberman, & Gearhart, 1987). In contrast to the Piagetian position, Vygotsky and his followers are concerned about different kinds of inputs, be these cast as everyday versus scientific, or as physical, social, cultural, linguistic, and symbolic.

Of special interest to us is the pairing of a constructivist position with the assumption that adults and other knowledgeable persons lead in creating relevant inputs (e.g., Rogoff & Wertsch, 1984). Adults, or others who possess knowledge of their culture's goods, are seen as guides and nurturers of children's constructivist tendencies. The younger the children, the more this is the case, presumably because they know less and thus are more in need of having their constructivist proclivities nudged in the right directions.

In treating adults (or others who know more than a novice) as agents of knowledge socialization, theorists must consider two issues. First, we must question whether it can be assumed that such individuals have both the presumed levels of motivation and the competence required for such a role. To be sure, there are studies wherein knowledgeable adults and peers function as described (e.g., Saxe et al., 1987; other chapters in this volume). However, families' ideas on how to divide household labor do not always entail the view that adults are all-knowing, all-benevolent, and suitably motivated (e.g., Goodnow, 1990). So the question remains open about the critical role of adults.

A second important issue is that the assumption about the critical role of adults may not be consistent with a constructivist theory of mind. To hold that the environment can be defined and offered by those already in the know is to flirt with (not necessarily intentionally) a variant of the Empiricist theory of the environment. To get around this potential pitfall, it is necessary to confront an apparent contradiction. If young children share no knowledge with adults from the outset, expert and novice need not converge on the same definition of what is a relevant environment. But it is clear that cultures do transmit their knowledge from one generation to the next.

If we allow some overlap in some knowledge domains between adults and young children, we can begin to eliminate the contradiction raised above. This is one reason we adopted a rational–constructivist position. But this move on its own is not enough. We still need to characterize environments that can support the growth of these early skeletons of knowledge, can explain how children learn about their Cultural Unconscious, and are consistent with the fact that children can learn new concepts, ones that presumably go beyond the range of initial skeletal principles. Our attempts to deal with these lacunae build on what we found when we looked at how exhibits in a museum for young children influence the kind and amount of child–adult interactions, especially in terms of the matter of informal ''teaching.'' We conclude that there are multiple environmental routes to knowledge acquisition, not all of which are equally suited to all kinds of learning.

LESSONS FROM A MUSEUM

Some Background Details

Our study of museum learning was conducted at the Please Touch Museum (PTM) in downtown Philadelphia. It serves a target population of children seven years of age or younger, which means its target clientele must be accompanied by responsible adults.

The museum attracts a fairly mixed racial and socioeconomic sample of school groups and families and operates at capacity about 50% of the time, receiving about 140,000 visitors per year. A somewhat high ($4.50 per individual) entrance fee is offset by memberships or scholarships and passes to low-income groups and families. PTM is located near two science museums (The Franklin Institute and the Academy of Natural Sciences), and families can use package tickets to visit all three museums on the same day.

PTM offers both special and permanent exhibits. There are benches and chairs throughout the museum. All floors at exhibit areas are carpeted, and visitors often sit or lie on the floor. Over the four years that we have been observing, exhibit areas have featured a grocery store, a doctor's office, an accountant's office, various forms of transportation, science materials, a television studio, an Indian village, a puzzle corner, a live-animal arena, areas to dress up in costumes and masks and put on stage shows, puppet shows, and a circus. There have been special exhibits on musical instruments, number concepts, scientific concepts, different cultures, block collections, toys from past decades (some from previous centuries), and fantasy. All exhibits are designed to encourage interactions, both between members of a family and with the props. The museum also has a book-store, runs symposia, conducts workshops for children and adults, and houses significant archival materials.

The Museum as a Natural Research Setting

PTM affords a rare research opportunity. One can observe adult–child interactions without asking caretakers to be with their children. The sense that the museum is like someone's living room or a "safe park" in a large downtown city area surely contributes to its popularity, as does the fact that adults and children move around and choose activities freely, *either as a family or not*.

To illustrate why we think it is important to observe how adults interact with young children without asking them to do so, consider the difference between observing parent–child interactions as a participant-observer in a museum and observing parent–child interactions as a guest-observer in a home. In the latter case, assuming that researchers succeed at encouraging the pair to be as natural as possible, the parent still knows she or he is in at least two roles: parent and participant in a study of parent–child interactions. On the assumption that adults are cooperative participants in the study, we should expect them to render their most competent performance (Orne, 1962). Therefore, such studies can inform us about baseline levels of competence. But to determine the extent to which this competence generalizes, studies run in different settings and under varied conditions are required.

Several investigators have observed successful interactions of turn-taking between a young child and a parent, in which the adults guided their young charges' efforts, for example, to work a puzzle (e.g., Wertsch & Stone, 1985). But what if the same child knew there was a cage containing a live rabbit behind her? What if the parent had a friend in the room and could sit and talk to the adult while the child played with the puzzle by herself? What if the adult would prefer to play with blocks and could wander off to do this while monitoring the child, who preferred to sit and play with the puzzle? Under these circumstances, the child might still succeed, might be at least as comfortable as when her parent does work closely with her, and might do her next puzzle more systematically (e.g., De-Loache, Sugarman, & Brown, 1985). How would we then characterize the adult's contribution to skill development?

These considerations led us to take advantage of PTM's willingness to allow us to be participant observers (see following discussion). We could step out of our usual research roles and *pass* (to use Goffman's term) as museum staff. The institution is such that children and adults encounter a wide choice of activities that afford opportunities for exploring and learning about new and unfamiliar things. In addition to these museum activities, we also know that such museums serve as places to meet friends, to get out of the rain, to watch other people, to have fun, to eat different foods, to snack on "junk," or to go when the family decides on an outing (e.g., Diamond, 1981).

The quality of PTM as a research site is enhanced by the fact that displays are designed to take into account children's viewpoints, abilities, and interests. For example, the counters in the "life-size" Grocery Store are 2 ft high and the mirrors are only 3 to 4 ft tall. Experts on early child development are consulted in developing exhibits, and children are observed using them. The goal is to encourage interaction with the materials and with other people. In short, PTM adheres to a constructivist philosophy, in addition to meeting some of our critical research design needs. It would have been hard to create a better setting ourselves.

Before starting our observations at PTM, we made regular visits, in part to get acquainted with the setting and in part to ease into our roles of participant-observers. At the museum we wore badges identifying us as museum staff (e.g., research advisor, docent, or intern), and we behaved accordingly. When we started to observe or tape, we used PTM permission procedures. When PTM collects its own data or sets up "photo opportunities," responsible adults are asked to sign consent forms that allow for research and educational use of any tapes, data, or related material. If permission is not forthcoming, the data are destroyed or simply not gathered. On those few occasions when we were asked what we were doing or whether we had special knowledge about the exhibits, we acknowledged our university connections. The rarity of such encounters adds to our confidence that visitors treated us as museum staff rather than special guests, such as celebrities, television crews, or newspaper reporters.

As described later in this chapter, PTM's cooperation and collaboration also made it possible for us to introduce exhibits that we designed.

Different Sites, Different Interaction Patterns

Just as the exhibits at the PTM varied in type, so too did the way visitors used them. Samples of interactions at the Grocery Store exhibit and the number exhibit (1-2-3 Go!) illustrate some of the differences.

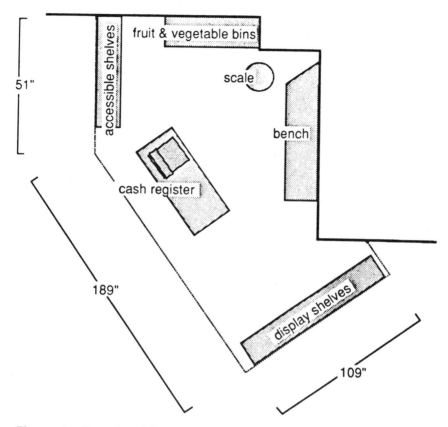

Figure 1 Floor plan of Grocery Store exhibit.

The Grocery Store: An everyday setting

In our culture, grocery stores are common everyday settings for children, especially young ones in the company of an adult. The Grocery Store at PTM, albeit close to life-size (Figure 1), is more like a neighborhood corner grocery than a supermarket. Still, the exhibit offers many of the familiar trappings one finds in both kinds of stores: shelves of food, boxed and canned goods, a scale, a checkout counter, and a cash register. The following excerpts from transcripts are based on recordings made with a flat microphone placed inconspicuously in the area.

Example 1 of grocery store talk

> [Speakers were a mother and her 2½-year-old daughter]
>
> Mother: Here's a shopping list. Look, what you have to do is find one of each picture. Tomato, lemon, pepper, corn, cucumber.
>
> Child: I try it.

Mother: Ohh, you're going to do it? Good girl. Why don't we put
           milk on your list? Let's go to the scale. We have to weigh
           it. Up, it weighs a quarter pound. How much? Hey, C—,
           you need a cucumber. You have a cucumber on your
           list.
Child: I don't want a cucumber on my list!
Mother: Well, I want a cucumber.
Child: And I can buy carrots.
Mother: First you have to put the food back, and I will help you.
           Here, put the carrots back where the pictures are, here.
           There's the picture of the carrots, so that's where the carrots
           go. Good, here's the other one, and the potato goes in there.
           Okay, here's a potato. Good girl. Here's an apple. Do you
           know where that goes?
Child: No . . .
Mother: Good girl. You put everything away. I'm proud of you.
Child: (*indistinguishable*) the shopping list.
Mother: Oh, you want to do the shopping?
Child: I wanna do that.
Mother: OK. OK, Miss, I would like 2 tomatoes. Would you ring
           up 2 tomatoes for me, please?
Child: I want to ring up popcorn.
Mother: I want popcorn, too. Thank you, that's a good idea. May
           I have popcorn?
Child: Here's . . . shopping (*indistinguishable*)
Mother: Thank you.
Child: Here.
Mother: Thank you.
Child: Here.
Mother: Thank you.
Child: Popcorn.
Mother: That's not popcorn. . . .

Example 2 of grocery store talk:

[The speakers were a mother, father, and their 4-year-old daughter]
Father: Are you going to get me some bananas? I need some ba-
           nanas. Let me have some food. Can I have some Campbell's
           soup? What else? Carrots?
Mother: Tuna. Get by the cash register.
Father: Hop up there so Mom can take a picture of you. Work the
           money.
Mother: Yeah, work the money.
Father: Work the money.
Mother: Work the money. Let me see ya.
Father: Coffee? What else? How 'bout some milk?
Child: All right. . . .

Both of the above transcripts show that parents do more in this setting than lead their children through the script of grocery shopping. They also organize the activity, in one case by encouraging their child to sort the different kinds of food and match three–dimensional replicas of the food to pictures of these that appeared on the bins. We documented this tendency of adults to introduce and organize children's activity in this area for a pilot sample of seven children (between 2 and 6 years of age) and the adults with them. Behaviors of children and adults were coded in three categories: (a) prompting, requesting, or ordering another to do something; (b) responding to another's behavior (e.g., fulfilling a request, saying "thank you" when given something); and (c) behavior independent of another's behavior. Of all the behaviors coded, 45.5% were adults' prompting, requesting, or ordering children to do something. This was by far the most frequent type of adult behavior.

Such characteristics of the interaction fit with the idea that learning occurs in natural settings because adults help structure the input for their charges (Greenfield, 1984). But some features of the interaction hardly support the idea that the young contribute actively to their own learning goals and environments. Adults in the above excerpts were very little inclined to give their children control of the interaction. Instead, they seemed determined to control the flow of events. In the first example, the mother seemed as much concerned that her daughter do the proper thing for the setting as that she have fun playing Grocery Store. When the list had a cucumber on it, the child had to get a cucumber. Before the child could buy a carrot, she had to put the carrot (plus lots of other vegetables) back where the mother thought it belonged. It remains to be determined whether such adult control served to teach.

Also of interest is the fact that talk about money, weighing, pricing, and so forth, was only at the most general level. In fact, adults said things that are decidedly inappropriate; one does not usually weigh cartons of milk, let alone talk about them in units such as pounds. If learning about quantitative matters did occur in this setting, it did so in the face of rather noisy data. Such observations are consistent with Durkin, Shire, Riem, Crowther, and Rutter's (1986) report that young children receive messy and errorful counting inputs. These observations also raise the possibility that inputs for learning about number and other quantities are more variable than we have assumed. Our observations of the 1-2-3 Go! special exhibit at PTM support this conjecture.

The How Many Box in the 1-2-3 Go! exhibit

In 1986, PTM mounted a special exhibit on numerical concepts. The 1-2--3-Go! exhibit included displays to encourage children to count, order, classify, match, establish one-to-one correspondence, use quantitative vocabulary, estimate, and assess or generate the cardinal number of collections. The How Many Box was one of the displays meant to support the latter activity.

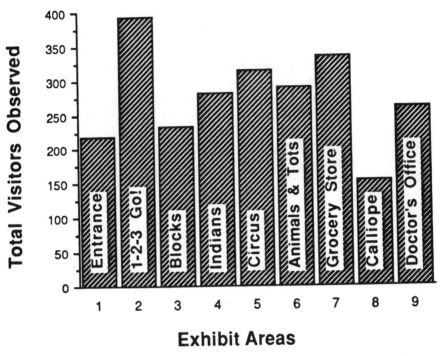

Figure 2 Distribution of visitors in different exhibit areas for observations collected from February to April, 1987.

To assess relative levels of interest in the 1-2-3-Go! exhibit, we regularly sampled the distribution of visitors at each exhibit area on the museum floor, keeping track of both the sex and age of those present during a sampling time (see Gelman & Massey, 1987 for more details). Our February to April 1987 samples of the total numbers of visitors in each of the museum areas listed in Figure 2 are typical of what we found. The 1-2-3-Go! exhibit was very popular, indeed about as popular as the Grocery Store.

Because such records showed that children and adults visited the number exhibits at the same time (Gelman & Massey, 1987), we went on to observe their interactions. Saxe et al. (1987) found that mothers who are asked to join their children in a number game are very likely to notice and then lead on from their children's mathematical goals. Children who experienced such interactions did better in the end than those who did not. The PTM setting allowed us to ask whether these tendencies generalize. For instance, do they appear when both participants have other things to do and/or do not think of themselves as cooperative participants in a research effort?

Our observations focused on the How Many Box, which was 3 ft high × 2 ft wide × 2 ft deep and had HOW MANY painted on each of its surfaces in large, black letters. In addition it had six lift-up doors on each of its vertical faces. Underneath the doors were pictures of various collections (e.g., eggs in an egg carton, legs on a chair, wheels on a bike, headlights on a car). Writing on each door completed the "How Many" question for the particular displays covered by that door (e.g., how many "headlights on a car," "legs on a chair," or "apples in this picture").

For children to use this exhibit as the designers intended, adults *had* to read the signs to them. Almost all children were preliterate. Some might think to count on their own. But they could also open and close the doors, repeatedly bang one door up and down, name the pictures, and so forth. To our surprise, adults usually did not read the few words on the sign (Gelman & Massey, 1987). Of the 43 adults observed in one set of observations, only one third asked the "How Many" question and even fewer (19%) counted or encouraged the children to count. In fact, 30% of the adults simply stood or sat off to one side while the children lifted and shut doors, labeled items, and so forth. Like Saxe et al. (1987), we found that when an adult read the signs and counted or encouraged counting on the part of their charge, that child was more likely to count than were other children who did not encounter such support. But we have to emphasize that such interactions were rare and seldom lasted long enough to guarantee that a child reached the intended goal—to determine the cardinal value of a given set. Apparently, adults— who surely are able to interact so as to encourage their children's interest in number activities—do not always choose to do so.

Different Domains: Different Transmission Environments?

Saxe et al.'s (1987) findings make it clear that parents are able to serve as *competent* teachers of early number skills. But do they take this role often enough to make a decisive difference in their children's learning? Do they do it when there is no one asking them to? It is possible that parents may not want to teach these skills and, like elementary school teachers, they may think that "experts in math" should do so instead (Stodolsky, 1988).

Recall that, although parents in the Grocery Store were quick to lead their children through details of the pertinent script, some details received more attention than others. Talk about the grocery list and what went into which bin was very specific. In contrast, talk about such matters as unit weights and details about cost took place at a more general or even inappropriate level. Is this yet more evidence that parents assume that details about quantity are for others (e.g., schools) to deal with? A similar set of questions emerges when we consider the way physics materials are treated in the context of the museum.

Our early attendance counts showed that the few physics items, mainly involving gears and inclined planes, were not popular at PTM. We sometimes saw a child stop to look and ask "What's this?", a question that usually was answered. But follow-up questions such as "How does it work?" typically led the adult to move on or redirect the child's attention to another exhibit. This contrasted dramatically with the kinds of interactions we saw between the same pairs in the Grocery Store, and struck us as rather odd. Surely the children knew less about mathematics and physics than grocery stores. Because the children were attracted to the former displays, one might even expect that adults would be more inclined to interact and "teach" at these. Given that just the opposite happened, it becomes necessary to consider the content of a domain as well as the situation in which adult–child interactions occur to understand how interactions between a knowledgeable individual and a novice serve the latter's cognitive development. These findings suggest that knowledgeable adults do not always engage in those activities that maximize the likelihood that their charges will learn about what they do not yet know.

When adults are in settings in which they can make choices, the degree to which they think of themselves as more or less competent to "teach" in a given domain probably influences the way they behave. Although we all have intuitive understandings in the math and science domains, often these understandings are not stateable, limited, or even wrong (McCloskey & Kargon, 1988). In contrast, scripts for the grocery store, taking a trolley, going to the doctor, and so forth are well known and understood (Schank & Abelson, 1977). Adults are masters of the everyday social and economic roles they play. Similarly, adults surely know the comparable setting-relevant vocabulary items that they "teach" young children, whereas they might not be as fluent with technical terms that are used in the math and physics domains. We live in a culture that assigns many different roles to adults. As members of this culture, we know whether or not a given activity is within our own purview, which activities are common to a large part of the culture, which are reserved for those with expertise, and so forth.

Knowledge about our everyday social institutions forms part of our common folk psychology and comes to be taken for granted (Bruner, 1989) and used to frame our explanations of how and why people interact in their sociocultural circle. Such kinds of interactions can and do go on without any discussion of how gravity influences the rate at which something falls down an inclined plane, or other scientific matters. True, discussions about mathematics or physics depend on fluency with such knowledge, but so do discussions about any specialized topic, be it economics, history, or literary criticism. Therefore, parents might be more concerned that their children master what every successful member of a group must know than that they master what parents think is specialized knowledge.

Additionally, the idea that specialized knowledge or language requires the participation of experts could itself contribute to the differences we have noted. Goodenough's (1987) account of how the Pulawait teach their young males to sail provides some evidence for this conjecture. This kind of learning is not embedded in the everyday activities of the group. Instead, the young men are required to attend special instruction meetings to memorize the names and movements of the stars. Only those who do well are allowed to continue and take instruction on the open water.

In sum, there are reasons to question the extent to which parents think they *should* serve in the role of teacher of all things. Even if they are competent in certain domains of expertise, they might still think it is not their primary role to pass on such knowledge to their children. They may be decidedly unwilling to delegate the teaching of "proper" behavior in public places such as grocery stores, and at the same time very willing to leave to others matters of science and math. If adults do not want to serve as teacher when it comes to "school" subjects, we need to expand on accounts such as that of Saxe et al. (1987) of how children join the ranks of the knowledgeable. Our next section details one strategy we have used to aid our efforts in this regard. We ask whether we could encourage children to focus their constructivist tendencies to learn about science in a museum. That is, we took on the task of trying to create exhibits that would support learning about science, even if children used the exhibit on their own.

THE TRY IT GALLERY: A JOINT VENTURE

Some Preliminaries

Our early observations that math and science exhibits were either unpopular or not used as they were intended prompted us to enter into a joint venture with PTM to develop a new exhibit area, the Try It Gallery. We chose displays on the basis of findings about the abilities and interests of young children, for example, simple machines that do not require an understanding of gravity or an explicit ability to explain the relationship between two states of an object or an event (Bullock, Gelman, & Baillargeon, 1982). We specifically included features that children should be able to assimilate. For example, since we know that young children are good at making predictions about the effects of changing simple physical causal events, we chose to design a display that allowed them to make predictions and experiment with conditions that might influence their predictions. We also tried to avoid exhibits that would elicit talk of misconceptions (McCloskey & Kargon, 1988); neither we nor PTM staff saw a need to create conditions that could elicit erroneous adult input. The name "Try It Gallery" was chosen, in part, to indicate that visitors were invited to try to participate in the scientific process: to make predictions and perform tests, to classify according to scientific criteria, to apply numbers to different settings, and so forth. Additionally, it signaled an agreement between us and the museum to work together to build, change, replace, or enhance particular displays in an effort to maximize the number of visitors sharing the designers' interpretation of the exhibits.

Given our argument that novices' interpretations of inputs do not necessarily converge with adults', PTM's agreement to this effect was especially important to us. We had every reason to expect to fail to accomplish our goal, which was, to generate conditions that children would interpret as we hoped they would. It is one thing to provide hands-on materials designed especially for young children and quite another to be sure that these objects will be used as intended. The objects themselves do not an experiment make. Blocks, tubes, balls, sticks, or pieces of wood serve a very large number of functions, depending on how one interprets them.

Trial One: Manipulatives Are Not Enough

From the start, the Try It Gallery met one important criterion of success. It was and continues to be one of the most popular areas in the museum. For example, our 1988 January through February counts of the total number of people in an area showed that it was the most popular exhibit of all. The Grocery Store and the adjoining Trolley Car area ranked second. Analyses of 19 counts on weekends and on a school holiday revealed that children and their parents were about equally likely to be in the area. This means that we can ask both whether the adults structured the children's use of particular exhibits and whether children interpreted them as designed. Our most detailed data on these questions came from an exhibit on motion, *The Racing Balls*, schematized in Figure 3.

The Racing Balls display

The exhibit consists of two identical large red cylinders wrapped with clear plastic tubing through which rubber balls can be rolled. The tubing wraps around one cylinder three times and around the other cylinder five times. This arrangement was chosen because it offers young children a way to generate an assessment or compare the amount of time it takes for the balls on each cylinder to travel through their respective tubes. By counting the loops in the tubing, a child could predict which ball would take longer or travel a greater distance. The tubing material was selected to minimize friction; similarly, we limited the grade of the fall to limit acceleration but make it possible for the balls to roll. To encourage preschoolers to predict and count the number of times the tubing wrapped around each cylinder, we placed a sign conspicuously on top of the cylinders in the exhibit. It suggested that visitors "race" two balls by putting one ball into the tubing at the top of each cylinder at the same time and seeing which arrived at the bottom first.

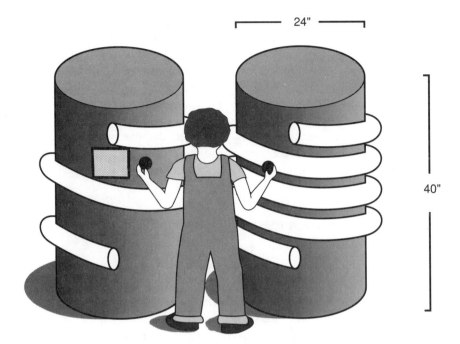

Figure 3   Schematic drawing of Racing Balls exhibit.

Preliminary findings. Our first effort to create an environment that would serve as an opportunity for young children to apply their existing scientific and mathematical knowledge to conditions that might expand their use of these was not successful. Although the Racing Balls were used a great deal, they were not used as we had hoped they would be. Adults rarely read the sign to their preliterate charges. Seldom did a child spontaneously make a comparison between the two cylinders. Perhaps worse yet, adults infrequently intervened to suggest this comparison to them. Instead, children tended to concentrate on one cylinder at a time, repeatedly putting a ball at the top of a tube, watching its progress through a tube, catching the ball, and putting it into the tube again and again and again. As we will see, adults' input at this exhibit was minimal. In some instances, they pointed out where the ball should have entered the tube, or they retrieved balls when they rolled away; otherwise, they sat on a nearby bench or leaned against the top of a drum or the closest wall.

Trial Two: Some Artifacts Speak for Themselves

Although it is known that adults do not usually read labels when in museums (e.g., Borun & Miller, 1980), it is an especially troublesome outcome when they fail to do so even when they are with preliterate children. The artifacts in the Try

It Gallery, unlike the boat and plane at a transportation exhibit, do not, on their own, afford the intended interpretation. Although children are inclined to take one look at a boat and get in it, they do not think to compare times of arrival of two moving objects. This situation led us to wonder what we could do to increase children's tendency to use our props as intended.

One straightforward way to do this is to tell children how to use the exhibit, which is what we hoped their adult companions would do when they read the "Race the Balls" sign on the top of each cylinder. Because parents neither read these signs nor talked about the ways to use the display, we decided to modify the exhibit to speak for itself.

Trial Three: A Decision to Show, as Well as Tell

Because our exhibit did not seem to interest the children in the possibility of predicting, comparing, and so forth, we decided to use a computerized script that would show and tell them to try such activities. We accomplished this by placing a Macintosh computer inside one of the cylinders that now had an opening in front for the screen (see Figure 3). In collaboration with MITECH Inc. and the design and education departments of PTM, we (particularly Massey and McManus) developed an audiovisual script designed to provide enough information to inform users about the goal of the exhibit and to encourage making predictions, testing predictions, and explaining the phenomenon.

As Figure 3 shows, the modified Racing Balls exhibit ended up with a computer screen and speaker placed at a child's level. These were activated when a sensor (under a rug) picked up the presence of a visitor at the exhibit. A cartoon-like black-and-white video illustration of a child at the exhibit then appeared on the screen, and at the same time a (digitized) female voice suggested that the child race the balls around the two cylinders to see which would reach the bottom first. The illustration showed a child placing one ball in each of the tubes that wrap around the cylinders. After an appropriate delay, the speaker asked which ball won and why. Again after a delay, the message and accompanying illustrations suggested counting the number of times the tubing wraps around each cylinder. Finally, it showed how the display would look if the tubes were unwrapped and pulled out straight to the side. It explained that the ball traveling through the 5-wrap tube has further to go and, therefore, takes longer.

The development of the computer's script was governed by two related principles. The first was that it would use the language of science. The second was that it should provide hints and clues in an order that suited a scientific inquiry. The idea was to engage constructivist tendencies but to leave to the users the choice of ways they then experimented with key variables.

Methods for data collection

Observations of visitors at the Racing Balls exhibit were collected at different times of day and different days of the week, both before and after the computer was added. Our previous studies indicated that it was important to sample across these different time periods because the number and kind of visitors to the museum varies with them. For example, school groups with relatively more children for the number of adults predominate on weekday mornings; entire families are common on weekends and holidays, when the museum is generally very crowded. Every child who approached the exhibit during an observation period became a target subject. Observations done during especially crowded times were videotaped and coded afterwards; otherwise, data were recorded with pencil and paper by one trained observer as described in the next paragraph. Adults accompanying children who approached the exhibit while it was being videotaped were asked for permission to videotape the child, using PTM's standard forms. We observed 163 children before the computer was added, and 104 children after the computer was in place. Table 1 shows the distribution by gender and approximate age and indicates the number of children accompanied by at least one adult.

We recorded our observations using forms like the one shown in Figure 4. The gender and estimated age of each target child, as well as anyone else present at the exhibit, were noted. A separate page was used to record each time a ball was put in a tube (or two balls were inserted simultaneously), and all pages for a given child were then put together to provide a record of the interactions occurring at the exhibit during the time that child was there. The characteristics of the target child and whoever else was present at the exhibit were indicated on the data sheets, and each exhibit-related activity was recorded, along with a code indicating who performed the activity. In addition, all verbalizations related to the exhibit were written down. For example, Figure 4 shows one of the data sheets for two children, a 5-year-old boy and a 3-year-old girl, who were at the exhibit with a male adult. While the girl held a ball up to the cylinder on the left and the boy held one up to the cylinder on the right, the adult said, "Ready, set, go," so they would place the balls in the tubes at the same time. When the first ball reached the bottom, the girl said (correctly) that she won, and the adult asked why the ball in the 5-wrap cylinder took longer. The boy then replied that it is because the tube is longer.

Effects of the computer

We present three kinds of "before and after" results. The first result is based on a general measure of ball-rolling tendencies, the remaining two on the extent to which visitors interacted with the exhibit as intended. Of these, one focuses on the rate at which children encountered examples of both balls starting together and rolling around the cylinders simultaneously. Unless this condition is met, it

Table 1

DISTRIBUTION OF CHILDREN BEFORE AND AFTER COMPUTER WAS ADDED
AS A FUNCTION OF AGE, GENDER, AND PRESENCE OR ABSENCE OF AN
ADULT

Characteristics of child	Less than 5 years (*n* = 22)	3 to 5 years (*n* = 120)	More than 5 years (*n* = 18)
	Before computer		
Sex of child			
Male	16	71[a]	12
Female	6	47[a]	9
Presence of at least one adult			
With adult	21	93	18
Without adult	1	27	3
	After computer		
Sex of child			
Male	7	51	11
Female	4	24	7
Presence of at least one adult			
With adult	8	50	15
Without adult	3	25	3

[a]Number of boys and girls in this group does not sum to the total *N* for the group because the gender
of two children could not be determined.

is unlikely that they could go on to experiment as intended. The second focuses
on whether or not talk at the exhibit was "scientific."

Mean number of ball-rolling events. The mean number of ball-rolling
events performed or witnessed by target children serves as an index of the amount
of physical engagement with the relevant materials. Often, more than one person
was present at the exhibit at the same time. We counted a target child as having
seen rolling balls, whether that child was responsible for the event or simply
watched another who was. (Either activity can serve as input for learning.) We
scored a ball-rolling event every time one ball rolled through one tube or two
balls rolled simultaneously through both tubes. Efforts to push the ball up the
tubing from the bottom were also scored as a ball-rolling instance.

A two-way (Presence vs. Absence of the Computer × Age) analysis of
variance was performed on these data. Children were divided into three age groups

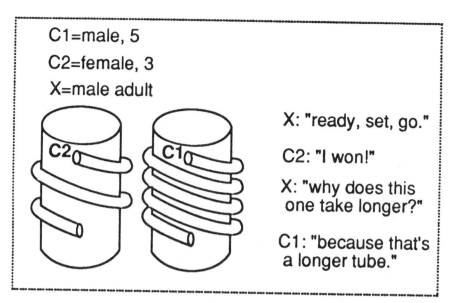

Figure 4 Sample data sheet used for observations at Racing Balls exhibit.

on the basis of the observer's estimates of age: younger than 3 years, 3 to 5 years, and older than 5 years. There were no significant effects or interaction. Children experienced approximately the same number of ball-rolling events before and after the computer was installed (Ms = 8.60 and 10.25, respectively). Interestingly, the mean number of ball-rolling events performed or witnessed did not vary significantly with age.

Experience with trials comparing balls simultaneously. Children have to witness or generate events in which the two balls start and roll around the cylinders simultaneously (hereafter referred to as *relevant comparison* trials) to get the point of the exhibit. Before the computer was in place, only 31% of the children received this kind of input. After the computer was in place, 76% of the children did. An analysis of variance (with Age and Computer Presence or Absence as between-subjects factors) of the mean number of times children performed or witnessed relevant comparison trials indicated that the computer introduced a reliable effect on this important variable, $F(1, 261) = 22.06, p < .001$. The means for children without and with the computer were .40 versus 2.17, respectively. There was also a main effect of age, $F(2, 216) = 5.49, p = .005$. The means for the three age groups in order of increasing age were .45, 1.97, and 1.43. Post hoc Tukey tests revealed that the mean for children in the 3-to-5-year age group was significantly greater ($p = .01$) than the mean for the children in the youngest age group.

Before the computer was placed in the exhibit, of the 31 children who were by themselves, only one saw a relevant comparison trial. Indeed, only 38% of the children with an adult saw at least one of these trials. After the computer was in place, even when children were alone, they either watched or generated relevant comparison trials about two thirds (64.5%) of the time. Having an adult present in the context of the computer-altered version of the display had some effect beyond the computer itself. Under this condition, 80% of the children saw at least one of the relevant comparison trials. This is further documented by the outcome of a two-way analysis of variance (with the between-subjects factors of Computer Present or Absence and At Least One vs. No Adults) of the mean number of relevant comparison trials children saw. There were main effects for the computer, $F(1, 263) = 53.34$, $p < .001$, and for the presence of an adult, $F(1, 263) = 3.78$, $p = .053$. Without minimizing this effect of adults, it is still noteworthy that children did much better when they were on their own at the computerized exhibit than when they were with an adult at the noncomputerized one.

Effects of computer on kind of talk. Given that the computer did get visitors to compare balls rolling around the two cylinders at the same time, we finally can ask whether we succeeded. Did children (either with peers or adults) now experiment with the display so as to assess the effects of different variables on the rate at which the two balls got to the bottom of their tubes? Analyses of the kinds of talk that children and adults generated in the exhibit area reveal that they did.

Some of our observations were videotaped, and others were recorded by hand. Either way, we tried as much as possible to record and compile all exhibit-relevant comments made by visitors. We divided all of the talk samples into two categories, *Procedural* and *Scientific*. Procedural talk included commands and questions concerning the balls (e.g., get the ball, where's a ball?, put it in there), instructions regarding courtesy (e.g., wait, watch out, your turn), and comments such as "around and around" or "here it comes." An excerpt was scored as Scientific if it included predictions or statements about the critical event, that is which ball "won"; offered or asked for a prediction or explanation; counted the number of times the tube wrapped around the cylinder; talked about differences in time, rate, or length; or made comments related to coordinating simultaneous trials (e.g., ready, go!). The following excerpts illustrate some of the differences between these two kinds of talk. The first example was collected before the computer was put in the exhibit and consists mostly of procedural statements, especially imperatives.

Example 1 of computer study talk

[Adult and child (3 to 4 yrs), *before* computer was installed.]

(*Adult does not read the sign and sits on bench; child stands in front of exhibit.*)

> Adult: Do you want to try it? Here's the ball. (*Adult gives ball to child.*) Put it in here. (*Adult indicates top of tubing on 3-wrap cylinder.*) Come here and wait. (*Adult and child watch as ball rolls through tube.*) It didn't make it. (*Ball bounced onto floor at bottom rather than landing in the finish box at the end.*) Try it again. (*Child again places ball in tubing at top of 3-wrap cylinder.*) It didn't make it again. Try one over here. (*Adult gestures to 5-wrap cylinder.*)

The following excerpt, recorded after the computer was operating, has much more talk about carrying out and interpreting the experiment. The kinds of comments made by this adult and child are typical of the kinds of things people talked about once the computer was in place.

Example 2 of computer study talk:

> [Adult and child (6 yrs), *after* the computer was installed.]
> (*Child, while attending to the computer, first places one ball in the tubing around the 5–wrap cylinder, then a ball in each tube simultaneously, then one ball in the 5–wrap tube again. Adult watches.*)
> Adult: Do the balls go the same distance?
> Child: Yes.
> Adult: Why do you say this? Look at how many times [it] goes around here . . . watch. (*Adult holds one ball at the 5-wrap tube while child holds the other at the 3-wrap tube.*) Ready? Go! (*They watch as the balls roll through the tubes.*) Your ball got to the bottom first. Why do you think your ball won?
> Child: Because my ball is faster.
> Adult: All right, then let's switch balls. (*They switch balls and repeat the procedure. Child is surprised*).
> Child: Mine won again! (*Adult has child sit down in front of cylinders to look at them.*)
> Adult: Which tube would be longer? (*Child does not answer.*) Try it again. (*They each take a ball and start them simultaneously again, this time with the child at the 5-wrap cylinder and the adult at the 3-wrap cylinder.*)

Separate analyses of variance were performed on the number of procedural verbalizations produced by children, the number of scientific verbalizations produced by children, the number of adult procedural verbalizations heard by each child, and the number of adult scientific verbalizations heard by each child. For each analysis, the Presence versus Absence of the Computer and Age (3 groups) served as independent variables. Results for each analysis follow.

For the procedural verbalizations produced by children, there was a marginal effect for the presence of the computer, $F(1, 261) = 3.64$, $p = .057$, with procedural verbalizations decreasing from a mean of .13 per child before the computer was present to .004 per child after. There was no effect of age and no interaction.

For scientific verbalizations produced by children, there were main effects for both the presence of the computer, $F(1, 261) = 4.88$, $p = .03$, and age, $F(2, 261) = 5.03$, $p = .007$. Children produced significantly more scientific verbalizations with the computer present ($M = .50$) versus absent ($M = .14$). Scientific verbalizations increased with age, from a mean of 0 in the youngest group, to .32 in the middle group, to .64 in the oldest group. A post hoc Tukey test indicated that the difference between the oldest and youngest age groups was significant ($p = .01$).

Only children who were at the exhibit with at least one adult were included in the analysis of adult procedural verbalizations heard by children. For this analysis, there was a main effect for the presence of the computer, $F(1, 199) = 4.97$, $p = .027$, with children hearing a mean of 1.43 procedural comments from adults before the computer was installed and .63 after. There was also a main effect of age, $F(2, 199) = 3.43$, $p = .034$. The number of procedural comments children heard from adults decreased with age group from 1.59 for the youngest children, to 1.06 for the middle group, to .44 for the oldest children. The difference between the oldest and youngest age groups was significant (post hoc Tukey test, $p = .05$). Age and presence of the computer did not interact.

The analysis of adult scientific verbalizations heard by children also included only children with at least one adult companion. The only significant result in this analysis was a main effect for the presence of the computer, $F(1, 199) = 22.76$, $p < .0001$. There was an increase in the number of scientific statements or questions adults addressed to children, from a mean per child of .42 before the computer was installed to 2.05 after it was installed.

An additional analysis of variance was performed to see whether having an adult present had an effect on children's tendency to talk scientifically. The computer reliably increased scientific talk in adults. Did the presence of an adult independently affect scientific talk on the part of children at the display? An analysis of variance using Presence versus Absence of the Computer and Presence versus Absence of at Least One Adult as between-subjects factors indicates that adult presence does *not* significantly affect children's tendency to talk scientifically, $F(1, 263) = .97$, $p = .326$. Once again, there was a main effect for the presence of the computer, $F(1, 263) = 9.12$, $p = .003$, and there was no interaction.

Summing Up

Adding the computerized script to our display dramatically altered the quality of children's and adults' behavior. It led to increases in the number of times children generated or saw two balls traveling around the cylinders simultaneously, it decreased the amount of procedural talk on the part of both children and adults, and it increased the amount of scientific talk observed for children and adults. In contrast, when left to their own devices, most adults did not attempt to demonstrate or "teach" at this exhibit. Although adults were more involved when the exhibit was supported by the computerized script, children could clearly proceed on their own or with other children. We still need to assess what children learned from this exhibit. Nevertheless, we finally achieved some success in our efforts to create an exhibit that children could interpret as intended, either on their own or with others.

We have argued that props in the environment need not constrain children's constructivist tendencies so that they follow the path we want them to. Even when we offer children signposts, we cannot be sure these will work. Our first effort to do this for one limited exhibit failed—despite the involvement of many kinds of relevant experts who worked an untold number of hours. In the end, it took still more people and a handsome commitment of funds to build a novel setting in which young children actively apply their armament of available science-relevant tools of inquiry and knowledge. We have made some genuine progress, but we are far from being able to specify in a systematic way what signposts will be effective for guiding conceptual development. Still, from this as well as the other work we have done at PTM, we have learned some lessons that apply to our goal. We turn to applying these lessons in our closing discussion of the nature of supporting environments for cognitive development, within a constructivist theory of mind.

CONCLUDING THEMES

The fact that constructivist theories grant young learners an active role in their own cognitive development means that novices and experts can disagree on the nature of relevant inputs. Given the difference between the knowledge of novices and of more mature learners, there must be times when our attention focuses on notably different inputs. Indeed, when novices benefit from domain-specific skeletal structures of knowledge, they can at times be better than adults at finding suitable inputs. Paradoxically, the young, who are novices in the sense of what they know, can sometimes be "experts" on the nature of relevant inputs. But how can one be an expert before mastering the material? Are there any principles that characterize these conditions?

Constructivist Principles of Supporting Environments

Principle One: Structures help define relevance

Constructivist theories are partial to structural accounts of knowledge. They assume that structures help individuals notice relevant data: Data that are consistent with available structures are recognized as members of the equivalence class of relevant inputs because they share the characteristics outlined by the organizing principles of the structure. Given this, when novices do have nascent knowledge structures, they can find relevant inputs. Their proclivities to take advantage of any conceptual structures they have, however skeletal these might be, means that they cannot help but find relevant inputs. This is because the organizing principles of the structures offer clues to what inputs will nourish development of the requisite body of knowledge. In fact, by serving to define the equivalence class of inputs that can feed further development within their domain, these nascent structures carry with them ways for identifying novel relevant inputs. Nascent structures foster their own development, because they underlie the ability to recognize relevant data and store them in a coherent way. For this reason, the paradox presented above is no longer a paradox. Children are, in fact, experts on the topic of relevant inputs, because they are actively constructing reality with whatever structures they have. These structures help them find and assimilate samples of the very inputs that can nurture their further development. Because adults, too, once started along the same trajectory, the odds are high that we and the children will converge on shared knowledge bases.

Noisy data can be sorted. Our observations at the museum, especially regarding the kinds of mathematical inputs children encounter, lead us to the conclusion that adults sometimes offer children noisy or even inappropriate data. How do children sort through the noisy data to find the good in the bad? Once again, the active use of available structures can accomplish the work. Data are noisy, impoverished, bad, or irrelevant because they are not exemplars of the equivalence class of acceptable inputs. Because they do not share the requisite pattern, they are not candidates for assimilation by the structure(s) in question. Indeed, structures of mind need not even notice irrelevant or noisy data.

Experts need not know the nature of relevant input. If relevance is defined by the structure of a target domain, it seems at least as important that children have opportunities that maximize their chances of encountering examples of the target domains when they are trying to learn about these than that they have tutors who offer expert input at a given time. Language learning provides an especially good example of this possibility.

Children are surrounded with examples of language simply because expert speakers use their language a great deal of the time. Similarly, those who know the social rules of a group or a culture display this knowledge repeatedly in their everyday activities; by "doing what comes naturally," expert knowers perforce generate examples of the pertinent data bases all the time.

Because there are always objects in the environment, and because there are always things that move on their own or do not, and so forth, there are domains for which the ubiquity condition applies. Hence, knowledgeable members of the community need not work on the creation of explicit lesson plans for novices to learn much about the physical world. Whenever they use the knowledge they have, they cannot help but generate exemplars that become part of the environment. When a novice's structures are able to assimilate these exemplars, the pertinent data are likely to be present, with or without the intentional involvement of others at that moment.

Principle Two: Redundancy is a good thing

The foregoing discussion neither assumes nor denies that adults offer the young the best possible learning data. If adults are more competent than others to generate examples repeatedly, or take care to see that their charges are in the right places at about the right time in their developmental agenda, they might best serve as providers. But we have already seen that even when adults are competent tutors, they might not display their competence for some domains. Therefore, it would seem foolhardy to require our acquisition model to treat competent parents as necessary agents of cognitive development. Rather, we should say that the more generally available the pertinent data, the better, whether or not any adults choose to present these data, because, the wider their availability, the more likely it is that there will be times and conditions when the child's structures and the environment in question are mutually compatible. In a sense, this is one way to characterize the successful Racing Balls exhibit. Children can get their clues about what to do from the television, from watching other children, from interacting with their parents, or from experimenting on their own. No one condition need be better than another, unless we can prove that some kinds of information can only be conveyed in certain ways.

Some readers will recognize in the preceding conclusion a variant of a principle of *frequency*. We emphasize that this principle is not the same one that is assumed by association theorists. First, the requirement in our principle of frequency is that there be frequent encounters with any exemplars that are structurally equivalent, not that there be frequent encounters with the exact same stimulus. Second, the principle we are proposing does *not* function to foster the gradual build up of habit strengths. Instead, it serves a maximizing function: The more opportunities children have to encounter the class of inputs to be learned, the greater are their chances of this happening in a timely way, that is, when they are able to recognize and use these encounters as relevant input data. When exemplars from the class of potentially relevant inputs are omnipresent, the odds favor more novices finding at least some relevant data and, therefore, converging on the abilities or concepts to be learned.

Language acquisition is a case in point. We know that speakers from different cultures vary in the extent to which they simplify their talk to beginning language learners. Therefore, the rates at which they generate certain kinds of utterances vary from one language community to another. Still, children all over the world master the syntax of their language group at about the same age (Schieffelin &

Ochs, 1986), presumably because children all over the world hear many examples of the surface structure of the syntax that underlies these outputs.

The case of language acquisition helps us place the principle of frequency in a broader context, that of the *principle of redundancy*. People seldom generate the exact same utterance. Nevertheless, they do produce many acceptable sentences, ones that reveal the implicit knowledge of syntactic principles that fluent speakers share. Put differently, sentences are patterns of sound that are isomorphic exemplars of the structure in question. It does not matter whether two examples of relevant data are the same in surface detail or whether these are produced by the same model. What matters is that they share the same structural characteristics, whether or not those who generate equivalent sentence frames know that they do. This is why our account of why a child will find the relevant data does not require explicit knowledge on the part of those who have already achieved expert levels of competence.

Implications of the redundancy principle. This principle has both theoretical and practical consequences. From a practical point of view, we already know that some of our guesses about relevant data will be wrong. Hence, if we focus on but one variant of possible inputs, we put young learners at risk of not learning. We are better advised to offer redundant data sets, ones that offer multiple routes to the learners. This practice is a way to try to maximize the chances of a child's finding a route that adult and child both deem relevant.

On the theoretical side, the preceding section helps sharpen some of the questions addressed by this volume. For example, the question of whether cognitive development has to occur in a social setting can be stated as follows: Are adults more likely to present multiple, redundant examples of the target body of knowledge? Are there other ways to accomplish the same goal? In either case, what class of inputs is made available in one way that cannot be so generated under different conditions? Our work at PTM, especially the experimental effort to use technology to encourage attention to what we thought was relevant, serves as an example of how one might proceed here.

Lessons From the Museum About Environments

Division of labor might be the rule

Earlier, we showed that, even when adults might be effective generators of relevant inputs, they might not choose to serve in this role. This possibility means that we should expect variability to be the rule on the question of how well at-home observations of parent–child interactions generalize to other settings. In a culture like ours, adults might prefer to share or even divide the labor of knowledge transmission. It remains to be determined whether there are some tasks of knowledge transmission that parents prefer to give away and others that they claim as their own. But we already know from the PTM work that parents may not insist

on claiming all of the ones that they could. Domains that focus on school matters are not claimed as readily as are those that bear on everyday scripts, even when we know that the parents would succeed in transmitting the material in question.

It also remains to be determined how effective parents' inputs are compared with those offered by others. Saxe et al. (1987) report benefits, even over short-term periods, when mothers do work on number games with their children. Still, it would be good to have data comparing what children learn about such matters when working on their own or watching television, or when interacting with their peers, their siblings, or other people they encountered. Might it be that any and all options for input will do (Atran & Sperber, 1987)? Might it even be that children have ideas of their own about suitable matches between their input needs and possible providers? We know many parents who complain that their children refuse their offers of homework help and turn to others instead. Protests that the teacher's way of doing things is different are common reasons for this in the first author's household.

Such possibilities present no problems for a constructivist theory that incorporates the principle of redundancy. Indeed, because we know that our culture is inundated with samples of mathematical artifacts, things we value, rules of interaction, and so forth, it makes sense to allow different adults to choose specializations when it comes to the job of knowledge transmission. Research is needed on whether it likewise makes sense to let the learners do some choosing.

The risk of failing to provide supporting environments

Ponder the consequences of a case in which parents preferred to give to others the job of knowledge transmission. For example, even though we can assume that parents would have been competent at helping their children with the Racing Balls exhibit, they did not. This was not a neutral decision in this case. First, the materials themselves did not suffice to render transparent to the children the intent of their use. Second, museums and schools often try to start children learning about things they will not encounter in everyday life. Third, because many exhibits are intentionally designed to introduce novel phenomena, it is less likely that the child will have pre-existing knowledge structures to apply. Therefore, novices are by definition more dependent on signposts. When knowledgeable people (parents or otherwise) either cannot or are not always motivated to generate or point these signposts out, learning in such cases is at risk. Had we not succeeded with our computer intervention, very few children would even have used the materials in the Racing Balls exhibit appropriately, let alone learned anything from the exhibit. Indeed, had we not watched what the children first did, we might not even have realized that the exhibit was a failure. It certainly was popular, and there was hardly a time that we did not see children enjoying themselves with it.

Although we were prepared to have the children's use of the exhibit diverge from what we had in mind, we were not prepared for how long it would be before

we reached a meeting of minds. It took two tries to achieve a workable exhibit. No matter how much collective knowledge we had about children and families of this age, the inclinations of preschoolers to count, to be interested in racing, to attend to moving objects, and so forth, we were not inoculated against failure. Most parents did not join the activities of their children, and the children used the items in ways that were not what we had in mind. It is important to emphasize that it took us a great deal of time, work, and experimenting to achieve the successes we did. As pleased as we are that we did this and succeeded, there is no escaping the fact that it was hard, conscious work. Although we always modified our plans in response to the children's reactions, one can hardly classify our efforts as spontaneous and immediate. It was not enough to be knowledgeable, benevolent adults in this situation, and we do not anticipate that it will be in the future. Devising relevant inputs for learning about novel phenomena is hard work— even when one is professionally qualified. It seems unreasonable to assume, then, that children's day-to-day cognitive development could proceed if it really were necessarily dependent on the input of close, personal socializing agents. It must be that there are multiple and redundant sources to which children can turn to find supporting environments for cognitive development.

A Comment on the "Roll" of Language

Without testing further variations in the *Racing Balls* displays, we cannot be sure that we had to have both video illustration and speech. Still, our best guess is that the video alone would not be as effective. One reason is that the combined output of animation plus speech offers redundant exemplars of some of the key features of the exhibit. Furthermore, some messages might require the use of language. Had we used only the video without speech in the Racing Balls exhibit, we think many children would have caught onto the idea of using two balls. But our goal was to teach more than this: We wanted children to engage in a mini-experiment, to use data and make predictions, to try to vary the outcomes, and even to get information about the way the exhibit worked. We wanted them to enter the world of science. When put this way, it could be that language had to be part of the communication. There are two reasons to so conjecture. As discussed earlier, objects on their own do not make a scientific experiment. Objects have to be interpreted in scientifically relevant ways for experimentation to happen. Second, mathematics and science have languages of their own, and to interpret objects correctly for use in mathematics and science, one has to use these languages. It is, in part, when one masters the languages within these domains that one has acquired a richer understanding of them (Kitcher, 1982).

These formal languages are very much the invention of mankind, as are many of the things we teach in schools. Given how much effort it took us to

develop one exhibit that did not assume such knowledge, it is unlikely that children's constructivist tendencies alone will suffice for learning math and science. To be sure, knowledgeable individuals can provide such inputs, but so can print, computers, and other media. Even here, then, it is necessary to ask what kinds of social and cultural inputs foster learning. We cannot simply assume that these have to be face-to-face interactions.

References

Atran, S., & Sperber D. (1987, June). *Language without teaching: Its place in culture.* Paper presented to the Fourth Annual Workshop on Culture, Schooling, and Psychological Development, Tel Aviv University, Tel Aviv.

Borun, M., & Miller, M. (1980). To label or not to label? *Museum News, 58,* 64–67.

Bruner, J. S. (1989, April). The state of developmental psychology. In D. R. Olson (Chair), *The contributions of Jerome S. Bruner to the study of child development.* Invited Symposium conducted at the meetings of the Society for Research in Child Development, Kansas City, MO.

Bullock, M., Gelman, R., & Baillargeon, R. (1982). The development of causal reasoning. In W. J. Friedman (Ed.), *The developmental psychology of time* (pp. 209–254). New York: Academic Press.

DeLoache, J. S., Sugarman, S., & Brown, A. L. (1985). The development of error correction in young children's manipulative play. *Child Development, 56,* 928–939.

Diamond, J. (1981). *The ethology of teaching: A perspective from the observation of families in science centers.* Unpublished doctoral dissertation, University of California, Berkeley.

Durkin, K., Shire, B., Riem, R., Crowther, R. D., & Rutter, D. R. (1986). The social and linguistic context of early number word use. *The British Journal of Developmental Psychology, 4,* 269–288.

Furth, H. (l966). *Thinking without language.* New York: The Free Press.

Gelman, R. (1990). First principles organize attention to relevant data and the acquisition of numerical and causal concepts. *Cognitive Science, 14,* 79–106.

Gelman, R., & Massey, C. (1987). The cultural unconscious as contributor to the supporting environments for cognitive development. Commentary on Saxe, Guberman, & Gearhart in the *Monographs of the Society for Research in Child Development, 52*(2, Serial No. 216), 307–317.

Goodenough, W. H. (1987). Traditional navigation in the Western Pacific: A search for pattern. *Expedition, 29,* 3–14.

Goodnow, J. J. (1990). The socialization of cognition: What's involved? In J. W. Stigler, R. A. Shweder, & G. Herdt (Eds.), *Cultural psychology: Essays on comparative human development* (pp. 259–286). Cambridge, England: Cambridge University Press.

Greenfield, P. M. (1984). A theory of the teacher in everyday life. In B. Rogoff & J. Lave (Eds.), *Everyday cognition: Its development in social context* (pp. 117–138). Cambridge, MA: Harvard University Press.

Karmiloff-Smith, A., & Inhelder, B. (1974–1975). If you want to get ahead, get a theory. *Cognition, 3,* 195–212.

Kitcher, P. (1982). *The nature of mathematical knowledge.* New York: Oxford University Press.

Landau, B., & Gleitman, L. (1985). *Language and experience: Evidence from the blind*

child. Cambridge, MA: Harvard University Press.

McCloskey, M., & Kargon, R. (1988). The meaning and use of historical models in the study of intuitive physics. In S. Strauss (Ed.), *Ontogeny, phylogeny, and historical development* (Vol. 2, pp. 49–67). Norwood, NJ: Ablex.

Newport, E. L. (1980). Constraints on structure: Evidence from American sign language and language learning. In W. A. Collins (Ed.), *Minnesota Symposium on Child Psychology* (pp. 93–124). Hillsdale, NJ: Erlbaum.

Orne, M. T. (1962). On the social psychology of the psychological experiment: With particular reference to demand characteristics and their implications. *American Psychologist, 17*, 776–783.

Pinker, S. (1989). *Learnability and cognition: The acquisition of argument structure.* Cambridge, MA: MIT Press/Bradford Books.

Rogoff, B., & Wertsch, J. V. (Eds.). (1984). *Children's learning in the "Zone of proximal development."* San Francisco: Jossey-Bass.

Saxe, G. B., Guberman, S. R., & Gearhart, M. (1987). Social processes in early development. *Monographs of the Society for Research in Child Development, 52*(Serial No. 216).

Schank, R. A., & Abelson, B. (1977). *Scripts, plans, goals and understanding.* Hillsdale, NJ: Erlbaum.

Schieffelin, B. B., & Ochs, E. (1986). Language socialization. *Annual Review of Anthropology, 15*, 163–191.

Stodolsky, S. S. (1988). *The subject matters: Classroom activity in math & social studies.* Chicago: University of Chicago Press.

Wertsch, J. V., & Stone, C. A. (1985). The concept of internalization in Vygotsky's account of the genesis of higher mental functions. In J. V. Wertsch (Ed.), *Culture, communication and cognition: Vygotskian perspectives* (pp. 162–179). Cambridge, England: Cambridge University Press.

CHAPTER 12

CULTURE AND SOCIALIZATION IN WORK GROUPS

JOHN M. LEVINE AND RICHARD L. MORELAND

The goal of this chapter is to analyze the role of socially shared cognitions in work groups. Although these cognitions are important determinants of group effectiveness, they have not received sufficient theoretical or empirical attention. Previous analyses have taken a rather narrow view of the nature and function of cognitions in work groups. Emphasis has been placed on the specific task knowledge that workers need to perform their individual jobs and on the formal mechanisms that professional trainers use in transmitting such knowledge. Much less attention has been paid to the broad task and social knowledge that workers need to participate fully in the life of the group and to the informal mechanisms that group members use in transmitting this knowledge to one another. We believe that an increased emphasis on these topics can produce important insights into work group functioning. Our chapter, therefore, will emphasize worker *socialization* rather than worker *training* (cf. Feldman, 1989).

For our purposes, a work group consists of three or more persons who interact regularly to perform a joint task, who share a common frame of reference, who have affective ties with one another, and whose behaviors and outcomes are interdependent. This definition is not meant to imply that all work groups are identical. They obviously differ in several important ways, including origin, struc-

Preparation of this chapter was supported by the Office of Educational Research and Improvement of the U.S. Department of Education and by the Andrew W. Mellon Foundation. Thanks are extended to Linda Argote for helpful comments on an earlier draft.

ture, type of task, and division of labor. Although these and other differences can influence how work groups function, they will not be emphasized in our discussion. Instead, we will focus on one of the defining characteristics of all such groups—the existence of a common frame of reference. This common frame of reference is often described as the group's *culture*.

Work group culture is critical to worker socialization, because a group's culture embodies the task and social knowledge that new members must acquire to participate fully in the life of the group. In the following sections, we will first describe the content of work group culture. Then we will discuss how group culture is acquired by newcomers. Finally, we will mention some unresolved issues regarding the culture of work groups and the transmission of cultural knowledge from oldtimers to newcomers.

THE CULTURE OF WORK GROUPS

Many different definitions of group culture have been offered (e.g., Fine, 1979; McFeat, 1974; Shrivastava & Schneider, 1984; Van Maanen & Barley, 1984), but two related perspectives are typically emphasized. First, culture is often viewed as a set of *thoughts* that are shared among group members. These thoughts guide group members' actions and provide a common interpretive framework for their experiences. Second, culture is often viewed as a set of *customs* that embody the thoughts that group members share. These customs serve to remind group members that their experiences can (and should) be interpreted in common ways.

Culture as Shared Thoughts

Those who view culture as a set of thoughts have devoted their efforts to cataloging the kinds of thoughts that members of the same work group share. These observers suggest that culture arises as workers struggle together to answer certain key questions about their group, its members, and the work they perform (see Figure 1).

Knowledge about the group

Some of the questions for which group members seek collective answers focus on the nature of their group. For example, workers often want to know what makes their group different from other groups (cf. Martin, Feldman, Hatch, & Sitkin, 1983; Shrivastava & Schneider, 1984; Van Maanen & Barley, 1984). Some work groups emphasize special characteristics, such as skills or bravery, that are common among their members but rare among outsiders. Smith (1977), for example, found that sailors aboard Great Lakes cargo boats and sailors aboard ocean-going cargo ships stressed different skills in describing themselves, although all of them worked at very similar jobs. Other work groups emphasize the sig-

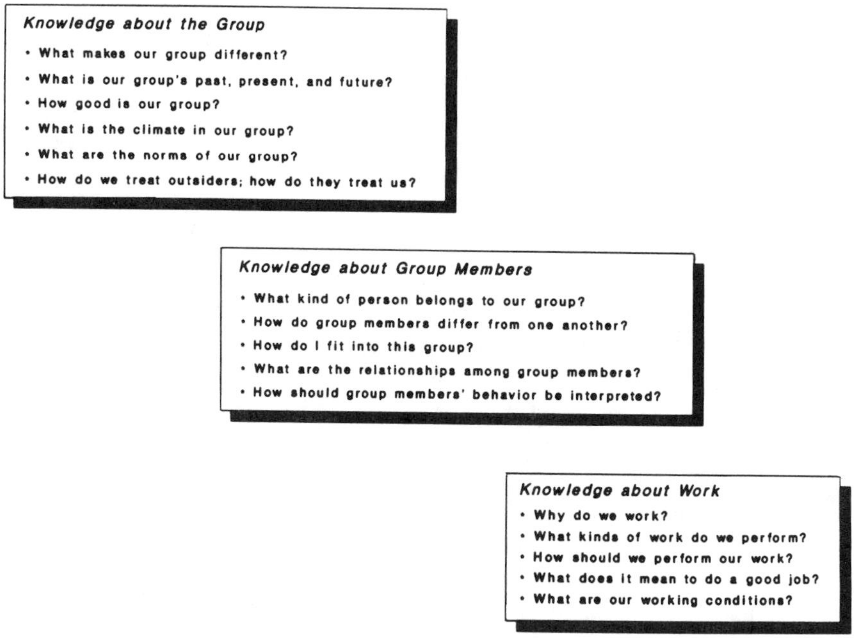

Knowledge about the Group
- What makes our group different?
- What is our group's past, present, and future?
- How good is our group?
- What is the climate in our group?
- What are the norms of our group?
- How do we treat outsiders; how do they treat us?

Knowledge about Group Members
- What kind of person belongs to our group?
- How do group members differ from one another?
- How do I fit into this group?
- What are the relationships among group members?
- How should group members' behavior be interpreted?

Knowledge about Work
- Why do we work?
- What kinds of work do we perform?
- How should we perform our work?
- What does it mean to do a good job?
- What are our working conditions?

Figure 1   Socially shared knowledge within work groups.

nificance of their jobs. Van Maanen (1973), for example, found that policemen stressed their role as a buffer between the dangerous world of criminals and the safe world of ordinary citizens. Workers who view their groups as unique acquire a stronger social identity and can engage in impression management more easily.

Workers may also ask questions about where their group has been in the past, where it is now, and where it is going in the future. Regarding the past, workers are often curious about the formation of their group, its prior members, and the critical events in its history. Regarding the present, workers are often curious about whether current conditions within their group are normal or abnormal (Van Maanen, 1977). Finally, regarding the future, workers are often curious about whether their group will improve or decline and how their group can best achieve its goals. As they gain a better understanding of their group's past, present, and future, workers may obtain a reassuring sense of predictability and control over the group.

Some of the most important questions that workers try to answer focus on the quality of their group. Such judgments are very subjective, because the quality of a group depends on the evaluative criteria applied (Fine, 1985). Sometimes these criteria are supplied or imposed by outsiders, but often they must be negotiated within the group. Some workers evaluate their group by comparing it with other groups that perform similar jobs, but such comparisons require complex decisions about which groups are appropriate targets for comparison, which aspects of the group ought to be evaluated in this way, and so on (Tajfel & Turner, 1979). Workers may also evaluate their group by comparing its quality now to what it was in the past or will be in the future, but these comparisons can be quite complex as well (Levine & Moreland, 1987). After evaluating their group, workers may also try to explain *why* it is good or bad. Once again, considerable negotiation may be required before workers can agree about the relative impact of different factors (cf. Brown, 1984; Leary & Forsyth, 1987). Finally, workers may develop collective strategies for coping with membership in a good or bad group. These strategies allow workers to resolve a variety of important issues, such as how the rewards of belonging to a good group or the costs of belonging to a bad one should be distributed among group members.

Workers may also have questions about the *climate* within their group. Some work groups have a warm climate, in the sense that decisions are made in a democratic manner and harmony is valued more than productivity. Other work groups have a cool climate. Workers generally prefer to belong to groups with warm climates, yet groups whose climates are cool may be tolerable as long as their members understand and agree about the kinds of relationships that they share with one another.

Workers often wonder what their fellow group members expect from them and what they can expect in turn from their fellow group members. As a result, they create and promulgate various social norms. These norms can be prescriptive or proscriptive and can focus on the thoughts, feelings, or behaviors of group members. Dressel and Petersen (1982), for example, found that male strippers in a local nightclub endorsed an elaborate "code of ethics" that governed their dance routines, interactions with audience members, and relationships with co-workers. Regardless of their focus, group norms can also vary in their acceptance, applicability, and rigidity. As a result, workers must learn who endorses a particular norm, to whom that norm applies, and what happens when someone violates the norm.

A final question that workers often try to answer is how their group relates to the world at large. Some work groups view outsiders positively and thus interact extensively with them. Sanders (1974), for example, found that bands of street musicians derived great pleasure from the approval that their music evoked from passersby. But other work groups view outsiders negatively and thus avoid interacting with them. Kauffman (1988), for example, found that prison guards felt trapped between angry prisoners and ordinary citizens who disdained their work. When a work group is embedded within a larger organization, workers must decide whether the organization as a whole supports their group, which people within the organization are likely to be helpful or harmful to the group, and so on (Gladstein, 1984). Many work groups cope with this complexity by closing their ranks and viewing all outsiders, even those who work for the same organization, with mistrust (e.g., Roy, 1952).

Knowledge about group members

Some of the questions for which group members seek collective answers focus on the characteristics of group members. For example, workers often develop a shared image of the prototypical member of their group (cf. Niedenthal, Cantor, & Kihlstrom, 1985). This person may be a current or former group member or someone entirely fictitious. In some work groups, additional prototypes representing the best and worst group members can also be found. Charles (1982), for example, found that forest rangers in Yellowstone National Park agreed that it was better to be a naturalist than a policeman. Prototypes reflecting specialized work roles can also be found within some groups. College faculty, for example, often share common images regarding the different kinds of people who make good teachers, researchers, or administrators.

Workers may also ask questions about the ways in which members of their group differ from one another. It is often important to know, for example, which group members possess the greatest work skills or are the most helpful. Information about such matters can be communicated in rather subtle ways. Zurcher (1965), for example, found that more experienced sailors aboard Navy ships were marked by their elaborate tattoos, specially modified uniforms, and use of shipboard argot. Aside from learning *who* is skillful or helpful, workers also need to know *how* such reputations are acquired within the group. Information about these matters can also be communicated in somewhat indirect ways (e.g., Nusbaum, 1978).

As workers learn more about one another, they may also obtain knowledge about themselves. Each person learns how he or she is viewed by the other group members and, through the process of reflected appraisal (Shrauger & Schoeneman, 1979), alters his or her self-image accordingly. Group members may also offer one another interpretative labels for their thoughts, feelings, and behaviors on the job. Through the process of self-attribution (Bem, 1972), each person again alters his or her self-image accordingly. Van Maanen (1973), for example, found that policemen often helped new recruits to cope with their fears about injury or death by labeling such feelings as *anger* or *excitement*. Recruits who accepted these labels were able to overcome their fears and perform their jobs more competently.

Workers are often interested not only in the characteristics of individual group members, but also in the relationships among group members. Most work groups contain complex social networks that bring people together or keep them apart. Some of these networks reflect feelings of liking or disliking among workers. There may be friendship cliques within the group or workers who are ostracized. Other social networks reflect patterns of communication among workers. Rumors, gossip, and other secrets may travel along established routes that include some workers but exclude others. Finally, some social networks reflect the ways in which workers perform their jobs. Whereas some workers labor alone, others may work together by sharing difficult tasks, offering advice, and correcting or concealing errors.

Finally, workers often seek information about how to interpret one another's behavior. Certain gestures, facial expressions, and slang can have special meanings that only group members understand. Roy (1955), for example, found that workers in a factory machine shop often teased one another, but that this teasing was interpreted as friendly rather than hostile behavior. Workers are especially anxious to understand the behavior of their leader (cf. Louis, 1980; Van Maanen, 1977) because of his or her power over them. Because of their power, leaders often interpret events for other group members, creating meanings that everyone is expected to share (cf. Gray, Bougon, & Donnellon, 1985; Pfeffer, 1981).

Knowledge about work

Finally, some of the questions for which group members seek collective answers focus on the work that they perform. For example, a key question asked by many workers is why they work at all. Some workers, who view their jobs as interesting or fulfilling, feel a strong intrinsic motivation to work (e.g., Katz, 1982). But other workers, who view their jobs as boring or unfulfilling, require strong extrinsic motivation to work (e.g., Zurcher, Sonenschein, & Metzner, 1966). Judgments about the attractiveness of various jobs can be very subjective, so they are often made collectively by the members of a work group (Salancik & Pfeffer, 1978). And once these judgments are made, they can affect workers in a variety of ways. Workers who regard their jobs as less attractive are generally less productive. Roy (1952), for example, found that radial-drill operators developed elaborate schemes for quota restriction and goldbricking and only worked hard when they needed extra money or were being observed by the foreman.

Some jobs are rather complex, in the sense that they involve a variety of tasks. Workers who perform these jobs must agree about what those tasks are and who will perform them, which tasks are most important, the order in which tasks must be completed, and so on (e.g., Zurcher, 1968). When workers perform a variety of tasks, some of those tasks may seem more "honorable" than others. Meara (1974), for example, found that butchers working at supermarkets regarded the skilled cutting of meat as their real work. Wrapping and pricing that meat and dealing with customers were regarded as necessary tasks, but unworthy of a butcher's talents.

Some jobs are also rather flexible, in the sense that they can be accomplished in several ways. Many workers develop special procedures that make their jobs easier, and these procedures are often shared with other members of their work group. Scribner (1984), for example, observed a group of preloaders who worked in a dairy warehouse assembling assorted products for shipment to local stores. Although many of the orders could be assembled in several ways, the preloaders consistently assembled orders in ways that required the least physical effort. Their skill in this regard was based on a relatively simple technique (available to every group member) for visualizing partial cases of a product and combining the contents of those cases mentally.

Many of the questions that workers ask involve the quality of their job performance. When jobs lack clear, objective performance standards, group members often decide among themselves whether someone is doing a job well or poorly. Berk and Berheide (1977), for example, found that many family arguments about housecleaning focus on whether something is really clean or still dirty. Aside from establishing performance standards, group members may also try to explain *why* some workers are better than others. Explanations for task performance are often embodied in stories that are told about previous or current members of the group (e.g., Berkman, 1978; Haas, 1977; Van Maanen, 1973). Finally, group members may wonder about the likely consequences of good or poor job performance. Information about these matters can also be found in stories. Martin, Feldman, Hatch, and Sitkin (1983), for example, found that the stories told by employees of several large business organizations addressed the same issues, such as whether promotion depends more on whom a worker knows than on what he or she knows and what happens to workers who make serious errors on the job.

Finally, workers are often curious about the conditions under which they perform their jobs. Some work groups, such as policemen (Van Maanen, 1973), operate in dangerous environments. As a result, their members must learn what those dangers are, where and when they are most likely to occur, and so on. Many work groups establish territories, and workers often negotiate how the space within a territory will be used (Konar, Sundstrom, Brady, Mandel, & Rice, 1982). Time pressures also affect many groups, whose members must learn to alter their working habits accordingly. Fine (1987), for example, found that professional cooks acknowledged various time pressures, such as which days of the week were busiest and how long it took to prepare certain items on the menu. Finally, issues of accountability arise in many work groups. Workers must learn who will evaluate their job performance and how those persons are best satisfied.

Culture as Customs

Culture can also be viewed as a set of customs—behavioral expressions of the thoughts shared among group members. Although customs take many different forms, we believe that most customs found in work groups can be classified as routines, accounts, jargon, rituals, or symbols.

Routines involve everyday procedures used by members of a work group. Habits and traditions are examples of routines; group norms can produce routines when members conform to those norms. Routines occur regularly and seem normal to workers, although they might appear odd to outsiders (cf. Haas, 1972; Roy, 1955; Zurcher et al., 1966). Zurcher and his colleagues, for example, found that hashers (workers in sorority kitchens and dining rooms) often created elaborate comedy "bits" based on silly metaphors for their work. Aside from alleviating boredom, a good bit also promoted group cohesiveness, facilitated the individuation of workers, and allowed the hashers to express hostility toward the women they served.

Accounts involve verbal descriptions of or explanations for matters that members of a work group find especially interesting. Stories told by workers or superstitions that they share are examples of accounts. Some accounts have a strong ideological flavor. Dressel and Petersen (1982), for example, found that male strippers seemed eager to justify their work as more than just a way to earn money. Their justification included claims that women have the same rights as men to watch strippers perform and that stripping is a misunderstood art form that deserves greater appreciation. By linking their work to larger social issues through an ideological account, the strippers were able to resolve some of the ambivalence that they felt about their jobs.

Jargon involves special words, phrases, or gestures that mean a lot to group members, but mean little or nothing to outsiders. Donovan (1920), for example, worked as a waitress in several Chicago diners. She noted that the staffs of these restaurants often spoke a special language that their customers could not understand. This jargon could have served at least two functions. Perhaps the workers felt a need to make it seem as though they were doing something special. Jargon may also have served to forestall critical comments from customers by creating a language barrier between customers and the staff.

Rituals are special ceremonies that group members carry out to mark the occurrence of significant events (cf. Trice & Beyer, 1984), including anniversaries, victories or defeats, changes in the status of group members, and arrivals to or departures from the group. Many work groups ritualize initiations of new members. Vaught and Smith (1980), for example, described some interesting rituals conducted by coal miners when a new man was assigned to their work teams. A length of wire was wrapped around the newcomer's genitals and attached to a heavy weight. The oldtimers tossed this weight to one another, threatening to drop it at any moment. Apart from some entertainment value, such rituals demonstrated to newcomers that their safety depended on the goodwill of fellow miners, and helped oldtimers estimate how newcomers might respond to the dangers of coal mining. The rituals thus promoted a sense of solidarity and trust among workers that enabled them to perform their jobs more safely.

Finally, *symbols* are material objects that possess a special meaning only group members can understand (Ornstein, 1986). Tools, costumes, and insignia are examples of symbols that might be found in work groups. Riemer (1977), for instance, found that apprentice electricians changed their tools as they became more experienced at their work. New workers brought many tools to work and purchased brands they could afford. But more experienced electricians carried only a few basic tools and bought only certain brands.

As these examples suggest, the customs of work groups can express the thoughts shared among group members in rather subtle and indirect ways. It may thus be difficult or impossible for an outsider to interpret those customs correctly. The culture of a work group can seem elusive and mysterious for other reasons as well. First, some groups have strong cultures, in the sense that knowledge is codified, widely shared among oldtimers, and embodied in customs, whereas other groups have cultures that are weak (Fine, 1979; Schein, 1984; Wilkins & Ouchi, 1983). Stronger cultures seem to develop in work groups that have (a) longer histories, (b) more stable and homogeneous memberships, (c) higher levels of outcome interdependence among members, (d) greater cohesiveness, and (e) more uncertain or threatening environments. In some work groups, culture may be too weak to detect or interpret clearly. Of course, one could simply ask workers to describe or explain their group's culture, but even then success would not be guaranteed. Culture is often tacit, an aspect of the group that is taken for granted by its members (Gregory, 1983; Van Maanen, 1980; Wilkins & Ouchi, 1983). And even if group members were aware of their culture, they might be unwilling to reveal it fully (Dandridge, Mitroff, & Joyce, 1980; Martin, 1982). Finally, it is important to note that culture is dynamic rather than static (Fine, 1979; Gray, Bougon, & Donnellon, 1985; Gregory, 1983; Van Maanen, 1977). The thoughts that are shared by group members and the customs through which those thoughts are expressed are constantly being revised and renegotiated.

Learning the culture of a work group clearly presents many problems, yet most people manage to solve those problems several times during their working lives. They attempt this feat every time they join a new work group. The socialization phase of group membership, when newcomers and oldtimers collaborate in the transmission of cultural knowledge, thus deserves special attention from researchers.

SOCIALIZATION IN WORK GROUPS

Work groups often need new members to maintain or improve their effectiveness. Attrition is inevitable in groups that exist for any length of time. Because attrition often leads to understaffing and thereby reduces the effectiveness of a group, new members must be recruited and trained to replace those who leave. Understaffing and reduced group effectiveness can also occur in the absence of attrition when a group's workload increases in size or complexity and current members are unable to adjust accordingly. Here, too, the recruitment and training of new members are essential.

We recently developed a model of group socialization that is helpful in analyzing how newcomers become full group members (Moreland & Levine, 1982, 1989). The model explains temporal changes in individual–group relations in terms of three basic processes: evaluation, commitment, and role transition. We assume that the group and the individual engage in an ongoing evaluation of how rewarding their relationship is compared with alternative relationships. On the basis of these evaluations, feelings of commitment arise between the group and the individual. Levels of commitment change in systematic ways over time, rising or falling to previously established decision criteria. When a decision criterion is crossed, a role transition takes place, the individual enters a new phase of group membership, and the relationship between the group and the individual changes. Evaluation proceeds, often along different dimensions, producing further changes in commitment and subsequent role transitions. In this way, the individual passes through five consecutive phases of group membership (investigation, socialization, maintenance, resocialization, and remembrance), separated by four role transitions (entry, acceptance, divergence, and exit).

The second phase of group membership, socialization, is particularly relevant to the concerns of this chapter. Socialization begins after the new member enters the group. During socialization, the group attempts to change the individual so that he or she can contribute more to the achievement of group goals, whereas the individual attempts to change the group so that it can better satisfy his or her personal needs. Insofar as these activities are successful, the individual experiences assimilation and the group experiences accommodation. If the commitment levels of both parties rise to their respective acceptance criteria, the individual undergoes the role transition of acceptance and becomes a full member. Socialization can be viewed as a struggle between the individual and the group regarding the type and amount of assimilation and accommodation that will take place. Part of this struggle focuses on the transmission of cultural knowledge.

Newcomers' Characteristics

Newcomers enter work groups with a variety of characteristics and experiences that influence their access and receptivity to the knowledge shared among old-timers. Several kinds of experiences can affect what newcomers know about a work group before entering it. These experiences include exposure to stereotypes about work groups of the same type (cf. Niedenthal, Cantor, & Kihlstrom, 1985), prior memberships in similar groups (e.g., Hopper, 1977; Jackson, Buglione, & Glenwick, 1988), contacts with previous and current group members (e.g., Decker & Cornelius, 1979; Quaglieri, 1982), and interaction with the group as a prospective member, client, or opponent (e.g., Premack & Wanous, 1985; Suszko & Breaugh, 1986). Regardless of its source, information about the group that is obtained prior to entry can vary in both accuracy and favorability. Insofar as the information is inaccurate or unfavorable, newcomers are likely to have difficulties in adapting to the group.

Once newcomers enter a work group, their motivation and ability to acquire information about the group can influence both the speed and depth of their learning. Motivation to acquire cultural knowledge can stem from a general desire to gain acceptance by any group or from a specific desire for acceptance by the group one has joined. A general desire for acceptance might be influenced by various dispositional characteristics, including sociability, need for affiliation, field dependence, and intolerance for ambiguity (e.g., Louis, 1980; Reichers, 1987). A specific desire for acceptance is influenced by the newcomer's level of commitment to the group (Moreland & Levine, 1982). A newcomer who is strongly committed to a work group will try to acquire whatever information he or she needs to help the group achieve its goals and to gain acceptance from other members. In contrast, a newcomer whose commitment to a work group is weak will be less motivated and may even actively avoid new information if it conflicts with his or her prior beliefs or threatens a preexisting social identity (Goodnow, 1990). Of course, the information that a newcomer acquires about a group may well alter his or her commitment to it.

A newcomer's ability to acquire cultural knowledge is influenced by his or her task and social skills. These skills can affect the acquisition of such knowledge in both direct and indirect ways. For example, the more task and social skills a newcomer possesses, the more easily he or she can learn whatever information is available in the group. Newcomers who possess task skills find it easier to comprehend and remember task-related information than do those who lack these skills. And newcomers who possess social skills (e.g., charm, empathy, sensitivity to nonverbal cues) find it easier to obtain information than do those who are socially unskilled. Less direct effects of task and social skills on the acquisition of knowledge by newcomers are also possible. For example, newcomers with stronger skills are more likely to be seen as valued group members, thereby eliciting higher commitment from oldtimers, than are newcomers with weaker skills. Because oldtimers want to assist newcomers to whom they are highly committed, skilled newcomers will be offered more inside information about the group than will their unskilled counterparts. Characteristics of newcomers, such as sex, race, personality traits, and values, may also affect oldtimers' commitment to newcomers, thereby increasing or decreasing their desire to share information with newcomers (Fairhurst & Snavely, 1983).

Newcomers' Tactics

After newcomers enter work groups, they can use a number of tactics to increase their access to the knowledge that oldtimers possess. These tactics include fulfilling oldtimers' expectations, seeking patrons within the group, and collaborating with other newcomers.

Research suggests that oldtimers expect newcomers to behave in particular ways and that they feel more commitment to newcomers who conform to these role expectations than they do to those who deviate. Oldtimers are more likely to share inside information about the group with newcomers to whom they are more committed. The role of a new member has four related aspects (Moreland & Levine, 1989). First, newcomers are expected to be anxious about their abilities and acceptance by oldtimers (e.g., Van Maanen, 1977). Second, newcomers are expected to be reserved in expressing their opinions and making suggestions about how the group should operate. Third, newcomers are expected to be dependent on oldtimers, imitating their behavior and asking them for advice (e.g., Feldman & Brett, 1983). Finally, newcomers are expected to conform, avoiding disagreements with oldtimers and adopting the group's perspective whenever possible (e.g., Snyder, 1958). When newcomers fulfill these expectations, they are more likely to elicit both commitment and information from oldtimers.

Another way that newcomers can acquire needed information is by utilizing patrons in the group. Several different kinds of patrons, varying in their levels of involvement with newcomers, can be found in work groups. The lowest involvement is exhibited by models chosen by newcomers as guides for behavior (e.g., Shuval & Adler, 1980; Weiss, 1978). Models are often unaware that they are being imitated by newcomers and make no effort to transmit information directly. Somewhat higher involvement is exhibited by trainers, who are assigned the job of handling newcomers by the group (e.g., Van Maanen, 1973). Although trainers feel responsibility for conveying information to newcomers, they often deal with several persons at once and thus fail to establish close relationships with any one of them. Still higher involvement is exhibited by sponsors, who bring newcomers into the group and thus feel a sense of responsibility for their success (e.g., Haas, 1974). Sponsors' concern for newcomers, often high immediately after entry, may decrease once newcomers are in the group for awhile. Finally, the highest involvement is exhibited by masters and mentors (cf. Blau, 1988). Although both master–apprentice and mentor–protege relationships often last for a long time and involve strong personal ties and mutual benefits, they differ in certain ways. Masters generally provide specific job instruction in exchange for assistance from their apprentices (e.g., Lave, 1988), whereas mentors generally provide career development help and psychosocial support without requiring immediate reciprocation from their protégés (e.g., Burke, 1984; Hunt & Michael, 1983).

So far we have emphasized how newcomers acquire information from oldtimers, but it is important to recognize that newcomers also provide information to one another. Because newcomers often share common problems, lack resources to solve these problems, and are somewhat fearful of oldtimers, they are likely to seek out one another for solace and support (e.g., Bell & Price, 1975; Van

Maanen, 1973, 1975). Once this contact is established, newcomers can provide mutual assistance in obtaining cultural knowledge (e.g., Burke & Bolf, 1986; Kram & Isabella, 1985). Such assistance occurs in various forms, some indirect and some direct. Indirect assistance includes imitation and social comparison (e.g., Levine & Moreland, 1987; Oldham, Kulik, Ambrose, Stepina, & Brand, 1986). Direct assistance includes provision of advice and collaboration in solving joint problems (e.g., Doise & Mugny, 1984; Schweiger, Sandberg, & Ragan, 1986). Of course, the information that newcomers provide to one another can be incorrect. When left to themselves, newcomers are likely to misjudge the group, their fellow members, or the work that they perform (Louis, 1980).

Oldtimers' Characteristics

Newcomers do not have total control over the transmission of cultural knowledge within work groups. Oldtimers, by virtue of their higher status and power, often regulate the type of information that newcomers receive, as well as when and how that information is transmitted. The motivation and ability of oldtimers to transmit such information can be influenced by their characteristics and experiences prior to the entry of newcomers.

Certain aspects of the group as a whole are often important in this regard. Oldtimers' motivation to transmit cultural knowledge can be influenced by the group's current success at attaining its goals and by newcomers' perceived like- lihood of contributing to goal attainment. When a group is failing because it does not have enough members or its members lack essential skills, oldtimers will feel greater commitment to newcomers and want to train them more quickly and efficiently. Commitment to newcomers and motivation to share information with them will be especially strong when oldtimers believe that newcomers either possess special skills that the group needs or can acquire these skills rather easily. Ironically, newcomers in a failing group may be unreceptive to the knowledge that oldtimers offer to share because of their own low commitment to the group.

The ability of oldtimers to transmit cultural knowledge can be influenced by the strength of their culture and by the group's prior experience with newcomers. Oldtimers in groups with strong cultures generally impart information more suc- cessfully to newcomers than do oldtimers in groups with weak cultures. When oldtimers have had prior experience with newcomers, they will also be better able to transmit information to them. Such experience allows oldtimers to estimate accurately what newcomers already know and how they will react to new infor- mation. Prior experience with newcomers can include earlier efforts to train similar persons and informal contacts with newcomers before they join the group.

Besides these aspects of the group as a whole, characteristics and experiences of individual oldtimers can also affect their transmission of cultural knowledge to newcomers. We have assumed so far that oldtimers are motivated exclusively by the desire to help newcomers become full group members. But oldtimers can be influenced by other motives as well. One such motive is the desire to enhance power and status. Because power and status are often associated with the possession of unique, or unshared, information, oldtimers may sometimes fail to share information that they have or pretend to possess information that they do not have. When oldtimers want to ingratiate themselves with group members who "own" some piece of information, they may even pretend not to possess information that they actually do have. A salad chef, for example, may pretend ignorance about the preparation of Sacher torte to avoid threatening the pastry chef's sense of expertise.

Other motives that might lead oldtimers to withhold information include the desire to punish newcomers (e.g., by withholding needed information), the desire to protect newcomers (e.g., by withholding information that other oldtimers do not like them), and the desire to sustain newcomers' motivation (e.g., by withholding information about the group's past failures). Motives that might lead oldtimers to share information include the desire to reward newcomers (e.g., by providing inside information) and the desire to build coalitions within the group. Of course, even when oldtimers want to share information, they may decide not to because they believe that the newcomer either already has the information (e.g., it seems obvious or someone else has probably imparted it), cannot comprehend it, or will not regard the information as credible.

Individual oldtimers may vary in their ability, as well as their motivation, to transmit cultural knowledge to newcomers. For example, some oldtimers may never have learned, or learned but then forgotten, critical aspects of group culture. Any information that these oldtimers transmit to newcomers is likely to be incorrect and, hence, detrimental. In contrast, other oldtimers with special expertise in certain areas of group culture (because of their interests or past experiences) may transmit information to newcomers that is correct and, hence, helpful.

Oldtimers' Tactics

Oldtimers can use various tactics to increase newcomers' knowledge of group culture. Some of these tactics affect newcomers' motivation to learn about the group, whereas others affect their access to and comprehension of cultural knowledge. A few tactics can have both kinds of effects.

Tactics that increase newcomers' motivation to learn about the group are frequently used during initiation ceremonies marking entry into the group. Some groups treat newcomers positively, welcoming them with parties, gifts, offers of aid and advice, and other special benefits (e.g., Lewicki, 1981; Schein, 1968). Newcomers who receive positive treatment may feel grateful to the group, thus increasing their desire to learn more about the group. In contrast, other groups treat newcomers negatively, forcing them to undergo harassment, degrading rituals, and even physical danger (e.g., Haas, 1972; Van Maanen, 1973; Vaught & Smith, 1980). Evidence suggests that harsh initiations often build strong commitment in new members. There are at least two possible explanations for this effect (Moreland & Levine, 1989). First, harsh initiations may cause newcomers to experience cognitive dissonance about their membership in the group, leading them to view the group more positively and feel more commitment to it. Second, harsh initiations may demonstrate to newcomers how ignorant they are of group norms, how incompetent they are at their jobs, and how dependent they are on oldtimers. These unpleasant revelations, in turn, may increase newcomers' desire to learn more about the group.

Once initiated, newcomers are subjected to a variety of other socialization tactics (see Moreland & Levine, 1989). One such tactic is "encapsulating" newcomers within a social milieu dominated by oldtimers. The goal of encapsulation is to increase newcomers' exposure to oldtimers who are willing and able to transmit group culture, and to decrease newcomers' exposure to other people who cannot or will not perform this function. Encapsulation can occur both during and after working hours. While on the job, oldtimers often closely observe newcomers to ensure that they are neither alone nor interacting with untrustworthy persons, such as other newcomers, marginal oldtimers, or outsiders. Oldtimers may also devote substantial energy to convincing newcomers that their previous identities, assumptions, and knowledge are no longer valid and, hence, must be replaced (Charles, 1982; Van Maanen, 1973). After working hours, oldtimers frequently try to spend leisure time with newcomers. These informal social interactions enable oldtimers to assess newcomers' cultural knowledge and to correct any of their misperceptions about the group.

Another common socialization tactic is encouraging oldtimers to serve as patrons for newcomers. The methods used to encourage these activities depend on the type of patronage involved. Regarding models, the group may try to ensure that all oldtimers conform to group norms, so that newcomers can observe the kind of behavior they are supposed to exhibit. Trainers are carefully selected, encouraged to learn newcomers' strengths and weaknesses, and rewarded on the basis of newcomers' performance. Sponsors are also held responsible for the performance of the newcomers they bring into the group, and oldtimers who have shown bad judgment about newcomers in the past are discouraged from sponsoring anyone else. Finally, masters and mentors are selected on the basis of their knowledge of group culture and rewarded on the basis of their apprentices' and proteges' performance.

A third socialization tactic is to train newcomers in a consistent manner. One mechanism for producing consistent training is to ensure that all oldtimers send the same signals to all newcomers. This is most likely to occur when oldtimers agree about what newcomers are supposed to learn and when they feel responsible for helping newcomers acquire this information. A second mechanism for producing consistent training is to ensure that successive newcomers are treated in the same way. This is most likely to occur when consistent selection criteria are used in recruiting new members and when the same oldtimers train successive generations of newcomers.

A final socialization tactic used by oldtimers is to assess periodically how much newcomers know about group culture and then deliver meaningful sanctions contingent on the quantity and quality of their knowledge. This assessment can be more or less formal, ranging from overt interrogations of newcomers to covert observations of their nonverbal behaviors. Among the more subtle assessment devices that oldtimers might use to assess newcomers' knowledge are telling an "ingroup" joke to see if newcomers laugh, having informers ascertain newcomers' true perceptions of the group, and tempting newcomers to violate group norms.

UNRESOLVED ISSUES

We have described the culture of work groups and discussed how cultural knowledge is transmitted from oldtimers to newcomers. Our analysis is based on two assumptions widely shared among those who study work group cultures. The first assumption is that most work groups develop cultures that are helpful rather than harmful (e.g., McFeat, 1974; Schein, 1984; Shrivastava & Schneider, 1984; Trice & Beyer, 1984). McFeat, for example, argued that culture promotes both the internal integration and the external adaptation of work groups. This argument reflects a kind of social Darwinism in which natural selection processes cause adaptive cultural elements to be retained, while maladaptive elements are lost. Although environmental pressures can clearly affect work groups in these ways, we are less optimistic about the outcome. In our opinion, work groups sometimes develop cultures that are harmless at best and dangerous at worst.

When a work group first forms, for example, its culture may be too weak to be very helpful or harmful. And it may take some time before natural selection can strengthen helpful cultural elements or weaken harmful ones. Frequent changes in the composition of a work group can also undermine the effects of natural selection by preventing a strong culture from developing. Finally, the environment within which a work group operates may change so rapidly that cultural change lags behind. As a result, cultural elements that were once helpful can become harmful (cf. Gray, Bougon, & Donnellon, 1985; Wilkins & Ouchi, 1983).

But even under the best conditions, some elements in a work group's culture may still be maladaptive. Group members can share thoughts (about their group, one another, or the work they perform) that limit their internal integration or external adaptation. Fine (1985), for example, noted that some sports teams fail because they attach too much importance to a single lost game. Players become despondent and underestimate the quality of their team. As a result, they later lose some games that they might otherwise have won. Ridgeway (1984) noted that ascribed status hinders the performance of many work groups. Female or Black workers are often mistakenly assumed to have less ability than they actually possess. As a result, they are not allowed to contribute as much to a group as they might, and the group's performance suffers accordingly. Finally, Haas (1977) noted that, when groups work in dangerous environments, their members often discourage any public expression of worry or fear. Over time, this can cause workers to ignore or forget about the real dangers of their job. As a result, they may take foolish risks, thereby increasing their own and others' chances of being injured or killed.

The fact that work groups can develop cultures that are harmful rather than helpful raises a serious issue. Instead of studying how newcomers acquire cultural knowledge, perhaps we should study how they produce cultural change. Unfortunately, only a few observers (e.g., Levine & Moreland, 1985; Sutton & Louis, 1987) have discussed the changes that newcomers produce in groups that they join. Some of these changes may be unintentional. The simple act of explaining group culture to newcomers, for example, may cause oldtimers to think more deeply about their beliefs and to alter some of them. And newcomers often ask disturbing questions or make unsettling references to other groups that can raise further doubts in the minds of oldtimers. Newcomers may also *try* to produce cultural change, especially when they are dissatisfied with the group. But change can be difficult to produce, because newcomers are usually less powerful than oldtimers. Success often depends on the balance of commitment within the group: Newcomers are more likely to produce cultural change when they elicit more commitment from oldtimers than they feel toward oldtimers. Of course, even when newcomers succeed in changing the culture of a work group, there is no guarantee that their innovation will prove to be helpful.

A second assumption widely shared among those who study work group cultures is that such groups function best when their members view the world from a common perspective. An effective work group is thus one whose members all think alike. For example, advocates of team development and quality circles in industrial settings commonly assume that shared information regarding interpersonal and task issues enhances group performance (e.g., Lawler & Mohrman, 1987; Woodman & Sherwood, 1980). Studies of the relationship between normative consensus and group performance suggest that performance is enhanced when group members endorse the same norms (e.g., Argote, 1989; Georgopoulos, 1965). Reviews of the group productivity literature routinely argue that the absence of shared knowledge about the distribution of members' skills, the failure of group members to exchange task-relevant information, and disagreements about performance strategies can all have negative consequences (e.g., Cummings, 1981; Hackman, 1987). Research on the relationship between group goals and performance emphasizes that performance is facilitated when realistic goals are shared among group members (e.g., Mackie & Goethals, 1987; Zander, 1985). And research on decision making in groups assumes that the quality of decisions is enhanced when all group members are fully apprised of all relevant information (e.g., Stasser & Titus, 1985; Vinokur, Burnstein, Sechrest, & Wortman, 1985).

Nevertheless, several lines of research suggest that maximally shared information can sometimes inhibit group performance. For example, research on group polarization suggests that sharing information in groups can produce more extreme decisions than individuals would reach if they worked alone (e.g., Isenberg, 1986; Laughlin & Early, 1982). Research on majority and minority influence indicates that sharing one's opinions with others can produce pressures to uniformity that lead to poor group decisions (e.g., Janis, 1982; Levine, 1989; Levine & Russo, 1987). Research on "social loafing," "free riding," and "sucker effects" suggests that group members' task motivation is weakened by the shared knowledge that individual performances will be combined to determine the group's overall performance (e.g., Harkins & Szymanski, 1988; Kerr & Brunn, 1983; Weldon & Gargano, 1988). Research on communication and performance indicates that too much information can sometimes overload the group's processing abilities (e.g., Foushee, 1984; Goodman, Ravlin, & Argote, 1986; Shaw, 1978). Finally, there is evidence that heterogeneity in task-relevant knowledge among group members can enhance their performance by increasing the probability that needed information will be available and by decreasing the cognitive demands placed on individual workers (e.g., Hackman, 1987; Wegner, 1987).

The fact that sharing cultural knowledge among group members sometimes harms rather than helps a work group raises another serious issue. In different situations, different distributions of knowledge within the group may be optimal. Or different kinds of knowledge may vary in their optimal distribution within the group. Unfortunately, very little is known about this issue, and few observers have even speculated about it. There is some agreement that broader distributions of knowledge are particularly beneficial to groups that operate in uncertain environments (cf. Pfeffer, 1981; Wilkins & Ouchi, 1983). In addition, the type of job performed by a work group and the status differences among its members may be important. Perhaps broadly distributed knowledge is more beneficial when (a) the group's job is unitary (all members do the same task) rather than divisible (different members do different tasks) and (b) the status differences among group members are small rather than large (Carley,

1990). These and related issues deserve further attention from researchers interested in socialization in work groups.

References

Argote, L. (1989). Agreement about norms and work-unit effectiveness: Evidence from the field. *Basic and Applied Social Psychology, 10*, 131–140.

Bell, C. G., & Price, C. M. (1975). *The first term: A study of legislative socialization.* Beverly Hills, CA: Sage.

Bem, D. J. (1972). Self-perception theory. In L. Berkowitz (Ed.), *Advances in experimental social psychology* (Vol. 6, pp. 1–62). New York: Academic Press.

Berk, S. F., & Berheide, C. W. (1977). Going backstage: Gaining access to observe household work. *Sociology of Work and Occupations, 4*, 27–48.

Berkman, S. C. J. (1978). "She's writing antidotes": An examination of hospital employees' uses of stories about personal experiences. *Folklore Forum, 11*, 48–54.

Blau, G. (1988). An investigation of the apprenticeship organizational socialization strategy. *Journal of Vocational Behavior, 32*, 176–195.

Brown, K. A. (1984). Explaining group poor performance: An attributional analysis. *Academy of Management Review, 9*, 54–63.

Burke, R. J. (1984). Mentors in organizations. *Group and Organization Studies, 9*, 353–372.

Burke, R. J., & Bolf, C. (1986). Learning within organizations: Sources and content. *Psychological Reports, 59*, 1187–1196.

Carley, K. M. (1990). Coordinating for success: Trading information redundancy for task simplicity. *Proceedings of the 23rd Annual Hawaii International Conference on System Sciences, 3*, 261–270.

Charles, M. T. (1982). The Yellowstone Ranger: The social control and socialization of federal law enforcement officers. *Human Organization, 41*, 216–226.

Cummings, T. G. (1981). Designing effective work groups. In P. C. Nystrom & W. H. Starbuck (Eds.), *Handbook of organizational design* (Vol. 2, pp. 250–271). Oxford: Oxford University Press.

Dandridge, T. C., Mitroff, I., & Joyce, W. F. (1980). Organizational symbolism: A topic to expand organizational analysis. *Academy of Management Review, 5*, 77–82.

Decker, P. J., & Cornelius, E. T. (1979). A note on recruiting sources and job survival rates. *Journal of Applied Psychology, 64*, 463–464.

Doise, W., & Mugny, G. (1984). *The social development of the intellect.* Oxford, England: Pergamon Press.

Donovan, F. R. (1920). *The woman who waits.* Boston: R. G. Badger.

Dressel, P. L., & Petersen, D. M. (1982). Becoming a male stripper: Recruitment, socialization, and ideological development. *Work and Occupations, 9*, 387–406.

Fairhurst, G. T., & Snavely, B. K. (1983). Majority and token minority group relationships: Power acquisition and communication. *Academy of Management Review, 8*, 292–300.

Feldman, D. C. (1989). Socialization, resocialization, and training: Reframing the research agenda. In I. L. Goldstein and Associates (Eds.), *Training and development in organizations* (Vol. 3, pp. 376–416). San Francisco: Jossey-Bass.

Feldman, D. C., & Brett, J. M. (1983). Coping with new jobs: A comparative study of new hires and job changers. *Academy of Management Journal, 26*, 258–272.

Fine, G. A. (1979). Small groups and culture creation: The idioculture of Little League Baseball teams. *American Sociological Review*, *44*, 733–745.

Fine, G. A. (1985). Team sports, seasonal histories, and significant events: Little League Baseball and the creation of collective meaning. *Sociology of Sport Journal*, *2*, 299–313.

Fine, G. A. (1987). Working cooks: The dynamics of professional kitchens. *Current Research in Occupations and Professions*, *4*, 141–158.

Foushee, H. C. (1984). Dyads and triads at 35,000 feet: Factors affecting group process and aircrew performance. *American Psychologist*, *39*, 885–893.

Georgopoulos, B. S. (1965). Normative structure variables and organizational behavior. *Human Relations*, *18*, 155–169.

Gladstein, D. (1984). Groups in context: A model of task group effectiveness. *Administrative Science Quarterly*, *29*, 499–517.

Goodman, P. S., Ravlin, E. C., & Argote, L. (1986). Current thinking about groups: Setting the stage for new ideas. In P. S. Goodman (Ed.), *Designing effective work groups* (pp. 1–33). San Francisco: Jossey-Bass.

Goodnow, J. J. (1990). The socialization of cognition: What's involved? In J. W. Stigler, R. A. Shweder, & G. Herdt (Eds.), *Cultural psychology: Essays on comparative human development* (pp. 259–286). Cambridge, England: Cambridge University Press.

Gray, B., Bougon, M. G., & Donnellon, A. (1985). Organizations as constructions and destructions of memory. *Journal of Management*, *11*, 83–98.

Gregory, K. L. (1983). Native-view paradigms: Multiple cultures and culture conflicts in organizations. *Administrative Science Quarterly*, *28*, 359–376.

Haas, J. (1972). Binging: Educational control among high steel iron workers. *American Behavioral Scientist*, *16*, 27–34.

Haas, J. (1974). The stages of the high steel iron worker apprentice career. *Sociological Quarterly*, *15*, 93–108.

Haas, J. (1977). Learning real feelings: A study of high steel nonworkers' reactions to fear and danger. *Sociology of Work and Occupations*, *4*, 147–170.

Hackman, J. R. (1987). The design of work teams. In J. Lorsch (Ed.), *Handbook of organizational behavior* (pp. 315–342). Englewood Cliffs, NJ: Prentice-Hall.

Harkins, S. G., & Szymanski, K. (1988). Social loafing and self-evaluation with an objective standard. *Journal of Experimental Social Psychology*, *24*, 354–365.

Hopper, M. (1977). Becoming a policeman: Socialization of cadets in a police academy. *Urban Life*, *6*, 149–170.

Hunt, D. M., & Michael, C. (1983). Mentorship: A career training and development tool. *Academy of Management Review*, *8*, 475–485.

Isenberg, D. J. (1986). Group polarization: A critical review and meta-analysis. *Journal of Personality and Social Psychology*, *50*, 1141–1151.

Jackson, J. M., Buglione, S. A., & Glenwick, D. S. (1988). Major league baseball performance as a function of being traded: A drive theory analysis. *Personality and Social Psychology Bulletin*, *14*, 46–56.

Janis, I. L. (1982). Counteracting the adverse effects of concurrence-seeking in policy-planning groups: Theory and research perspectives. In H. Brandstatter, J. H. Davis, & G. Stocker-Kriechgauer (Eds.), *Group decision making* (pp. 477–501). London: Academic Press.

Katz, D. (1982). The effects of group longevity on project communication. *Administrative Science Quarterly*, *27*, 81–104.

Kauffman, K. (1988). *Prison officers and their world*. Cambridge, MA: Harvard University Press.

Kerr, N. L., & Brunn, S. E. (1983). Dispensability of member effort and group motivation losses: Free-rider effects. *Journal of Personality and Social Psychology, 44*, 78–94.

Konar, E., Sundstrom, E., Brady, K., Mandel, D., & Rice, R. (1982). Status demarcation in the office. *Environmental Behavior, 14*, 561–580.

Kram, K. E., & Isabella, L. A. (1985). Mentoring alternatives: The role of peer relationships in career development. *Academy of Management Journal, 28*, 110–132.

Laughlin, P. R., & Early, P. C. (1982). Social combination models, persuasive arguments theory, social comparison theory, and choice shift. *Journal of Personality and Social Psychology, 42*, 273–280.

Lave, J. (1988). *Cognition in practice.* Boston, MA: Cambridge University Press.

Lawler, E. E., & Mohrman, S. A. (1987). Quality circles: After the honeymoon. *Organizational Dynamics, 15*, 42–54.

Leary, M. R., & Forsyth, D. R. (1987). Attributions of responsibility for collective efforts. In C. Hendrick (Ed.), *Group processes: Review of personality and social psychology* (Vol. 8, pp. 167–188). Newbury Park, CA: Sage.

Levine, J. M. (1989). Reaction to opinion deviance in small groups. In P. Paulus (Ed.), *Psychology of group influence* (2nd ed., pp. 187–231). Hillsdale, NJ: Erlbaum.

Levine, J. M., & Moreland, R. L. (1985). Innovation and socialization in small groups. In S. Moscovici, G. Mugny, & E. Van Avermaet (Eds.), *Perspectives on minority influence* (pp. 143–169). Cambridge, England: Cambridge University Press.

Levine, J. M., & Moreland, R. L. (1987). Social comparison and outcome evaluation in group contexts. In J. C. Masters & W. P. Smith (Eds.), *Social comparison, social justice, and relative deprivation: Theoretical, empirical, and policy perspectives* (pp. 105–127). Hillsdale, NJ: Erlbaum.

Levine, J. M., & Russo, E. M. (1987). Majority and minority influence. In C. Hendrick (Ed.), *Group processes: Review of personality and social psychology* (Vol. 8, pp. 13–54). Newbury Park, CA: Sage.

Lewicki, R. J. (1981). Organizational seduction: Building commitment to organizations. *Organizational Dynamics, 10*, 42–21.

Louis, M. R. (1980). Surprise and sense making: What newcomers experience in entering unfamiliar organizational settings. *Administrative Science Quarterly, 25*, 226–251.

Mackie, D. M., & Goethals, G. R. (1987). Individual and group goals. In C. Hendrick (Ed.), *Group processes: Review of personality and social psychology* (Vol. 8, pp. 144–166). Newbury Park, CA: Sage.

Martin, J. (1982). Stories and scripts in organizational settings. In A. Hastorf & A. Isen (Eds.), *Cognitive social psychology* (pp. 255–305). New York: Elsevier.

Martin, J., Feldman, M. S., Hatch, M. J., & Sitkin, S. B. (1983). The uniqueness paradox in organizational stories. *Administrative Science Quarterly, 28*, 438–453.

McFeat, T. (1974). *Small-group cultures.* New York: Pergamon Press.

Meara, H. (1974). Honor in dirty work: The case of American meat cutters and Turkish butchers. *Sociology of Work and Occupations, 1*, 259–283.

Moreland, R. L., & Levine, J. M. (1982). Socialization in small groups: Temporal changes in individual-group relations. In L. Berkowitz (Ed.), *Advances in experimental social psychology* (Vol. 15, pp. 137–192). New York: Academic Press.

Moreland, R. L., & Levine, J. M. (1989). Newcomers and oldtimers in small groups. In P. Paulus (Ed.), *Psychology of group influence* (2nd ed.) (pp. 143–186). Hillsdale, NJ: Erlbaum.

Niedenthal, P. M., Cantor, N., & Kihlstrom, J. F. (1985). Prototype-matching: A strategy for social decision-making. *Journal of Personality and Social Psychology, 48*, 575–584.

Nusbaum, P. (1978). A conversational approach to occupational folklore: Conversation, work, play, and the workplace. *Folklore Forum, 11*, 18–28.

Oldham, G. R., Kulik, C. T., Ambrose, M. L., Stepina, L. P., & Brand, J. F. (1986). Relations between job facet comparisons and employee reactions. *Organizational Behavior and Human Decision Processes*, *38*, 28–47.

Ornstein, S. (1986). Organizational symbols: A study of their meanings and inferences on perceived psychological climate. *Organizational Behavior and Human Performance*, *38*, 207–229.

Pfeffer, J. (1981). Management as symbolic action: The creation and maintenance of organizational paradigms. In L. L. Cummings & B. M. Staw (Eds.), *Research in organizational behavior* (Vol. 3, pp. 1–52). Greenwich, CT: JAI Press.

Premack, S. L., & Wanous, J. P. (1985). A meta-analysis of realistic job preview experiments. *Journal of Applied Psychology*, *70*, 706–719.

Quaglieri, P. L. (1982). A note on variations in recruiting information obtained through different sources. *Journal of Occupational Psychology*, *55*, 53–55.

Reichers, A. E. (1987). An interactionist perspective on newcomer socialization rates. *Academy of Management Review*, *12*, 278–287.

Ridgeway, C. L. (1984). Dominance, performance, and status in groups: A theoretical analysis. In E. Lawler (Ed.), *Advances in group processes* (Vol. 1, pp. 59–93). Greenwich, CT: JAI Press.

Riemer, J. W. (1977). Becoming a journeyman electrician: Some implicit indicators in the apprenticeship process. *Sociology of Work and Occupations*, *4*, 87–98.

Roy, D. F. (1952). Quota restriction and goldbricking in a machine shop. *American Journal of Sociology*, *57*, 426–442.

Roy, D. F. (1955). "Banana Time": Job satisfaction and informal interaction. *Human Organization*, *18*, 158–168.

Salancik, G. R., & Pfeffer, J. (1978). A social information processing approach to job attitudes and task design. *Administrative Science Quarterly*, *23*, 224–253.

Sanders, C. R. (1974). Psyching out the crowd: Folk performers and their audiences. *Urban Life and Culture*, *3*, 264–282.

Schein, E. H. (1968). Organizational socialization and the profession of management. *Industrial Management Review*, *9*, 1–15.

Schein, E. H. (1984). Coming to a new awareness of organizational culture. *Sloan Management Review*, *25*, 3–16.

Schweiger, D. M., Sandberg, W. R., & Ragan, J. W. (1986). Group approaches for improving strategic decision making: A comparative analysis of dialectical inquiry, devil's advocacy, and consensus. *Academy of Management Journal*, *29*, 51–71.

Scribner, S. (1984). Studying working intelligence. In B. Rogoff & J. Lave (Eds.), *Everyday cognition: Its development in social context* (pp. 9–40). Cambridge, MA: Harvard University Press.

Shaw, M. E. (1978). Communication networks fourteen years later. In L. Berkowitz (Ed.), *Group processes* (pp. 351–361). New York: Academic Press.

Shrauger, J. S., & Schoeneman, T. J. (1979). Symbolic interactionist view of self-concept: Through the looking-glass darkly. *Psychological Bulletin*, *86*, 549–573.

Shrivastava, P., & Schneider, S. (1984). Organizational frames of reference. *Human Relations*, *10*, 795–809.

Shuval, J. T., & Adler, I. (1980). The role of models in professional socialization. *Social Science and Medicine*, *14*, 5–14.

Smith, M. E. (1977). Don't call my boat a ship! *Anthropological Quarterly*, *50*, 9–17.

Snyder, E. C. (1958). The Supreme Court as a small group. *Social Forces*, *36*, 232–238.

Stasser, G., & Titus, W. (1985). Pooling of unshared information in group decision making: Biased information sampling during discussion. *Journal of Personality and Social Psychology*, *48*, 1467–1478.

Suszko, M. K., & Breaugh, J. A. (1986). The effects of realistic job previews on applicant self-selection and employee turnover, satisfaction, and coping ability. *Journal of Management, 12*, 513–523.

Sutton, R. I., & Louis, M. R. (1987). How selecting and socializing newcomers influences insiders. *Human Resource Management, 26*, 347–361.

Tajfel, H., & Turner, J. C. (1979). An integrative theory of intergroup conflict. In W. G. Austin & S. Worchel (Eds.), *The social psychology of intergroup relations* (pp. 33–47). Monterey, CA: Brooks-Cole.

Trice, H. M., & Beyer, J. M. (1984). Studying organizational cultures through rites and ceremonials. *Academy of Management Review, 9*, 653–669.

Van Maanen, J. (1973). Observations on the making of policemen. *Human Organization, 32*, 407–418.

Van Maanen, J. (1975). Police socialization: A longitudinal examination of job attitudes in an urban police department. *Administrative Science Quarterly, 20*, 207–228.

Van Maanen, J. (1977). Experiencing organization: Notes on the meaning of careers and socialization. In J. Van Maanen (Ed.), *Organizational careers: Some new perspectives* (pp. 15–45). New York: Wiley.

Van Maanen, J. (1980). Career goals: Organizational rules of play. In C. B. Derr (Ed.), *Work, family, and the career* (pp. 111–143). New York: Praeger.

Van Maanen, J., & Barley, S. R. (1984). Occupational communities: Culture and control in organizations. In B. M. Staw & L. L. Cummings (Eds.), *Research in organizational behavior* (Vol. 6, pp. 287–365). Greenwich, CT: JAI Press.

Vaught, C., & Smith, D. L. (1980). Incorporation and mechanical solidarity in an underground coal mine. *Sociology of Work and Occupations, 7*, 159–187.

Vinokur, A., Burnstein, E., Sechrest, L., & Wortman, P. M. (1985). Group decision making by experts: Field study of panels evaluating medical technologies. *Journal of Personality and Social Psychology, 49*, 70–84.

Wegner, D. M. (1987). Transactive memory: A contemporary analysis of the group mind. In B. Mullen & G. Goethals (Eds.), *Theories of group behavior* (pp. 185–208). New York: Springer-Verlag.

Weiss, H. M. (1978). Social learning of work values in organizations. *Journal of Applied Psychology, 63*, 711–718.

Weldon, E., & Gargano, G. M. (1988). Cognitive loafing: The effects of accountability and shared responsibility on cognitive effort. *Personality and Social Psychology Bulletin, 14*, 159–171.

Wilkins, A. L., & Ouchi, W. G. (1983). Efficient culture: Exploring the relationship between culture and organizational performance. *Administrative Science Quarterly, 28*, 468–481.

Woodman, R. W., & Sherwood, J. J. (1980). The role of team development in organizational effectiveness: A critical review. *Psychological Bulletin, 88*, 166–186.

Zander, A. (1985). *The purposes of groups and organizations*. San Francisco: Jossey-Bass.

Zurcher, L. A. (1965). The sailor aboard ship: A study of role behavior in a total institution. *Social Forces, 43*, 389–400.

Zurcher, L. A. (1968). Social psychological functions of ephermeral roles: A disaster work crew. *Human Organization, 27*, 281–297.

Zurcher, L. A., Sonenschein, D. W., & Metzner, E. L. (1966). The hasher: A study of role conflict. *Social Forces, 44*, 505–514.

PART FIVE

COLLABORATING AT WORK

CHAPTER 13

THE SOCIAL ORGANIZATION OF DISTRIBUTED COGNITION

EDWIN HUTCHINS

DISTRIBUTED COGNITION

In the history of anthropology, there is scarcely a more important concept than the division of labor. In terms of the energy budget of a human group and the efficiency with which a group exploits its physical environment, social organizational factors often produce group properties that differ considerably from the properties of individuals. For example, Wittfogel, (1957; cited in Roberts, 1964) writing about the advent of hydraulic farming and oriental despotism, says

> A large quantity of water can be channeled and kept within bounds only by the use of mass labor; and this mass labor must be coordinated, disciplined, and led. Thus a number of farmers eager to conquer arid lowlands and plains are forced to invoke the organizational devices which—on the basis of premachine technology—offer the one chance of success; they must work in cooperation with their fellows and subordinate themselves to a directing authority. (pp. 17–18)

The research on which this chapter is based was supported by the independent research program of the Navy Personnel Research and Development Center, San Diego; by the Personnel and Training Research programs, Psychological Sciences Division, Office of Naval Research, under Contract No. N00014-85-C-0133; and by a fellowship from the John D. and Catherine T. MacArthur Foundation. The views and conclusions presented in this chapter are those of the author and should not be interpreted as necessarily representing the official policies, either expressed or implied, of the sponsoring agencies.

Thus, a particular kind of social organization permits the efforts of individuals to combine in ways that produce results—in this case, a technological system called *hydraulic farming*—that could not be produced by any individual farmer working alone. This kind of effect is ubiquitous in modern life, but it is largely invisible to us. The skeptical reader may wish to look around right now and see whether there is anything in the current environment that was not either produced or delivered to its present location by the cooperative efforts of humans working in socially organized groups. The only thing I can find in my environment that meets this test is a striped pebble that I found at the beach and carried home to decorate my desk. Every other thing I can see from my chair is not only the product of coordinated group rather than individual activities but is also *necessarily* the product of group rather than individual activity.

All divisions of labor require some distributed cognition in order to coordinate the activities of the participants. Even a simple system of two men driving a spike with hammers requires some cognition on the part of each to coordinate his own activities with those of the other. When the labor that is distributed is cognitive labor, the system involves the distribution of two kinds of cognitive labor: the cognition that is the task, and the cognition that governs the coordination of the elements of the task. In such a case, the group performing the cognitive task may have cognitive properties that differ from the cognitive properties of any individual.

Given the importance of social organization and the division of labor as transformers of human capacities, it is something of a surprise that the *division of cognitive labor* has played a very minor role in cognitive anthropology. There have been few analogous investigations of the many ways in which the cognitive properties of human groups may depend on the social organization of individual cognitive capabilities. In recent years there has been increasing interest in intracultural variability, the question of the distribution of knowledge in a society (Romney, Weller, & Batchelder, 1986; Boster, 1985, this volume). For the most part, this work has addressed the question of the reliability and representativeness of individual anthropological informants and is not oriented toward the question of the properties of the group that result from one or another distribution of knowledge among its members.

The notion that a culture or society, as a group, might have some cognitive properties differing from those of the individual members of the culture has been around since the turn of the century, most conspicuously in the writings of the French sociologist Emile Durkheim (1893/1949; 1915/1965) and his followers, and largely in the form of programmatic assertions that it is true. This is an interesting general assertion, but can it be demonstrated that any particular sort of cognitive property could be manifested differently at the individual and group levels? Making a move in that direction, Roberts (1964) suggested that a cultural group can be seen as a kind of widely distributed memory. Such a memory is clearly more robust than the memory of any individual and undoubtedly has a much greater capacity than any individual memory has. Roberts even speculated on how retrieval from the cultural memory might be different from individual memory retrieval and how changing social organizational devices might be required to continue to support memory retrieval functions in increasingly complex cultures. Roberts explored these issues in a comparison of four American Indian tribes. Information retrieval (scanning) at the tribal level among the Mandan was held to be more efficient than among the Chiricahua because "The small geographical area occupied by the tribe, the concentrated settlement pattern, the frequent visiting, the ceremonial linkages, made even informal mechanisms [of retrieval] more efficient" (1964, p. 448).

Roberts noted that the tribal level information retrieval processes of the Cheyenne had properties different from those of the Mandan or Chiricahua, and linked the properties to particular features of social organization.

> If the membership of a council represents kin and other interest groups in the tribe, each member makes available to the council as a whole the informational resources of the groups he represents. . . . Councils have usually been viewed as decision-making bodies without proper emphasis on their function as information retrieval units. (Roberts, 1964, p. 449)

In the sentences just cited, Roberts attributes the differences in retrieval efficiency at the group level to variables such as group size, the pattern of interactions among individuals, the distribution of knowledge, and the time course of interaction. How could we demonstrate the effects of variables such as these? Even this small number of variables defines a very large parameter space. To investigate that space experimentally and tease out the effects of each of these variables and their possible interactions with each other is a very expensive proposition.

Still, it seems important to come to an understanding of the ways that the cognitive properties of groups may differ from those of individuals. In the comparison of the physical accomplishments of pre- and post-hydraulic agriculture societies, it is obvious that the differences in physical accomplishment are due to differences in the social organization of physical labor rather than to differences in the physical strength of the members of the two societies. Similarly, if groups can have cognitive properties that are significantly different from those of the individuals in the group, then differences in the cognitive accomplishments of any two groups might depend entirely on differences in the social organization of distributed cognition and not at all on differences in the cognitive properties of individuals in the two groups.

This chapter describes an attempt to use computer simulation modeling to explore the social organization of distributed cognition. The advantages of this technique are that experiments can be constructed and run cheaply and quickly. Furthermore, the computer modeling technique permits a degree of control over independent variables that is not attainable in empirical studies, and the processing of the "individuals" in computer models can be examined (dissected, really) in a way that is not possible with human subjects.

The disadvantage is that computer models are always abstractions from real systems, and the degree to which we believe the results are informative about human phenomena depends on how well we think the abstraction captures the important aspects of the phenomena being modeled. There is ample room for doubt about the cognitive fidelity of the models presented in this chapter, and I will try to present these doubts and the problems of the model honestly in the discussion that follows.

Despite its many problems, computer modeling of this type may help to suggest new hypotheses about the nature of systems of socially distributed cognition (or whatever else is being modeled). Such models may also help us develop new understandings of phenomena that are well known but may not have previously been seen as related. Finally, they may direct our attention to certain parts of the huge parameter space for further empirical investigations. That is, such models may help us decide where to spend precious empirical research resources.

To test the notion that the cognitive properties of groups differ from those of the individuals who comprise them, we need to focus on some particular cognitive property that is generally agreed to be a property of individual cognition, and then develop some way to show that whether that property is or is not manifested by a group depends on the social organization of the group. For the purposes of this study, we will use the phenomenon known as *confirmation bias*.

CONFIRMATION BIAS IN THE FORMATION OF INTERPRETATIONS

Confirmation bias is a propensity to affirm prior interpretations and to discount, ignore, or reinterpret evidence counter to an already formed interpretation. It is a bias to confirm an already held hypothesis about the nature of the world. This is a commonsense notion. We talk about the difficulty of changing someone's mind, once it is "made up." The importance of "first impressions" is an obvious corollary of our folk belief in this principle. There is also compelling scientific evidence on the generalizability of confirmation bias across such areas as attribution (Anderson, Lepper, & Ross, 1980), personality traits (Hastie & Kumar, 1979), logical inference tasks (Wason, 1968; Wason & Johnson-Laird, 1972), beliefs about important social issues (Lord, Lepper, & Ross 1979), and scientific reasoning tasks (Fleck, 1979/1935; Tweney, Doherty, & Mynatt, 1981, parts III & IV).

To the extent that this propensity to stick with prior interpretations and discount disconfirming evidence frequently leads people to persevere in faulty interpretations of the nature of the world, this tendency seems maladaptive. After all, knowing what is going on in the environment is an important ability for any creature, and, in general, the more complex the creature, the more complex is that creature's sense of what is in the environment. For very complex creatures like human beings, a property of cognitive processing that prevents us from finding better interpretations once we have a "good" one would seem very maladaptive. Why, then, would such a property survive? Clearly, there must be a trade-off here between the ability to move from one interpretation to a better one and the need to have an interpretation—*any interpretation*—in order to coordinate with events in the environment. A system that maintains a coherent but suboptimal interpretation may be better able to adapt than a system that tears its interpretations apart as fast as it builds them.

This propensity is widely accepted as a general feature of *individual cognition*. If it represents a sometimes infelicitous trade-off between keeping a poor interpretation and having no interpretation at all, one wonders if it might not be possible for a group of individuals, each of whom has this propensity, to make a different sort of trade-off. That is, might a group be organized in such a way that it is more likely than any individual alone to arrive at the best of several possible interpretations, or to reject a working interpretation when a better one is present? The plan for the remainder of this chapter is to accept confirmation bias as a property of individual cognition and then to ask what properties it might produce in systems of socially distributed cognition. What I hope to show is that the consequences of this property of individual cognition for the cognitive capabilities of groups of humans depend almost entirely on how the group distributes the tasks of cognition among its members. That is, some ways of organizing people around thinking tasks will lead to an exacerbation of the maladaptive aspects of this property of mental systems, whereas other forms of organization will make an adaptive virtue on the group level of what appears to be an individual vice.

INTERPRETATION FORMATION AS CONSTRAINT SATISFACTION

Many important human activities are conducted by systems in which multiple actors attempt to form coherent interpretations of some set of phenomena. Some of these systems are small, being composed of only a few individuals, but others are very large. The operation of complex systems is often accomplished by teams. A shift of nuclear power plant operators, an aircraft flight crew, or the bridge team on a large ship are each a small system in which multiple individuals strive to maintain an interpretation of the situation at hand. The complexity of a system may make it impossible for a single individual to integrate all the required information. Or the several members of the group may be present because of other task demands but, nevertheless, be involved in distributed interpretation formation. Management teams in business and government are also systems of distributed interpretation formation, as are juries in the court system. A community of scientists may be the best example of a very large scale system in which a group strives to construct a coherent interpretation of phenomena.

Forming an interpretation is an instance of what computer scientists call a *constraint satisfaction problem*. Any coherent interpretation consists of a number of parts; call them *hypotheses*. Some of the parts go together with each other or support each other, whereas others exclude or inhibit each other. These relationships between the parts of the interpretation are called *constraints*. The following example is taken from Perrow's book, *Normal Accidents*:

> On a beautiful night in October 1978, in the Chesapeake Bay, two vessels sighted one another visually and on radar. On one of them, the Coast Guard cutter training vessel *Cuyahoga*, the captain (a chief warrant officer) saw the other ship up ahead as a small object on the radar, and visually he saw two lights, indicating that it was proceeding in the same direction as his own ship. He thought it possibly was a fishing vessel. The first mate saw the lights, but saw three, and estimated (correctly) that it was a ship proceeding toward them. He had no responsibility to inform the captain, nor did he think he needed to. Since the two ships drew together so rapidly, the captain decided that it must be a very slow fishing boat that he was about to overtake. This reinforced his incorrect interpretation. The lookout knew the captain was aware of the ship, so did not comment further as it got quite close and seemed to be nearly on a collision course. Since both ships were traveling full speed, the closing came fast. The other ship, a large cargo ship, did not establish any bridge-to-bridge communication, because the passing was routine. But at the last moment, the captain of the *Cuyahoga* realized that in overtaking the supposed fishing boat, which he assumed was on a near parallel course, he would cut off that boat's ability to turn as both of them approached the Potomac River. So he ordered a turn to the port.[1]

The two ships collided, killing eleven sailors on the Coast Guard vessel. The captain's interpretation contained a number of hypotheses: that the other ship was small, that it was slow, and that it was traveling in the same direction as his own ship. These hypotheses were linked with a set of observations—the ship presented a small image on the radar; it appeared (to the captain) to show two lights; the distance between the ships was closing rapidly—to form a coherent interpretation in which the hypotheses were consistent with each other and with the observations. Several of the hypotheses of the mate's interpretation are in direct conflict with some of the hypotheses in the captain's interpretation. For

---

[1] From *Normal Accidents* (p. 215) by C. Perrow, 1984, New York: Basic Books. Copyright 1984 by Basic Books.

example, the hypothesis that the ships are meeting head-on and the hypothesis that one is overtaking the other are mutually exclusive.

A good interpretation is one that is both internally consistent and in agreement with the available data. Evidence from the world makes some of the hypotheses of the interpretation more or less likely. Those hypotheses that are directly driven by evidence have constraining relationships to other hypotheses for which there is, perhaps, no direct evidence. For example, in the ship collision described above, there is no direct evidence concerning the speed of the other vessel. That hypothesis is derived from the hypothesis that the Coast Guard ship is overtaking the other and the observation that the distance between the ships is closing rapidly. If those two things are true, the other ship must be moving slowly. The job of forming an interpretation can thus be seen as attempting to assign likelihoods to the various hypotheses in such a way that the constraints among the hypotheses and between the hypotheses and evidence in the world are as well satisfied as is possible.

Our project in this chapter is to develop a framework for describing these situations and the factors that control the cognitive properties of these socially distributed systems. We would like to develop an abstraction that is pertinent to the phenomena and that captures the similarities among a number of classes of distributed interpretation formation in spite of the diversity of details out of which they are composed. The account we want should explicitly address the issue of the formation of interpretations and the ways that interpretations can be influenced by evidence from the environment as well as by evidence communicated by other actors in the setting. It should allow us to look at what is going on inside individuals and also what is going on between them, and should allow us to characterize both the properties of individuals and those of systems composed of several individuals.

Constraint Satisfaction Networks

A particular kind of connectionist network called a *constraint satisfaction network* provides a rough model of individual interpretation formation. A constraint satisfaction network is a

> . . . network in which each unit represents a hypothesis of some sort
> (e.g., that a certain semantic feature, visual feature, or acoustic feature is
> present in the input) and in which each connection represents constraints
> among the hypotheses. Thus, for example, if feature B is expected to be pres-
> ent whenever feature A is, there should be a positive connection from the unit
> corresponding to the hypothesis that A is present to the unit representing the
> hypothesis that B is present. Similarly, if there is a constraint that whenever A
> is present B is expected *not* to be present, there should be a negative connec-
> tion from A to B. If the constraints are weak, the weights should be small. If
> the constraints are strong, then the weights should be large. Similarly, the in-
> puts to such a network can also be thought of as constraints. A positive input

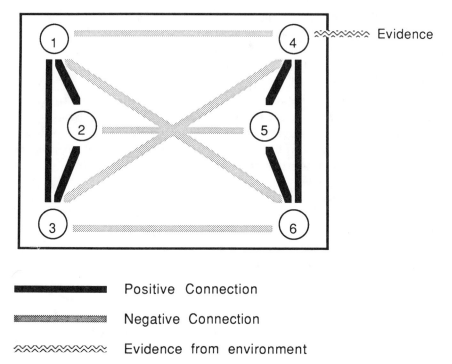

Positive Connection

Negative Connection

Evidence from environment

Figure 1   A simple constraint satisfaction network composed of six units. Evidence in
the environment that supports a particular hypothesis is implemented as the
addition of activation to the unit that represents that hypothesis. This network
receives evidence that supports the hypothesis represented by unit 4.

to a particular unit means that there is evidence from the outside that the relevant feature is present. A negative input means that there is evidence from the
outside that the feature is not present.[2]

With each unit adjusting its activation (likelihood of being true) on the basis
of the activations of its neighbors and the strengths of the connections to those
neighbors, such a network will eventually settle into a state in which as many
constraints as possible will be satisfied.

Imagine a network in which there are two clusters of units. (See Figure 1.)
Among the units within each cluster there are positive connections. Thus, each
cluster of units represents a set of hypotheses that are consistent with each other.

[2]From "Schemata and Sequential Thought Processes in PDP Models" by D.E. Rumelhart, P.
Smolensky, J. L. McClelland, & G. E. Hinton. In *Parallel distributed processing: Explorations in
the microstructure of cognition: Vol. 2. Psychological and biological models* (pp. 8–9) edited by J. L.
McClelland, D. E. Rumelhart, & the PDP Group, 1986, Cambridge, MA: MIT Press. Copyright 1986
by MIT Press. Reprinted by permission.

All of the connections that go from a unit in one cluster and a unit in the other cluster are negative. This means that the hypotheses represented by the units of one cluster are inconsistent with the hypotheses represented by the units of the other cluster. When such a network tries to satisfy as many constraints as it can among the hypotheses, it will end up with all the units in one cluster highly active and all the units in the other cluster inactive. That is, it will arrive at an interpretation in which one set of hypotheses is considered true and the other is considered false. Once having arrived at such a state, the network will be very insensitive to evidence that contradicts the interpretation already formed. Notice that there are two kinds of patterns here: the pattern of interconnections among the units and the pattern of activation across the units. An interpretation of an event is a particular pattern of activation across the units, for example, the state in which all the units of the left-hand cluster are active and all the units in the right-hand cluster are inactive. The stable interpretations of the network are determined by the pattern of interconnectivity of the units. In this case we have carefully arranged the connection strengths so that there will be just two stable interpretations.

In the ship collision scenario presented above, we can assume that the captain and the mate share the schema for interpreting the motion of other ships on the water. Seeing two lights supports the hypothesis that one is viewing the stern of the other ship; seeing three supports the hypothesis that one is meeting it head-on. If one ship is overtaking another, a rapid closing of the distance to the other ship supports the hypothesis that it is going slowly. The mate would doubtless endorse these constraints among hypotheses. But he reached a different interpretation, because he "saw" different evidence than the captain saw. In the computer simulation model, sharing the schema will be expressed as sharing the pattern of connections among the units. Sharing the interpretation will be expressed as having the same pattern of activation across the units.

For the network shown in Figure 1, an interpretation is a pattern of activation across the six units of the network. Each unit represents a hypothesis, and the connections among units represent supportive or competitive relations among the hypotheses represented by the units. In this network, units 1–3 support each other and units 4–6 support each other. The units in each of these clusters inhibit the units in the other cluster. The network has two coherent interpretations: one in which units 1–3 are active while units 4–6 are inactive, and another in which units 4–6 are active and units 1–3 are inactive.

Because each of the six units can have any value between zero and one, the space of possible interpretations for this network is, thus, a six-dimensional space. Unfortunately, it is very difficult to visualize events in six dimensions; however, this six-dimensional space can be mapped into two-dimensional space. Because it is possible to compute the euclidian distance of any pattern of activation from the patterns of activation of the two good interpretations, it is possible to

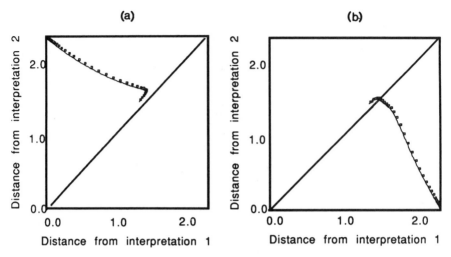

Figure 2   The trajectories of a single network in interpretation space.

build a space in which the two dimensions are *distance from interpretation one* and *distance from interpretation two*. Thus, the location of any pattern of activation can be plotted in space in terms of its nearness to the two good interpretations. For example, the pattern of activation in which every unit has an activation value of 0.5 is equally distant from the two good interpretations. The plotting of positions in interpretation space is of no computational consequence; it simply makes the motion of the networks visible. Note also that not all locations in the space are possible and that the fact that two networks are at the same location in the space does not mean that they have the same pattern of activation. Figure 2 shows the interpretation space plotted in two dimensions. The X-axis shows the distance of the current interpretation from interpretation 1. The Y-axis indicates the distance of the current interpretation from interpretation 2. Thus, for example, the lower right-hand corner is as close to interpretation 2 as is possible and as far from interpretation 1 as possible. It therefore represents the location of interpretation 2. The diagonal line is everywhere equidistant between the two interpretations. The track of the network is shown in time. Its position is plotted at equal time intervals, so the distances between the plotted positions are proportional to the speed at which the network's interpretation is changing. The network shown in Figure 2, panel *a* began slightly nearer to interpretation 1 than to interpretation 2. It began moving, slowly at first, away from both interpretations; then it turned toward interpretation 1 and picked up speed. Finally, it made a slow approach to interpretation 1. The same network is shown in Figure 2, panel *b*, but this time it has evidence from the environment in favor of interpretation 2. Even though it began slightly predisposed to interpretation 1, it was swayed by the evidence from the environment and went to interpretation 2.

Three variables determine the behavior of the isolated network. First, there is the pattern of interconnectivity of its units. This is the network's schema of the phenomena about which the interpretation is formed. Second, there is the initial pattern of activation across its units. This is the network's preconceptions about the state of affairs in the world. This pattern can be seen in the trajectories of networks in interpretation space as the point at which a network starts. Third are the external inputs to particular units of the network. This represents the evidence directly in favor of or against particular hypotheses that are parts of the interpretations. The trajectories shown in Figure 2 demonstrate the effects of these variables.

Communities of Networks

The behavior of a single constraint satisfaction network mimics, in a rough way, the phenomenon of confirmation bias as it is observed in individual human actors. Even more complicated versions of these networks could provide more accurate models of confirmation bias. The simple networks presented here are close enough to serve my present purpose, which is finding a simulation that allows researchers to explore the relationships among properties of individuals and properties of groups. To make such an exploration, I will create and examine the behavior of communities of networks. This may not seem to be the most obvious strategy to pursue. Because the processing in connectionist networks is distributed across units in a network, and the processing in a system of socially distributed cognition is distributed across a number of people, there is a strong temptation to adopt a superficial mapping between the two domains, in which units in a network are seen as corresponding to individual people and the connections among units are seen to correspond to the communication links among people. In this way, a single network would be taken as a model of a community of people. There are many problems with this mapping, and I do not have space to deal with them here. Let me simply issue the warning that this most obvious mapping is quite likely a dead end and suggest instead that the real value of connectionism for understanding the social distribution of cognition will come from a more complicated analogy in which individual people are modeled by whole networks or assemblies of networks, and systems of socially distributed cognition are modeled by communities of networks. The latter approach is the one I have taken here.

Parameters of the Models

What happens in a system in which there are two or more constraint satisfaction networks, each trying to form an interpretation? A system composed of two or more nets has at least seven parameters that are not present when we consider

Table 1

PRINCIPAL PARAMETERS OF SIMULATION MODELS AND FEATURES OF
INDIVIDUAL AND GROUP PROCESSING THEY REPRESENT

In the model	In a human system
Distributions of properties of individual nets	
Pattern of interconnectivity among units in the net	Schemata for phenomena
External inputs to particular units in the net	Access to environmental evidence
Initial pattern of activation across units in the net	Predispositions, current beliefs
Parameters that characterize the communication among nets	
Pattern of interconnections among the nets in the community	Who talks to whom
Pattern of interconnectivity among the units of communicating nets	What they talk about
Strengths of connections between nets that communicate	How persuasive they are
Time course of communication	When they communicate

only a single network. Three of these parameters have to do with the distribution
of structure and state across the individual members of a community of networks.
The other four concern the communication among the networks in the community.
The nature of these parameters and the features of real communities to which,
for the purposes of the model, they are intended to correspond are shown in
Table 1.

Distributions of individual properties

The pattern of connectivity among the units within a network defines the *schema*
for the event to be interpreted. Thus, the first additional consideration is the
distribution of event schemata across the members of the community. Clearly a
system in which all the networks have a consensus about the underlying structure
of the domain of interpretation is different from one in which different networks
have different patterns of constraint among the hypotheses. As a simplifying
assumption, we will assume that all the networks have the same underlying constraint structure. This is simply an implementation of the ethnographer's fantasy
that all the individuals have the same schemata for the events to be interpreted
(Boster, Chapter 10 in this volume). In the ship collision situation, it appears that
the captain and the mate shared the schemata for interpreting the motion of other

ships. But, consensus on schemata is not the same thing as consensus about the interpretations of events. Two individuals could have the same schema for some phenomenon and still reach different interpretations of events.

As we have seen, the nets may receive inputs directly from an environment. The *distribution of access to environmental evidence* is an important structural property of a community of networks. If all nets in the community have the same underlying patterns of constraints among hypotheses and all receive input from the same features of the environment, all networks in the community will arrive at the same interpretation. If different networks have access to different inputs from the environment, they may move to very different interpretations of the world.

At any point in time, the pattern of activity across the units in a particular network represents the current state of belief of that network. A coherent interpretation is a pattern of activation that satisfies the constraints of the connections among units. When a community of networks is created, it may be created so that different nets have different patterns of activation. Thus, the third parameter concerns the *distribution of predispositions* across the networks in the community. The initial activations in these simulations are always low; that is, the individuals do not start with strong beliefs about the truth of any of the hypotheses.

Communication parameters

In such a system, we must consider at least four additional parameters that describe the communication between the networks. For the sake of simplicity, we will model the communication between networks as external inputs applied directly to the units in each network. If a particular node in one network is, for example, highly active, then some fraction of that activity may be applied as an external input to the corresponding node in some other network. Thus, in this model, communication between individual nets is represented by direct communication of the activation levels of units in one net to units in another net (see Figure 3). This is based on the assumption that real communication about belief in a hypothesis from one individual to another should have the effect of making the activation level of the hypothesis in the listener more like the activation level of the hypothesis in the speaker. This simplification is very problematic because it ignores the fact that communication is always mediated by artifactual structure.

One communication parameter describes the *pattern of interconnections among the networks* in the community. This corresponds to the patterns of communication links in a community of people. Each particular network in the community may communicate with some subset of the other networks in the community.

Each network that communicates with another does so by passing activation from some of its own units to the corresponding units in the other network. The *pattern of interconnectivity among the units of communicating networks* determines which of the units of each network pass activation to their corresponding numbers

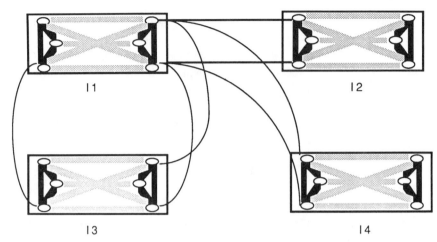

Figure 3   Communication among the individual networks. This figure illustrates three
of the four communication parameters: the *pattern of interconnections among
the networks* (who talks with whom), *pattern of interconnectivity among the
units of communicating nets* (what they talk about), and the *strengths of
connections between nets that communicate* (how persuasive they are). The
last communication parameter, the *time course of communication* (when they
communicate), is not represented in this figure. The combination of parameters shown in this figure is intended only to show the range of possible
communicative patterns within a group. Subsequent simulation experiments
explore the cognitive consequences of a variety of patterns.

in the other networks. This corresponds to a determination of what the networks
can talk to each other about. It could be thought of as a limitation on vocabulary
that permits the networks to exchange information about only some of the hypotheses that participate in the interpretations.

Recall that a network passes only a fraction of the activity of its unit to the
corresponding unit in another network. This fraction of the activity of a unit in one
net that is applied as an external input to the corresponding unit in the other network
may be called the *persuasiveness* of the source; it determines how important it is for
a unit to agree with its corresponding unit in the other network relative to the
importance of satisfying the constraints imposed by other units in its own net.

The final community level parameter is the *time course of communication*.
This refers to the temporal pattern of the exchange of external inputs between the
nets. This can vary from continual exchange of external inputs to no communication at all. In between these extremes are an infinite number of patterns of
connection and disconnection. Again, it would be possible to have a different
time course of communication for every connection between the nets, and even
to have the persuasiveness of each connection be a function of time, but for
simplicity, this too will be considered a global parameter, with all connections
either on or off at whatever strength they have been assigned at any point in time.

SOCIAL ORGANIZATION AND THE COGNITIVE PROPERTIES OF GROUPS

Now we have the simulation pieces required to make an exploration of the relationships among the properties of the individuals and of the group with respect to confirmation bias.

The Commonsense Architecture of Group Intelligence

It is frequently assumed that the best way to improve the performance of groups is to improve the communication among the members of the group, or, conversely, that what is lacking in groups is communication. In the fourth novel of the Foundation series, *Foundation's Edge*, Isaac Asimov (1982) describes a world, Gaia, that is a thinly disguised Earth in the distant future. The original concept of Gaia was developed by James Lovelock and referred only to the notion that the entire biosphere of the earth could be taken to be a single self-regulating organism. Asimov has extended the Gaia concept to the cognitive realm. On Asimov's planet, every conscious being is in continuous high bandwidth communication with every other. There is but one mind on Gaia, a very powerful mind, one that can do things that are beyond the capabilities of any individual mind.

One might question whether this is really an advisable way to organize all that cognitive horsepower. Our simulations provide us with a means to answer this question. They indicate that more communication is not always *in principle* better than less. Under some conditions, increasing the richness of communication may result in undesirable properties at the group level.

Consider a simulation experiment in which we vary only the persuasiveness of the communication among nets (see Figure 4). (Recall that this is implemented by changing the strength of the connections between units in one net with corresponding units in other nets.) We begin with a community of networks in which all the nets have the same underlying constraint structure, all have the same access to environmental evidence, and each has a slightly different initial pattern of activation from any of the others. Furthermore, all the networks communicate with each other, all the units in each network are connected to all the units in the other networks, and the time course of communication is continuous. This can be regarded as a model of mass mental telepathy. Under these conditions, when the communication connection strength (persuasiveness) is zero, the nets do not communicate at all, and each settles into an interpretation that is determined by its initial predispositions (see Figure 4, *a*). If we start the community again, this time with a nonzero persuasiveness, each individual network moves toward the

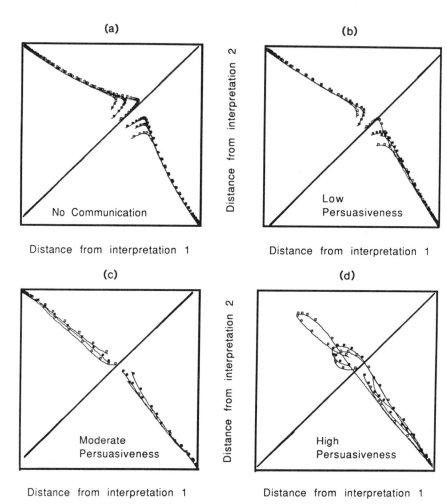

Figure 4   The trajectories of a group of six individuals in interpretation space. Each
panel in this figure represents the same six individuals starting in the same
locations. The persuasiveness of the communication among them is manipulated; all other parameters are held constant.

interpretation that it had moved to in the absence of communication, but now it
does so more quickly. If we keep restarting the community, each time increasing
the persuasiveness, the velocity of the nets in conceptual space increases even
more. The nets hurry in groups to the available interpretations (some to one, some
to the other) and, once there, they respond only a little to additional evidence
from the environment (see Figure 4, *b*).

   As the internetwork connection strength is increased even more, undecided
individuals may be drawn back to their original interpretations (see Figure 4, *c*).

With the persuasiveness turned up even more, the nets that start out toward a minority interpretation are drawn back by the emerging consensus, and all of them rush to the same interpretation. Having arrived at that interpretation, they remain there, absolutely unmoved by any amount of evidence from the environment (see Figure 4, *d*). At high levels of persuasiveness, this system thus manifests a much more extreme form of confirmation bias than any individual alone would manifest. In retrospect, it is easy to see why. When the level of communication is high enough, a community of such nets that receive similar inputs from the world, and that start near each other in the interpretation space, behaves as one large net. Wherever the nets go in interpretation space, they go hand in hand and stay close together. Because they are in continual communication, there is no opportunity for any of them to form an interpretation that differs much from that of the other. Once in consensus, they stay in consensus even if they have had to change their minds to reach consensus. When the strengths of the connections between networks is increased to a point where it far outweighs the strengths of the connections within networks, the nets all move to a shared interpretation that is incoherent. In this condition, the importance of sharing an interpretation with others outweighs the importance of reaching a coherent interpretation.

Returning to Gaia, we see that a mega-mind such as that described by Asimov would be more prone to confirmation bias than any individual mind. It might be a mind that would rush into interpretations and, once having formed an interpretation, would manifest an absolutely incorrigible confirmation bias. Is it possible for communication ever to be rich enough in a real human community to lead to this sort of group pathology? Perhaps. Even within individual networks, as a coherent interpretation forms, units representing hypotheses that have no direct support in the world receive activation from neighboring units, and a whole coherent schema is filled in. This well-known effect in individual cognition seems even more powerful in some group settings. Buckhout (1982) asked groups to produce composite descriptions of a suspect in a crime that all had witnessed. He reported, "The group descriptions were more complete than the individual reports but gave rise to significantly more errors of commission: an assortment of incorrect and stereotyped details" (p. 122). In this situation, it seems that the members of the group settled into an even more coherent interpretation than they would have acting alone. That is just what happened to the networks in the simulation.

Of course, this extremely tight coupling represents a defective case. In the next section, I consider cases in which there follows some interesting distribution of access to evidence, in which the communication connection strengths are moderate, in which the pattern of interconnectivity is partial (that is, where we do not talk about everything we know, only about some of the important things), and in which the time course of communication follows some pattern other than being continuously on.

Producing a Diversity of Interpretations

The problem with confirmation bias is that it prevents an organism from exploring a wider range of possible interpretations. Although the first interpretation encountered may well be the best, a search of the interpretation space may reveal another one that better fits the available evidence. How can this search be accomplished? I have already shown that, in the absence of communication, the interpretations formed by the individual networks—as each exhibits its own confirmation bias—depend on the three parameters that characterize the individual nets: the underlying constraint structure, the access to environmental evidence, and the initial pattern of activation. If a community is composed of individuals that are different from each other in terms of any of these parameters, various members of the community are likely to arrive at different interpretations. Thus, diversity of interpretations is fairly easy to produce, as long as the communication among the members of the community is not too rich.

ORGANIZATIONAL SOLUTIONS FOR REACHING DECISIONS

Some institutions cannot easily tolerate situations in which the group does not reach a consensus about which interpretation shall be taken as a representation of reality. In some settings, it is essential that all members of the group behave as though some things are true and others are false, even if some of the members have reservations about the solution decided upon. The members of aircraft crews, for example, must coordinate their actions with each other and with a single interpretation of the state of the environment, even if some of them doubt the validity of the interpretation on which they are acting. Such institutions may face the problem of guaranteeing that a shared interpretation is adopted in some reasonable amount of time.

Hierarchy

A common solution to the problem of reaching a decision is to grant to a particular individual the authority to declare the nature of reality. This arrangement is especially clear in settings where the relevant reality is socially defined (e.g., the law), where an important state of affairs (e.g., guilt or innocence) exists only because some authority, such as a judge, says it exists. But this solution is also adopted with respect to physical realities where time pressures or other factors require a commitment to a particular interpretation. This second case comes in two versions: one in which the other members of the community may present evidence to the authority, and one in which the authority acts autonomously. I will now describe two simulation experiments on this theme.

Hierarchy without communication

Suppose we let all members of the group attempt to form an interpretation but give only one network the authority to decide the nature of reality for all members of the group. The cognitive labor of interpreting the situation may be socially distributed in a way that permits an exploration of more alternatives in the interpretation space than would be explored by a single individual with confirmation bias. But if the alternative interpretations never encounter each other, the wider search might as well have never happened. The decision reached by the group is simply the decision of an individual. One might imagine this as a sort of "king" or "dictator" model, but lack of communication can also bring this state of affairs about in situations that are not supposed to have this character. The ship collision discussed earlier is an example of a case in which the correct interpretation of a situation arose within a group, but somehow never reached the individual who had the authority to decide around which model of reality the group must organize its behavior.

Hierarchy with communication

This situation is modeled in the simulation by changing the communication pattern so that one of the networks (the one in the position of authority) receives input from all the others, but the others do not receive external inputs from each other. In the simulation under these conditions, the network that is the authority will follow the weight of the evidence presented to it by the other networks. As the other networks move in interpretation space, the center of gravity of the weight of evidence presented by the other networks also moves. Depending on the persuasiveness with which the other networks communicate with the authority, it may be pulled to one interpretation or another, or even change its mind about which is the better interpretation. The authority thus becomes a special kind of cognitive apparatus, one that tracks the center of gravity of the entire community in conceptual space at each point in time. At very high levels of persuasiveness, this authority network may find the evidence for both interpretations compelling and may be drawn to a state in which it has high activations for the units representing all the hypotheses in both interpretations.

Consensus

Unanimity or nothing

Imagine a world in which each network can only attend to one aspect of the environment at a time, but all networks communicate to each other about the interpretations they form on the basis of what they are attending to. Suppose further that there is more information in the environment consistent with one interpretation (I will call it the best interpretation) than with another. In this situation, any single individual acting alone will reach the best interpretation only when that individual happens to be attending to some aspect of the environment that is associated with that interpretation, or when the individual happens to be predisposed to that interpretation. If there are many networks and the aspect of the environment each network attends to is chosen at random, then on average more of these networks will be attending to evidence in support of the best interpretation than any other interpretation, because, by definition, the best interpretation is the one for which there is most support. If the networks in such a group are in high bandwidth communication with each other from the outset, they will behave as the Gaia system did, rushing as a group to the interpretation that is closest to the center of gravity of their predispositions, regardless of the evidence. If, however, they are allowed to go their own ways for a while, attending to both the available evidence and their predispositions, and then communicate with each other, they will first sample the information in the environment and then go (as a group) to the interpretation that is best supported. In Figure 5, the networks explore the interpretation space during a period in which they are not communicating strongly, and two of the networks come close to interpretation 1. As the level of persuasiveness rises, they are drawn to a consensus with the majority of the networks that have settled on interpretation 2. Not only is the behavior of each individual different in the group setting than it would have been in isolation but also the behavior of the group as a whole is different from that of any individual, because the group, as a cognitive system, has considered many kinds of evidence, whereas each individual considered only one.

The simulations indicate two problems with this mode of resolving the diversity of interpretations. First, if some individuals arrive at very well-formed interpretations that are in conflict with each other before communication begins, there may be no resolution at all. They may simply stay with the interpretations they have already formed. Sometimes such "hard cases" can be dislodged by changing the distribution of access to evidence in the community to give stubborn networks direct access to evidence that contradicts their present interpretation. However, this may only drive the network to a state in which it has no coherent interpretation of the situation. Figure 6 depicts such a situation. At the beginning of this simulation, the networks are not communicating with each other at all. As time goes on, the persuasiveness with which they communicate increases rapidly. The networks ultimately arrive at a consensus, but the interpretation on which they agree does not fit either of the coherent interpretations.

Demographics of conceptual space: voting

Another set of methods for establishing an interpretation to be acted on by a group relies on measuring the demographics of the community in conceptual space. We can imagine the starting state as being one in which the members of the group

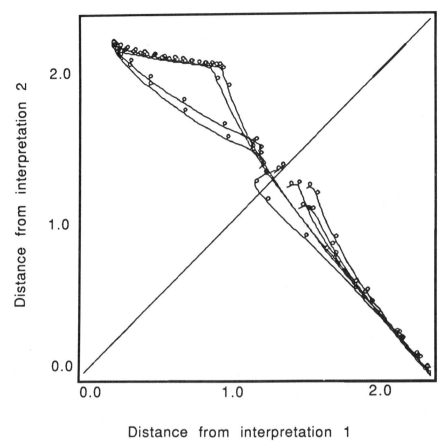

Figure 5   Generation of diversity followed by consensus. In these simulations, the
networks start out not communicating. As time goes on, the persuasiveness
with which they communicate increases.

are sprinkled around in the conceptual space. The starting location of each member
is defined by the preconceptions it has about the situation. Some may begin closer
to one interpretation, some closer to another. As each member tries to satisfy the
constraints of its internal schemata and the available external evidence, it moves
in conceptual space. This movement is usually toward one of the coherent interpretations defined by the underlying schemata. As we saw above, if the members
of the community are in communication with each other, they may influence each
other's motion in conceptual space. A mechanism for deciding which interpretation
shall be taken as a representation of reality may be based on the locations of the
members of the community in conceptual space. If a majority are at or close to
a particular interpretation, that interpretation could be selected as the group's
decision. This is, of course, a voting scheme.

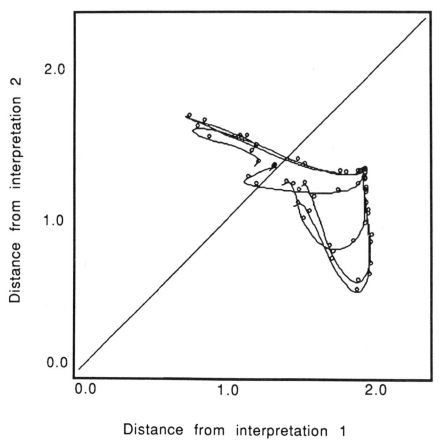

Figure 6   High persuasiveness may lead to an incoherent interpretation.

A majority rule voting scheme is often taken to be a way of producing the same result as would be achieved by continued negotiation, but which short-cuts the communication. In our simulations, we see that voting does not always produce the same results as would be achieved by further communication. That this is so can easily be deduced from the fact that the result of a voting procedure for a given state of the community is always the same, whereas a given state of the community may lead in the future to many different outcomes at the group level, depending on the time course and bandwidth of subsequent communication.

A Fundamental Trade-off for Organizations

Many real institutions seem to embody one or another of these methods for first generating and then dealing with diversity of interpretation. Obviously, real social institutions come to be organized the way they are for many reasons. For example, the political consequences of various schemes for distributing the authority to choose a definitive interpretation are important aspects of the actual implementation of any institution. I do not claim that institutions are the way they are because they produce particular kinds of cognitive results. My point is, rather, that social organization, however it may have been produced, does have cognitive consequences that can be described. By producing the organizations we observe—largely ones in which there are explicit mechanisms for resolving diversity of interpretations—perhaps social evolution indicates that, in some environments, chronic indecision may be much less adaptive than some level of erroneous commitment. This may be the fundamental trade-off in cognitive ecology. The social organization, or more precisely the distribution of authority to define situations as real, determines the location of a cognitive system in the trade-off space. Where the power to define the reality of situations is widely distributed in a "horizontal" structure, there is relatively more potential for diversity of interpretation and more potential for indecision. Where that power is collected in the top of a "vertical" structure, there is less potential for diversity of interpretation but also more likelihood that some interpretation will find a great deal of confirmation and that disconfirming evidence will be disregarded.

Where there is a need for both exploration of an interpretation space and consensus of interpretation, we typically see two modes of operation. One mode trades off the ability to reach a decision in favor of diversity of interpretation. The participants in the system proceed in relative isolation and in parallel. Each member may be subject to confirmation bias, but, because they proceed independently, the system as a whole does not manifest confirmation bias. The second mode breaks the isolation of the participants and exposes the interpretations to disconfirming evidence, hopefully avoiding erroneous perseverence of an interpretation when a better one is available. This mode trades off diversity in favor of the commitment to a single interpretation that will stand as the new reality of the situation. The two modes are frequently separated in time and marked by different social structural arrangements.

SUMMARY

In this chapter, I have tried to take some tentative steps toward a framework for thinking about cognitive phenomena at the level of groups. My simulation models are both a kind of notation system that forces me to be explicit about the theoretical constructs that I claim produce the phenomena of interest, and a dynamic tool for investigating a universe of possibilities. The simulations show that, even while holding the cognitive properties of individuals constant, groups may display quite different cognitive properties depending on how communication is organized within the group and over time. Groups can be better at generating a diversity of interpretations than any individual is, but having generated a useful diversity, they then face the problem of resolving it. From the perspective presented here, several well recognized kinds of social organization appear to provide solutions to the problems of exploring a space of interpretations and of discovering the best available alternative.

In the simulations presented here, the effects of group level cognitive properties are not produced solely by structure internal to the individuals or by structure external to the individuals. Rather, the cognitive properties of groups are produced by an interaction between structures internal to individuals and structures external to individuals. All human societies face cognitive tasks that are beyond the capabilities of any individual member. For example, even the simplest culture contains more information than could be learned by any individual in a lifetime (Roberts, 1964; D'Andrade, 1981), so the tasks of learning, remembering, and transmitting cultural knowledge are inevitably distributed. The performance of cognitive tasks that exceed individual abilities is always shaped by a social organization of distributed cognition. Doing without a social organization of distributed cognition is not an option. The social organization that is actually used may or may not be appropriate to the task. It may produce desirable properties or pathologies. It may be well defined and stable or shifting by the moment, but there will be some form of organization whenever cognitive labor is distributed, and the form that organization takes will play a role in determining the cognitive properties of the system that performs the task.

References

Anderson, C. A., Lepper, M. R., & Ross, L. (1980). The perseverance of social theories: The role of explanation in the persistence of discredited information. *Journal of Personality and Social Psychology, 39,* 1037–1049.

Asimov, I. (1982). *Foundation's edge.* New York: Ballentine Books.

Boster, J. S. (1985). Requiem for the omniscient informant: There's life in the old girl yet. In J. Doughert (Ed.), *Directions in cognitive anthropology* (pp. 177–197). Urbana: University of Illinois Press.

Buckhout, R., (1982). Eyewitness testimony. In U. Neisser (Ed.), *Memory observed: Remembering in natural contexts* (pp. 116–125). San Francisco: W. H. Freeman & Co.

D'Andrade, R. (1981). The cultural part of cognition. *Cognitive Science, 5,* 179–195.

Durkheim, E. (1949). (G. Simpson, Trans.) *The division of labor in society.* Glencoe, IL: Free Press. (Original work published 1893)

Durkheim, E. (1965). (J. W. Swain, Trans.) *The elementary forms of the religious life.* New York: Free Press. (Original work published 1915)

Fleck, L. (1979). *The genesis and development of a scientific fact.* (T. J. Trenn & R. K. Merton, Trans.). Chicago: University of Chicago Press. (Original work published in German, 1935)

Hastie, R., & Kumar, P. (1979). Person Memory: Personality traits as organizing principles in memory for behavior. *Journal of Personality and Social Psychology, 37*, 25–38.

Lord, C., Lepper, M., & Ross, L. (1979). Biased assimilation and attitude polarization: The effects of prior theories on subsequently considered evidence. *Journal of Personality and Social Psychology, 37*, 2098–2110.

Perrow, C. (1984). *Normal accidents.* New York: Basic Books.

Roberts, J. (1964). The self-management of cultures. In W. Goodenough (Ed.), *Explorations in cultural anthropology: Essays in honor of George Peter Murdock* (pp. 433–454). New York: McGraw Hill.

Romney, A. K. , Weller, S. C., & Batchelder, W. H. (1986). Culture as consensus: A theory of culture and informant accuracy. *American Anthropologist, 88*(2), 313–338.

Rumelhart, D. E., Smolensky, P., McClelland, J. L., & Hinton, G. E. (1986). Schemata and sequential thought processes in PDP models. In J. L. McClelland, D. E. Rumelhart, & the PDP Group (Eds.), *Parallel distributed processing: Explorations in the microstructure of cognition: Vol. 2. Psychological and biological models* (pp. 7–57). Cambridge, MA: MIT Press.

Tweney, R., Doherty, M., & Mynatt C. (1981). *On scientific thinking.* New York: Columbia University Press.

Wason, P. C. (1968). Reasoning about a rule. *Quarterly Journal of Experimental Psychology, 20*, 273–281.

Wason, P. C., & Johnson-Laird, P. N. (1972). *Psychology of reasoning: Structure and content.* London: Batsford.

Wittfogel, K. (1957). *Oriental despotism: A comparative study of total power.* New Haven: Yale University Press.

CHAPTER 14

COGNITIVE AND SOCIAL
PROCESSES IN DECISION MAKING

REID HASTIE AND NANCY PENNINGTON

INTRODUCTION: THE JUROR AND JURY DECISION TASKS

A remarkable number of decisions in our culture are made in small groups. These decisions range from informal, relatively trivial decisions concerned, for example, with where a family will spend its holiday weekend, to more grave and significant decisions, such as whether a defendant will receive a death penalty sentence or whether our nation will engage in armed conflict with another nation. Two general justifications are often cited for the use of a group decision process. First, there is an assumption that pooling individuals' points of view or knowledge relevant to a decision will produce a more complete pattern of evidence or preferences and, therefore, provide a firmer foundation for the ultimate decision. Second, there is an assumption that the group decision process leads to more satisfaction on the part of individuals engaged in the decision and, hence, to greater commitment to carry out the plan of action selected by the decision makers.

Both of the general justifications for making group decisions depend on assumptions about the value and extent to which cognitions will be shared socially. First there is an assumption that information concerning facts and values is distributed across individuals who participate in the decision and is not fully shared before the group meets. The decision process is assumed to include the pooling of information concerning what is true, what is morally right, and what is preferred, producing a more complete set of pieces of the puzzle than could be available to any individual decision maker working alone. Thus, the prospect of socially sharing information is at the heart of the first justification. Second, there is a notion that if the group solves the decision problem together, individuals will share a vision or conception of the conclusion once the solution is reached. The higher level of socially shared consensus after a group decision will mean that individual commitment to the selected course of action will be greater following group discussion.

The small decision-making group that we have studied extensively is the petit trial jury. Jury decision making is one of the few social events in which members of different social classes and ethnic groups get together to perform a complex intellectual task in a small group. Juries are also an attractive subject for study by social scientists, because they are important, common, and the conditions under which they operate are well defined by tradition and legal statutes.

LEVELS OF ANALYSIS

This chapter focuses on three levels of analysis. The first level refers to the decision-making behavior of individual jurors. This is the familiar level of cognitive analysis and is really a description of the sequence of mental processes an individual juror goes through in trying to reach a decision about the verdict in a criminal case. Most jurors seem to perform the task of reaching an individual decision when they are listening to a case, just before they begin deliberation. For example, Hastie, Penrod, and Pennington (1983) found, on the basis of observations of jurors in mock-jury studies and surveys following deliberations of real juries, that 80% to 90% of the jurors had a definite opinion about the verdict they favored before deliberation began. This level of analysis corresponds to the level of analysis that cognitive psychologists aspire to in most of their research, the level that could be compared with the trace produced by a computer program model that simulates a human subject's performance on the cognitive task.

When we turn to a consideration of the behavior of groups and individuals' behavior within groups, a second and a third level of analysis are relevant to the present discussion. One level is the level of description of the social events that occur during deliberation. This is *not* a theoretical description at a level that characterizes the cognitive events that occur within individual jurors' minds. Rather, it is a level of description of the observable events that occur in social interaction among jurors over the course of their deliberation.

The third level of analysis that we might aspire to in group decision making is an analysis of the cognitive psychologies of individual jurors in the context of social interaction in deliberation (rather than isolated from social interaction, as in our analysis of individual juror predeliberation decision making). Very little research on group decision making attempts to reach this level of analysis, at least on the empirical side. There is speculation, however, about what the cognitive processes of individual jurors within the context of· group deliberation might be like, and recent models for jury decision making often begin with a model of individual cognition in the context of group deliberation (cf. Hastie et al., 1983; Kerr, 1981; Stasser & Davis, 1981).

Our first task in this chapter is to describe the individual psychology of juror decision making at the first descriptive level, the level of cognitive processes. Next, we will describe the process of group decision making at the level of the social events occurring during deliberation. We will then speculate about the third level, individual cognition in the context of a decision-making group.

INDIVIDUAL JUROR DECISION MAKING

On the basis of empirical research on juror decision making, we have concluded that a general three-stage model describes the process a typical juror goes through on his or her way to a decision (See Figure 1 for an overview of the model; see Pennington & Hastie, 1986, 1987, 1988 for the details). First, the juror evaluates the evidence and constructs a mental summary of the evidence in the form of a narrative story. Second, the juror comprehends the judge's instructions concerning the legal verdict alternatives that are available as decision categories. Third, the juror attempts to find a match between his or her story summary of the evidence and a verdict category in order to classify the story in the category it best fits.

According to this model, there are two routes to a Not Guilty verdict in a criminal case. First, the story summary may best fit the features defining the legal Not Guilty verdict. For example, a juror may have concluded that a summary of the evidence in a murder trial is a "self-defense" story, and this story would match the judge's description of the Not Guilty By Reason of Self Defense verdict definition. Second, if no classification seems to provide a good match between the story and the verdict categories, the juror (as instructed by the judge) responds with a verdict of Not Guilty (no decision).

We have called this general three-stage model an *explanation-based model* of juror decision making because of the central role played by the summary of the evidence (which we consider an explanation) created by the juror during the first, or "Story Construction," stage of his or her reasoning toward a verdict. The cognitive processes that occur during the first stage of individual decision making—the formation of a summary of the evidence—are the common processes that occur when a person attempts to make sense of other, not legally significant social events as they occur in everyday life. This stage is initiated at the beginning of the presentation of trial evidence, and jurors assign meaning to trial evidence

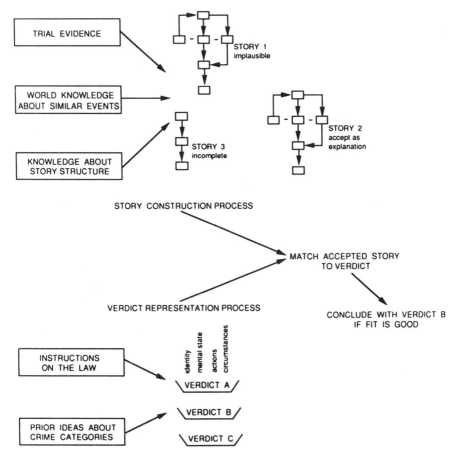

Figure 1   An overview of the explanation-based "Story Model" for individual juror decision making.

by incorporating it into one or more plausible accounts or narrative stories that explain the events witnesses testify about at the trial. Although there is considerable variation across individual jurors in the degree of elaboration of the constructed stories and in whether alternate stories are constructed, the typical juror concludes this stage of the decision process with a single dominant story in mind (Kuhn, Pennington, & Ledbetter, 1983). General knowledge about the structure of human social action (in our culture), often described by psychologists as an *episode schema*, is used to organize the events according to the causal and intentional relations among them that are explicit or implicit in the witnesses' testimony or are inferred by the juror.

The pervasiveness and significance of narrative structure in legal settings has been noted by anthropologists studying dispute resolution in non-Western societies (E. Hutchins, personal communication; J. Roberts, personal communication). In some cultures, laws or codes for conduct are represented and passed from generation to generation in the form of stories. Similarly, when a dispute is resolved in some cultures, the resolution is expressed as a story that prescribes events that should follow a transgression or conflict. Attorneys interested in winning cases in Western societies have also noticed that narrative structures play a special role in legal persuasion. For example, a popular trial tactics textbook (Mauet, 1981) advises attorneys to make a deliberate choice as they begin preparing for trial between a case presented in narrative form and one presented in a logical argumentative form.

Briefly, the episode schema jurors use to comprehend the events described by witnesses involves the following component processes: (a) imposing relations between events that the juror believes occurred (we emphasize causal relations such as the concepts of initiates, results in, enables, reason for); (b) structuring the evidence in a hierarchy of embedded episodes composed of relations such as those just mentioned; (c) at the highest level of the hierarchy, formulating the organizational structure as a general episode schema representing the most important events that the juror believes happened; and (d) elaborating components of the highest level episode structure in terms of more detailed event sequences, which then compose lower levels of the organizational hierarchy.

The second stage of the decision process, Verdict Representation, is usually not initiated until the trial judge presents instructions to the jurors at the end of the trial. At this point, the juror attempts to comprehend and learn the decision alternatives available by law. This involves the mental representation of each verdict alternative as a category frame with defining features and an associated decision rule specifying their appropriate combination (in terms of disjunctions and conjunctions of features). For example, features in a verdict category such as first degree murder include the following: *identity*—the defendant is the person who is the agent of the victim's death; *intent to kill*—the defendant intended to kill the decedent; *a purpose formed*—the defendant had time before the killing occurred to form the purpose of performing the acts that would result in death; *insufficient provocation*—the defendant's actions were not provoked by a legally mitigating circumstance (e.g., the defendant was in fear of bodily harm); *an interval elapsed* between the formation of the purpose and the action that resulted in death—there was at least a momentary pause between the time when the defendant was alleged to have formed the purpose of killing and the time at which the killing action occurred; *the killing was in pursuance of the original resolution* or purpose; and, finally, *the killing was unlawful*—again, no mitigating or excusing circumstances were present. This list of seven features taken in conjunction defines the legal category of first-degree murder. Similar conceptual analyses can be performed for most common criminal verdict categories.

The third stage in the decision process, Classification, involves the juror's attempts to find a match that allows him or her to classify the episode–story structure in one of the verdict categories by matching features in the verdict category against events or relationships that the juror believes are true and has stored in the representation of the story. When the juror attempts to find a match between the story and the verdict category, the jurors also attempt to apply the judge's procedural instructions concerning presumption of innocence and standard of proof. Thus, if no good match is found, the presumption of innocence dictates that the juror should return a verdict of Not Guilty, or, if a good match is found, final classification depends on the juror's belief that each of the elements (features of the category) of the verdict is established beyond a reasonable doubt by evidence from the trial.

Our program of empirical research (Pennington & Hastie, 1986, 1987, 1988) has established that, in typical felony trials (e.g., murder trials and armed robbery trials), the story model we have outlined provides a good description of the cognitive processes that a juror engages in to reach a verdict decision. It is plausible that the narrative mode of reasoning that is central in juror decision making is adopted in anticipation of the social interaction that will occur during the consensus-seeking deliberation process that follows. Interestingly, as far as our research shows, it does not seem to matter whether or not jurors expect to engage in social interaction requiring explicit justifications for their verdicts (Tetlock & Kim, 1987). In some of our studies, mock jurors expected to explain their verdict decision to at least one other person or to engage in jury deliberation, whereas in other studies there were no such expectations. In either condition, however, the jurors exhibited the narrative mode of reasoning that we have found is typical. This implies, at least for members of our culture, that reasoning about social events in terms of story forms is natural and relatively easy. An interesting speculation is that individual cognition is shaped by inculturation during development so that well-socialized members of our culture reason when they are alone in a fashion that will be congenial to sharing judgments and the reasoning that led to those judgments (Freyd, 1983). It seems that one such form is the narrative or story mode that we have observed repeatedly in our analyses of juror decision making (cf. Bruner, 1986).

THE JURY DELIBERATION PROCESS

In a parallel research program, we have attempted to develop descriptive models of the social events that occur during jury deliberation. Most of this research has involved experimental studies of the behavior of mock jurors in a simulated jury deliberation. These are "high-fidelity" simulations in which jurors, sampled from the population of available jurors in courthouses in the Chicago and Boston areas, are exposed to the standard procedures and instructions that would accompany a typical jury trial. However, these ''jurors'' viewed a film of a reenacted criminal trial instead of an actual ''live'' trial. These mock juries took from 30 minutes to approximately 380 minutes to deliberate before a verdict was rendered or a hung, deadlocked conclusion was reached.

Perhaps the most fundamental questions that need to be addressed about shared cognition are: Who is sharing information and what kind of information is shared? For juries deliberating verdicts in serious felony cases, some general characteristics of information-pooling behavior are known from our research. First, there are definite role effects and individual differences in who talks. Better educated jurors, jurors in elite occupation groups, and higher-income jurors (these groups tend to overlap) talk more than jurors on the lower socioeconomic end of these dimensions. Gender is related to amount of talking, with the average male juror talking about one and one-half times as much as the typical female juror. Interestingly, this differential has held since at least the 1950s in American juries (Strodtbeck & Lipinski, 1988). Jurors' age is also related to the rate at which they participate, with relatively old (over 60) and relatively young (under 25) jurors participating at lower rates than middle-aged jurors. The foreman role also carries with it a norm of higher participation, with foremen typically speaking two to three times more than the average nonforeman.

When participation rates are ordered from highest to lowest and a participation rank curve is plotted, it assumes the characteristic negatively accelerating form that has been observed in dozens of other small groups (Bales, Strodtbeck, Mills, & Roseborough, 1951; Stephan & Mischler, 1952). Similarly, when participation rates are plotted against faction size, larger factions do more talking than small factions, but *each member* of a large faction does proportionately less talking than members of small factions. One interpretation of the participation rank curve and the faction size effect on individual speaking rates is that there is a limited amount of relevant information to be pooled in the jury and that there is a norm to avoid repetition of redundant information. Thus, for a juror in a large faction, many of the relevant arguments will be made by others in the faction, and there will be less for any single person to say.

With reference to the contents of deliberation, about half of the discussion is spent on the facts of the case, reviewing and evaluating testimony about what happened and its implications for a verdict. About one quarter of the discussion is concerned with the law, what it means, and its relationship to the facts. About 15% of the discussion is devoted to such activities as organizing the group process, discussing what the jury should discuss, deciding when to take votes, and administering votes. The residual, about 10% of the total discussion, does not clearly fit any task-relevant category, although some of it is devoted to social amenities that can have a substantial influence on the group's ability to reach consensus.

Two Models of Jury Deliberation

Jury deliberation was less systematic than individual decision making, and we have concluded that two models are necessary to describe the social process: an *evidence-driven deliberation style* and a *verdict-driven deliberation style* (each exhibited by about one third of the mock juries we observed; the remaining one third did not fit any simple classification by style; see Figures 2 and 3 for overviews of these models; see Hastie et al., 1983, pp. 163–166 for more details).

The evidence-driven deliberation sequence is essentially a recapitulation of the events that we have described for an individual juror's reasoning to a verdict, but at the group level. Juries exhibiting this deliberation style begin discussion by attempting to reach consensus about what happened in the circumstances relevant to the crime events. Usually, at the start of deliberation, individual jurors have reached different conclusions about the underlying sequence of narrative events in the true story of what happened. During this first stage of deliberation (usually consuming one third to one half of the total deliberation time), jurors pool information about their alternate versions of what happened and attempt to influence one another to reach consensus on a single group story of what happened.

This portion of deliberation is fairly distinct from the remaining portions of deliberation in which "stages" get mixed up a bit. In a typical evidence-driven jury, no votes on the verdict are taken during these early stages of discussion, and it is difficult to identify which verdicts are favored by which jurors and the relative sizes of juror factions who support alternate verdict choices.

In the last half of deliberation, jurors socially perform the second and third stages ascribed to the individual juror in the explanation-based model. The jury attempts to reach agreement about the definitions and ordering of the alternate verdict categories available to them and at the same time attempts to classify the story of what happened into one of these categories. In contrast to the reasoning of individual jurors, there is considerable discussion of procedural instructions from the judge about matters such as the standard of proof ("beyond reasonable doubt" in criminal cases). During this second phase of deliberation, voting occurs at a higher rate than during the early phase, when the focus was on consensus about evidence. Of course, juries frequently fail to reach consensus on a single story, even after an hour or more of discussion in the early phases of deliberation, and this complicates discussion and impedes progress toward consensus when the jury turns to the task of specifying the verdict decision categories and making a classification. In this second phase, jurors aligned in factions debate with one another about the appropriate classification and the definitions of the verdicts.

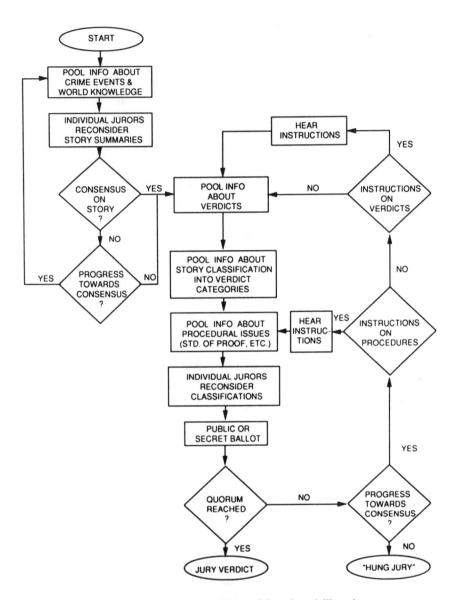

Figure 2   Summary of events in an evidence-driven jury deliberation.

We labeled the alternate pattern of social events in deliberation that emerged from our observational analyses the verdict-driven style because in this pattern, discussion is organized by verdicts from the beginning of deliberation. In a jury

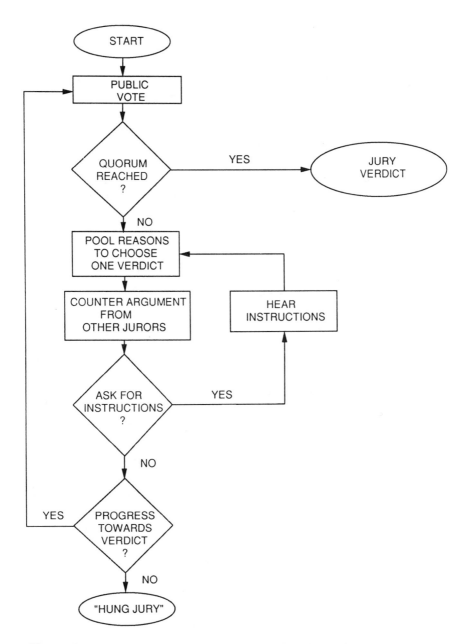

Figure 3 Summary of events in a verdict-driven jury deliberation.

that assumes this deliberation style (in contrast with evidence-driven deliberations), the early events usually involve determining who is associated with which verdict, through either the mechanism of voting or discussion. Once factions are defined, deliberation proceeds with jurors who favor one faction or another citing evidence that they believe discriminates between verdict alternatives or favors their faction's verdict. Thus, from the beginning there is an adversarial character to the discussion.

In verdict-driven deliberations, there is less of a tendency for jurors to spell out complete narratives concerning the events that occurred, and more of a contrasting tendency to cite evidence in a piecemeal fashion organized by the verdicts or elements of the verdicts that are under dispute. One result of deliberation in a verdict-driven style is that individual jurors show less consensus at the end of deliberation on the events that they believe occurred at the time of the crimes. Of course, consensus is not perfect among evidence-driven jurors, but it is higher than among verdict-driven jurors.

An important issue for research on socially shared cognition concerns the appropriate measurement of agreement or shared cognition. In our jury research, after juries had rendered a verdict we asked jurors to respond to a questionnaire inquiring about nine key issues attorneys had indicated ought to be the focus of consideration in rendering an appropriate verdict. In one murder case used in our research, for example, a key issue concerned whether the victim had accidently stumbled onto the defendant's knife during a violent quarrel or whether the defendant had deliberately and aggressively stabbed the victim. We asked our jurors, after deliberation, what they believed was the truth on this issue, as well as on eight others. Then for each jury we calculated the percentage of agreement across jurors on each of the nine issues. So, for example, on the issue of ran-onto-the-knife versus stabbed-with-the-knife, if 9 (of 12) jurors indicated that they believed the defendant had aggressively stabbed the victim, we would note 75% agreement on this one of nine key issues. After calculating the percentage of agreement on each of the nine issues separately for a single jury, we took the average agreement across the nine issues for that jury. Thus, we had 69 numbers, one for each of our mock juries, indicating percentage of agreement across nine key issues underlying the decision by the 12 jurors on each jury. In general the values of this index were high, averaging over 80%.

One interesting conclusion, given our distinction between the two deliberation styles, is that evidence-driven juries tended to conclude with higher agreement rates (88% agreement) than did verdict-driven juries (79% agreement). The difficult question arises when we try to conceptualize an appropriate control group to use as a base line for comparison of agreement rates produced by social interaction in a jury. One simplistic control comparison is between chance agreement rates and the agreement rates obtained among individuals who deliberated in juries. The chance agreement rate is 50%, and we noted that jury agreement rates were typically over 80%. Another more interesting comparison is provided by creating noninteracting sets of 12 jurors by sampling jurors from 12 different juries and then calculating the agreement rate for these jurors who never talked with one another about our case. Here the agreement rates are approximately 68%, definitely lower than the 80 + % agreement rates among jurors from a single interacting jury. However, we are not sure if either of these comparison groups provides more illumination on socially shared cognition in small group decision processes. We think the question of what an interesting comparison would be must wait for an answer until theories about the processes and consequences of socially shared cognition have been developed.

We wondered why the verdict-driven style, so different from the evidence-driven individual decision process, appears in jury deliberation. The most obvious difference between the individual and group decision-making tasks derives from the requirement of a quorum or unanimous consensus on the group decision; this requirement, of course, does not apply to the individual's decision task. We think that the goal of consensus drives juries toward the verdict-driven deliberation style with its focus on achieving sufficient consensus to render a group verdict.

Although it is plausible that some individual jurors engage in an internal debate in which different parts of their minds play competing roles in proposing and defending verdicts, this is uncommon among even the brightest and apparently most fair-minded jurors. Even the most even-handed jurors tend to organize the evidence from a case in memory around a single narrative story. To the extent that they acknowledge differences from their favorite narrative structure, the differences are stored as deviations rather than fully formed alternate stories.

This contrast between the individual inability to entertain alternate constructions of the evidence and the tendency, at least in typical felony trials, for different individuals to have constructed different unitary conceptions of the evidence produces one of the signature phenomena of jury deliberation: the surprise and discomfort that arise when jurors enter deliberation and discover that other jurors believe dramatically different versions of what happened. Again and again in our observations of jury deliberation, we found that individual jurors were surprised that not everyone saw the case exactly as they did.

A General Model of Consensus-Seeking Processes

In observing deliberation processes in a jury, we observed three general classes of social mechanisms manifested in jurors' efforts to persuade one another to reach consensus. As a rule, efforts to reach consensus involve individual jurors' attempts to convince other jurors to agree with them. Occasionally, we observed jurors acting as brokers, advocating a compromise solution that was not the advocates' personal favorite solution or the favorite solution of the jurors whom the advocate attempted to convince to change. But in criminal jury deliberations of the type we have observed, this compromise solution advocacy was relatively rare. (We might expect compromise to be more common in groups making decisions that are less "categorical" and more "continuous," as, for example, when civil jurors attempt to reach agreement about the degree of responsibility to be attributed to a party in a lawsuit or about the size of a monetary award that is appropriate to provide a civil suit plaintiff.)

Returning to our observations of jurors attempting to reach group consensus in mock juries, we found that three mechanisms appeared again and again as social influence tactics in the consensus-seeking process (see Levine, 1989 and Levine & Russo, 1987, for introductions to social psychological research on consensus-seeking processes in small groups). First, jurors attempted to persuade one another to shift from verdict to verdict with arguments about facts or the proper inferences to be drawn from facts (including references to testimony, events the jurors claimed had occurred based on the testimony, and the judge's instructions about the facts of the law). As noted earlier, arguments about the facts of the law (e.g., the definitions of the verdict categories given by the judge) were the locus of most opinion changes in our jury deliberations. Of course, jurors share large amounts of information about the testimony and their beliefs about events referred to in the testimony, especially in evidence-driven juries. So our first mechanism for consensus-seeking processes is the pooling of information relevant to the truth about events or the law under discussion.

Second, jurors used appeals to values, right conduct, and other exhortations of a moral or exemplificatory nature. Some of these appeals were implicit in the sense that one might infer that the verdict favored by most jurors is the most socially acceptable or appropriate verdict. But many of these arguments take the form of discussions of the appropriate role of the juror in the criminal justice system or the morally appropriate treatment of members of certain groups in society (e.g., people like the defendant). This consensus-seeking mechanism is closely related to Deutsch and Gerard's (1955) normative social influence process. It appeals to jurors' values rather than their beliefs about the truth.

Third, we saw evidence for a collection of social behaviors that we will label *direct reward and punishment*. For example, when a large faction opposed a few holdouts toward the end of deliberation, it was common for members of the large faction to derogate the holdout jurors' characters, reasoning abilities, and motivations. This mechanism was not identified as a distinct social influence mechanism by Deutsch and Gerard, but its action was clearly apparent in research by Festinger and his colleagues (1950, 1954) and by Schachter (1951) on group dynamics. Thus, we witnessed three major social influence mechanisms: information exchange, appeal to moral values, and punishment–reward.

It is interesting to examine recent models of behavior in consensus-seeking groups and to note that analysis at the level of these mechanisms has been eschewed in favor of a reliance on more general summary variables in mathematical models. For example, Davis (1973), Hastie et al. (1983), Kerr (1981), Latane and Wolf (1981), and Stasser and Davis (1981) have all focused on faction size as the effective variable producing opinion change within small groups. For the most part, however, they have not modeled the mechanisms that might make faction size an effective cause or predictor of the outcome of group deliberation (Stasser & Davis, 1981, provide the most discerning analyses of the alternate mechanisms).

As one of "the offenders," we admit that a more elementary level of analysis, modeling the incidence and effects of more specific social influence mechanisms, would be desirable in theoretical treatments of the interaction processes in small decision-making groups. Recently Stasser (1988) presented a computer simulation model (DISCUSS) that takes a step in the right direction by predicting opinion change as the result of (simulated) information exchange during discussion. We heartily endorse the move to this level of analysis and think of Stasser's model as the bellwether theoretical development in current theoretical treatments of small decision-making groups.

Although we have not moved far in this direction, we would like to sketch our plans to modify our own simulation model of consensus-seeking processes in small decision-making groups. Figure 4 provides a flow chart summary of the events that occur during one run of a simulated jury in our model, JUS (name given to the computer simulation model described herein; for more detail, see Hastie et al., 1983, pp. 175–226). If we focus on the events that occur in the theoretical model as it "deliberates" in an effort to reach consensus on an appropriate verdict, the group process emerges from a simple model of individual decision processes that is repeated in the simulation for each juror in the model's jury. At any point in time, each juror is in one of a discrete set of belief states corresponding to legal verdicts (including an undecided state).

The process of opinion change is conceptualized as a decision to stay in the current state or move to another state. Two factors determine the probabilities that a juror will move to another state or stay in the current state. First, stubborn jurors will be less likely to move from one verdict to another than less resistant jurors. Our assumption is that *stubbornness* is determined by three classes of factors: (a) individual character (some jurors are more stubborn than others); (b) confidence of juror in the current verdict opinion based on his or her cognitive evaluation of the evidence (some jurors are more strongly convinced than others by the evidence for their verdict); and (c) payoffs that the juror perceives are associated with the alternate decision options. For example, jurors will value harsher verdicts less than more lenient verdicts if they are concerned about the loss associated with convicting a person of too severe a crime (or, worse, convicting an innocent defendant).

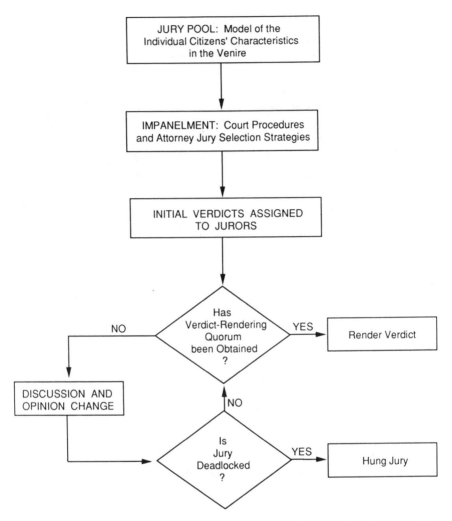

Figure 4   An overview of the "JUS" computer simulation model of jury decision making. From *Inside the Jury* (p. 181) by R. Hastie, S. Penrod, and N. Pennington, 1983, Cambridge, MA: Harvard University Press. Copyright 1983 by Harvard University Press. Adapted by permission.

Second, a faction's power to retain old members is an increasing but negatively accelerating function of its size. Similarly, a faction's power to attract new members increases with size according to the same "diminishing returns" rule. This omnibus factor is assumed to reflect the influence of information exchange, pressures to conform, and desires to escape social punishment or receive social reward. Recently, we reconceptualized this factor as reflecting an assessment (by the individual juror) of the probability that each faction will win deliberation.

Thus, our model of opinion change is an implicit utility theory model in which the juror is assumed to combine (a) the *subjective probability* that a faction will win deliberation with (b) the *value* assigned to each faction according to its cognitive appeal as the correct verdict and according to a characterological factor, stubbornness, associated with a desire not to change from the current faction.

In versions of the model under development, we are sharpening the representation of the probability factor (the perceived probability that a faction will win deliberation) and the value factor (the desirability that the juror associates with each verdict's winning). These two factors *parallel* the classic distinction between normative and informational modes of social influence (Deutsch & Gerard, 1955). We are also extending the model to include the generation of events such as persuasive (informative) arguments and punishment (and reward) to describe the fine-grained mechanisms of social influence in deliberation.

Larger factions will have greater capacity to generate persuasive arguments and social reward and punishment, but the relationship would not be perfect and would not be linear. For example, in a typical criminal trial there is a limited pool of plausible arguments that can be generated for one verdict or another. As factions get larger, there will be a tendency for the cognitive resources of more members to be able to generate or retrieve more arguments for the faction's point of view, but because of redundancy in individual jurors' reasoning processes about the case (particularly among jurors who have similar conceptions of the evidence and its implications), adding jurors to an already sizable faction will not increment the argument-generating capacity of that faction in a direct or linear manner.

DYNAMICS OF INDIVIDUAL VERSUS GROUP DECISION MAKING

One way to compare the processes of decision making at the individual and group levels is to attempt to identify the variables that predict initial opinions and changes of opinions in the two contexts—always focusing on changes of an individual's opinion.

Our research on individual decision making has not focused on where differences in verdicts ultimately originate from. Rather, we have concluded that the form of the story constructed by the individual plays a central *mediating* and (we claim) causal role in determining the ultimate decision. We are not so sure why different jurors construct different stories in the first place, although we have some speculations based on analyses of the contents of jurors' think-aloud protocols collected while they are making their decisions.

The pattern and character of the inference processes that occur when individual jurors construct stories do not vary systematically with their verdicts. And there are not systematic differences in individual jurors' comprehensions of the verdict category alternatives or the procedures (e.g., conceptions of the meaning of "beyond reasonable doubt") that they apply to make the classification decision. What does seem to discriminate are the premises that different jurors believe apply to human behavior in the social world.

For example, one characteristic difference between jurors who favor harsher (e.g., first-degree murder) verdicts and jurors who favor more lenient verdicts (e.g., not guilty by reason of self-defense) derives from differences among jurors' beliefs about male aggressiveness and the habits of individuals of various social classes that involve the possession of dangerous weapons. In the murder case used as a stimulus in one third of our research, one belief about the social world that discriminates between harsh- and lenient-verdict jurors concerns inferences made when a juror learns that the defendant was carrying a knife at the time of a fight that resulted in a murder charge. Jurors from lower-income social classes do not find a defendant's possession of a knife during a fight remarkable; they believe that men from the defendant's social class habitually carry knives. More colloquially, they believe lower-class men carry weapons of various types as a routine habit, just in case an event arises in which they might need to defend themselves. Of course, these jurors are likely to believe that the defendant had no special purpose in mind that motivated his possession of the knife, and they conclude that the defendant acted in self-defense or was surprised and acted in the heat of passion when the fateful killing occurred.

On the other hand, jurors from upper-income social classes who live in wealthier neighborhoods find the fact that the defendant was carrying a knife as being of special significance and as the basis to infer a murderous intention. Again, in colloquial terms, people from more genteel society regard the defendant's possession of a knife as a remarkable event and are likely to infer a special motivation, for example, that the defendant intended to injure or kill the victim when he decided to carry the knife. Thus, these jurors are likely to argue for a harsh verdict, first-degree murder, that requires an inference that the defendant had formed a plan and was executing the plan with a specific goal of injuring or killing the decedent.

Thus, we attribute differences between jurors in the ultimate verdict to differences in their story structures, and, in turn, we attribute these differences in stories to jurors' beliefs concerning social events and the motivations associated with them.

If we consider the events that cause jurors' changes of opinion during deliberation, we reach a different conclusion about which factors are critical in determining individual jurors' verdicts. We conducted an analysis of the contents of discussion that occurred during the two minutes of deliberation just before an individual juror declared to the group that he or she had changed his or her opinion about the proper verdict. Again, as an illustration of an empirical analysis of an issue relevant to socially shared cognition, we will review the method we used to identify the types of information pooled that had substantial (causal) influence on jurors' verdict preferences in deliberation. We kept track of jurors' preferred verdicts over the course of deliberation, using their public and private votes and any oral statements they made that unequivocally indicated they had changed their opinions about the proper verdict. When a juror indicated that his or her opinion had changed, we stopped the tape, rewound for two minutes, and performed a content analysis on the discussion that occurred in the two-minute interval before the juror's verdict changed. We then sampled another two-minute segment of deliberation from a period in the discussion when no jurors changed their opinions.

When we compared the content of the before-change two-minute segments and the no-change control segments, we found that discussion of the law, including definitions of the verdicts and the meaning and proper application of legal procedures (e.g., the beyond reasonable doubt standard of proof), was significantly higher during the intervals preceding changes. In contrast there was a tendency (but not a statistically reliable one) for discussion to include more references to the evidence about the events and facts of the matter to be decided during the no-change control segments.

Thus, we found that discussion preceding changes of opinion tended to focus not on what had happened in the crime circumstances, but rather on the law, including definitions of the verdict categories and the appropriate procedures the jurors should apply when determining if a standard of proof had been met. Thus, in the context of group deliberation, the factor that predicted what verdicts jurors would favor (or change to favor) was discussion of the definitions of the verdict categories or the appropriate classification rules that should be applied to determine the fit of a story to a verdict. During group deliberation, jurors would not change their opinions about what had happened (the crime events), but they would change their minds about how those events should be classified legally, either by changing their minds about the definitions of the verdict categories or by changing their opinions about the definition of a term such as *beyond reasonable doubt*. The apparent potency of the discussion of verdicts and story classification procedures was particularly prominent in verdict-driven juries and somewhat less prominent as a predictor of opinion change in evidence-driven juries.

CONCLUDING REMARKS

This chapter is a tentative contribution to the topic of socially shared cognition in small decision-making groups. The most important implication of our research is that we need to base our speculations and future theories about socially shared

cognition on systematic *empirical* investigations of these phenomena. Our research illustrates some initial solutions to problems of how socially shared cognition can be observed and measured. We have developed operational methods to describe the structure of socially shared beliefs about the causal events underlying testimony in legal trials. We have presented some methods to index the extent to which members of a small group agree on these underlying cognitive conceptions. And we have attempted to measure the impact of shared information on opinion changes among members of a small consensus-seeking group.

Considerable work remains to be done to develop scientific concepts to describe intraindividual cognitive processes, interindividual social processes, and the relations between these two levels of analysis. But we believe that a constant emphasis on operational, empirical definitions will promote the most efficient development of theories of socially shared cognition.

References

Bales, R. F., Strodtbeck, F., Mills, T., & Roseborough, M. (1951). Channels of communication in small groups. *American Sociological Review*, *16*, 461–468.

Bruner, J. S. (1986). *Actual minds, possible worlds*. Cambridge, MA: Harvard University Press.

Davis, J. H. (1973). Group decision and social interaction: A theory of social decision schemes. *Psychological Review*, *80*, 97–125.

Deutsch, M., & Gerard, H. B. (1955). A study of normative and informational social influences upon individual judgment. *Journal of Abnormal and Social Psychology*, *51*, 629–633.

Festinger, L. (1950). Informal social communication. *Psychological Review*, *57*, 271–282.

Festinger, L. (1954). A theory of social comparison processes. *Human Relations*, *7*, 117–140.

Freyd, J. J. (1983). Shareability: The social psychology of epistemology. *Cognitive Science*, *7*, 191–210.

Hastie, R., Penrod, S. D., & Pennington, N. (1983). *Inside the jury*. Cambridge, MA: Harvard University Press.

Kerr, N. L. (1981). Social transition schemes: Charting the group's road to consensus. *Journal of Personality and Social Psychology*, *41*, 684–702.

Kuhn, D., Pennington, N., & Ledbetter, B. (1983). Adult thinking in developmental perspective. In P. Baltes & O. Brim (Eds.), *Life-span development and behavior* (Vol. 5, pp. 157–195). New York: Academic.

Latane, B., & Wolf, S. (1981). The social impact of majorities and minorities. *Psychological Review*, *88*, 438–453.

Levine, J. M. (1989). Reaction to opinion deviance in small groups. In P. Paulus (Ed.), *The psychology of group process* (2nd ed., pp. 187–231). Hillsdale, NJ: Erlbaum.

Levine, J. M., & Russo, R. M. (1987). Majority and minority influence. In C. Hendrick (Ed.), *Group processes: Review of personality and social psychology* (Vol. 8, pp. 13–54). Newbury Park, CA: Sage.

Mauet, T. A. (1981). *Fundamentals of trial techniques*. Boston: Little, Brown.

Pennington, N., & Hastie, R. (1986). Evidence evaluation in complex decision making. *Journal of Personality and Social Psychology*, *51*, 242–258.

Pennington, N., & Hastie, R. (1987). *Explaining the evidence: Further tests of the Story Model for juror decision making.* Unpublished manuscript, University of Chicago.

Pennington, N., & Hastie, R. (1988). Explanation-based decision making: Effects of memory structure on judgment. *Journal of Experimental Psychology: Learning, Memory, and Cognition, 14,* 521–533.

Schachter, S. (1951). Deviation, rejection, and communication. *Journal of Abnormal and Social Psychology, 46,* 190–207.

Stasser, G. (1988). Computer simulation as a research tool: The DISCUSS model of group decision making. *Journal of Experimental Social Psychology, 24,* 393–442.

Stasser, G., & Davis, J. H. (1981). Group decision making and social influence: A social interaction sequence model. *Psychological Review, 88,* 523–551.

Stephan, F., & Mischler, E. (1952). The distribution of participation in small groups: An exponential approximation. *American Sociological Review, 17,* 598–608.

Strodtbeck, F. L., & Lipinski, R. M. (1988). *Women jurors, then and now.* Unpublished manuscript, University of Chicago, Social Psychology Laboratory.

Tetlock, P. E., & Kim, J. I. (1987). Accountability and judgment processes in a personality prediction task. *Journal of Personality and Social Psychology, 52,* 700–709.

PART SIX

THE INDIVIDUAL IN SOCIOCOGNITIVE CONTEXT

CHAPTER 15

SHARING COGNITION THROUGH COLLECTIVE COMPREHENSION ACTIVITY

GIYOO HATANO AND KAYOKO INAGAKI

In this chapter we will examine two important questions in constructive group interaction: how a collective attempt to acquire knowledge takes place, and how much knowledge comes to be *shared* (acquired in common) through this attempt. We will be concerned particularly with the generation, revision, and elaboration of explanations for a set of facts, a rule, or a procedure. In other words, our focus is collective comprehension activity and the sharing of its product by group members.

As will be shown, a large number of members of a group can be involved in enduring, coherent discourse about a target issue. Moreover, the group may generate "respectable" cognitive products, for example, a plausible explanation, that any individual member is unlikely to produce. The first question we will explore is how this phenomenon is possible.

The second question we will examine is: How much of the knowledge offered during the discourse is acquired by members differing in prior knowledge and in the extent of participation? When they do not know who knows best, how can group members pick out valid pieces of information and reject others? If the

The authors would like to thank Naomi Miyake, Keiko Takahashi, and James Wertsch for reading and commenting on an earlier version of this chapter. We also thank all the participants of the conference on socially shared cognition for their vocal and silent evaluative reactions to our presentation based on the earlier draft.

collective attempt succeeds in producing a plausible explanation about the target, is it acquired by all or almost all the members?

This chapter consists of three parts. First, we will examine in what type of groups constructive interaction is likely to occur. After discussing a few conditions necessary for a group to engage frequently in constructive interaction, we will offer a prototype of such interaction: a class taught by Hypothesis-Experiment-Instruction. Second, we will present some experimental data related to the above two questions. We will rely primarily on our own research findings but will refer to studies by our Japanese colleagues as well. Finally, we would like to propose our own answers to these questions in speculative ways.

Before turning to these three major parts, however, is is important to define terminology. Throughout this paper *comprehension* is defined as the solution of the problem of "the 'how' and 'why' of the connections observed and applied in action" (Piaget, 1978). In other words, to *comprehend* means to achieve insight (*nattoku* in Japanese) or to find satisfactory explanations for the occurrence of a series of events, the validity of a rule, or the success of a procedure. *Comprehension activity* is a term for the process of achieving insight and thus, as described in Collins, Brown, and Larkin (1980) and Hatano and Inagaki (1987), includes generating inferences, checking their plausibility (by seeking further information from outside or by retrieving another piece of stored information), and coordinating pieces of old and new information, all to build an enriched and coherent representation of what is going on behind a given set of information, a representation that will serve as the basis for insight.

Sometimes comprehension activity is an individual enterprise initiated when a person becomes aware that his or her comprehension is inadequate, although within his or her reach, and is terminated when this person feels he or she has found satisfactory explanations (Hatano & Inagaki, 1987). On other occasions, comprehension takes a collective form. At least some members of a given group become interested in the how and why and ask a question or invite others' comments on their own relevant ideas. The committed members go on by presenting additional information they have gathered, drawing attention to pieces of shared information that seem to support their ideas, and so forth, until all group members are satisfied with some proposed explanations or are convinced that no plausible explanation is forthcoming (or are just bored with the activity). The exact nature of this activity will be discussed in greater detail later.

WHERE SHALL WE LOOK FOR CONSTRUCTIVE GROUP INTERACTION?

It is now generally accepted that social interaction plays an important role in the acquisition of knowledge. However, constructive interaction, that is, the collective invention of knowledge that none of a group's members has acquired or is likely to produce independently, occurs frequently only in some types of groups. We think the following four parameters are important to characterize such groups.

Horizontal in Terms of the Flow of Information

Of the two distinguishable types of interactions, many more researchers have studied *vertical* interaction (represented by adult–child interaction), partly because of the influence of Vygotsky (1978). Current conceptualizations of apprenticeship (Collins, Brown, & Newman, 1989) also concern interaction that is vertical in nature. These researchers assume that one member (i.e., the developed person) continues to be more capable than the other (i.e., the developing individual) at every moment of interaction. Moreover, they have paid much more attention to the reproduction than to the invention of knowledge, if not simply the transmission of knowledge from the more mature to the less mature.

We believe that the construction of knowledge through social interaction can be observed much more often in the other type of interaction, that is the *horizontal* (as in peer interaction). Speaking generally, the less mature member in vertical interaction is not highly motivated to construct knowledge, because he or she believes that the other member possesses or can construct that knowledge more easily (Inagaki, 1981). Even when asked for an explanation, he or she will concentrate on looking for the more capable member's desired answer, instead of figuring it out, as is often observed between a teacher and student. The more mature member may offer some explanation but is unlikely to elaborate or revise it, because the idea is not challenged in interaction.

In contrast, in horizontal interaction, members' motivation to disclose their ideas tends to be natural and strong, because no authoritative right answers are expected to come immediately. Therefore, the members often express fearlessly a variety of ideas, which are likely to be examined, sorted out, and elaborated in interaction. What is critical here is the horizontality in terms of (perceived) expertise as to the target issue among those who participate in the exchange of ideas.

Characterizing a relationship as *horizontal* does not exclude the possibility that some members are more capable than others at some given moment. It only means that roles among members are changeable in interaction. Thus the vertical–horizontal distinction should be taken as a continuum rather than a dichotomy.

Three or More Members

We maintain that, although "two heads are better than one," dyads are far from optimal for the construction of knowledge, and that it is preferable to study interactions in groups consisting of at least three and preferably a few more persons. In other words, we believe that the presence of a third party is an essential component of group process through which knowledge is constructed. Even when only two persons are actively involved in discussion or debate, they seldom ignore other people. Instead, they often talk to the third party or audience, because it may have the potentially deciding vote.

The presence of an audience can enhance the collective construction of knowledge for social and cognitive reasons. Socially, it makes discussion or debate livelier and more enduring, because discussion or debate becomes an intellectual game for gaining supporters to form the majority. Cognitively, it divides the roles of proposing and evaluating ideas among the members. Third parties give, either explicitly or implicitly, clues for evaluating arguments offered by the proponent and opponent: The proponent and opponent can evaluate how persuasive their ideas are by observing reactions of the audience. This is certainly easier than monitoring their own arguments by reflection only.

Does the presence of an audience always facilitate the construction of knowledge? Certainly not. It may lead those speakers who care about the audience's reactions too much to avoid any risky or adventurous attempt and may undermine their motivation for knowing. It may also induce superficial or even sensational arguments if speakers "play to a gallery." We believe, however, that the presence of an audience tends to be advantageous for the construction of knowledge to the extent that the audience is rational.

Involvement of Empirical Confirmation

We assert that, because comprehension activity includes seeking further external information, constructive group interaction usually includes seeking information from outside the group. As Piagetians have revealed (e.g., Doise & Mugny, 1984), although social interaction per se may enable its participants to acquire knowledge, it probably does so only when the correct idea is so salient that it comes out promptly to solve cognitive conflict produced by the interaction. People are not always ready to incorporate information offered by others. Unless the information is persuasive in terms of logic or given by someone known to be an authority, people, especially those forming the majority, will not assimilate the information until external feedback proves its plausibility. Miyake's study (1986) has shown that empirical confirmation by inspection played a significant role in facilitating joint comprehension of how a sewing machine makes stitches, even for her academically sophisticated subjects.

Furthermore, we believe that constructive group interaction is often induced when group members talk about a set of clearly articulated alternatives that are falsifiable by empirical means. In other words, the construction of knowledge occurs often when group activity is "situated" in a specific context. Otherwise, sharing the meaning of what is discussed requires much effort and cost. People may agree (or disagree) prematurely with very different interpretations about the target. For example, our unpublished study revealed that, when asked to comprehend jointly why a given series of steps was needed to make *bonito sashimi*, dyads of female college students rarely spent more than 10 minutes developing an answer. They thought they had comprehended and that their comprehension was shared. Only when asked whether the same procedure should be followed under slightly different conditions was the discrepancy in their interpretations uncovered.

Room for Individual Knowledge Acquisition

A group as a whole usually has a richer data base than any of its members for problem solving. It is likely that no individual member has acquired or has ready access to all needed pieces of information, but every piece is owned by at least one member in the group. For example, when a dyad of two experts—one in the language in which a target passage is written and the other in its content—is required to translate a written passage, their joint product is much better in quality than either of the individual products (Sugimoto, 1988). Thus, if pieces of information distributed among a group's members are aptly collected, group problem solving should be more effective than individual enterprise.

However, problem solving by a group may not result in all individual members' acquisition of its product. Individual group members may not be able to solve on their own a problem that they have solved collectively. Pieces of information distributed among members can be used to solve a given problem without being coordinated into a new piece of knowledge in each member's head. This is because the knowledge has not been invented or represented in an explicitly stated and usable form for individuals.

Individual knowledge acquisition is possible in everyday life in loosely organized groups that are supposed to fulfill several different functions, even when knowledge acquisition itself is not the primary goal. Because human beings have an intrinsic motivation to understand (Hatano & Inagaki, 1987), they are likely to seek the meaning of what they and others do in the group and, thus, to get relevant pieces of knowledge without any explicit request to do so. However, this motivation can be undermined by the expectation of extrinsic rewards, external evaluation, or even the authorized "right" answer (Hatano & Inagaki, 1987). Moreover, because engaging in comprehension activity is seldom the shortest or quickest way to solve a specific problem, it is discouraged when efficiency in getting the solution is emphasized.

Therefore, we assume that, if the group activity is to pursue goal(s) other than knowledge acquisition, if the procedure to achieve the goal(s) has been well established, and if the group's members are required to perform the procedure with utmost efficiency, the members are not likely to engage in persistent comprehension activity. As a result, they are not likely to advance their individual knowledge even when they are repeatedly involved in the group. Readers will find this assumption plausible if they imagine themselves working in a factory under the Taylor system or in a military unit in which what each person should do is specified in detail. Collective problem solving occurs in these groups, but not the collective construction of knowledge.

SHARING COGNITION IN A GROUP: AN EXAMPLE

One concrete example of a group in which constructive interaction takes place is a class taught by a Japanese science education method called *Hypothesis–Experiment–Instruction* (Itakura, 1967), originally devised by K. Itakura and used in science classes in elementary and junior high schools. The following procedure is usually adopted with this method:

1. Pupils are presented with a question having three or four answer alternatives. The question specifies how to confirm which alternative is right.

2. Pupils are asked to choose one answer by themselves.

3. Pupils' responses, counted by a show of hands, are tabulated on the blackboard.

4. Pupils are encouraged to explain and discuss their choices with one another.

5. Pupils are asked to choose an alternative once again. They may change their choices.

6. Pupils are allowed to test their predictions by observing an experiment or reading a given passage.

A teacher, after presenting the problem, acts as a chairperson or moderator who tries to stay neutral during students' discussion. Thus, although he or she has control over what kinds of activities students engage in, none of the discussion participants is regarded as more capable or expert than any other. Throughout the interaction, information flows horizontally. In step 4 above, students are often engaged in lively discussions in a large group of 40 to 45 people. Several students may express their opinions often, but a majority of them tend to participate vicariously in the discussion, nodding or shaking their heads or making brief

Table 1

TABULATION OF PUPILS' RESPONSE FREQUENCIES BEFORE AND AFTER
DISCUSSION

Response	Before discussion	After discussion
(a) Spring becomes shorter	12	21
(b) Spring becomes longer	8	5
(c) Spring retains its length	14	8

Note: From ''Facilitation of Knowledge Integration Through Classroom Discussion'' by K. Inagaki, 1981, *The Quarterly Newsletter of the Laboratory of Comparative Human Cognition, 3*, No. 2, p.27. Copyright 1981 by LCHC. Reprinted by permission.

remarks. There is empirical confirmation in step 6 that can demonstrate clearly which answer alternative is correct. Moreover, discussion in step 4 is about which alternative will prove to be correct in step 6: in other words, discussion is situated in the context of empirical confirmation.

The group is not expected to perform this task efficiently. Rather, its members are expected to acquire knowledge, because this method is for learning science and, above all, for learning basic concepts and principles in science. However, unlike the dyads in Miyake (1986), students are not explicitly asked to achieve comprehension as a final task outcome. They are encouraged only to discuss which alternative is correct. Enduring comprehension activity is initiated primarily by their being presented a problem, the answer alternatives of which represent plausible yet erroneous ideas (i.e., common misconceptions held by pupils) as well as the correct answer, and is amplified through discussion.

Consider the following example from the first lesson on buoyancy, taught by Mr. Shoji to fifth graders (Inagaki, 1981). Mr. Shoji started the lesson with a question: ''Suppose that you have a clay ball on one end of a spring. You hold the other end of the spring and put half of the clay ball into water. Will the spring (a) become shorter, (b) become longer, or (c) retain its length?'' Response frequencies before discussion are shown in Table 1.

As you can see, each alternative was chosen by several students, indicating that all three alternatives were plausible to the students. The following are examples of reasons for choosing alternative *a*, *b*, or *c* that were given by students before entering the discussion:

(a) ''The water has the power to make things float. Therefore, I think the water will make the clay ball float to some extent.'' ''I feel myself lighter in water. I have this experience when I take a bath.''

(b) ''The spring will be longer because the clay ball will sink.'' ''Because the water will be absorbed into the tiny particles which the clay ball consists of.''

(c) "The nature of the clay will not change when we put it into the
water." "The water has the power to make completely immersed things
float, but not if they are only half immersed."

The teacher then elicited group discussion by encouraging students to give
counter arguments against other opinions. Students actively engaged in discussion,
refuting other opinions or defending their own. For example, one of the supporters
of *a* opposed a supporter of *c* by saying, "Your opinion is strange to me. You
said, 'The weight of the clay ball will not change because it is only half immersed
in water.' But you know, when a person's head is above the water, his weight is
lighter in water." Another supporter of *a* said, "I don't agree with the idea that
the clay ball is as heavy in water as in air. I think the water has the power to
make things float." One of the supporters of *c* objected: "Even if the water has
the power to make things float, the clay ball will not float, I suppose." Another
student supporting *a* insisted, "If the clay is a very small lump, I think the water
can make it float."

After the discussion, the teacher retabulated the pupils' responses by asking
whether there were any pupils who had changed their choices. As shown in Table
1, opinions of supporters of option *a* made nine students change their predictions,
but about 40% of the students still had incorrect predictions. Finally, the pupils
observed an experiment to test their predictions. The result supported the pupils
who had chosen alternative *a*.

Which arguments made by the supporters of *a* might have won over some
of their classmates before the demonstration? Could the remaining supporters of
b or *c* incorporate these arguments after the demonstration? To our regret, no
detailed information is available about the individual cognitive processes or social
dynamics involved in discussions by the above class. (Generally speaking, there
have been only a few analytic studies on Hypothesis–Experiment–Instruction. We
will present one of them in the next section.)

Let us discuss briefly the representativeness of our example, that is, a class
taught by Hypothesis–Experiment–Instruction, for constructive interaction in general. Can we observe more or less similar interactions among "just plain folks"
(Lave, 1988)? We think it is likely that ordinary people, as well as students,
engage in a collective attempt to determine which of the alternative ideas confronting them is best, although they pick out their own problem and propose their
own alternatives instead of being presented a ready-made problem and answer
alternatives. In our daily conversation, for example, we may talk about such things
as which bar serves the best *sushi* and what is the fastest route for going to Dokkyo
University from Chiba University. Although we are not primarily interested in
the problem of *why*, we may try to formulate some justifications for our choice.
We also believe it is universal across cultures that groups of people discuss their
own choices and elaborate their explanations for their choices through discussion,

although how well the Hypothesis–Experiment–Instruction method works may be culture-bound.

SOME EXPERIMENTAL FINDINGS

Motivational and Cognitive Effects of Discussion

Our earlier studies on constructive interaction aimed at examining the effectiveness of the Hypothesis–Experiment–Instruction method for Japanese school children. All of these studies were typical group comparisons between experimental and control subjects, and we did not analyze in detail either collective comprehension activity or patterns of sharing. However, the findings can serve as a basis for constraining the range of answers to the questions we posed at the beginning of this chapter.

Let us consider one study (Inagaki & Hatano, 1968) in which fourth graders received a science lesson concerning the conservation of weight when sugar is dissolved in water. Subjects were randomly divided into experimental and control groups (44 and 43 students, respectively) on the basis of their performance on the target task at pretest. Two thirds of the members in each group were non-conservers. In the experimental condition, the six steps outlined previously were followed in groups of about 20 students each, whereas in the control condition, steps 3, 4, and 5 were omitted. Thus, the difference between the conditions was in the extent of the exchange of ideas among the pupils, or more specifically, of the information about who (or how many students) supported each of the alternatives and how they justified their choices, not in the amount of authoritative information given.

Using audiotapes and relying on informal observations, we obtained group protocols, that is, transcribed sequences of members' utterances (with salient nonverbal behaviors recorded). Unlike individual thinking-aloud protocols, group protocols are too coarse to allow us to analyze all major mental events occurring in any individual's brain, even when he or she speaks very often and the group is very small. Utterances in a group are almost always preceded by editing and, thus, cannot be taken as concurrent indexes of mental events. The larger the group, the more editing is done and the longer is the delay. However, these protocols suggest at least two elements to be included in the answer to our first question regarding how a collective attempt to acquire knowledge takes place.

First, students' enduring comprehension activity was pushed forward by their social, or more specifically "partisan," motivation, as well as by cognitive or "epistemic" motivation. In other words, their collective attempt is not a "pure" comprehension activity but aims at winning an academic competition as well as at comprehension. As soon as the whole group was divided (psychologically, not

spatially or socially) into a few parties according to their choice of answer alternatives, the students seemed to be motivated to work for the party they belonged
to, that is, to collect more supporters and eventually win the argument by per-
suading all others. Most of the utterances were arguments against other parties
that ranged from pointing out errors in reasoning to noting overlooked facts that
they thought were critical. Speakers often gave signs of solidarity to supporters
who had chosen the same alternative, and the supporters returned signs of agreement. When their prediction proved to be correct, students were quite excited and
again exchanged signs of companionship. When it turned out to be wrong, they
were greatly disappointed but tried to console each other.

        This is not to say that the classroom discussion was driven solely by the
competitive desire to be academic winners. Epistemic motivation, the desire to
know and understand, remained strong and underlay all the partisanship. In addition to the general situational emphasis on individual learning, the freedom to
change one's prediction and, thus, one's affiliation to a party, and also the agreed
reliance on experiment as the means for confirming or disconfirming predictions
seemed to enhance this motivation. Thus, the students were all seeking to share
better comprehension, as well as competing between parties.

        The second element that the protocols suggest is that this partisanship made
pupils' comprehension activity more effective, because it served to divide the task
into several manageable parts. It is hard for any individual to collect arguments
both for and against each alternative and to assess them impartially. In collective
comprehension activity, participants do not have to do this. Supporters of one
alternative have only to try to defend it (offer arguments "for") by elaborating
justifications, because supporters of other alternatives naturally try to criticize
them (propose arguments "against"). In fact, in response to other parties' criticisms, most committed supporters could think of more plausible and sophisticated
explanations than they had had at the beginning, while maintaining a more or less
consistent standpoint. Moreover, assessing the strength of each argument, which
would have been very hard to do on a purely cognitive basis, was helped by social
cues. The effectiveness of one's own or a comrade's argument could be judged
by whether it made opponents silent or attracted more supporters. Here reactions
of the third party would also be considered. Unlike the arrangement of partners
in Miyake's experiment (1986), the division of labor in this experiment was
possible in part on a competitive basis.

        Division of labor was also possible within a party. Because those students
belonging to the same party shared many relevant opinions, they could easily add
to or elaborate what had been said by their comrades. The students could make
their explanation increasingly clear, more persuasive, and more detailed in the
course of discussion, although each of the individual contributors added only a
little.

Let us derive suggestions from this study for our second question regarding how much knowledge is shared through collective comprehension activity. In contrast to the few shifts in the choice of alternatives before the experimental confirmation, when given a posttest immediately after the observation of the experiment, all but a few of the previously mentioned children in the experimental condition acquired conservation responses to the target sugar-and-water task, as did most of the control condition children. Moreover, the experimental condition children could give adequate explanations about why the weight of dissolved sugar was conserved more often than could the control condition children. For example, 26% of the experimental subjects gave atomistic or quasiatomistic explanations, whereas none of the control subjects gave such reasons. In addition, experimental subjects showed greater progress in applying the principle of weight conservation to a variety of situations.

However, what experimental subjects could learn depended on what had been discussed, especially what explanations had been offered by the proponents of the correct alternative. For example, most of the atomistic reasons given at the posttest were found in one class in which one of the students had justified his prediction of the conservation of weight by relying on atomism (i.e., a lump of sugar consisted of a large number of very small particles, and these particles still existed in water). It is reasonably clear that explanations offered in group discussion could be assimilated when students were given external feedback informing them which alternative was correct. In other words, through collective comprehension activity, they had been able to share a set of possibly correct explanations despite apparent opposition. Thus, effects of group discussion must vary from class to class, because the content of the discussion necessarily varies.

Analyses of Group Protocols

Our recent studies have been concerned with individual *learning history*, that is, how each student in a group elaborates or revises his or her idea by incorporating and reacting to information presented in discussion. Therefore, the results of these studies are more informative concerning the two questions posed at the beginning of this chapter. One of these studies (Inagaki & Hatano, 1989) dealt with characteristics of monkeys in relation to their lives in a tree.

First, three experimental groups of about 20 fifth graders each read a short passage about relationships between animals' characteristics and their ways of living, using lions and moles as examples. Next, they were given a problem in multiple choice form about the monkey's characteristics. An example problem was: "Do the thumbs of monkeys' forefeet oppose the other 'fingers' (like in human hands) or extend in parallel to other 'fingers' (like in human feet)? How about the thumbs of their hind feet?'' Answer alternatives included: (a) the thumbs are never opposing; (b) the thumbs are opposing only in the forefeet; and (c) the thumbs are opposing in both fore and hind feet. [Alternative (c) is correct.] Then, pupils' response frequencies were tabulated on the blackboard, and group discussion followed. After about 15 minutes of discussion, the pupils chose an answer alternative once again. (These three steps correspond to steps 3–5 in our earlier studies.) Finally, students were given a short passage stating the correct answer, instead of observing an experiment. This passage described only the relevant facts about monkeys and contained no explanations about why these characteristics had evolved. The control condition was also provided to assess how likely it was that those pupils would construct knowledge without social interaction. Three control groups of about 20 pupils read the same passage immediately after they chose, for the first and only time, an answer alternative to the multiple choice problem.

We again made group protocols, and this time they were supplemented by retrospective data obtained by a questionnaire given after the group interaction. In addition to the points made in the preceding section, the following pieces of evidence were obtained for the presence of the partisan motivation. First, in the questionnaire, 47 of the 65 experimental students (72%) nominated no one belonging to other camps as having stated reasonable but not agreeable opinions. Second, only 11 children out of the 65 (17%) changed their predictions at the second choice (before the feedback). Third, levels of confidence were significantly elevated after the discussion, and there was also significantly elevated interest in reading the passage. This combination clearly contradicts Berlyne's theory (e.g., 1963), which attributes curiosity to uncertainty, and suggests that both confidence and interest reflect children's commitment to their party more than their cognitive incongruity.

Learning Histories of Vocal and Silent Participants

After reading the passage about the characteristics of monkeys, both experimental and control subjects were asked in a questionnaire format to explain why monkeys had a thumb opposing other fingers. When the degree of elaborateness of the explanations was rated on a 4-point scale, the experimental subjects gave significantly more elaborate explanations than did the control subjects [Mean rated score for the experimental group was 1.88 with an SD of 1.04, and was 1.44 with an SD of 1.06 for the control group, $t(126) = 2.36$, $p < .05$], by connecting the given facts in the passage to some of the ideas expressed in discussion.

However, this picture as a whole does not tell much about the variety of learning histories. Even within the experimental condition, there occurred different series of learning events for different groups and different students, and the overall

Table 2

DEGREE OF ELABORATENESS OF EXPLANATIONS GIVEN BY EACH TYPE OF
PARTICIPANT AFTER DISCUSSION

Type of participant	N	M	SD
Majority-vocal	18	2.22	0.85
Majority-silent	33	1.58	1.05
Minority-vocal	7	2.29	0.88
Minority-silent	7	2.00	1.10

difference of the experimental subjects from the control subjects reflects only in
a global fashion the aggregate of these histories.

Discussions developed differently in the three experimental groups, depending on the distribution of the children's initial responses, which were tabulated
on the blackboard. In Group A, supporters of option b formed the majority (three
students supported option a, 13 students option b, and five students option c) and
spoke most actively. Their opinion, that thumb-opposing forefeet would be convenient for grasping a branch or an object, but thumb-opposing hind feet would
be inconvenient for walking, dominated the discussion. In Group B, supporters
of options b and c were in the mainstream with competing pluralities (four students
chose option a, 10 students option b, and eight students option c). Discussion in
this group was on the monkey's hind feet, and the two sides stood evenly divided
at the end of the session. In Group C, supporters of a and b were most numerous
(10 students chose option a, 10 option b, and two option c). Their arguments
were exclusively between two opinions, that is, "A monkey has thumb-opposing
forefeet because they are convenient for grasping an object," and "A monkey
should not have such feet because they are not good for walking."

Each of the subjects in the three experimental groups was placed into one
of four cells of a 2 x 2 design, according to whether the subject belonged to the
majority (of combined pluralities) or minority at the beginning of the discussion
and whether the subject spoke at least once or not at all during the discussion.
These groups were compared in terms of rated elaborateness of their explanations
(See Table 2). A two-way ANOVA indicated that the explanations given by vocal
participants were slightly more elaborate than those of silent ones, and the minority
participants' explanations were as elaborate as those of the majority participants.

This suggests that the vocal participants tended to be somewhat more involved in the discussion and thus better able to integrate various pieces of information than the silent participants. However, some vocal participants belonging
to the majority failed to give elaborate explanations on the posttest. Even when
they started with good ideas, they did not seem to have learned much, probably

because they belonged to the mainstream during the discussion, and the difference between their prediction and many others' ideas seemed small.

Although silent participants tended not to learn as much from discussion, some of them actively tried to find agent(s) who spoke for them in discussion, and if they could, they tended to give elaborate explanations afterward. M.Y., described in the next paragraph, is representative of such children. Even when silent participants (such as T.I., described after M.Y.) could not find such an agent because they belonged to a minority, some of them seem to have responded with their opponents' arguments in mind and elaborated their explanations by incorporating challenging ideas into their initial choice.

M.Y. (a boy) from Group B belonged to the majority; he chose b before the discussion. In the questionnaire he referred to two vocal supporters of b as those whose opinions had been the same as his. At the same time he named a girl who had supported c as a proponent of a reasonable explanation. He did not change his prediction and his curiosity and confidence after the discussion increased. His explanation on the posttest was rated elaborate: "A monkey cannot climb a tree nor grasp an object unless its fore and hind feet are thumb-opposing." This suggests that he incorporated information from the supporter of c when he read the material and found out that his idea was correct for the forefeet but not for the hind feet.

T.I. (a girl) from Group A did not try to find an agent in discussion; she did not name anybody whose opinion had been plausible. She chose alternative c both before and after the discussion, and wrote in the questionnaire that she had not changed her answer because she had been confident in herself. Her explanation on the posttest was, "Because [monkeys] have not walked on the ground often, [their feet] have become suitable for holding on to branches." Because no control group pupils gave such explanations, we can infer that she was responding to the argument by supporters of b, who made up the majority, that "thumb-opposing hind feet are inconvenient for walking."

DATA-CONSTRAINED SPECULATIONS

How Collective Comprehension Activity Takes Place

In the following paragraphs, we will discuss how collective comprehension activity takes place with some success even among students who are academically unsophisticated, basing our discussion on the data presented above. Our answer to the first question we posed in this chapter is as follows: Collective comprehension activity often takes place when cognitive motivation and social motivation work in a concerted fashion. The activity is performed successfully when it is divided, on the basis of social motivation, between proponents, opponents, and a third party, as well as within each party.

Collective comprehension activity is different from individual comprehension activity in its social nature in the dual sense: (a) it is energized by social (partisan) motivation; and (b) there are social constraints on which part of the hypothesis space is explored and what types of evidence are considered. Our studies clearly demonstrated that social motivation made collective comprehension activity lively, enduring, and cheerful. The studies also showed that the partisan motivation gave a basis for effective division of labor in the pursuit of comprehension. It enabled students to take partial charge of the hard task of collecting and evaluating arguments both for and against each alternative between parties and within each party.

Partisan motivation, however, is by no means the sole motivation for collective comprehension activity. Comprehension activity, whether it is collective or individual, is induced by epistemic curiosity or motivation for comprehension. In this sense, the activity is radically different from ordinary party politics, which is almost exclusively driven by partisan motivation. The epistemic motivation is amplified, not superseded, by the partisan motivation, because in the constructive group activities one's affiliation with a party is cognitively based and is changeable depending on cognitive change, and the group discussion proceeds under the shared metacognitive belief in empirical confirmation as the means to decide which answer is correct.

The collective comprehension activity examined so far has at least two components in common with the collective scientific discovery by children in day care that we studied earlier (Inagaki & Hatano, 1983). First, in both cases, information seeking was initiated not only by epistemic curiosity but also by social motivation: the desire to help one's party win in the collective comprehension activity and the desire to induce a socially useful event in the collective discovery. Second, in both cases, knowledge could be acquired through group interaction, although group members did not yet have enough cognitive capability to do so by themselves, mainly because the task of knowledge acquisition was divided into easier steps. Although the two cases differed in many aspects—for example, the children in day care could not formulate a hypothesis verbally—they can shed light on the how and why of the occurrence of a collective attempt to acquire knowledge and its success.

How Much Knowledge is Shared

As for the knowledge acquired through group discussion, our experimental data suggest three points. First, students often produce knowledge that can seldom be acquired without such interaction. Second, what a majority of them acquires varies from group to group, even when the interaction is induced by one and the same procedure. Third, knowledge differs considerably, even among those students who have been in the same group. Therefore, we must conclude that two processes are involved in the construction of knowledge through interaction: (a) individual invention of knowledge, motivated by group interaction; and (b) assimilation of information proposed by others in the preceding interaction, with some individual editing.

Group discussion often induces individual comprehension activity following it; that is, it motivates people to collect more pieces of information about the issue of the discussion and to understand the issue more deeply. Our cognitive Berlynean theory (Hatano & Inagaki, 1987) assumes that, when people recognize that their comprehension is not yet adequate, they are likely to engage in activity for seeking adequate comprehension, as long as they believe the target is worth understanding and its adequate comprehension is within reach. Group discussion on an issue is likely to make students recognize that their comprehension is not adequate. In the course of discussion, students may be surprised to find out that there exists a number of ideas that are plausible although different from their own. In addition, they may be perplexed by being unable to decide which of the alternative ideas is most tenable. More important, when asked for clarification of their views or when they are directly disputed, students may become aware of the lack of co-ordination among the bits of knowledge they possess. Through these processes, students often begin to feel a healthy dissatisfaction with the adequacy of their comprehension.

At the same time, group discussion offers much information valuable for deepening comprehension if one assimilates it aptly. Because group members have been exposed to plausible explanations in the process of discussion, they can revise or elaborate their knowledge easily by incorporating some of them when the feedback reveals the falsity of their predictions.

Our data strongly suggest that silent members may be actively participating. They can learn much by observing the ongoing discussion or debate carefully. This is often characterized as a vicarious process, but it is more than that. In a sense, these students are all trying to find an agent, someone who really speaks for them. A good agent or vocal participant can articulate what a silent member has been trying without success to say and, through clarity of expression, can confirm the validity of the assertion for everyone involved. Such a participant not only persuades opponents but also convinces supporters that they are on the right track.

We would like to emphasize that, although not competent enough to understand the target issue without group activity, people usually try to interpret and incorporate what has been achieved collectively. Unless they are alienated workers in factories under the Taylor system or are required to execute a piecemeal procedure according to a given manual, they seek comprehension about what they as individuals are doing and how the entire system is working.

However, we would also like to emphasize that comprehension is essentially a private achievement, because exactly what and how much explanation is satisfactory may vary from individual to individual. Moreover, there can usually be at least several plausible interpretations and explanations for a given set of facts, rules, or procedures. In fact, Miyake (1986) found that, even after an hour-long joint comprehension activity that resulted in a subjective feeling of complete sharing, members of dyads, when individually queried, gave very different explanations.

Thus our answer to the second question we posed can be summarized as follows: People who have been involved in collective comprehension activity need not have uniform representations; they may well have different ways of comprehension. However, many of those ways of comprehension can be achieved only after constructive interaction—more accurately, interaction in a particular group in which the participants have expressed certain opinions. Only in this sense can we claim that they share comprehension through their collective attempt.

References

Berlyne, D. E. (1963). Motivational problems raised by exploratory and epistemic behavior. In S. Koch (Ed.), *Psychology: A study of a science* (Vol. 5, pp. 284–364). New York: McGraw-Hill.

Collins, A., Brown, J. S., & Larkin, K. M. (1980). Inference in text understanding. In R. J. Spiro, B. C. Bruce, & W. F. Brewer (Eds.), *Theoretical issues in reading comprehension* (pp. 387–407). Hillsdale, NJ: Erlbaum.

Collins, A., Brown, J. S., & Newman, S. E. (1989). Cognitive apprenticeship: Teaching the crafts of reading, writing, and mathematics. In L. B. Resnick (Ed.), *Knowing, learning, and instruction: Essays in honor of Robert Glaser* (pp. 453–494). Hillsdale, NJ: Erlbaum.

Doise, W. & Mugny, G. (1984). *The social development of the intellect*. Oxford, England: Pergamon Press.

Hatano, G., & Inagaki, K. (1987). A theory of motivation for comprehension and its application to mathematics instruction. In T. A. Romberg & D. M. Stewart (Eds.), *The monitoring of school mathematics: Background papers, Vol. 2: Implications from psychology; outcomes of instruction. (Program Report 87-2)* (pp. 27–46). Madison: Wisconsin Center for Education Research.

Inagaki, K. (1981). Facilitation of knowledge integration through classroom discussion. *The Quarterly Newsletter of the Laboratory of Comparative Human Cognition, 3,* 26–28.

Inagaki, K., & Hatano, G. (1968). Motivational influences on epistemic observation. *Japanese Journal of Educational Psychology, 16,* 191–202. (In Japanese with English summary)

Inagaki, K., & Hatano, G. (1983). Collective scientific discovery by young children. *The Quarterly Newsletter of the Laboratory of Comparative Human Cognition, 5*, 13–18.

Inagaki, K., & Hatano, G. (1989). *Learning histories of vocal and silent participants in group discussion*. Paper presented at the annual meeting of the Japanese Psychological Association, Tsukuba, Japan. (in Japanese)

Itakura, K. (1967). Instruction and learning of concept "force" in static based on Kasetsu–Jikken–Jigyo (Hypothesis–Experiment–Instruction): A new method of science teaching. *Bulletin of National Institute for Educational Research, 52*, 1–121. (in Japanese)

Lave, J. (1988). *Cognition in practice*. Cambridge, England: Cambridge University Press.

Miyake, N. (1986). Constructive interaction and the iterative process of understanding. *Cognitive Science, 10*, 151–177.

Piaget, J. (1978). *Success and understanding*. London: Routledge and Kegan Paul.

Sugimoto, T. (1988). *Substantive and linguistic knowledge in translation*. Paper presented at the annual meeting of the Japanese Cognitive Science Society, Osaka. (in Japanese)

Vygotsky, L. S. (1978). *Mind in society*. Cambridge, MA: Harvard University Press.

CHAPTER 16

SOCIAL INTERACTION AS APPRENTICESHIP IN THINKING: GUIDANCE AND PARTICIPATION IN SPATIAL PLANNING

BARBARA ROGOFF

In this chapter, I use the metaphor of apprenticeship to argue that children's cognitive development involves guided participation with other people in handling the intellectual tools and societally organized goals of their culture. I will focus on the development of children's planning skills in the context of interaction with their parents and peers.

Although there are obvious differences between apprenticeships involving mature learners and guided participation involving young children (such as the attention span and background knowledge of the learners), the apprenticeship model is attractive for several reasons:

1. Apprentices are active in gathering information and practicing skills as they participate in skilled activities. Children are active in observing and participating in the activities of those around them and are motivated to participate more centrally.

This paper adapts material presented in my recent book *Apprenticeship in Thinking: Cognitive Development in Social Context* (New York: Oxford University Press). It was written during my Fellowship at the Center for Advanced Study in the Behavioral Sciences in 1988–1989, supported by the National Science Foundation (#BNS87-00864), the Spencer Foundation, and a Faculty Fellow Award from the University of Utah. The research reported here has been supported by the National Institute of Child Health and Human Development (#16793).

2. The learning of apprentices is structured by practices developed by their predecessors to meet societally valued goals. Learning to sew, cook, weave, heal, navigate—all involve becoming skilled in the use of tools and inventions of previous generations that both reflect and shape societal goals. This aspect of apprenticeship provides a parallel with the importance of recognizing that children's cognitive development involves learning to use the intellectual tools of their society (e.g., literacy, mnemonic devices, conventions for representing space) to handle culturally valued activities and goals (e.g., in U.S. schooled populations, efficient planning and organizing lists of information to be remembered).

3. Apprentices are assisted in their learning by communication and involvement with more skilled people—experts and more advanced apprentices—who help determine how to divide the activity into subgoals that a novice can begin to handle, as well as provide pointers on how to handle the tools and skills required. (Note that *expertise* is a relative term; experts are more skilled than novices and have some degree of vision regarding the organization of a skill, but they are not finished developing themselves.) The roles of experts with novices parallel the roles of caregivers and peers who help children's cognitive development by collaborating with them in determining the activities in which children participate and their level of participation, as well as guiding their efforts to handle intellectual tools and skills in the context of joint involvement.

4. Apprentices seldom learn alone. In addition to being involved with more skilled practitioners, apprentices often learn in a community of relative novices (such as fellow graduate students, classmates, siblings, or other novice weavers). Interaction with and observation of other novices provides challenge, support, collaborative puzzling out of problems, and models of learning in progress.

My research on children's cognitive development stresses the mutual involvement of children and their partners in arranging for children's activities and in jointly handling problem solving. It also emphasizes the societal context of the tools available and the skills promoted as they derive from a culture's history and reflect cultural goals both for the direction of individual development and the aims of particular activities. The cultural context of cognitive development and of social interaction requires attention to the specifics of the skills to be learned, the goals to be reached, and the shared activities in which children and others participate.

Vygotsky's (1978, 1987) ideas have served as a source of inspiration to this perspective, through his suggestion that individual cognitive development is embedded in a sociocultural environment that provides tools for thinking and partners who are skilled in the use of such tools. Vygotsky argued that children's interactions with others in the ''zone of proximal development'' provide children with the opportunity to carry out cognitive processes jointly that are more advanced than they could manage independently, and that this joint problem-solving process serves as the basis for children's subsequent independent efforts.

My concept of *guided participation* (Rogoff, 1990) is an effort to extend Vygotsky's notion of the zone of proximal development. I stress that children are active in participating in activities (centrally or, to use Lave's term in this volume, *peripherally*) with guidance from more skilled people. Both participation and guidance are mutual efforts of children and their caregivers or companions; neither can be attributed to an individual alone. Children participate *with others* who facilitate or challenge them in the process, or at least permit children's presence, with mutual adjustments in roles. In their mutual engagement, children and their partners manage activity with guidance of children's efforts, with varying degrees of asymmetry between the participants in responsibility for providing and seeking guidance, and with varying goals for development in differing cultural communities.

Guided participation necessarily involves subtle communication between people as to what new information is needed or appropriate and how it can be made compatible with current levels of skill and understanding. Children and their social partners build bridges from children's current understanding to reach new understanding through processes inherent in communication. They structure problem solving in a way that provides children with a level of support and challenge that comfortably stretches their skills, whether the goal is teaching and learning or simply managing a practical situation. Guided participation involves transfer of responsibility for handling more complex features of a problem as children develop skill and is, hence, a dynamic process of structuring and supporting development.

Guided participation relies on tacit communication and distal arrangements based on practical considerations, as well as on explicit face-to-face interaction that may be designed as instructional. In addition to dialogue that aims to assist children's learning, guided participation involves casual conversation that is not explicitly didactic, subtle nonverbal and verbal forms of interaction, and distal arrangements for children's activities. The determination of the scenario and cast of characters in children's daily lives, managed by children and their caregivers in their cultural context, is a very powerful aspect of guided participation in access to and involvement in skilled activities. The routine arrangements and interactions between children and their caregivers and companions provide children with thousands of opportunities to observe and participate in the skilled activities of their culture. Through repeated and varied experience in supported routine and challenging situations, children become skilled practitioners in the specific cognitive activities of their communities.

In this chapter, I present research exploring how guided participation channels the development of children's skill in planning efficient imaginary routes. The research, focusing on middle-class U.S. children aged 4 to 5 years and 6 to 9 years, examined the roles of both guidance and participation in skilled planning and the extent to which children and their partners succeeded in sharing their thinking processes as they worked together.

It is important to note that our research focused on one cultural group—middle-class Americans, a group of obvious interest to its members. The cognitive skills, intellectual tools, valued approaches, and interactional practices of this group are likely to differ from those of other cultural groups. For example, not all cultural communities may value planning imaginary routes in advance of action to maximize efficiency of the routes rather than minimizing effort in the planning; not all would use the specific tools for spatial planning that were utilized in this research (e.g., drawing routes with colored pencils on maps or counting blocks). In addition, people from many groups would not be interested in playing with puzzles to plan efficient imaginary errand trips or avoiding dead ends in mazes for the sake of an interested researcher; and many would not feel comfortable with adults and children working together as approximate equals or explicitly stating their planning tactics.

GUIDANCE AND PARTICIPATION IN SPATIAL PLANNING

To examine the role and processes of guidance as well as participation in cognitive activities, we observed children planning collaboratively with others and then examined how they handled similar problems independently. We used spatial planning tasks because the planning and collaboration processes are more visible in these tasks than they would be in some other kinds of planning tasks. Specifically, our planning tasks involved children in devising efficient imaginary routes in two-dimensional spatial layouts, with tasks resembling the errand planning task used with adults by Hayes-Roth and Hayes-Roth (1979).

Our data examining the relationship between collaborative spatial planning and children's subsequent independent performance did not show unqualified advantages of social interaction. The findings suggest that having a problem-solving partner may not yield benefits for later independent problem solving unless the partners engage in shared, skilled problem solving. Because the results differ somewhat for young children and older children in our spatial planning tasks, we first report the research for the older ages, 6 to 9 years, and then for the younger ages, 4 and 5 years. Efficient planning of future actions may be more difficult for young children to share with another person than other cognitive activities that provide concrete support for the shared decision making, as in remembering categories or lists of items.

OLDER CHILDREN'S GUIDANCE AND PARTICIPATION IN PLANNING

Our studies with 9-year-old children consistently showed the advantages of working with a skilled partner compared with working with a partner less skilled in

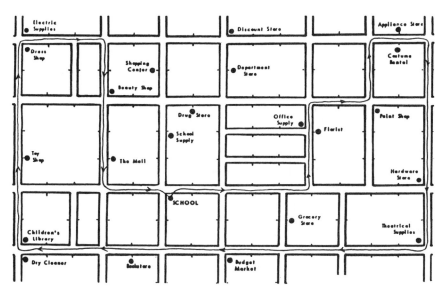

Figure 1   Map of imaginary downtown area for errand-planning task, showing an optimal route from the school, around town to pick up items, and back to school. From "Influence of Adult and Peer Collaborators on Children's Planning Skills" by B. Radziszewska and B. Rogoff, 1988, *Developmental Psychology*, *24*, p. 842. Copyright 1988 by the American Psychological Association. Reprinted by permission.

planning. We used peers as less skilled partners in this research to provide a contrast with working with adults, who are more skilled in these errand planning tasks. (The results are not assumed to apply to situations in which peers are skilled or in control. I take up the question of the value of peer interaction after describing the findings in which they serve as less skilled partners than adults.)

Collaborating With Parents or Peers

In the first study of this series, we found that 9-year-old children gained more skill in imaginary errand planning from collaborating with parents than with 9-year-old partners (Radziszewska & Rogoff, 1988). Partners were given a map of an imaginary downtown (Figure 1) and two lists of errands (Table 1) and were asked to plan a trip to get materials for a school play. Each partner had a list of five items to be picked up; the partners needed to coordinate their planning of the route so that the driver could make one trip efficiently (to save gasoline).

To produce an optimal route, subjects needed to devise a plan incorporating the stores at which visits were mandatory (i.e., to get items available from only one store) and to decide which of two alternative stores it would be most efficient to include for items involving a choice of stores (e.g., "glue from the Drug Store

Table 1

TWO LISTS OF ERRANDS USED ON ONE TRIAL OF THE ERRAND-
PLANNING TASK

First Partner's List

- ☑ silk flowers from the *Florist*
- ☑ uniforms from the *Theatrical Supplies*
- ☑ belts from the *Dress Shop*
- ☑ wallpaper from the *Discount Store* or *Hardware Store*
- ☑ acrylic paper from the *School Supply* or *Bookstore*

Second Partner's List

- ☑ hair spray from the *Beauty Shop*
- ☑ repaired stereo from the *Appliance Store*
- ☑ stage decoration from the *Children's Library*
- ☑ paint brushes from the *Paint Shop* or *Shopping Center*
- ☑ glue from the *Drug Store* or *Toy Shop*

Note: From "Influence of Adult and Peer Collaborators on Children's Planning Skills" by B. Radziszewska and B. Rogoff, 1988, *Developmental Psychology, 24*, p. 842. Copyright 1988 by the American Psychological Association. Adapted by permission.

or from the Toy Shop''). The map was the same for all trials, and the optimal route was similar, but the lists of items were different for each trial. Partners planned two trips together; then each planned a trip independently.

The collaborative planning of adult–child dyads was much more sophisticated than that of peer dyads. The peer dyads planned by making decisions on a step-by-step basis, as is common in children's individual planning (Brown & DeLoache, 1978; Friedman, Scholnick, & Cocking, 1987; Magkaev, 1977). The peer dyads usually proceeded by identifying the store closest to the current location and checking to see if it was on either of the lists, which produced much less efficient routes. Adult–child dyads planned longer sequences of moves, averaging 4.9 stores per move decision compared with the peer dyads' average sequences of 1.3 stores. Almost half of the adult–child dyads planned the whole route at once, whereas none of the peer dyads did so. Adult–child dyads were also twice as likely to explore the layout before making moves, often marking the choice and no-choice stores with different colors and symbols to facilitate planning an optimal route. Furthermore, adult–child dyads were 11 times as likely to verbalize planning strategies.

During collaboration with adults, children usually participated in the more sophisticated planning strategies organized by the adults. Statements of strategy came almost exclusively from adults, but the sophisticated planning decisions were made jointly between the adults and children.

Differences between the performances of the children who performed well and those who performed poorly after collaborating with adults appeared to relate to the extent of participation and guided decision making with the adults during collaboration. For example, one child who performed extremely well on the posttest worked with a mother who stated her strategy and initiated efforts, such as marking the stores in different colors and finding the tentative route between the mandatory stores. After the mother's initiations, the daughter continued the strategies under her mother's supervision, with the daughter taking more responsibility by the second trial. In contrast, another child who had more difficulty on the posttest had worked with a mother who simply ordered her daughter to find and mark the stores and then dictated the whole route, offering little explanation and not stating the strategy. The daughter obediently followed all directions. In the second trial, the daughter had no greater responsibility; the mother planned and drew the route on her own, with few comments.

The interaction between peers resembled that of the adult–child dyads in which the children subsequently performed poorly. Often the more skilled peer partners dominated decision making, ignored their partner, and communicated little. In one peer dyad, for example, one child dominated decision making. He made most of the moves, occasionally pushing the other boy's hand off the map and generally ignoring his partner's attempts to participate. Interested only in knowing if his partner had a given store on his list, he returned to work alone, occasionally stating the need to look for the next closest store. There was little coordination or communication between the children; while one child made most of the moves, the other considered his own moves.

It seems that planning with a skilled partner provides an opportunity for children to participate in the use of skills that are in advance of those they can manage independently, and that such collaboration enhances children's later independent planning. Children who had worked with adults produced routes that were about 20% shorter than those of children who had worked with peers, and they appeared to have appropriated specific aspects of the sophisticated planning strategy they had practiced with adults. For example, 14 of the 16 children from adult–child pairs started the individual trial by searching for and marking the choice and the mandatory stores on the map, a common strategy in the collaborative trials of these children with adults, whereas only 1 of the 16 children from peer dyads marked the stores in advance of making moves.

These results are similar to those of Ellis and Rogoff (1982, 1986), who found that 6- to 7-year-old children who had worked with adults performed better on a later independent version of a memory and classification task than did the children who had worked with 8- to 9-year-old teachers. The pairs of children focused on immediate actions in a step-by-step approach. The children working with other children often had to perform the task with minimal guidance or were excluded from decision making as the child-teacher took over the task, frequently without even looking to see if the learner was watching. This contrasted with the guidance and shared decision making observed in adult–child dyads, which usually involved discussion of the rationale for decisions and participation of the children in decisions and in preparation for later independent management of the task. Of the children who had interacted with adults, those whose interactions involved both guidance regarding decision-making rationales and participation in decision making performed better on the later individual task (Rogoff & Gauvain, 1986).

Although the differences between having a peer partner and having an adult partner were striking in both the collaborative processes and the later independent performance in the planning task of Radziszewska and Rogoff (1988), as well as in the earlier memory and classification task of Ellis and Rogoff (1982, 1986), the advantage of working with adults could be attributed to adults' skill in the task and/or to the processes of guidance and participation involved in adult–child interaction. The study described next examined the role of children's partners' expertise in errand planning and the guided participation of children in skilled planning processes.

Collaborating with Partners Varying in Errand-Planning Expertise

Radziszewska and Rogoff (in press) compared children's interaction with adults and with peers, using one group of peer partners with no special preparation and another group of peer partners trained to use the optimal strategy in the errand-planning task prior to their collaboration with the target children. The collaborative planning of the trained peers and the adults involved equally sophisticated planning strategies (i.e., planning sequences of moves rather than single steps) and produced equally efficient routes, whereas the collaborative planning by untrained peer dyads involved less sophisticated planning strategies and produced less efficient routes.

When they later planned routes by themselves, target children who had collaborated with adults performed better than those who had worked with either trained or untrained peers. The advantage of working with adults versus working with trained peers appeared to result from both the guidance and the participation of children working with adults. Although dyads involving adults and those involving trained peers were similar in the sophistication and efficiency of their collaborative planning, dyads with adults frequently involved explanation of the optimal strategy or strategic thinking aloud, forms of guidance that were almost nonexistent in the peer dyads (whether the peers were trained or not). In addition, almost all the children working with adults were active participants, observing or participating in decisions, whereas fewer than half of the children working with trained peers were active participants. Although children working with untrained peer partners were more active in decision making than were children with trained peer partners, the unavailability of a partner skilled in errand planning meant that there was not a basis for guidance or observation of more skilled planning. Thus it appears that neither a partner's skill in errand planning nor children's participation alone was as useful as participating with guidance in skilled imaginary errand planning.

This view is substantiated by correlations between the individuals' posttest performance and their prior experiences during the collaborative planning trials. Good posttest performance by target children was related to production of good routes on collaborative trials, active involvement of children in planning decisions, and communication of the optimal strategy in joint planning.

POTENTIAL ADVANTAGES OF PEER INTERACTION IN OTHER SITUATIONS

Our findings that working with an adult yields greater skill in errand planning than working with a peer contrast with Piaget's speculation (1977) that peer interaction would provide greater learning than adult–child interaction, because of the greater possibility for exploration of ideas with peers.

A suggestion derived from Damon (1984; Rogoff, 1990) may incorporate the seemingly conflicting results of our adult–peer comparisons and Piagetian studies with peers: In learning to handle a skill that does not require a transformation of perspective, interaction with more skilled partners may be most useful, whereas in making a serious shift of perspectives, interaction among equals may provide a more effective forum for development. Development that involves a transformation of perspective (as in Piagetian conservation tasks) requires an individual to give up a current understanding to reach a new perspective, and may be supported best by an exchange of ideas on an equal basis, with partners considering each other's views to reach conclusions. Two studies of moral reasoning support the assumption that peer discussion involves greater consideration of partners' ideas than does adult–child discussion, and that such equal contribution and evaluation of ideas between peers may lead to shifts in children's perspectives (Kruger, 1988; Kruger & Tomasello, 1986).

What about situations in which peers and adults work in a peer domain? The initial purpose of using peers in the errand-planning studies was to have a comparison group working with less skilled partners to contrast with collaboration with skilled adult partners; thus our comparisons of adult–child interaction versus peer interaction are unlikely to generalize to peer interaction in tasks in which peers are especially skilled or that they regard as in the domain of peer activities (rather than in the domain of adult–child activities), such as play and exploration.

Research situations are usually managed by an adult researcher who sets the problem, the goals, and the rules for the people being observed, removing these activities from analysis and limiting the roles of the observed participants who might otherwise redefine the problem, the goals, or the rules. To examine the unique role of peer interaction will require researchers to work outside adult territory, where we have focused on interactions with goals and means defined in advance by adult researchers.

It is of interest to study naturalistic interaction between peers in tasks they do well and/or choose for themselves, tasks that peers might teach each other or collaborate on when away from adult influence. As an approximation of this situation, Jonathan Tudge and I are currently investigating peer and adult–child collaboration on learning two spatial planning computer games with which novice 9-year-old children were more comfortable than were novice adults.

DIFFICULTIES AND IMPORTANCE OF SHARED DECISIONS FOR YOUNGER CHILDREN

When we attempted to extend the research on guided participation in errand planning to younger ages, we encountered some unanticipated difficulties. The 4- and 5-year-olds working with adult partners were no more effective in learning to plan routes than were those who worked alone, except perhaps when the children and their partners truly shared decision making. For younger children, it may be particularly difficult to participate in planning decisions that require shared thinking without the support of concrete actions and supports.

Maze Route Planning

In two studies in progress (in collaboration with Jamie Germond and Barbara Radziszewska), 4-year-olds who worked alone in a practice session were at least as skilled in planning maze solutions as matched children who solved the practice mazes with their mothers' assistance. During the practice session, children either worked by themselves with their mothers seated nearby or worked on an equal number of mazes with their mothers' assistance (Figure 2).

In both the original study and a replication (designed to decrease instructions from the experimenter that we thought might have made the mothers' help unnecessary), children who worked alone and those who had their mothers' assistance in the practice phase solved an equal number of mazes in the posttest, with an equal degree of advance planning.

We are currently doing a third version of this study, with mazes differing in the degree to which advance planning is appropriate, to see whether this dif-

Figure 2   A 4-year-old assisted by her mother in planning a route through a maze of intermediate difficulty in the maze-planning task.

ference makes mothers' assistance more useful to the children in distinguishing when to plan in advance and when to plan opportunistically during action, a skill that is difficult for 4-year-olds (Gardner & Rogoff, 1990). The mazes have either short look-ahead or long look-ahead alleys to vary the relevance of advance planning before beginning to draw the route. We are interested in seeing whether adult assistance will aid young children in learning to fit planning strategies to the circumstances. Preliminary analyses suggest that, as in the first two studies, there is no advantage of adult assistance for young children in this task.

Figure 3   Two 5-year-olds planning the route through the model grocery store to pick
up five grocery items as efficiently as possible. The child on the left has just
entered the door of the store with the miniature shopper. In front of the
children, out of view of the camera, the children have cards with five pictures
identical to five of the pictured grocery items on the "shelves" of the store.

Grocery Store Route Planning

In another study involving young children in spatial planning, there was a similar
lack of differences between children who had worked alone and those who had
worked with a partner. In this study, 5-year-olds were asked to devise routes to
pick up grocery items (presented in a pictorial list) without backtracking through
the aisles of a three-dimensional model store (Gauvain & Rogoff, 1989; see Figure
3). Children who had worked alone on planning efficient routes through the store
performed as well later as did children who had worked with peers or with their
mothers. Simply having a partner did not increase the efficiency of routes planned
by these children.

However, the children who shared decision making in their interactions with
partners (rather than working independently or dividing the task into independent
turns) performed better than did children who had worked alone and better than
children who had a partner but had not worked jointly. These results, although
correlational, support the idea that participation in joint decision making is an

important aspect of the interactional situation. The presence of a partner may be irrelevant, unless the partners truly share their thinking processes in problem solving.

Why Might Young Children Not Benefit From Interaction With a Skilled Partner?

Piaget's suggestion that young children have difficulty coordinating problem solving with another person (Piaget, 1977; Azmitia & Perlmutter, 1989) may explain the lack of benefits of having a partner in these tasks at this age—unless the partners actually manage to share in decision making.

In some situations, the presence of a partner may be a distraction, requiring attention to the division of labor and to social issues, rather than providing support. Some tasks may be difficult to coordinate with another person, and this may especially be the case for young children.

The maze-planning tasks that we have used may be particularly difficult for young children to work on collaboratively. Such planning may be relatively inaccessible both to reflection by the individual and to discussion or joint attention in action. Maze planning provides limited concrete contexts for description and instances to point to in conversation or demonstration, because it deals with future events. It may be more difficult to share decision making or understanding of a problem that deals with abstract concepts or future events than to participate in cognitive activities dealing with concrete, present referents.

It may be easier for young children to share thinking processes in memory tasks, learning pieces of information that are physically presented, than it is in planning tasks requiring discussion of future possibilities and strategies for coordinating several possible actions. This idea is supported by our results with several memory tasks in which children assisted by adults showed benefits in their memory performance. In a pilot study, 4-year-old children remembered slightly more items in a free recall task when their parents were encouraged to assist them in learning the list of items than when their parents were instructed to present the list without elaboration as in standard laboratory procedures (Mistry & Rogoff, 1987). In two studies, 5-year-olds benefitted from guidance by an experimenter who followed specific scripts varying in extent of guidance and child participation in learning and remembering the category rationale for a set of common items (Goncu & Rogoff, 1987).

There do not seem to be general difficulties for young children in profiting from social interaction, because they benefit from working with others in remembering as well as in language development and object construction (Adams, 1987; John-Steiner & Tatter, 1983; Nelson, Denninger, Bonvillian, Kaplan, & Baker, 1984; Snow, 1984; Wood, Wood, & Middleton, 1978). I attribute the findings for young children in the maze-planning tasks to task-specific challenges for young children in sharing the process of developing efficient plans in which they must deal with coordination for the future. This is supported by the evidence linking young children's skill in independent errand planning with having actually shared in making decisions regarding routes in the model grocery store.

CONCLUSIONS

The results point to the importance of considering the nature of participation in decision making rather than simply assuming that the presence of an adult is an advantage. Simply being with a skilled adult may have no link to children's learning. However, guided participation in which children are involved in active observation or joint skilled decision making seems to relate to children's appropriation of the skilled processes for their later independent performance in similar problems.

Together, the results with older and younger children suggest that shared thinking is a central feature of social interaction that allows children to take advantage of the bridging, structuring, and transfer of responsibility that I have suggested as processes involved in guided participation. Children appear to benefit from engaging in decision making with partners who have skills in the task at hand. They gain from both guidance and participation, shared processes in which children's and adults' roles are inseparable.

Just as research on language development points to the importance of joint attention and of expansions of young children's attempts to communicate, building on children's interest and level of skill, research on the development of spatial planning skills suggests that a crucial aspect of social interaction for children's later use of a skill is the extent to which children participate in skilled, shared problem solving as involved observers or decision makers with support.

The importance of shared problem solving as a forum for cognitive development becomes crucial when we conceptualize how children's involvement in socially structured problem solving relates to their skilled activity when working independently. In contrast with views that present the process as one of internalization, with modeled information being transferred across a barrier from a social partner to the inside of the child, or with information being transmitted, I see the process as one of appropriation (Rogoff, 1990) in which through participation, children transform their understanding and skill in solving the problem. Children's appropriation of their role in shared decision making shows up in their later efforts in similar problems, changed through their guided participation in skilled activity.

As children participate in the skilled activities practiced around them, their role in the activity requires stretches to handle new aspects of the task. Such stretches in the context of engagement in communication and shared activity make it possible for children to handle aspects of problem solving that were previously not possible for them; from their participation in shared problem solving, children appropriate approaches they can use the next time they meet a similar problem. As Wertsch and Stone (1979, p. 21) put it, "The process *is* the product."

Children participate as apprentices in structured and supported problem solving, contributing to decisions and actively observing others. Rather than receiving a packaged lesson to internalize as a result of this involvement, children's participation itself changes their understanding. Apprentices, in contributing to and actively observing skilled practice, adjust to handle the situation and appropriate from their involvement in the shared activity skills and knowledge that they may apply in later situations that they see as similar.

References

Adams, A. K. (1987, January). *"A penguin belongs to the bird family": Language games and the social transfer of categorical knowledge.* Paper presented at the Third International Conference on Thinking, Honolulu.

Azmitia, M., & Perlmutter, M. (1989). Social influences on young children's cognition: State of the art and future directions. In H..Reese (Ed.), *Advances in child development and behavior: Vol. 22* (pp. 89–144). New York: Academic Press.

Brown, A. L., & DeLoache, J. S. (1978). Skills, plans, and self-regulation. In R. S. Siegler (Ed.), *Children's thinking: What develops?* (pp. 3–35). Hillsdale, NJ: Erlbaum.

Damon, W. (1984). Peer education: The untapped potential. *Journal of Applied Developmental Psychology, 5,* 331–343.

Ellis, S., & Rogoff, B. (1982). The strategies and efficacy of child versus adult teachers. *Child Development, 53,* 730–735.

Ellis, S., & Rogoff, B. (1986). Problem solving in children's management of instruction. In E. Mueller & C. Cooper (Eds.), *Process and outcome in peer relationships* (pp. 301–325). New York: Academic Press.

Friedman, S. L., Scholnick, E. K., & Cocking, R. R. (Eds.). (1987). *Blueprints for thinking: The role of planning in psychological development.* Cambridge, England: Cambridge University Press.

Gardner, W., & Rogoff, B. (1990). Children's adjustment of deliberateness of planning according to task circumstances. *Developmental Psychology, 26,* 480–487.

Gauvain, M., & Rogoff, B. (1989). Collaborative problem solving and children's planning skills. *Developmental Psychology, 25,* 139–151.

Goncu, A., & Rogoff, B. (1987, April). *Adult guidance and children's participation in learning.* Paper presented at the meeting of the Society for Research in Child Development, Baltimore.

Hayes-Roth, B., & Hayes-Roth, F. (1979). A cognitive model of planning. *Cognitive Science, 3,* 275–310.

John-Steiner, V., & Tatter, P. (1983). An interactionist model of language development. In B. Bain (Ed.), *The sociogenesis of language and human conduct* (pp. 79–97). New York: Plenum.

Kruger, A. C. (1988, March). *The effect of peer and adult–child transactive discussions on moral reasoning*. Paper presented at Conference on Human Development, Charleston, South Carolina.

Kruger, A. C., & Tomasello, M. (1986). Transactive discussions with peers and adults. *Developmental Psychology, 22*, 681–685.

Magkaev, V. K. (1977). An experimental study of the planning function of thinking in young school children. In M. Cole (Ed.), *Soviet developmental psychology: An anthology* (pp. 606–620). White Plains, NY: M. E. Sharpe.

Mistry, J., & Rogoff, B. (1987, April). *Influence of purpose and strategic assistance on preschool children's remembering*. Paper presented at the meeting of the Society for Research in Child Development, Baltimore.

Nelson, K. E., Denninger, M. S., Bonvillian, J. D., Kaplan, B. J., & Baker, N. D. (1984). Maternal input adjustments and non-adjustments as related to children's linguistic advances and to language acquisition theories. In A. D. Pellegrini & T. D. Yawkey (Eds.), *The development of oral and written language in social contexts* (pp. 31–56). Norwood, NJ: Ablex.

Piaget, J. (1977). Les opérations logiques et la vie sociale [Logical operations and social life]. In *Etudes sociologiques* [Sociological studies] (pp. 143–171) by J. Piaget. Geneva, Switzerland: Librairie Droz.

Radziszewska, B., & Rogoff, B. (1988). Influence of adult and peer collaborators on children's planning skills. *Developmental Psychology, 24*, 840–848.

Radziszewska, B., & Rogoff, B. (in press). Children's guided participation in planning errands with skilled adult or peer partners. *Developmental Psychology*.

Rogoff, B. (1990). *Apprenticeship in thinking: Cognitive development in social context*. New York: Oxford University Press.

Rogoff, B., & Gauvain, M. (1986). A method for the analysis of patterns illustrated with data on mother–child instructional interaction. In J. Valsiner (Ed.), *The role of the individual subject in scientific psychology* (pp. 261–290). New York: Plenum.

Snow, C. E. (1984). Parent–child interaction and the development of communicative ability. In R. Schiefelbusch & J. Pickar (Eds.), *The acquisition of communicative competence* (pp. 69–107). Baltimore: University Park Press.

Vygotsky, L. S. (1978). *Mind in society: The development of higher psychological processes*. Cambridge, MA: Harvard University Press.

Vygotsky, L. S. (1987). *Thinking and speech* (N. Minick, Trans.). In R. W. Rieber & A. S. Carton (Eds.), *The collected works of L. S. Vygotsky* (pp. 37–285). New York: Plenum.

Wertsch, J. V., & Stone, C. A. (1979, February). *A social interactional analysis of learning disabilities remediation*. Paper presented at the International Conference of the Association for Children with Learning Disabilities, San Francisco.

Wood, D., Wood, H., & Middleton, D. (1978). An experimental evaluation of four face-to-face teaching strategies. *International Journal of Behavioral Development, 2*, 131–147.

CHAPTER 17

COLLABORATIONS AMONG TODDLER PEERS: INDIVIDUAL CONTRIBUTIONS TO SOCIAL CONTEXTS

CELIA A. BROWNELL AND MICHAEL SEAN CARRIGER

The idea that much of what children know and understand about the world is acquired in social contexts has gained increasing currency among developmental psychologists, fueled in particular by the rediscovery of Vygotsky's work (Wertsch, 1985). Although this perspective has long historical roots within developmental psychology (cf. Brownell, 1989), its impact was eroded in the last few decades by interest in more traditional Cartesian questions of what develops within the individual mind as a function of solitary activity in the world. Now development again is coming to be viewed as an interpersonal process as well as an intrapersonal one. Researchers have begun to realize that not only are knowledge, strategies, and skills used in social contexts, they are also acquired during social commerce.

SOCIAL PROCESSES OF KNOWING

Part of what scholars wish to know, of course, is *what* children acquire in the cultural contexts in which they participate—what is the nature of their changing knowledge, skill, and activity, whether situated in the culture of the school, the farm, the shopping mall, the birthday party, the family, or the peer group. Another important part of what scientists wish to know, and the focus of much recent research, is *how* knowledge gets transmitted, shared, and acquired. What are the social processes of knowing?

One of the primary means of addressing these questions has been to manipulate the social situation and to identify cognitive outcomes. Children's problem-solving performance, language production, or skill acquisition, for example, have been measured before and after a variety of manipulations of the child's social context, including peer tutoring, parent–child interaction, and peer collaborations. In other words, researchers have treated social contexts as independent variables and have hoped to discern those aspects of social contexts that have important consequences for learning or development.

Variations in the "context of measurement," for example, can produce systematic variations in judgments about children's knowledge (Perret-Clermont, chapter 3 in this volume; Siegal, chapter 2 in this volume). Thus, depending on apparently minor differences in the task or the social aspects of the experimental setting, children's presumed universally developing abilities appear more or less robust, reliable, or universal. The social context here becomes a "window" onto the development of competence. Different windows give different views, and no single window gives a complete view.

Similarly, variation in "contexts of acquisition" can produce systematic variations in what is acquired. Thus, particular aspects of the social context serve to scaffold, guide, or channel development, partly by defining and interpreting the child's world for him or her as the child encounters it, and partly by structuring, facilitating, and challenging the child's activity in the world (Rogoff, this volume, 1990; Winegar, 1989).

Social contexts are, by definition, composed of individuals, whose interactions define the context. Thus, to understand the role of contexts in development means to know both the characteristics of the individuals who constitute any given context and the processes of interaction that depend, in part, on the particular individuals involved. The social construction of knowledge is dynamic and dialectical (Hinde & Stevenson-Hinde, 1987), because, although individuals' development cannot be fully understood outside the contexts in which it is embedded, contexts themselves cannot be understood without knowing the characteristics of the component individuals and how these characteristics govern the social processes that influence development.

We must, therefore, study social context as dependent variable as well as independent variable. The social context must become the *object* of explanation as well as the *source* of explanation. To do this, we must consider what children bring to the social situation and how children's knowledge, motives, biases, affect, and activity in the setting constrain the interactional processes that guide their development. These elements structure the social interchange and thereby contribute to the social construction of knowing.

Relationships and Development

Social relationships are the contexts in which knowledge and expertise are acquired and consolidated (Hartup, 1986; Hinde, Perret-Clermont, & Stevenson-Hinde, 1985). Hartup (1989) has distinguished two broad classes of relationships that are presumably culturally universal: vertical (between individuals of differing knowledge and social power) and horizontal (between individuals of similar knowledge and social power). These two kinds of relationships have consistently been shown to serve different functions in children's development.

Although some psychologists equate Vygotskian notions with vertical relationships and Piagetian notions with horizontal relationships (cf. Musatti, 1986), many important questions are hybrids of these theoretical stances. For example, we would like to know what kinds of cognitive conflict might be engendered in the *expert* who apprentices, scaffolds, or guides the skill acquisition of the novice. How does a mother's knowledge change by participating in her child's development? On the other hand, we would also like to know how two novices jointly solving a problem scaffold one another (cf. Brown & Palincsar, 1989; Ellis & Rogoff, 1986). Seldom, if ever, do two learners know precisely the same thing at the same time, even in horizontal relationships. How do children monitor, support, and challenge one another in their respective momentary zones of competence when they work and play together? Although vertical and horizontal relationships contribute differently to development, the social processes that affect change are not given by the form of the relationship alone. Children themselves contribute differently to both vertical and horizontal relationships as they develop. In so doing, they systematically change the contexts or the relationships in which they participate.

Likewise, individual differences among children at a given developmental point can affect the relationships in which these children grow. For example, whereas all children may be generally "tutor-prone" (Bruner, 1972), there are also individual differences in children's willingness and ability to participate as "tutees" (e.g., Matas, Arend, & Sroufe, 1978; Strayer & Moss, 1987). This variability, in turn, results in different sets of dynamics in children's vertical relationships and no doubt also in their horizontal relationships (Hartup & Brownell, 1988). This goes beyond the notion that adults provide different scaffolds in reaction to a child's changing competence. The argument here is that relationships are mutually influenced by both partners. Children actively manage and shape the very relationships that also shape them (cf. Hinde & Stevenson-Hinde, 1987; Rogoff, in press; Valsiner, 1987).

Thus, our position is that children participate in a variety of structurally different relationships that have different effects on development because of the different interactional processes characterizing them. At the same time, children bring their own developmental and individual characteristics to these relationships. Hence, the processes that are presumably universal within horizontal or vertical relationships, by virtue of the structural features of these relationships, also possess unique variation contributed by the children themselves who participate. It is these individual contributions to social contexts on which we focus in this chapter.

Peer Collaborations

The particular relationship context we have chosen to study is peer relationships, and within these relationships we focus on collaboration. From the perspective of contextual influences on development, peer relationships are not studied as often as parent–child relationships. Several scholars have, nevertheless, recently argued that peer contexts are central to the child's social construction of reality (Azmitia & Perlmutter, 1989; Damon & Phelps, 1989; Mueller & Cooper, 1986).

Peer collaborations capture well the emphasis in this volume on the bidirectional nature of social and cognitive processes in development. On the one hand, children's collaborations are fundamentally *social* in nature. They encompass motivational and affective factors. They are founded on a repertoire of particular social behaviors, including expressive behavior and communicative behavior. They depend on two or more people interacting with one another dynamically, mutually regulating behaviors that possess meaning in the context of the social exchange. For example, my taking a puzzle piece from your pile is an act with a different meaning when we are cooperating at putting the puzzle together than when we are not. At the same time, collaboration is also fundamentally *cognitive* in nature. It requires goal recognition or definition, planning of behavior around the goal, adopting effective goal-related strategies, monitoring and changing goal-directed behavior, and so on.

Collaborations also include *bidirectional* influences between social and cognitive processes. First and most simply, the cognitive elements of problem solving have to be coordinated with another person through social means. The planning, monitoring, motivating, and regulating of behavior have to happen on the interpersonal plane as well as through intrapersonal processes. Second, the actual processes of coordination—the dynamics of social interaction—are often hypothesized to change the nature of the cognitive events in social problem solving as compared with solitary learning (Rogoff, 1983; see Azmitia & Perlmutter, in press, for a recent review of peer collaborations). Concomitantly, the knowledge and skills brought by each of the participants to the collaboration will affect the processes of coordination.

The focus of this chapter is on the earliest social collaborations among peers. If social interaction "creates the mind," as Mead, Vygotsky, and others have argued, then early interactions in horizontal relationships should contribute as much as those that occur in vertical relationships. Nevertheless, the sharing of knowledge among young peers must be a different event, governed by different social processes, than collaborations between parents and young children.

Most of the research on collaborative problem solving in young children has emphasized adult–child interaction among preschoolers (Azmitia & Perlmutter, in press). The assumption seems to be that young children cannot jointly regulate the planning and strategy formation that are necessary for effective problem solving, and, therefore, they depend on "other-regulation." But there is a small literature on early peer interaction that suggests that between 18 and 24 months a transition may occur in children's social competencies to permit cooperation and the establishment of "shared meanings" with each other (Brenner & Mueller, 1982; Eckerman, Didow, & Davis, 1989; Eckerman & Stein, 1982; Goldman & Ross, 1978; Ross & Lollis, 1987). Thus, rather than studying socially skilled individuals who possess a wide repertoire of interactional skills, including how to coordinate behavior with someone else, where the question is how these two skilled individuals coordinate their knowledge through language and skilled interaction, we are exploring the genesis and early development of these skills of coordination, largely through nonverbal means.

Our data address two specific questions. First, when do children become able to collaborate to solve a problem together, and what do these early collaborations look like? Second, what do developmental differences in social understanding contribute to these early collaborative efforts? We pursued these questions using dyads of children between 12 and 30 months old, children who are just beginning to show interest and some rudimentary skills in peer interaction. One reason for examining these ages for the origins of collaboration is that peer interaction is just emerging in the second year. But another—and perhaps more interesting and compelling—reason to look at the second year is that this is the time when the young child begins to differentiate *self* from *other* as independent causal agents and to form complex relations among events.

How do these changes relate to the origins of collaboration? If we think of collaboration as establishing joint goals and referents and adjusting one's own behavior to fit or coordinate with another's toward a joint goal, it becomes difficult to conceive of true collaboration without recognition of both self and other as causal agents, as autonomous initiators and controllers of behavior. In other words, although the very young infant can participate in social interaction under the direction of a parent, he or she is not truly a contributor, we would argue, until able to join planfully and intentionally in the interactions of another, actively affecting the other's behavior and the course and outcome of the interaction and, thereby, the collaborative process of knowledge acquisition. Individuals who do not recognize that another person can cause things to happen autonomously cannot join their efforts intentionally to reach a common, shared goal. Although some scholars of infant development claim that the youngest infants are capable of intersubjectivity between minds of interactants, there is much controversy on this matter. Many other scholars of early social development argue that the appearance of intersubjectivity in young infants is a convenient social construction by parents and adults who must interact with the socially naive infant (e.g., Dunn, 1982; Kaye, 1982; Schaffer, 1984). Regardless of the disposition of this controversy among scholars of infant–adult interaction, however, the evidence on early peer interaction supports the emergence of intersubjectivity during the second year.

HOW TODDLERS COLLABORATE

We will report data from a study of collaborative problem solving in 12-, 18-, 24-, and 30-month-olds that focused on the relationship between collaboration and the development of self–other differentiation, or decentration. We paired 16 children at each age, who were unfamiliar with one another, in dyads to solve a simple cooperation problem. The children were also individually administered a pretend-play task that indexed their ability to represent the causal autonomy of animate replicas (i.e., their ability to pretend that a doll or stuffed animal could control its own actions). This task is a well-established means of estimating early self–other differentiation.

There were three cooperation problems, all similar in operation. Each dyad received one problem and had 7 minutes to solve it. Each problem required one child to push a piston (or lever or rotating handle) through a clear plexiglass box to get access to some small animals placed in a cup attached to the end of the handle (or piston or lever). However, by the strategic placement of springs and plexiglass barriers, the child's access was blocked as he or she operated the handle. Furthermore, if the child released pressure on the piston (or lever or rotator), it would slip back inside the box. This apparatus, therefore, required a second child to retrieve the animals. To do so, the second child had to position himself or herself opposite the first and reach for the animals as the first child made them available. The problems thus required the coordinated action of two children for solution. The children had to adopt complementary roles spatially by positioning themselves opposite one another at the apparatus, and they also had to adopt complementary roles temporally, with one child pushing the handle and holding it extended while the second child retrieved the animals. Once children solved the problem, they were permitted to play with the animals briefly, whereupon the apparatus was reloaded, and they were asked to solve it again.

The pretend-play task to index self–other differentiation involved experimenter modeling of five short scenarios with dolls or stuffed animals as the actors (e.g., going to bed, eating breakfast), after which the child was asked to imitate the experimenter's actions. As with the elicited imitation procedure used in language development research, children will typically imitate at their highest level of competence, even if it is lower than that represented in the modeled scenario. We coded four levels of children's imitations, as previously established in the literature. At Level 1, the lowest level, the child cannot pretend with animate replicas at all and instead pretends that he himself is the agent. For example, if the experimenter models giving the doll a drink of juice, the child imitates by pretending to drink juice himself or herself. At Level 2, the child can represent another as a recipient of her actions but does not pretend that others can control their own behavior (e.g., the child gives the doll a drink, but cannot pretend that the doll holds the cup and drinks by itself). At Level 3, the child represents others as active agents of their own behavior (e.g., puts the cup in the hands of the doll for the doll to drink by itself). At this point, one can infer that the child is able to represent other people as initiators and controllers of behavior and events in the world, independent of the child's own actions, desires, or interests. At Level 4, the child can represent two dolls autonomously interacting with one another (e.g., one doll gives another doll a drink).

We derived two measures: (a) the highest level imitated by the child across scenarios, and (b) a composite decentration score, which was the number of different actions imitated at each level (e.g., two actions imitated at Level 1 and one action imitated at Level 2 sums to a score of 4; two actions at Level 2 and one at Level 3 sums to a score of 7).

From the cooperative problem-solving tasks, we coded several behaviors that were meant to index attempts to coordinate behavior with a partner. We counted the number of solutions to the problems and latency to solution. We also coded (a) the children's movements around the apparatus, both to the same side as the partner and to the opposite side from the partner; (b) the frequency that a child manipulated the handle with a pause for the partner versus manipulations without a pause; (c) the frequency that one child anticipated the appearance of the animals as the partner operated the handle; (d) commands; (e) compliance versus resistance; (f) displacement by one child of the partner; and (g) simple exploration. We then created a composite coordination score by summing the variables of manipulate + pause, anticipate animals, commands, and compliance with command, and dividing the sum by all on-task behavior.

We conducted analyses in three steps. The first step was a fairly global description of the cooperative problem-solving behavior of the children (paired in dyads). The second step was a more detailed analysis of particular kinds of behaviors and intercoordinations of behavior that might, together, describe the collaborative process more convincingly. The final step was an assessment of relations between collaboration and decentration.

Table 1

SOLUTION CHARACTERISTICS AS A FUNCTION OF AGE

Solution	Age			
characteristics	12 months	18 months	24 months	30 months
Number of solutions per dyad	.00	.50	4.80	4.50
Coordinated behavior (proportion)	.03	.20	.38	.33
Type 1 solutions (proportion)	—	.80	.18	.05
Type 2 solutions	—	.20	.52	.40
Type 3 solutions	—	.00	.30	.55

Collaborative Solutions

When we consider children's ability to solve the problem collaboratively, we see
clear age differences, both in their success rates and in the means by which they
achieved success (see Table 1). No 12-month-olds and only half the 18-month-
olds solved the problem, whereas all of the 24- and 30-month-olds solved it. In
fact, most of the older dyads solved the problem multiple times. In contrast, those
18-month-olds who managed to solve the problem once were never able to re-
achieve the solution, suggesting, perhaps, that their initial solutions were accidental. We should note that all dyads engaged in problem-solving behavior, and
all manipulated the apparatus in such a way as to have been able to achieve an
individual solution had the springs and barriers not prevented it. What this suggests,
then, is that the difficulty for the younger children was in figuring out how to
work together to a common end. As will become evident, there were differences
among the older children as well in the degree to which they were able to coordinate
their behavior. That is, although children older than 12 months solved the problem
together, the particular solutions they used were more or less collaborative.

Except for the 12-month-olds, there were no age differences in movements
around the task, either to the same side (e.g., to join, displace, or imitate the
partner) or to the opposite side (e.g., to complement the partner's behavior).
However, there were differences for the proportion of problem-solving behavior
that was coordinated with the partner's behavior. Children in the two older age
groups (24 and 30 months) coordinated their behavior with one another a much
greater proportion of the time than did children in the two younger age groups.
There were no differences in proportion of coordinated behavior, however, between 18-month-olds who solved the problem and 18-month-olds who failed to

do so. Once more, this suggests that the 18-month-olds solved the problem by accident, not by actively coordinating their behavior.

We decided to examine the children's collaborations in more detail, partly because it was possible to solve the problems accidentally and partly because we wished to understand what was happening socially during these problem-solving attempts. We focused on several specific aspects of the collaborative process: solution styles, solution times, monitoring one another's task-related behavior, attempts to influence one another's goal-directed behavior, and responses to violations by the partner of appropriate goal-directed sequences.

Solution styles

Consider the following example of a solution. Child A pushes the handle and holds it in its extended position, looks at the animals as they appear in the hole on the other side of the plexiglass barrier, tries to reach through the plexiglass to get them, and then, while still holding the handle, looks away, distracted by something else happening in the room. Child B, meanwhile, has ignored Child A's activity on the task and is busy exploring the screws that hold things together; moments earlier, he had tried to reach through the hole to get the animals but was unsuccessful. Now he looks up from his exploration, notices that the animals are at the opening, and runs over to get them. As B exclaims his delight, A returns attention to the task, joins B, and they share the animals. This would have been counted as a solution, and technically it is cooperative, because two children did together what one child could not do alone. But it is not really collaborative, because these children worked independently of each other. There is little sense here of joint regulation of behavior, of trying to coordinate two separate roles, or of sharing any kind of knowledge.

On the basis of exchanges such as these, we determined the major ways that children actually solved the problem. There were three main ways, and these differed in their apparent planfulness or intentionality. Type 1 solutions involved simply reaching into the box (through the small hole in the end or the top), without any consideration of what the partner was doing. This was a sort of independent exploration of the problem and an attempt to solve it alone. In fact, the child could not get the animals this way. But if the partner pushed the handle, also independently exploring the problem, and this happened to put the first child in contact with the animals, he could remove them. Type 2 solutions occurred when a child retrieved the animals *after* the partner manipulated the handle and held it. But again, still opportunistically, the second child simply noticed that the animals were available and got them out. Type 3 solutions involved anticipating the partner's action with the handle. In this case, one child stood next to the hole where the animals would become available and clearly waited for the partner to push the handle; the child placed his or her hand, head, or body in an expectant position, such as holding his or her hand next to the hole where the animals would appear, and did so when the partner was about to push the handle.

There are clear changes with age in the children's use of these solution styles. As Table 1 shows, 80% of 18-month-olds' solutions were of the direct reaching, accidental variety (Type 1), and none of their solutions was of the anticipatory variety (Type 3). By 30 months, only 5% of solutions resulted from reaching directly into the hole (Type 1), and 55% included anticipation of the partner's behavior (Type 3). The 24-month-olds were in between. They anticipated the partner's behavior some of the time (30%) (Type 3), but mostly they were doing solutions that were more opportunistic (Type 2). This suggests, again, that 18-month-olds' solutions were almost entirely accidental; 24-month-olds' solutions were anticipatory some of the time and were seldom a simple by-product of reaching directly through the hole for the animals; and not until 30 months were children regularly aware of and likely to consider the activities of the other child.

Solution times

For joint and collaborative problem solving, most writers have suggested that the partners in the collaboration have to establish either implicitly or explicitly a common problem-solving space, or a mutual agreement about how the problem is to be approached and defined. If mutual agreement is established early in a dyad's encounters with the problem, we would expect to see a decline in solution times for successive solutions, and indeed we do for those dyads that achieve multiple solutions.

For both 24- and 30-month-olds, the time it took to solve the problem decreased over successive solutions, suggesting that some sort of mutual agreement had been established in the first solution. This implies that, even if the first solution was opportunistic for these young children, subsequent solutions probably were not. Presumably, the children used the first solution to establish agreement about how to solve the problem, and they figured out how to coordinate their behavior relative to one another as well as relative to the goal.

However, there may be alternative explanations for a decrease in solution time. For example, each child could have figured out individually which behavior worked and then simply have repeated that behavior in later solutions. Without the trial-and-error characteristic of the first solution attempt, solution times would decrease. That would be different from what we mean by joint agreement here: that both children understand that their efforts are independently directed to the same reference point, and that they make some effort to coordinate their actions. In communication, for example, speakers establish a common reference point and check with each other to be sure they are referring to the same shared "space," unless shared reference is assumed to be based on common experience or memory (see the chapters in this volume by Clark & Brennan and Krauss & Fussell). If speakers discover that reference has not been shared, one of them stops to repair

Table 2

EXTENT TO WHICH TODDLERS MONITORED PARTNER DURING
SOLUTION ATTEMPTS

	Age		
Monitoring	18 months	24 months	30 months
Monitor peer	10.90	10.50	10.20
Monitor/both on task	6.30	7.40	8.30
Monitor/one on task	4.70	3.40	1.70
Monitor peer/hold handle (proportion)	.04	.11	.19

the problem (see Schegloff, chapter 8 in this volume, for an extended discussion of communication repairs).

In this study, we did not have the luxury of explicit verbalizations about the child's own or the partner's behavior that would have revealed the children's thinking about their relations, as we do with older children and adults. Therefore, we were forced to use more indirect means to infer that the children were indeed collaborating or, alternatively, that we could not be certain that they were. Furthermore, we can seldom be certain that a single pattern decisively reveals real collaboration in this age group. Rather, we must seek a converging pattern of results. Other interactive processes, then, must be examined to determine if these young children were collaborating with one another and to provide insights into the processes of collaboration.

Monitoring partner

If children are aware of one another as actors, as we contend they must be if they are engaging in truly collaborative efforts, then they should look at each other to monitor the other's behavior as it relates to their joint efforts. In fact, they do monitor each other, but the frequency of looking at each other does not change with age (see Table 2).

But looking at each other can serve many functions besides monitoring task-relevant behavior. In particular, it can serve purely social functions. One way we began to tease apart these two functions was to separate looking at one another when both children are on task from looking at each other when only one child is on task and the other child is playing off task or is conversing with another person in the room. As shown in Table 2, it becomes clear that with age the children are more likely to monitor one another when they are both working on the task than when one is off task. This suggests that the older children are attempting to establish or monitor joint task-related efforts, whereas the younger children are more likely to be monitoring one another for social reasons.

Table 3

ATTEMPTS TO INFLUENCE PARTNER'S BEHAVIOR

Influence attempts	Age		
	18 months	24 months	30 months
Frequency of influence	83	98	77
Gesture to other (proportion)	.70	.64	.31
Indirect verbalization to other (proportion)	.30	.31	.21
Direct verbalization to other (proportion)	.00	.05	.31

To make this conclusion stronger, we narrowed down the circumstances under which we would expect monitoring to be functional for coordinated activity and determined whether older children's gazes at each other were more likely to occur in that context. Specifically, we determined whether monitoring the partner was more likely to occur when the partner was manipulating and holding the handle. The pattern in Table 2 makes it clear that older children were more likely to engage in this problem-related sort of monitoring of each other than were younger children.

Influence attempts

A still more direct collaborative process is that of attempting to influence the activity of one's partner as it relates to the common goal. We identified three types of influence that are progressively more directive. A *gesture* was any goal-directed gesture, such as pointing to or waving at the apparatus or animals inside. This behavior can serve at least two different purposes. It may simply reflect the child's efforts to direct his or her own attention, as a slightly more public version of Vygotsky's private speech, or it may be intended to direct the partner's attention to some part of the apparatus or to direct the partner to act on some part of the apparatus. For example, older children would sometimes combine a command such as "Do it! Do it!" with a wave at the other child to move over to the other side of the task and perform the appropriate action. An *indirect verbalization* was a task-related verbalization directed to the other child but not an explicit request or command for action (e.g., "I see it"; "Here it comes"). Thus, as with gestures, this might be interpreted by the other child as a directive but need not be interpreted in this way. A *direct verbalization* was an explicit request or command to the other child to perform a task-relevant behavior (e.g., "Look!"; "Get it!"; or "Do it!").

The data show that there was no change with age in the absolute frequency of influence attempts (see Table 3). Rather, the form of influence attempts changed with age, from less direct to more direct. That is, by 30 months, almost one third of the children's attempts to influence one another were by commands and requests for goal-directed action.

Although it might be argued that these findings are confounded with language development more generally, such reasoning cannot be applied to the 24-month-olds. Normally developing 2-year-olds are very capable of saying things such as "Go there," or "Get it." In fact, both 18- and 24-month-olds used indirect verbalizations. Hence, although the 18-month-olds' lack of direct influence attempts may be language related, the transition between 24 and 30 months must certainly be due to something else. It seems that the 30-month-olds were trying to influence the operation of the task *through* influencing their partner's behavior. They were explicitly trying to coordinate their own goal-directed behavior with their partner by altering their partner's behavior as well as their own. The younger children verbalized about the task, but they did not attempt to influence the partner to act. We would speculate that the 30-month-olds were more aware of the relations between their own and their partner's behavior, and were purposefully attempting to coordinate those relations in the service of a common goal.

Response to violations by partner

Finally, we reasoned that children who were trying to coordinate their behavior with each other should react to their partner if the partner violates the appropriate sequence of events for solution. Reacting *to* the partner suggests that the child is aware that the partner has disrupted the joint effort. In contrast, the child who has simply learned the appropriate individual behaviors to get the job done, without regard for the partner's role in the job, should simply try another nonsocial, problem-related behavior if the partner violates the appropriate solution sequence. For this child, the peer is not truly a collaborator in the enterprise.

A violation was identified as the expected event in the solution sequence not occurring when both children were on task, regardless of whether either child appeared to recognize this as a violation. Violations tended to be of two basic types: The child manipulating the handle let go of it after pausing, often as the partner reached for the animals; or the child on the receiving end failed to reach for the animals while the partner was holding the handle and waiting for the animals to be retrieved.

The pattern of responses and their relation to age are quite striking. Data were not analyzed for 18-month-olds, because of their low frequency of violations. First, 30-month-olds were far more likely to look at the partner when she or he violated the sequence of events; 80% of 30-month-olds, but only 20% of 24-month-olds, looked at their partners at least once following a violation by the partner. In Table 4, the data are presented as a proportion of all violations that elicited a look at the partner, and there are clear age differences. These differences are not due to lower base rates in younger children of either violations or gazes

Table 6

SOLUTION CHARACTERISTICS AS A FUNCTION OF DYAD TYPE

	Dyad type[a]		
Solution characteristics	2–2	2–3	3–3
Number of dyads with single solution	5.00	7.00	5.00
Number of dyads with multiple solution	1.00	6.00	4.00
Type 1 solutions (proportion)	.50	.11	.16
Type 2 solutions (proportion)	.50	.59	.42
Type 3 solutions (proportion)	.00	.30	.42
Frequency of coordinated behavior	16.60	24.30	30.30

[a]2–2 = both children at Level 2 decentration (other represented as passive recipient of child's actions); 3–3 = both children at Level 3 (other represented as active agent of its own behavior); 2–3 = one child at Level 2, one at Level 3.

child to be able to represent the other as an active agent for the dyad to solve the problem more than once. In other words, for the dyad to re-achieve the solution, suggesting that solutions were purposeful and intentionally coordinated, at least one child in the pair had to be able to represent the other as causing his or her own behavior. When we look at how the dyad solved the problem (the type of solution), we see a similar pattern. Dyads in which both children were at Level 2 never solved the problem using the most advanced solution type—anticipating the partner's behavior. Again, having at least one child in the pair at Level 3 appeared to be necessary to achieve this kind of solution. When both children were at Level 3, they seldom used the most primitive solution style. The frequency of coordinated behavior also varied with the makeup of the dyad. Thus, children's differential understanding of self–other relations within a dyad was related to the dyad's performance. Children bring different abilities and understanding to collaborations, even the very earliest ones, and these differences seem to affect both the processes and the outcomes of collaborative problem solving.

CONCLUSIONS

We can offer several conclusions from these data. Most important, children under 3 years old *can* collaborate with one another to solve simple problems. They are neither too egocentric nor too socially unskilled to establish joint goals and to adjust their behavior in the service of these goals. We are led to conclude that peer social contexts may emerge as important influences quite early in children's development.

Nevertheless, there are also clear progressions with age in very young children's ability to collaborate with one another. As they get older, children become better able to comprehend the behavior and intentions of another, as well as better able to affect the other's behavior and to communicate about their own behavior and desires. We are additionally led to conclude, then, that age-related social and cognitive skills contributing to peer collaborations influence what and how children learn from these collaborations.

Finally, within collaborations, individual differences in the collaborators' social and cognitive skills influence the outcomes of the collaborations, even among very young children. Thus, collaborative abilities and collaborative processes *develop*. Our understanding of socially shared cognition must, therefore, depend on our understanding of what develops and how it develops.

We have studied the joint regulation of behavior in a social context in which there is no expert to scaffold or guide the children's skill acquisition. Instead, knowledge or skill must be coconstructed in this context. Children acquire the skills they use in such coconstructions through their participation with others, building understanding by relating. Relatively few principles or mechanisms have been proposed to account for this sort of acquisition. Hence, a major task for future research will be to discover the social processes of knowing, among even the youngest children.

Numerous questions are raised by these data. Because children contribute to the relationships in which they participate, we wonder how differences in social experience, as well as in dominance, sociability, effectance motivation, and similar factors, affect their peer encounters. At this age, perhaps such factors are irrelevant. On the other hand, perhaps they contribute more to these early collaborations than do the age-related skills studied here. The data also raise questions about communicative and collaborative processes themselves, particularly because many of these children are minimally verbal. What social and communicative cues can young children recognize, and to which ones do they respond? How, exactly, do they go about establishing and repairing shared reference and negotiating meaning? And, finally, there are larger, broader questions involved, such as how general such collaborations are, what spontaneous collaborations during freeplay look like at this age, and what the earliest peer collaborations contribute to children's understanding.

It is not unique to speculate that peer exchanges may facilitate the differentiation and understanding of self versus other. However, no one has addressed such questions among the youngest peer collaborators. Nor have researchers addressed how understanding derived from early peer collaborations might contribute to other kinds of collaborations, such as those with siblings or parents. It is also possible that peer collaborations may only contribute to particular aspects of development, or that they may be effective contributors only at particular points in development (cf. Azmitia & Perlmutter, in press; Damon & Phelps, 1989). It would be worthwhile to explore how and when early peer collaborations serve to enculturate children's thinking, social skills, and relationships.

In conclusion, these data suggest that how children jointly structure peer collaborations and what children take away from these collaborations will differ as a function of what children bring to them. Children's social and cognitive competencies will mediate contextual influences on their development. Our conclusions about social influences on young children's development, then, must take into account both age-related and child-specific contributions to the action of such social influences. The sources of these individual contributions will, of course, themselves be social, cultural, and historical in origin.

Hence, the model of development to be ultimately derived must be multi-causal, reciprocal, and perhaps dialectical: Social contexts do not in any autonomous way create the child, because children themselves shape the action of social contexts at the same time as contexts shape them. Individuals are determined by the relationships in which they participate, and those relationships are simultaneously determined by the participating individuals. Culture and history create us at the same time that we create them. Simple unidirectional causal models, then, are inadequate and inaccurate. Moreover, individual psychological function cannot be reduced to social processes. And social processes cannot be reduced to the sum of individual psychological functions. The best we can do, within our current conceptual and empirical frameworks, is to select part of this complex network of interwoven processes for investigation. For our part, we have begun to explicate how the toddler contributes to the collaborative enterprise; next we must begin to inquire about what collaborations contribute to toddlers' development.

References

Azmitia, M., & Perlmutter, M. (1989). Social influences on children's cognition: State of the art and future directions. In H. Reese (Ed.), *Advances in child development and behavior: Vol. 22* (pp. 89–144). New York: Academic Press.

Brenner, J., & Mueller, E. (1982). Shared meaning in boy toddlers' peer relations. *Child Development, 53*, 380–391.

Brown, A. L., & Palincsar, A. S. (1989). Guided, cooperative learning and individual knowledge acquisition. In L. B. Resnick (Ed.), *Knowing, learning, and instruction: Essays in honor of Robert Glaser* (pp. 393–453). Hillsdale, NJ: Erlbaum.

Brownell, C. (1989). Socially shared cognition: The role of social context in the construction of knowledge. In L. T. Winegar (Ed.), *Social interaction and the development of children's understanding* (pp. 173–205). Norwood, NJ: Ablex.

Bruner, J. (1972). The nature and uses of immaturity. *American Psychologist, 27*, 1–28.

Damon, W., & Phelps, E. (1989). Strategic uses of peer learning in children's education. In T. Berndt & A. Ladd (Eds.), *Peer relationships in child development* (pp. 135–157). New York: Wiley.

Dunn, J. (1982). Comment: Problems and promises in the study of affect and intention. In E. Tronick (Ed.), *Social interchange in infancy* (pp. 97–206). Baltimore: University Park Press.

Eckerman, C., Didow, C., & Davis, L. (1989). Toddlers' emerging ways of achieving social coordinations with a peer. *Child Development, 60,* 440–453.

Eckerman, C., & Stein, M. (1982). The toddler's emerging interactive skills. In K. Rubin & H. Ross (Eds.), *Peer relationships and social skills in childhood* (pp. 41–72). New York: Springer-Verlag.

Ellis, S., & Rogoff, B. (1986). Problem solving in children's management of instruction. In E. Mueller & C. Cooper (Eds.), *Process and outcome in peer relationships* (pp. 301–345). New York: Academic Press.

Goldman, B., & Ross, H. (1978). Social skills in action: Analysis of early peer games. In J. Glick & A. Clarke-Stewart (Eds), *The development of social understanding* (pp. 177–212). New York: Gardner Press.

Hartup, W. (1986). On relationships and development. In W. Hartup & Z. Rubin (Eds.), *Relationships and development* (pp. 1–26). Hillsdale, NJ: Erlbaum.

Hartup, W. (1989). Social relationships and their developmental significance. *American Psychologist, 44,* 120–126.

Hartup, W., & Brownell, C. (1988). Early social development: Transitions and concordances. *Eta Evolutiva, 29,* 5–17.

Hinde, R., Perret-Clermont, A., & Stevenson-Hinde, J. (Eds.). (1985). *Social relationships and cognitive development.* New York: Oxford University Press.

Hinde, R., & Stevenson-Hinde, J. (1987). Interpersonal relationships and child development. *Developmental Review, 7,* 1–21.

Kaye, K. (1982). *The mental and social life of babies.* Chicago: University of Chicago Press.

Matas, L., Arend, R., & Sroufe, L. (1978). The relationship between quality of attachment and later competence. *Child Development, 49,* 547–556.

Mueller, E., & Cooper, C. (Eds.) (1986). *Process and outcome in peer relationships.* New York: Academic Press.

Musatti, T. (1986). Early peer relations: The perspectives of Piaget and Vygotsky. In E. Mueller & C. Cooper (Eds.), *Process and outcome in peer relationships* (pp. 25–53). New York: Academic Press.

Rogoff, B. (1983). Thinking and learning in social context. In B. Rogoff & J. Lave (Eds.), *Everyday cognition* (pp. 1–18). Cambridge, MA: Harvard University Press.

Rogoff, B. (1990). *Apprenticeship in thinking: Children's guided participation in culture.* New York: Oxford University Press.

Rogoff, B. (in press). Joint socialization of development by young children and adults. In M. Lewis & M. Feinman (Eds.), *Social influences on behavior.* New York: Plenum Press.

Ross, H., & Lollis, S. (1987). Communication within infant social games. *Developmental Psychology, 23,* 241–248.

Schaffer, H. (1984). *The child's entry into a social world.* London: Academic Press.

Strayer, F., & Moss, E. (Eds.). (1987). *Development of social and representational tactics during early childhood.* Montreal: La Maison d'Ethologie de Montreal.

Valsiner, J. (1987). *Culture and the development of children's action.* New York: Wiley.

Wertsch, J. (1985). *Culture, communication and cognition: Vygotskian perspectives.* Cambridge, England: Cambridge University Press.

Winegar, L. T. (Ed.). (1989). *Social interaction and the development of children's understanding.* Norwood, NJ: Ablex.

CHAPTER 18

PROBLEMS OF DIRECTION IN SOCIALLY SHARED COGNITION

WILLIAM DAMON

With some notable exceptions, the study of human cognition has traditionally focused on individual problem solving and on test-taking of one kind or another. But in recent years, social scientists have found this focus inadequate for capturing thinking in all its variety and have turned instead to examinations of cognition in real-life settings and in social interaction. These efforts have broadened psychologists' vision of how thinking is composed and from what sources it derives. Moreover, as part of such efforts, a number of scholarly disciplines (such as anthropology, sociology, linguistics, and economics) have contributed importantly to a cognitive science once dominated by laboratory psychology.

The current convergence by a diverse group of scholars on the notion of socially shared cognition represents a promising new direction in such efforts. Like other social scientists at this time, I have found this notion to have conceptual appeal; however, I also have found some things missing in its current application. My main concerns are developmental ones. I shall illustrate my concerns first with reference to the closely related notion of *situated* cognition that has recently captured the imagination of the cognitive science community; I will then comment on the overlapping construct of socially shared cognition at the center of the present volume.

In the several guises that it has assumed, situated cognition has come to convey a number of loosely associated ideas. First, the term has been used to denote practice-centered knowledge, as distinct from knowledge that is abstract, decontextualized, and rule-bound. Second, the term has been used to suggest a scientific approach that views thinking as a form of action rather than merely as disembodied and solipsistic reflections. Third, the term has been used to assert that all cognition is embedded in historical, cultural, and social–relational contexts. In this sociocultural application, cognition is seen to be spawned by social interaction and communication. In use, it is seen to be widely distributed across individuals and collectives.

The chapters in this volume demonstrate how rapidly these ideas are spreading among contemporary scholars interested in the dynamics of human thinking. There are those, of course, who will reply that today's praxis-based and socially sensitive approaches to thinking are simply reinventing wheels already designed by the likes of Dewey, Mead, Vygotsky, and others back to Aristotle. It has been suggested that some contemporary theorizing seems unaware of intellectual traditions that may have delved into similar issues in greater depth (Wineburg, 1989). Yet I find much that is new and illuminating in the recent reincarnations of the old notions. Good ideas have value in themselves, apart from their location in scholarly tradition. It is not always necessary to appreciate the historical context of an idea—even in cases where, ironically, the idea has something to do with appreciating the historical context of ideas.

Nevertheless, the current formulations of pragmatism, contextualism, and social constructionism in the study of cognition raise some nagging questions. I do not claim that these questions have been wholly answered in prior theory and research. But it may be that some questions have been addressed in a more satisfying manner because they have been more clearly recognized. In this chapter, I shall focus on a question related to socially shared cognition that I believe has been left dangling of late: What part does individual development play in the social construction of knowledge?

This question is not as straightforward as it may first appear, because it includes a number of distinct and even unrelated concerns. Some of these concerns are biological and psychological, having to do with the nature of mental life and its transformation over the life span. Others are social and communicational, having to do with the ways in which persons influence one another's ideas and the ways in which cultures are transmitted, preserved, and changed. And others are ideological, having to do with the values through which we determine what types of change to call progressive in a developmental sense.

The developmental question, therefore, breaks out into several subqueries: What do individuals bring with them to the interactional settings in which knowledge is constructed (or coconstructed)? Reciprocally, what do they take away in a lasting sense from such settings? Are there regular patterns connected with aging that influence what individuals may bring along (e.g., can we expect that 4-year-olds generally will go about coconstructing knowledge differently from 10-year-olds)? Is there something special about *developmental* change; that is, are there transformations in individual or cultural ideas that we may call *progress*? If so,

large units of candy, price them appropriately, and even adjust for a continually changing inflation rate. At the same time, these children had very little formal schooling and practically no adeptness with written numeric orthography. Their behavior seems perfectly functional despite their ignorance of the standard tools of mathematical discourse.

Saxe, however, refrained from claiming that these precocious candy merchants have acquired an idyllic state of mathematical competence. Rather, he pointed out that their conventional numeric illiteracy is indeed a real handicap, even if it does not put them at a disadvantage in the world of street candy selling. It is a handicap because these young mathematicians will need a working knowledge of formal symbol systems if they are to make progress in algebra, geometry, calculus, and all other forms of higher math.

It is easy to romanticize the unschooled skill, particularly when charming examples of spontaneous intelligence are found among people previously suspected to be incapable. Social scientists who have observed the impressive adaptive skills of people once thought to be ''primitive'' (ranging from *paisanos* to children to people indigenous to underdeveloped areas) have done just that. But leveling the differences between spontaneous skill and formal instruction makes better romantic fiction than social science.

The developmental benefits of formal instructional experiences have long been familiar to psychologists and educators. It was, ironically enough, Vygotsky who wrote one of the most lucid accounts of such benefits. (The irony is that Vygotskian theory somehow has come to represent an approach that reduces the value of knowledge to its social-contextual significance, without the implication that some forms of knowledge are developmentally superior to others; yet Vygotsky's own writings have an unmistakable developmental thrust.) Vygotsky wrote of the gap between what he called *spontaneous* and *scientific* concepts (Vygotsky, 1962). Spontaneous concepts arise directly from a child's own experience and are fully imbued with the vivid meaning and flavor of that experience. Scientific ones (among which Vygotsky included social scientific, literary, and historical ideas, as well natural science concepts) are learned as part of a systematic package of formal instruction. The full range and complexity of higher-order thinking only becomes available to a child through schooling experiences that impart scientific concepts. Certain learning acts, therefore, are imbued with a developmental priority, in the sense that they enable learners to acquire advanced thinking abilities.

When the term *development* is used rigorously (i.e., with explicit reference to the formation of increasingly advanced systems) rather than loosely (i.e., to mean merely any sort of change during ontogenesis), it makes people uncomfortable because of the values that are inevitably implied. Who is to say what is *advanced*, or what represents *progress*? Yet such values choices are unavoidable if we are to look critically at any intellectual achievement, let alone if we are to participate in any planned intervention. My point here is that such choices need not reflect someone's arbitrary set of biases. Rather, they can be made on the objective grounds of functionality. The defining and selecting of functions, of course, is a matter of value and, therefore, subjective; but the determination of how well a given behavior serves an already defined function can be an objective and reliable procedure. Once, therefore, the desired functions of thought are defined, the developmental directions by which we assess change can be readily identified and calibrated. Of course, there will always be some discrepancy in how scientists define the functions, but there will also be a great deal of shared consensus.

The important thing is to begin with a careful consideration of criteria for determining developmental direction, to avoid approaching cognitive phenomena without clear standards of analysis. Most educators, for example, recognize and value the features of thought that have been called, variously, *higher-order, complex, abstract, propositional, critical, hypothetical/deductive, hierarchical, formal, or systematic.* This value provides a common standard of analysis through which acts of learning may be consistently evaluated. With this approach, the question of implicit values in any statement of developmental direction can be addressed and unambiguously resolved. Of course, the nature of the resolution will vary across domains and functions of knowledge.

SOCIAL INFLUENCE AND PSYCHOLOGICAL DEVELOPMENT

For a developmentalist, the study of socially shared cognition has many attractions, one of which is the opportunity to understand how social relationships contribute to cognitive growth. Recent ethnographic studies of adult–child interactions are cases in point (Rogoff, 1986). Through observations of adults coaching children in practical skills, Rogoff and her colleagues identified some key features of social interchange that foster children's skill acquisition. Rogoff called the interactive bridge-building processes that she observed *guided participation.*

Not all social relationships have the same characteristics and, similarly, not all cognitive achievements have the same qualities. The promise of focusing on socially shared cognition is that it will enable us to link the characteristics of particular social relations with the quality of cognitive achievement that grows out of them. It is clear, for example, that guided participation is a special form of social interchange. It cannot provide a model for every learning engagement that children experience, because children also acquire knowledge in other social relationships with differing characteristics. The interesting question is whether there are systematic links between certain types of social interaction and certain types of cognitive achievement.

One answer to this question is being provided by a recent wave of theoretical and empirical writing on children's peer learning. Since the time of Piaget's work on moral judgment, the notion that peer relations spawn conceptual products different from adult–child relations has circulated among developmentalists (Piaget, 1965/1932). In Piaget's moral theory, *heteronomous* concepts arise from adult–child relations characterized by unilateral respect and constraint, whereas *autonomous* ones arise from peer relations that are based on mutual respect and equality. Youniss (1980) traced a similar notion through Sullivan's writings on peer "chumship." In all of these sources, there is the sense that peer interactions present special learning opportunities for children because they encourage an active exchange of ideas between equal partners who need not defer to one another's intellectual authority.

In recent years, there have been several empirical extensions of these notions into the cognitive realm (see Damon, 1984, and Damon & Phelps, 1989, for reviews). Generally, researchers have found that peer relations can induce certain types of conceptual insight that are often resistant to adult–child instruction. These are conceptual insights that require radical shifts in previous operating assumptions. Examples range from Piagetian conservation tasks to the notion of proportionality that underlies many ratio problems in mathematics and the physical sciences (Damon & Phelps, 1989; Perret-Clermont, 1980). Peer relations can foster deep insights of this sort because they can provide a context for discovery learning within a framework of social support.

I say *can* foster and *can* provide because there are many important distinctions to be made between different kinds of peer interactions. Research has shown that such distinctions themselves can affect the quality and quantity of learning that takes place within the relationship. For example, peer interactions can differ in their degree of conflict (Bearison, Magzamin, & Filardo, 1986), in their degree of mutuality and equality (Berndt, 1987), and in their patterns of reciprocal discourse (Damon & Killen, 1982). Too much or too little conflict, low levels of mutuality and equality, and unbalanced, asymmetrical discourse patterns can mitigate against the productive learning environments typically established in children's peer relations. Each of these within-relationship qualities, independently or in conjunction with one another, can be more determinate of a peer relationship's propensity to foster learning than the simple fact that it occurs between agemates.

The same, I believe, can be said about adult–child relationships. Certainly not all learning interactions between adults and children have the characteristics of guided participation. Although we do not yet have good data on this, it seems intuitively evident that many other adult–child relational patterns play a role in children's cognitive growth. Guided participation may be the most effective, and justifiably it has been singled out for careful analysis. But there are other patterns that may stimulate learning in complementary and even essential ways. In lieu of systematic observational data on these other patterns, I offer a personal anecdote from my own parental experience.

A few weeks before my daughter's 12th birthday, I took her on a trip to Texas with me. I have a fairly typical parental relationship with my daughter, in the sense that I have tutored her on many practical skills and conceptual problems over the years. For example, I have taught her some things about how to play the guitar, how to cook chili, and how to solve problems in combinatorial logic. Guided participation is a good characterization of these interactions. But our interchanges during this recent trip had some very different features.

During the trip, I took my daughter into a hands-on science museum in El Paso and then across the border into Ciudad Juarez. During these visits, two noteworthy episodes of socially shared cognition occurred. The first centered on a very difficult mathematical enigma in the science museum. The second centered on a Mexican toy in which eight blocks were linked by string in a mysterious and surprisingly dynamic arrangement. Suffice it to say that neither my daughter nor I had a good initial grasp of how either puzzle worked. But our behavior while trying to figure out each puzzle is, I believe, instructive.

At the museum, we plunged into the math problem much like eager novices in a peer collaboration. Our interaction bore many of the qualities that developmentalists have found in such interchanges (Damon, 1984; Damon & Phelps, 1989; Brownell, this volume). For example, we jointly generated and tried out new ideas, corrected and questioned one another, suggested experiments to test the other's solutions, forced each other to verify and justify our conclusions, and reminded one another of information arising from earlier trials. Some of our behavior was as primitive as the peer interactions of very young children: Neither of us was above grabbing the display objects from the other when we thought we had a bright idea. While we were working together on the puzzle, the ideas that I expressed were not noticeably better than my daughter's. Eventually, however, she became bored or frustrated by our apparent lack of progress and went off to another exhibit. I stuck with the puzzle, finally got it, and then insisted that my daughter sit through a detailed explanation of the steps that I had taken.

The second episode occurred a day later while my daughter was playing with her new toy from Mexico. As she was exploring the mysteries of the device, the string broke and the blocks came apart. The problem then became how to put it back together. She asked for my help, and we worked on it jointly. Again, while we were working together, our interactions looked very much like a classic peer collaboration, with many of the same features that characterized our joint efforts in the museum. This time, however, it was I who became frustrated and gave up. Maria stayed the course and succeeded in repairing her toy. Still, unlike me in the museum, she was either unable or unwilling to provide an explanation of her achievement.

In both of these episodes, there was joint and solitary experimentation in combination with some mix of collective and individual reflection. To an undetermined extent, there was learning by both parties. That is, we each became able to do something that had previously stymied us. I do not know whether this was learning of a more fundamental and useful sort than in the cottage cheese incident cited earlier. That would depend on whether our new understanding provided a base of transfer to other problems that we had previously approached in a less efficient or satisfactory manner. This naturalistic incident did not include such a test. But some insight certainly was generated.

Although these learning engagements took place between an adult and a child, the interactions bore more of the characteristics of peer collaboration than of guided participation. As in most adult–child relations, a pattern of adult tutoring child had been firmly established during adult and child's history together. In the present episodes, however, this pattern asserted itself only once: when I (unlike my daughter) insisted on explicating for her benefit what I had learned.

I have described this episode here to illustrate three points concerning socially shared cognition and its relation to learning. First, even when learning is fostered through processes of social communication, individual activity and reflection still play a critical role. Sometimes, as the theme of this volume asserts, individual activity may build on collective questions and insights. Other times, however, individual activity actually may need to resist the collective illusions created by a group. From experimental social psychology, Moscovici's (1976, 1980) great studies that turned the Asch and Milgram conformity paradigm on its head offer a memorable empirical demonstration of this point. Any paradigm that assumes a one-way, deterministic relation between the collective and individual knowledge construction is overly simplistic. Individuals often need to separate themselves from groups in order to seek truth, and groups often learn from individuals who have separated themselves in just this way. Consider, for example, lonely geniuses and prophets who are pariahs in their time. (Moscovici, interestingly, cites Freud as *his* model of social influence—the disregarded individual ultimately shaping the collective perspective.) We must make sure that our models of socially shared cognition do not lose sight of such phenomena by veering too far toward a collective determinism.

My second point is that the qualities of a social exchange that foster learning are more interaction-specific than relationship-specific. In the psychological literature, much has been made of the distinction between adult–child and child–child relations, but the critical distinction does not always correspond with this split. Rather, it is the guided versus collaborative quality of the interactions that makes a difference. The nature of that difference is still a matter of conjecture, but one possibility is that guided interactions lead to the acquisition of practical skills, algorithms, and other modeling type products of cultural transmission, whereas collaborative interactions lead to the deep transformations of conceptual insight engendered by discovery learning. If so—or if other critical distinctions obtain—the distinctions seem to be rooted more in the nature of the learning interaction than in the constituency of the overall relationship. Adults can have both collaborative and guided interactions with the same child, as in the case of my daughter and me. We know, too, that children do not always collaborate with one another as peers. Often one child will assume a leadership role and guide another child through the acquisition of a skill.

My third point partially hedges my second point. Relationships do have a strong reality of their own, deriving from the historical legacy of their existence over time. Specific interactions within relationships are never independent of this overarching reality (see Hinde, 1981, for a fuller statement of this point). The formidable relational history between my daughter and me emerged when I found myself explaining to her, in didactic fashion, the fruits of my own reflections. When it was her turn to do so, again consistent with our history together, she demurred.

Before leaving these basic social-relational issues, there is a fourth point— a methodological aside—that I would like to insert in the context of the example just offered. This pertains to the validity of case material for analyses of cognitive growth through socially shared cognition. Of course, I realize that the tale of my daughter and me is a mere anecdote rather than a systematic case study. But I would argue that, if it had been done properly, it could contribute a kind of evidence that has been missing from the usual normative study of children's learning. Moreover, it is a kind of evidence that is especially needed in the study of socially situated cognition. Idiographic treatments of learning can help us understand the complex role of multiple social influences in a way that experimental isolations of single variables cannot. (See Allport, 1942, for a discussion of how case material can serve this goal in the social and natural sciences.) Contemporary science has come to see idiographic approaches as less scientific than normative ones. Perhaps this is because quantification has come to stand as an easy substitute for conceptual rigor. But any paradigm that stresses deep interpenetration of multiple social forces into cognitive functioning can ill afford to ignore rich data sources that open windows onto such forces.

INDIVIDUAL EXPERIENCE AND DEVELOPMENTAL CONTINUITY

For all the theoretical benefits offered by emphases on socially shared or situated cognition, there is at least one theoretical danger. Such approaches do not readily lend themselves to capturing the continuity of individual experience over time. Although it does not necessarily need to do so, the current focus on the contextual shaping of cognitive performance has tended to obscure the contributions of prior experience to that performance. Yet intellectual acts are affected not only by

situation described above. In one of our subsequent studies using this situation, we found that 56% of the children markedly increased their awareness of fairness issues (Damon & Killen, 1982). This compared with 34% and 20% of children in control groups not exposed to *in vivo* peer discussions (the 34% group being one that was individually tutored by an adult on a similar but hypothetical set of issues).

Interestingly, the children who changed in the course of the peer debate did not always come away claiming that equality was the final answer to all justice problems. Rather, many of them saw their equal solution to the group problem as a situation-specific response with some practical and moral value, and said that, in other situations, they might adopt a meritorian or benevolent solution that deviated from absolute equality. The social learning, therefore, was not always of a direct sort in which the child simply came away with a mental copy of the group solution. More likely, the group engagement triggered a process of reflection that led eventually to judgmental change as varied as the individuals who experienced it.

In these data, we see individual development fostered, guided, but not quite directed by social influence. For some children, the peer debate forced a choice that posed a new possibility for them—equality of treatment. The debate gave other children a chance to hear and discuss alternatives, some of which they would ultimately consider more morally satisfying than equality, although in the end they would choose equality as a way to resolve their current situation. For still others (a large minority of 44%), the situation provided no grounds for enhancing their moral reasoning in any detectable way. The experimental situation was the same for all subjects and certainly had some impact on all subjects, yet registered differently on the moral awareness of different individuals. As always, the fact, extent, and nature of intellectual change were only partly socially determined.

The challenge for the future is to arrive at a better understanding of how social and developmental forces work together in the formation of human behavior. The problem for our field is that we have very few theoretical models or experimental paradigms that do full justice to both the social and the developmental. Compounding this problem, there has been an uncomfortable tendency among opposing camps to fight for the primacy of the social or the developmental as a means of asserting the superiority of a particular approach. Although this struggle may have some value for the contenders, it is hard to see how genuine progress can be made in this manner. Vygotsky reputedly once said, "Social psychology *is* developmental psychology." Although I have never been able to track down a reference for this possibly apocryphal comment, I still like the vision that it conveys. This volume and the conference from which it arose reflect this spirit. To the extent that such a spirit prevails in future investigations, we have some interesting work in store for us.

References

Allport, G. W. (1942). *The nature of personal evidence in the social sciences*. New York: Social Science Research Council Monograph.

Bearison, D., Magzamin, S., & Filardo, E. (1986). Socio-cognitive conflict and cognitive growth in young children. *Merrill-Palmer Quarterly, 32*, 236–245.

Berndt, T. (1987). Conversations between friends: An appraisal of processes and theories. In J. Gewirtz & W. Kurtines (Eds.), *Social interaction and moral development* (pp. 212–237). New York: Wiley.

Brown, J. S., Collins, A., & Duguid, P. (1989). Situated cognition and the culture of learning. *Educational Researcher, 18*(1), 32–42.

Damon, W. (1984). Peer-based education: The untapped potential. *Journal of Applied Developmental Psychology, 5*, 331–343

Damon, W., & Killen, M. (1982). Peer interaction and the process of change in children's moral reasoning. *Merrill-Palmer Quarterly, 28*, 347–367.

Damon, W., & Phelps, E. (1989). Strategic uses of peer interaction in children's education. In T. Berndt & G. Ladd (Eds.), *Peer relationships in child development* (pp. 114–147). New York: Wiley.

Hinde, R. A. (1981). On describing relationships. *Journal of child psychology and psychiatry, 17*, 1–19.

Lave, J. (1988). *Cognition in practice*. Cambridge, England: Cambridge University Press.

Moscovici, S. (1976). Social influence and social change. *European Monographs in Social Psychology* (No. 10). London: Academic Press.

Moscovici, S. (1980). Toward a theory of conversion behavior. In L. Berkowitz (Ed.), *Advances in experimental social psychology* (pp. 32–42). New York: Academic Press.

Palincsar, A.S. (1989). Less charted waters. *Educational Researcher, 18*(4), 5–7.

Perret-Clermont, A.-N. (1980). *Social interaction and cognitive development in children*. London: Academic Press.

Piaget, J. (1965). *The moral judgment of the child*. New York: The Free Press. (Original work published in 1932)

Rogoff, B. (1986). Adult assistance of children's learning. In T. E. Raphael (Ed.), *The contexts of school-based literacy* (pp. 86–110). New York: Random House.

Saxe, G. B. (1988a). Candy selling and math learning. *Educational Researcher, 17*, 14–21.

Saxe, G. B. (1988b). The mathematics of child street vendors. *Child Development, 59*, 1415–1425.

Vygotsky, L. S. (1962). *Thought and language*. Cambridge, MA: MIT Press.

Wineburg, S. (1989). Remembrance of theories past. *Educational Researcher, 18*(4), 7–10.

Youniss, J. (1980). *Parents and peers in child development*. Chicago: University of Chicago Press.

CHAPTER 19

CONCLUSION

MICHAEL COLE

When I attended the conference from which the chapters in this volume were drawn, it was my strong impression, an impression reinforced by additional readings in the course of preparing these comments, that the organizers (now editors) were unusually successful in provoking a fruitful discussion of basic issues in psychological theory with important implications for the application of theory to practice, particularly the practice of education. The impetus for this gratifying outcome was, appropriately enough, found in the core concept in the conference's organizing theme, socially shared cognition, and most particularly in the ambiguities of the term *sharing*.

The simple expedient of referring to Webster's Dictionary reveals something of the Janus-headed nature of this concept. On the one hand, *sharing* means to "receive, use, experience in common with another or others." This is the sense of *share* in force when we ask that two children share the use of the family TV or when two adults share a taxi. On the other hand, *share* also means to divide or distribute something, as in "Would you like to share this batch of cookies?" or "Who is willing to share the burden of this committee work?"

What makes the concept really interesting with respect to the notion of *sharing cognition* is that sharing often means both "having in common" and "dividing up" at the same time (as a reexamination of the examples just given will show). This possibility raises all sorts of interesting questions for cognitive psychologists: What does it mean for a cognitive process to occur both *in* and

Preparation of this manuscript was facilitated by grants from the Carnegie and Spencer Foundations. I wish to thank Yrjo Engestrom for his comments and suggestions.

between individuals? Insofar as cognition is shared in the distributed sense, where might it be located? In the social group? In the culture? In the genes?

These are not totally fanciful questions. Each is asked (and answered) in one or more of the chapters in this volume. Moreover, as these chapters show, when psychologists become concerned with deciding what part of cognition is held in common and what part is divided up, and when they take the additional steps of asking about the locus and origins of the shared and distributed parts of cognition, they are easily led to ask questions and conduct research that calls into question the analytic apparatus of psychology as a discipline and, correspondingly, its relationship to other social sciences.

Very roughly speaking, I detect three orientations among the contributors with respect to the general theoretical and methodological implications of the notion that human thought processes could, in some sense, be shared or distributed among people. First, there are those who see no particular challenge to their ongoing scientific practices; the social sharing of knowledge or the circumstances of social interaction can simply be added to the array of factors already known to influence individual thought. At the other extreme are those who believe that the concept of individual cognition dominating contemporary psychology is so thoroughly confused that it calls for a fundamental realignment of scientific effort; in an important sense, these authors argue, human cognition consists of the interaction of individual, social, and cultural processes and must be studied systemically in terms of all these aspects simultaneously. To accomplish such a synthesis, at least interdisciplinary research and perhaps even a new scientific discipline seem to be required.

Between these two extremes, several contributors appear to consider the implications of the notion of socially shared cognition to be an open question. Starting from one or another disciplinary orientation, these investigators seek to extend our knowledge of human cognition through investigation of the conditions of its sharing in concrete cases, with minimal concern for interdisciplinary work or paradigmatic reform.

To make the implications of the contrasting viewpoints as clear as possible, I will first discuss chapters written within the normative framework of standard social science practice. Each of these chapters accepts the assumption that cognition is an inside-the-head phenomenon, each makes what I consider to be an interesting contribution to the issue of socially shared cognition, and each displays certain strengths of the normative approach. Second, I will discuss two chapters from within this tradition of research that raise important questions about its limitations. Third, I will take up those chapters offering the most serious challenge to cognitive psychology. On the basis of this brief review, I will offer some observations on prior programs of research relevant to this discussion (focusing on work by members of the Laboratory of Comparative Human Cognition), suggest some methodological implications of taking seriously the notion that culture is an important locus of shared cognition, and conclude with some remarks about the implications for educational theory and practice of taking seriously the proposition that cognition is culturally mediated and socially shared (in all senses of that term).

THE NORMATIVE FRAMEWORK

According to the traditional understanding of the division of scientific labor that created the social sciences in the late 19th century, psychology was the study of individual human thought (Boring, 1950). The precise approach to this object of study was disputed among psychologists. Some thought of cognition in terms of the content of consciousness and favored introspection as a methodology; others eschewed the study of consciousness in favor of behavior and related their laws to observable actions. In principle, however, the possibility of isolating individual psychological processes through the use of controlled experimental procedures was widely accepted. Thus, although behaviorists could (and did) criticize Wilhelm Wundt and his descendants for their lack of scientific rigor in using introspective reports as evidence of internal, cognitive processes, the tradition of studying human subjects by presenting them with carefully measured stimuli under carefully controlled standardized conditions, and of attributing to individuals the psychological laws derived from relations between stimulus input and behavioral output (e.g., the wiggle of an EEG recorder, a hand motion, a sequence of words) remained.

In an important sense, acceptance of individual human behavior (reborn in the 1960s as the individual human mind) as the unit of analysis for psychology rendered the notion of socially shared cognition a contradiction in terms, or perhaps simply a methodological confusion. The sociologist Emile Durkheim, whose ideas on this topic were referred to by a few of the participants, made the point with special clarity in a classic statement of why individual thought must be strictly separated from cognition considered as a social phenomenon:

> If, as we may accept, the synthesis and *sui generis* which every society
> constitutes yields new phenomena, differing from those which take place
> in the individual consciousness, we must also admit that these facts re-
> side exclusively in the very society itself which produces them, not in its
> parts—that is, its members. Thus they are in this sense external to indi-
> vidual minds considered as such. . . . Thus we have a new justification
> for the separation which we have established between psychology
> proper, which is the science of the individual mind, and sociology. So-
> cial facts do not differ from psychological facts in quality only: *they
> have a different substratum.* . . . (Durkheim, 1938/1896, xvi)

Anthropology, another social science with justified claims to the study of human thought, adhered to a complementary point of view, according to which it contributed to an understanding of the *content* of thinking while ceding to psychology the study of thought *processes*. (Such historical agreements lie behind Wertsch's remark in chapter 5 of this volume that the notion of socially shared cognition sparks resonances among representatives of other social science disciplines and Schegloff's attribution in chapter 8 of an interest in the *process*, not the content, of sharing to psychologists.)

This intellectual division of labor has had its detractors from the time it was first proposed, but it has proved exceedingly durable. The premise that cognition is something unique to individuals survived what has become known as the *cognitive revolution* of the late 1950s and 1960s, during which psychologists began to make inferences about cognitive processes that intervene between stimulus and response. These processes were attributed to individual human beings as patterns of information processing that occur "in the head." In the still-ubiquitous block diagrams that populate introductory psychology textbooks and professional journals, stimuli are registered at the periphery of the body, transported through sensory organs to the brain, where they are processed (e.g., transformed and stored), leading at some later moment(s) to output registered as some kind of action that influences the surrounding environment.

Psychologists who adopt this inside-the-head view of cognition may, of course, talk about socially shared cognition. Two people may, for example, have the same knowledge about a given domain, or they may share a common pool of potential information and engage in a division of problem solving responsibility. But to adopt terminology used by both Jean Lave (chapter 4) and James Wertsch (chapter 5), the sharing that occurs in this framework does not break down the basic distinction between individual and social. Most often the part of cognition that is considered social is simply added on to the preexisting, individual processes. Consequently, analysts who adopt this approach to socially shared cognition need not deviate from the methodological frame that has ruled experimental psychology for the past hundred years.

Sharing as Division of Cognitive Labor

My first example of application of standard experimental approaches to socially shared cognition is provided by the work of Brownell and Carriger (chapter 17). These investigators formulated a question about the psychological capacities (skills) within each participant that underlie (give rise to) successful joint activity. They addressed this problem by constructing an apparatus that could be manipulated by children as young as 12 months but that required collaborative manipulation by two children. They then observed how children between the ages of 12 and 30 months coped with this task. In addition, they presented each child with a separate task designed to assess individual ability to represent dolls as active agents in a pretend-play task. As described in their chapter, they found that collaboration grows markedly in the second year of life as children become better able to coördinate with their partners, and that this increased coordination is linked to the ability to represent others as active agents as the result of universal onto-genetic factors influencing the cognitive apparatus inside each individual child. Their observations were, at least implicitly, meant to apply to representational capacities in general, not just to those manifested in the special situation they constructed.

A second example of socially shared cognition as a division of cognitive labor is provided by Hatano and Inagaki's study (chapter 15) of small group interactions focused on various science problems. In this case, each group shared a particular belief about the answer with other group members but was in conflict with members of other groups who held different beliefs. The investigators identify several ways in which lack of shared understanding might have a positive impact on individual problem solving. First, the division into groups gave rise to "partisan motivation," which supplemented the desire to know and understand, sustaining highly directed problem solving. Second, group members intuitively worked out useful divisions of cognitive labor, providing internal criticism and elaboration of arguments. Third, social cues such as the ability to silence opponents provided feedback supporting assessment of the effectiveness of one's argument.

An interesting feature of Hatano and Inagaki's study was that children were not required to arrive at a shared understanding (consensus), but only to elaborate their arguments as fully as possible before they were given an opportunity to "see for themselves" by testing their predictions in concrete activity. Hatano and Inagaki reported that very often discussion by itself failed to produce conversions, but succeeded in sensitizing students to the feedback from their subsequent empirical tests.

The picture that one gets from this research, as well as from early studies described by Perret-Clermont and her colleagues (chapter 3) in which dyads attempted to solve various conservation tasks (see later discussion), is that although new levels of comprehension are a private achievement, such achievements can be markedly facilitated by properly organized social interaction.

The same remarks apply to the research reported by Rogoff (chapter 16). In each of the cases she describes, the age and skills of the target child's partners constitute independent variables whose differential effects in an individual posttest indicate the way in which experience with a particular division of cognitive labor influences later problem solving when the child must assume virtually all responsibility.

The results of these studies in no way challenge standard psychological theory. Rather, they appear to extend well-known phenomena into potentially useful areas of educational practice, suggesting conditions under which it is likely to be productive to have children working together.

Sharing as Having *or* Putting *in Common*

The other side of the sharing coin that has come in for study within the dominant research paradigm on cognition is based on the commonsense notion that people who use a common language or are members of the same culture will thereby share the contents of thought in the form of shared knowledge. However, this knowledge will not be totally shared; no one knows everything about one's own culture. Consequently, in addition to studying what people have in common in terms of cognitive content, it is interesting to study the dynamics of how the amount of shared content can be modified for particular purposes (such as holding a conversation or engaging in joint problem solving).

The first, *having* aspect of socially shared cognitive content has been intensively studied by cognitive anthropologists, represented in chapter 10 by James Boster. His data extend this line of research in a provocative direction, suggesting that for the domain of living organisms there are universal structures in our experience as human beings that result in pancultural similarities in our judgments of what goes with what in the world around us. In effect, this form of socially shared cognition arises from homo sapien's shared phylogenetic history coded in the structure of our genetic makeup. Culture-specific expertise may modify these structures under certain conditions, but by and large, the data indicate, the constraints imposed by humans' perceptual–cognitive apparatus (understood as our phylogenetically common physical structures) and structure inherent in the natural world (within which we evolved as a species) are sufficient to guarantee a common foundation of shared knowledge with which to regulate our daily interactions.

It is worth mentioning that, although this research might be interpreted as being only about sharing of cognitive content, it has clear implications for such important cognitive processes as inference and problem solving, because the internal organization of the categories provides different people with a shared notion of "what goes with what" in the world around them. As Shweder (1977) argued convincingly in another context, there is a strong tendency for people to confuse *likeness* with *likelihood* in their reasoning about the world, so it seems entirely plausible to conclude that sharing conceptual categories will result in similar patterns of inference in a variety of problem-solving circumstances.

The work of Krauss and Fussell (chapter 9), which extends earlier work by Krauss and others, would also appear to point to the cognitive process implications of Boster's results by showing how people use knowledge about shared categories and their bases to make inferences about what attributes of objects will be salient for specified categories of interlocutors. Using this information, people are more effective in seeking shared understandings by tailoring their communicative utterances accordingly. Nonetheless, as the work of Schegloff (chapter 8) and that of Clark and Brennan (chapter 7) amply illustrate, the process of "putting in common'' unavoidably requires ongoing work, at least some of which, any psychologist would agree, is cognitive in nature.

DOUBTS ABOUT THE DOMINANT PARADIGM

In this section, I turn to contributions that raise doubts about the general applicability of the paradigm underpinning the research discussed thus far and, by extension, doubts about the conception of socially shared cognition that it supports.

The chapter by Perret-Clermont, Perret, and Bell (chapter 3) richly illustrates the kinds of difficulties with standard experimental-psychological methods that I have in mind. The "two generations" of research described in that chapter correspond roughly to the differences in approach to the question of socially shared cognition to which I referred at the beginning of my remarks. In Perret-Clermont and her colleagues' "first generation" research, a sharp distinction was made between the social and the cognitive; the research problem was to determine "how social factors affect cognitive performances and how individuals actively utilize social resources to solve given problems" (p. 42). This research produced interesting support for early speculations by Piaget that the give and take of peer interactions could, under the right circumstances, disequilibriate children and provide experiences from which a new stage of understanding could develop. (There is much more to these results, of course; the reader should refer to the original reports for a specification of the precise conditions that seemed to promote development. See also converging evidence provided by Martin, 1985, and Tudge, 1985.)

Although successful at one level, certain unexpected secondary effects of the change in procedure to allow for peer interaction forced a change in the researchers' overall understanding of their subject matter. In particular, they were disquieted by the repeated finding that under a heterogeneous set of conditions, sex and social class variations in cognitive performance that were routinely obtained with standard testing procedures disappeared. In addition, presumably irrelevant changes in the content or conduct of the problem were observed to change children's performance. These variations were not mere surface phenomena; a generalized change in operatory level of the kind that ought to have required months or years seemed to occur in the course of a single experimental session.

These results led Perret-Clermont and her colleagues to question the sharp distinction they had been making between the social and the cognitive. They began to wonder if the standardized tasks they presented might not reflect differences in communicative competence or interpretation of adult discourse rules. Their observations led not only to further questions about the interpretive processes that constitute the child–experimenter interaction (and, hence, the task) but also to questions about the impact of schooling on development and, ultimately, to the second generation of research in which the unit of analysis is the social interaction rather than the individual's behavior as specified by the experimental procedures.

The subsequent series of studies focused on variations in the content and context of interactions between experimenter and subject in test-like situations and the social organization of classroom interactions. With respect to the testing situations, the researchers found that a myriad of what they refer to as *socio-cognitive* aspects of the testing situation influence children's interpretation of the task and, thereby, their behavior. For some populations, special staging of the task (e.g., having two dolls share juice in a conservation of liquid problem) improved performance; for some it did not. For some populations, performance was improved by preceding assessment with a cooperative game; for others it was not.

Perret-Clermont et al. also observed that adults routinely fail to follow the testing script in a rigid way but modify their behavior in a continuing negotiation of the task situation with the children. These deviations from the standard script did not appear to be superfluous noise. Rather, the adults seemed to be negotiating the conduct of the testing in ways that are necessary to establishing cooperation. But they had the unfortunate effect of undermining the analyst's ability to specify cognitive processes in the child vis-a-vis the normative task.

The major methodological thrust of Perret-Clermont, Perret, and Bell's work on face-to-face cognitive testing is strongly supported by Siegal (chapter 2), who demonstrates in a particularly convincing way that small children are quite sensitive to discourse maxims such as "be cooperative" and "be polite." He shows that various experimental procedures that have been developed to test children's understandings of such concepts as number and identity systematically seduce young children into giving answers that mislead adults about their knowledge of the concept domain of interest to the adult.

Anyone reading these studies cannot help but come away convinced of the truth of Perret-Clermont and her colleagues' admonition that "It is important to understand to what extent so-called cognitive development is dependent on the acquisition of sociocognitive knowledge in specific contexts" (p. 42).

Most relevant to the theme of this volume, the work of the Geneva group and of Siegal forces a radical reconsideration of how to locate the cognitive, not only in the one-on-one testing situation and the classroom but in any circumstances. Clearly, aspects of cognitive performance that once were attributed to psychological processes within individual children emerge as joint accomplishments between people, that is, as socially shared.

The question then becomes, what new kind of scientific enterprise is required to deal adequately with the acquisition (and use) of sociocultural knowledge in specific contexts viewed not as the independent invention of the child, but as a socially shared and distributed form of cognitive activity emerging from, and constituting, joint activity?

NEW DIRECTIONS: TOWARD CONTEXT, ACTIVITY, AND SITUATION

Several participants independently noted the contrast that Perret-Clermont and her colleagues drew between their first generation research (in which they made a strict distinction between the individual and the social, assuming that the performances they observed were a context-free property of the individual children) and the second generation research (where processes of interpretation and socially oriented problem solving were given prominence). In each case, these participants' remarks were accompanied by criticism of the dominant paradigm of psychological research and by suggestions for alternative scientific practices.

James Wertsch (chapter 5) refers to the "disturbing tendency" of psychological research to investigate the individual removed from social or cultural context. Like myself and my colleagues, Wertsch turns to the ideas of the Soviet sociohistorical school for inspiration. This choice proves attractive, as Damon points out in chapter 18, because this school of psychology assumes that joint mediated activity is the proper unit of psychological analysis and, hence, is inherently socially shared (Lektorsky, 1984).

Addressing these same issues from the perspective of anthropology, Shirley Heath (chapter 6) and Jean Lave (chapter 4) take a different path. Heath draws a contrast between laboratory experiments in which cognitive psychologists focus on the "syntactic, context-free logic of reasoning" and studies of learning in "natural learning sites [that] shape the semantic and situational constraints of reasoning in basic ways" (p. 103). She does not suggest a specific recipe for psychology, but offers ethnographic observation as an essential antidote to laboratory experiments. Lave, whose work can be considered an extended commentary on the difference between the dominant paradigm of cognitive research and an alternative, synthetic new paradigm, cites in support of her approach Ragnar Rommetveit's (1987, p. 78) assertion that the standard paradigm "seems to rest on the assumption that the world can be exhaustively analyzed in terms of context-free data or atomic facts and captured in a semantically closed language." Her methodology combines ethnographic observation, historical and institutional analysis, and, in some cases, experimentation derived from observation as complementary ways to contextualize her data.

When such criticisms of standard psychological approaches are translated into new theoretical and methodological practices, they appear to push psychologists into new, poorly charted territory. Before taking up the implications for psychologists of committing oneself to a radical vision of socially shared cognition, I will summarize earlier decades of research that bear on the issues raised in the current volume, including research by myself and my colleagues.

A LITTLE HISTORY

As Damon notes in chapter 18, the notion that cognition needs to be considered as situated or embedded in its socio-cultural-historical context has gained some adherents among cognitive scientists. Damon is correct in pointing out that modern enthusiasm for such ideas often appears to be cut off from its historical roots. My own view is that this particular history is important to understand, because it is one of the most certain constraints limiting the reinvention of the mistakes of prior generations. (After all, if the previous versions of such ideas were deserving of such merit, why don't *they* represent the dominant paradigm? And if they were found inadequate, why are we wasting our time with them now?)

Links to the Classics

I believe it is important to recognize that all three progenitors mentioned by Damon—Dewey, Mead, and Vygotsky—explicitly rejected the positivist division of labor that created experimental psychology and the other social sciences in the 1880s and 1890s. In particular, they rejected the division between "natural" and "human" sciences upon which laboratory experimental methods and claims about context-free psychological processes are based. Mead, it is worth noting, studied in Germany with Wilhelm Dilthey, champion of a historically grounded interpretive approach to human psychology (Dilthey, 1988), whereas the Soviet sociohistorical theorists explicitly set themselves the task of surmounting the division of psychology into two incoherent branches (Luria, 1979). In doing so, they acknowledged their debt not only to Dewey but also to Janet, James, and several seminal thinkers whose ideas are increasingly remembered in the contemporary psychological literature.

There is no space here to pursue the threads linking anthropological, sociological, and psychological theorizing about the social and cultural constitution of mind (see Lave, 1988; Laboratory of Comparative Human Cognition [LCHC], 1983 for partial accounts), but it is worth noting that such important thinkers as S. F. Nadel (1951) and Meyer Fortes (1938) argued powerfully for "person-acting" and shared social spheres as units of analysis for the study of mind in relation to its sociocultural constituents. Roger Barker's (1968) notion of a synomorphic relationship between behavior and setting remains highly relevant, although widely ignored by today's advocates of similar views (Lave, 1988 being a notable exception). Somewhat later, Aaron Cicourel and his colleagues (1974) demonstrated with great clarity that "standardized" tests and experiments are, in reality, intricately negotiated and manifestly *non*standard forms of social interaction whose dynamics and structure must be understood in terms of the social contexts of which they are a constituent part.

Some Personal History

My own involvement with such issues grew out of the disorienting experience of being assigned the task of identifying cultural barriers to modern mathematics education among tribal people living in rural Liberia (Gay & Cole, 1964). As summarized in various publications, the crosscultural literature is replete with discussions of the methodological dilemmas that arise once one begins to suspect that experimental cognitive tasks are special kinds of culturally mediated social interaction and not privileged windows on the mind. One extended example from our research illustrates the kind of merry chase that can begin when, like Perret-Clermont and her colleagues, one finds that modifications of the content and context of standardized cognitive tasks, with no change in the underlying logic, can lead rapidly to stage-like changes in individuals' manifested cognitive abilities.

In this cycle of experiments, we arranged for people from rural areas of Liberia whose culture has no tradition of writing or formal schooling to solve a task requiring them to draw what appeared to be a simple inference based on an experience created in the experimental context (see Cole, Gay, Glick, & Sharp, 1971 for details).

The apparatus we began with was borrowed from Tracy and Howard Kendler, who had used it extensively in studies with children in the United States (Kendler & Kendler, 1967). It consisted of a box with three panels, each covered by a flap. The flaps could be lifted one at a time or all together to display the panels singly or as a unit.

The task was presented as follows. First, the subject was taught that pushing a button on the left panel would yield a marble. Then she or he was taught that pushing a button on the right panel yielded a ball bearing. Next the two side panels were closed and the center panel opened to reveal a window through which could be seen a piece of candy, a slot, and a small tray at the bottom. The subject was handed the ball bearing and marble and told that one of them, if dropped into the slot, would yield the candy. Rarely did anyone require more than a few practice trials to master these three component tasks. Once this phase of the procedure had been mastered, all three panels were opened simultaneously for the first time; the subject was told that now the task was to obtain the candy, which could be kept.

Eight-year-old American children had been reported to handle this problem tolerably well, and 12-year-olds handled it with apparent ease, but very few nonliterate Liberian adolescents or young adults seemed capable of solving it, although they learned the component tasks with apparent ease. What was the source of the problem?

To answer this question, we began by substituting objects with which these people had everyday experience for the Kendlers' somewhat strange-looking box. First we substituted distinctively different matchboxes in which color-coded keys could be found for the side panels, the ball bearing, and the marble, and a locked box was substituted for the center panel. By opening the correct matchbox and taking the correct key, the subject could unlock the lock and obtain the candy. In this version of the task, 90% of the subjects, including young children, solved the task, most of them with no prompting from us.

By varying several aspects of this task in subsequent studies, we found that the crucial factor blocking performance was unfamiliarity in the initial link in the problem. Although it may seem somewhat bizarre, we found that subjects readily solved these problems, even when they were asked to obtain color-coded keys from the matchboxes and drop them into the slot in the Kendler apparatus, but not if they had to obtain the same keys from the apparatus and then use the correct one to open a lock. Moreover, when we repeated these manipulations with American children, we found that kindergartners who failed to display inferential ability with the Kendler apparatus had no trouble with our matchbox "problem isomorph."

Such results are by no means isolated cases (see Cole & Means, 1981; LCHC, 1983, for reviews and discussion). In a great many (but not all) cases, it can be demonstrated that, with appropriate manipulations of the content and context of a standard cognitive task, dramatic changes in performance can be obtained, so that cognitive processes initially assumed to be absent in some population could be shown to be present but evocable under conditions other than those provided by the initial experimental procedures. These results led us to the conclusion that one had to study the cultural context of learning and thinking and to connect one's experimental procedures to the activities and associated contexts that had accumulated historically in the culture in question (Gay & Cole, 1964; Cole et al., 1971).

This change in orientation, where the starting point for psychological analysis became the indigenous organization of activity (whether in a classroom, test, rice field, or children's game), forced on us the absolute necessity of arriving at a deeper understanding of the ways that such activities are organized and, in particular, of understanding more deeply the role of culture in that process.

Limited Influences

By and large, this line of work seemed to have little direct impact on our contemporaries, except for crosscultural psychologists who acknowledged our methodological critique while deploring the absence of integrating theory in our work (e.g., Jahoda, 1980). The only line of influence I could detect was that it reinforced a parallel movement within domestic studies of child development, inspired by irritation among American and British learning theorists with Piagetian claims about the meager cognitive capacities of young children and infants (Bryant, 1974; Donaldson, 1978; Gelman, 1978; Gelman & Baillargeon, 1983). Yet, paradoxically perhaps in light of the emphasis on social sharing in this volume, the overall impact of this intracultural, ontogenetic work has been to reinforce existing theories that place cognition inside individual heads. Instead of making the context of interaction in relation to the culture an object of study, intracultural, developmental psychologists proceeded to strip the context of its response demands, inventing procedures to allow one to assess infants' expectations (e.g., "representations of psychological tasks") with minimal response demands. This line of work has now succeeded in pushing the rudiments of elementary psychological processes back into early infancy (some would claim to birth) through the use of dishabituation techniques that require no more than a baby's ability to attend to a series of stimulus presentations.

What has not been taken up so systematically, but is the aspect of the problem that has continued to be of central concern to my colleagues and me, is the issue that Perret-Clermont and her colleagues refer to as a problem of how children gain access to relevant knowledge, not in the form of illusions of causality (Leslie, 1986) or the earliest appearance of number (Starkey, Spelke, & Gelman, 1990) but in the form of culturally elaborated systems of knowledge, such as the theory of mechanical causality favored by the Greeks, medieval notions of temperature, or the Oksapmin system of arithmetic calculation (For a similar point, see Karmiloff-Smith, 1989).

It is presumably the case that, by virtue of their common human heritage, people all over the world are born with the same pool of elementary representational capacities. These basic capacities are then differentially organized and elaborated into complex systems of higher psychological functions, depending on the actual activities in which people engage. These activities, in turn, depend crucially on the historical and cultural circumstances in which people live.

When one turns to this aspect of the problem—the way in which children come to acquire the complex systems of knowledge that organize joint activity among people in *any* culture—the issue of socially shared cognition jumps to the forefront, because nothing is so certain than that those systems of knowledge are not "in" the child's head to begin with. Whatever the mechanisms of their acquisition, they cannot be acquired in a sociocultural vacuum. Hence, if one is to study human cognition as it is encountered in normal human adults, it is necessary to start not with cognitive processes abstracted from their context, but with the structure of activity that provides the functional matrix of and structural constraints on their acquisition.

NEEDED: A PSYCHOLOGICALLY USEFUL THEORY OF CULTURE

Space clearly does not permit me to elaborate on all these points, so I will focus on only one area that I believe needs serious elaboration if convincing new methodologies for the study of socially shared cognition are to emerge. I believe it is crucial to emphasize that the two analytic categories we label *individual* and *social* are constituted in a unique medium—human culture. It is my impression that a good deal of what gets lumped under the *social* category in the term *socially shared cognition* is actually cultural rather than (or in addition to) social. I emphasize this point because a failure to distinguish between cultural and social contributions to the social sharing of cognition leads, in my opinion, to an unfortunate recreation of that dualistic approach to the individual and the social that has led to many fruitless decades of debate among psychologists and makes it impossible to elucidate the dynamics of developmental change.

Two examples, one a famous thought experiment proposed by the anthropologist, Gregory Bateson, the other an empirical example taken from the transcript of parents greeting their daughter at birth, will serve to make clear why a distinction between the social and the cultural is vital to understanding human cognition.

Structure in the Medium: Culture as Tool

As Emanuel Schegloff points out in his contribution to this volume (chapter 8), cognition is shared not only among minds, but also among minds and the structured medium within which minds interact. "The world of interaction," he writes

> has its own structures and constraints. Its shape not only bears on the fate of acts, messages, utterances once they are enacted by persons (or subjects). It enters into the very composition, design, and structuring of conduct and is part and parcel of whatever processes—cognitive or other—are germane to the very conception and constitution of acts, messages, or utterances in the first instance. (pp. 153–154)

This point was made brilliantly by Bateson (1972) in a discussion of mind as a cybernetic relationship between individuals and their ecologies.[1] Human cognition, he maintained, extends beyond the skin to include at least the tools through which humans interact with their environments. Bateson's thought experiment is posed as follows:

> Suppose I am a blind man, and I use a stick. I go tap, tap, tap. Where do *I* start? Is my mental system bounded at the handle of the stick? Is it bounded by my skin? Does it start halfway up the stick? Does it start at the tip of the stick? (p. 459)

Bateson goes on to argue that such questions are nonsensical unless one is committed to including in one's analysis not only the man and his stick, but also the environment in which he finds himself and his purposes. When the man sits

---

[1] I would like to thank Charles Goodwin and Sandro Duranti for reminding me of this example and of the central importance of Bateson's ideas to the discussion of socially shared cognition.

down to eat his lunch, the stick's relation to mind has totally changed, and then forks and knives become relevant. In short, the border of the mind cannot reasonably be drawn at the skin (or any sense organ, locally considered). Moreover, the precise ways in which mind is distributed depend crucially on the tools through which one interacts with the world, which in turn have been shaped by one's cultural past as well as one's current circumstances and goals. The combination of goals, tools, and setting (or perhaps *arena* in Lave's, 1988, terminology) constitutes simultaneously the *text* and the *con-text* of behavior and the ways in which cognition can be said to be distributed in that context. The full set of resources for constructing contexts may be one useful synonym for the elusive concept of culture.

Culture as Constraint: The Future in the Present

Although Bateson's thought experiment is useful in jolting one into realizing the important senses in which mind is distributed into the tools or media through which we interact with the world, it is simplified in several ways. Sticks, after all, are among the most primitive of tools; Bateson's analysis would need generalizing to include all variety of artifacts, including, of course, human language, to draw out its full implications. Moreover, his example only implicitly includes other people as part of the mental system under consideration (e.g., those who built the streets, cooked the meal). Because my goal here is to separate analytically the cultural and the social for purposes of better understanding the social contributions to socially shared cognition, I will leave Bateson's thought experiment and choose an example that epitomizes for me a key way in which the social and cultural interact to create human minds.

Pediatrician Aiden Macfarlane (1977) published several transcripts of the reactions of parents when they first saw their newborn child and discovered its sex. Consider such simple comments as "I shall be worried to death when she's eighteen" or "It can't play rugby" (said of another girl). In these examples, the adults interpreted the biological characteristics of the child in terms of their own past (cultural) experience. In that experience it is "common knowledge" that girls do not play rugby and that when they enter adolescence they will be the object of boys' sexual attention, putting them at various kinds of risk. Using this information derived from their cultural past and assuming implicitly that there will be cultural stability, the parents projected a probable cultural future for the child: She will be sought after by boys, causing her father anxiety or she will not participate in a form of activity (rugby) requiring strength and agility that is the special preserve of boys. Then (and this is crucial for understanding the contribution of culture to socially shared cognition), the parents organized the child's *present* environment in terms of their projection of the child's *future*. In this process, a purely hypothetical, mental entity, the adult's expectations about the future constraints their child would face, are transformed into movement and talk, materially constituted constraints on the child's experience of the world in the present. This materialized version of cultural expectations is perhaps best known from studies in which adults, totally ignorant of the real gender of a newborn, treated it quite differently, depending on its symbolic or cultural "gender" by, for example, bouncing "boy" infants (those wearing blue diapers) and attributing "manly" virtues to them, but treating "girl" infants (those wearing pink diapers) in a gentle manner (Rubin, Provezano, & Luria, 1974).

Macfarlane's simple example also demonstrates an important distinction between the social and the cultural, and motivates the special emphasis placed on the social origins of higher psychological functions by sociohistorical psychologists (Cole, 1988; Rogoff, chapter 16 in this volume; Vygotsky, 1978; Wertsch, chapter 5 in this volume). As Macfarlane's transcripts clearly demonstrate, human nature is social in a sense different from the sociability of other species, because only a culture-using human being can reach into the cultural past, project it into the future, and then carry that (purely conceptual) future into the present in the shape of beliefs that then materially constrain and organize the present sociocultural environment of the newcomer.[2]

SOME IMPLICATIONS FOR RESEARCH AND PRACTICE

Once one adopts the view that cognition refers not only to universal patterns of information transmission that transpire inside individuals but also to transformations, the forms and functions of which are shared among individuals, social institutions, and historically accumulated artifacts (tools and concepts), the enterprise of cognitive psychology undergoes a dramatic change.

First, as several contributors to this volume point out, there is likely to be a shift in the psychological unit of analysis away from the organism in an environment to two or more human beings acting in a culturally mediated setting. Although it is not clear just how this unit should be characterized (as situated cognition, joint mediated activity, or "person-acting-in-a-setting"), the urge to define and use a unit that avoids reduction to either the individual mind or the social group is clear enough. There are several formulations of this shift among the chapters in this volume. In addition, the important recent work of Engestrom (1987), Lave (1988), and Suchman (1987) is highly relevant.

---

[2]The process being described here in phenomenological terms is, I believe, a rather strict analogue to the process of *back propagation*, which plays a central role in connectionist learning models of the kind discussed in Hutchins' chapter. Technical demonstration of the special properties of back propagation contributed by culture awaits simulations only alluded to as yet by Hutchins.

Second, a socioculturally shared or distributed view of cognition requires one to look on even a two-person psychological test as a culture-specific form of activity, which itself has to be located within its cultural context (Cicourel et al., 1974; Cole, Dore, Hall, & Dowley, 1978; Cole & Means, 1981; McDermott, Orasanu, & Boykin, 1977; Scribner, 1975). Moreover, such a view leads one to discover the intricate ways in which individuals share and distribute cognitive processing on a moment-to-moment basis (Cole, Hood, & McDermott, 1978; Cole & Traupmann, 1981).

A natural concomitant of the points I have just mentioned is an appreciation of the need to consider what geneticists refer to as "levels of the environment." That is, to take a familiar example from the domain of education, forms of interaction called *psychological tasks* must be seen as embedded in (i.e., constituting and constituted by) such "levels of context" as the classroom lesson, the routine of the school day, the prescribed curriculum, the social institution of the school, and the community of which the school is part (Bronfenbrenner, 1979; Cole & Griffin, 1987; LCHC, 1989).

Third, belief that cognition is often or always jointly constructed by people acting in culturally organized contexts (adults acting alone and without tools may or may not be an exception, depending on one's particular theory) motivates the study of people in a variety of activity settings and militates against the acceptance of a particular kind of activity (e.g., schoolroom lessons or psychological tests) as a privileged source of information about cognition. Hence, Heath (chapter 6) focuses on Little League activities as teaching and learning contexts with properties that appear admirable enough to provide a critical focus on school-based activity, if not a substitute for it. Lave (1988, see chapter 4 in this volume) shows how the kind of learning and thinking involved in becoming a midwife, a tailor, an effective dieter, or a recovered alcoholic represents forms of shared cognition that are systematically suppressed in formal schooling. Gelman and Massey (chapter 11) provide very revealing contrasts in parent–child interaction from their studies of behavior in museums and Hastie and Pennington (chapter 14) provide a provocative analysis of jury behavior. The chapter by Levine and Moreland (chapter 12) indicates that similar analyses applied to the organization of work groups are likely to yield rich results (see, for example, Engestrom, 1990). In sum, this line of research (see also Newman, Griffin, & Cole, 1989) shows that cognitive psychological analysis can start from observing the organization of activity traditional to a society while maintaining scientific rigor.

Properly conceived simulations and experiments, and classrooms and lessons, should not be overlooked as sources of knowledge about cognition simply because of overzealous claims for their efficacy. As many have remarked, classrooms and written tests are a part of the everyday experience of millions of children and adults, so understanding the nature of the thinking that is required, promoted, or stunted in such settings is a legitimate area of inquiry, even as one may seek to criticize such institutions and practices as a member of society. Similarly, as Hutchins's contribution to the current volume indicates, simulations that model "social sharing" of cognition can help to specify the conditions under which two or more people working together produce more effective cognitive products than individuals working in (relative) isolation.

Finally, views that promote the study of thinking as situated in activity and conditional on context provide a principled approach to research in, and reform of, classroom instruction. As discussed more fully in Cole and Griffin (1987), LCHC (1989), and Newman, Griffin, and Cole (1989), many researchers reject approaches that break activity down into its elements and emphasize highly controlled individual seatwork, and favor approaches that feature activity-centered teamwork and interaction, as well as solitary or large group activities. Similarly, because the classroom and the individual lesson are not viewed as isolated from the school as a whole and the community in which they are located, one can begin to address links between contexts and institutions in a serious manner as part of a research program on the organization of instruction (LCHC, 1989).

The fact that such a program is part of a long historical tradition of activity-centered pedagogy should not detract from its appropriateness. Perhaps, as Damon suggests, we are in danger of simply making a turn around the perpetual cycle resulting from dualistic standoffs between individualism and collectivism, reductionism and wholism, and so on. I prefer to think that, if we come to grips theoretically and empirically with the phenomenon of cultural mediation, we can experience the kind of spiral of development that will permit us to deal more successfully with the pressing problems we confront as a society and a species.

References

Barker, R. (1968). *Ecological psychology: Concepts and methods for studying the environment of human behavior*. Stanford: Stanford University Press.

Bateson, G. (1972). Form, substance, and difference. In G. Bateson (Ed.), *Steps to an ecology of mind* (pp. 448–468). San Francisco: Chandler.

Boring, E.G. (1950). *A history of experimental psychology*. New York: Appleton-Century-Crofts.

Bronfenbrenner, U. (1979). *The ecology of human development*. Cambridge, MA: Harvard University Press.

Bryant, P. (1974). *Perception and understanding in young children*. New York: Basic Books.

Cicourel, A., Jennings, K. H., Jennings, S. H. M., Leiter, K. C. W., MacKay, R., Mehan, H., & Roth, D. R. (1974). *Language use and school performance*. New York: Academic Press.

Cole, M. (1988). Cross-cultural research in the socio-historical tradition. *Human Development*, *31*, 137–157.

Cole, M., Dore, J., Hall, W. S., & Dowley, G. (1978). Situational variability in the speech of preschool children. *Annals of the New York Academy of Science, 318,* 65–105.

Cole, M., Gay, J., Glick, J. A., & Sharp, D. W. (1971). *The cultural context of learning and thinking.* New York: Basic Books.

Cole, M., & Griffin, P. (1987). *Contextual factors in education: Improving science and mathematics education for minorities and women.* Unpublished manuscript, Wisconsin Center for Education Research, Madison, WI.

Cole, M., Hood, L., & McDermott, R. P. (1978). *Ecological niche picking: Ecological invalidity as an axiom of cognitive psychology* (Tech. Rep.). San Diego: University of California, Laboratory of Comparative Human Cognition.

Cole, M., & Means, B. (1981). *Comparative studies of how people think: An introduction.* Cambridge, MA: Harvard University Press.

Cole, M., & Traupmann, K. (1981). Comparative cognitive research: Learning from a learning disabled child. In W. A. Collins (Ed.), *Minnesota Symposium on Child Development* (Vol. 14, pp. 125–154). Hillsdale, NJ: Erlbaum.

Dilthey, W. (1988). *Introduction to the human sciences.* Detroit: Wayne State University Press.

Donaldson, M. (1978). *Children's minds.* New York: W. W. Norton.

Durkheim, E. (1938). *The role of sociological method.* Chicago: University of Chicago Press. (Original work published 1896)

Engestrom, Y. (1987). *Learning by expanding.* Helsinki: Orienta-Konsultit Oy.

Engestrom, Y. (1990). *Learning, working, and imagining.* Helsinki: Orienta-Konsultit Oy.

Fortes, M. (1938). Social and psychological aspects of education in Taleland. *Africa, 11*(Suppl.), 1–64.

Gay, J., & Cole, M. (1964). *The new mathematics and an old culture.* New York: Holt Rinehart.

Gelman, R. (1978). Cognitive development. *Annual Review of Psychology, 29,* 297–332.

Gelman, R., & Baillargeon, R. (1983). A review of some Piagetian concepts. In P. Mussen (Ed.), *Handbook of child psychology* (Vol. 3, pp. 167–230). New York: Wiley.

Jahoda, G. (1980). Theoretical and systematic approaches in cross-cultural psychology. In H. C. Triandis & W. W. Lambert (Eds.), *Handbook of cross-cultural psychology* (Vol. 1, pp. 69–141). Boston: Allyn & Bacon.

Karmiloff-Smith, A. (1989). Commentary. *Human Development, 32,* 272–275.

Kendler, T. S., & Kendler, H. H. (1967). Experimental analysis of inferential behavior in children. In L. P. Lipsitt & C. C. Spiker (Eds.), *Advances in Child Development and Behavior* (Vol. 3, pp. 157–190). New York: Academic Press.

Laboratory of Comparative Human Cognition. (1983). Culture and cognitive development. In P. H. Mussen (Ed.), *Handbook of child psychology* (Vol. 1, pp. 295–356). New York: Wiley.

Laboratory of Comparative Human Cognition. (1989). Kids and computers: A positive vision of the future. *Harvard Educational Review, 59,* 73–86.

Lave, J. (1988). *Cognition in practice.* New York: Cambridge University Press.

Lektorsky, V. A. (1984). *Subject, object, cognition.* Moscow: Progress Publishers.

Leslie, A. M. (1986). Getting development off the ground: Modularity and the infant's perception of causality. In P. van Geert (Ed.), *Theory building in developmental psychology* (pp. 405–437). Amsterdam: Elsevier.

Luria, A. R. (1979). (A. R. Luria, M. Cole, & S. Cole, Eds.). *The making of mind: A personal account of Soviet psychology.* Cambridge, MA: Harvard University Press.

Macfarlane, A. (1977). *The psychology of childbirth.* Cambridge, MA: Harvard University Press.

Martin, L. (1985). The role of social interaction in children's problem solving. *Quarterly Newsletter of the Laboratory of Comparative Human Cognition, 7*(2), 40–45.

McDermott, R. P., Orasanu, J., & Boykin, W. (1977). A critique of test standardization. *Social Policy, 8*, 61–67.

Nadel, S. F. (1951). *Foundations of social anthropology.* London: Cohen & West.

Newman, D., Griffin, P., & Cole, M. (1989). *The construction zone: Working for cognitive change in school.* New York: Cambridge University Press.

Rommetveit, R. (1987). Meaning, context and control. *Inquiry, 30*, 77–79.

Rubin, J. Z., Provezano, F. J., & Luria, Z. (1974). The eye of the beholder: Parents' view of sex of newborns. *American Journal of Orthopsychiatry, 44*, 512–519.

Scribner, S. (1975). Situating the experiment in cross-cultural research. In K. F. Riegel & J. A. Meacham (Eds.), *The developing individual in a changing world: Historical and cultural issues* (pp. 316–321). The Hague: Mouton.

Shweder, R. A. (1977). Likeness and likelihood in everyday thought: Magical thinking in judgments about personality. *Current Anthropology, 18*, 637–648.

Starkey, P., Spelke, E. S., & Gelman, R. (1990). Numerical abstraction by human infants. *Cognition, 36*, 97–127.

Suchman, L. A. (1987). *Plans and situated actions: The problem of human–machine communication.* Cambridge, England: Cambridge University Press.

Tudge, J. (1985). The effect of social interaction on cognitive development: How creative is conflict? *Quarterly Newsletter of the Laboratory of Comparative Human Cognition, 7*(2), 33–40.

Vygotsky, L. S. (1978). *Mind in society.* Cambridge, MA: Harvard University Press.

NAME INDEX

Numbers in italics refer to listings in reference sections.

418

SUBJECT INDEX